T0293575

This essential guide teaches you all of the verbal-based critical and logical reasoning skills you need for the Verbal and Data Insights sections of the GMAT. It also covers all of the necessary strategies and processes to answer the Reading Comprehension and Critical Reasoning problem types found on the Verbal section of the GMAT.

Acknowledgements

A great number of people were involved in the creation of the book you are holding.

Our Manhattan Prep resources are based on the continuing experiences of our instructors and students. The primary author for this edition was Stacey Koprince, who determined what strategies to cover and how to weave them into a cohesive whole.

David Mahler and Jeff Vollmer served as the primary editors during the writing phase. Mario Gambino and Helen Tan served as a sounding board during the writing phase, vetting both ideas and content. Mario Gambino managed production for all images.

Prakash Jagannathan managed the production work for this guide, with the help of editors Shaheer Husanne Anwar Ali, Arunsanthosh Kannan, and Chitra Shanmugam. Once the manuscript was done, Stevonnie Ross edited and Rebecca Berthiaume proofread the entire guide from start to finish. Carly Schnur and Andrea Repole designed the covers.

Retail ISBN: 978-1-5062-9221-2
Retail eISBN: 978-1-5062-9222-9
Course ISBN: 978-1-5062-9223-6
Course eISBN: 978-1-5062-9224-3

GMAT™ Strategy Guides

GMAT All the Quant and Data Insights

GMAT All the Verbal

GMAT Foundations of Math

GMAT Advanced Quant

July 2, 2024

Hello!

Thank you for picking up a copy of *All the Verbal*. I hope this book provides just the guidance you need to get the most out of your GMAT studies.

At Manhattan Prep, our goal is to provide the best instructors and resources possible. If you have any questions or feedback, please do not hesitate to contact us.

Chat our Student Services team on our website, email us at gmat@manhattanprep.com or give us a shout at 212-721-7400 (or 800-576-4628 in the United States or Canada). We try to keep all our books free of errors, but if you think we've goofed, please visit manhattanprep.com/GMAT/errata.

Our Manhattan Prep Strategy Guides are based on the continuing experiences of both our 99th percentile instructors and our students. The primary author of the 8th Edition All the Verbal guide was Stacey Koprince and the primary editors were David Mahler and Jeff Vollmer. Project management and design were led by Prakash Jagannathan, Mario Gambino, and Helen Tan.

Finally, we are indebted to all of the Manhattan Prep students who have given us excellent feedback over the years. This book wouldn't be half of what it is without their voice.

And now that *you* are one of our students too, please chime in! I look forward to hearing from you. Thanks again and best of luck preparing for the GMAT!

Sincerely,

Stacey Koprince
Director, Content & Curriculum
Manhattan Prep

TABLE OF CONTENTS

The GMAT Mindset

The GMAT is a complex exam. It feels like a strictly academic test—math, reading comprehension, data analysis, logical reasoning—but at heart, the GMAT is really a test of your *executive reasoning skills*.

Executive reasoning is the official term for your ability to make decisions in the face of complex and changing information. It makes sense, then, that graduate management programs would want to test these skills. But *how* does the GMAT test executive reasoning skills? Understanding this will impact both how you study for the GMAT and the decisions you make as you're taking the test.

Here's the first big difference compared to school tests: Your teachers tested you on material they fully expected you to know how to handle. They never put something on the test that they *expected* you to get wrong.

But the GMAT will actually do this! The GMAT wants to know how well you make decisions regarding when to invest your limited time and mental energy *and* when *not* to. When you see something that will take too long or be too hard, do you let yourself get sucked in? Or do you say, "No, thanks!" and walk away?

In other words, the GMAT is testing you on how well you make business decisions. No good businessperson invests in every single opportunity that comes along. Rather, an effective businessperson evaluates each opportunity, saying yes to some and no to others.

That's what you're going to do on the GMAT, too. You will invest in a majority of the problems presented to you, but you *will also* say no to some—the ones that look too hard or seem like they'll take too long to solve. These are literally bad investments.

The GMAT is Adaptive

Here's the next big difference compared to school tests: The GMAT adapts to you as you take it, offering easier or harder questions based on how you're doing on the test. Ideally, you'll do well on the material that you know how to answer in a reasonable amount of time. Your reward? Eventually, you'll earn questions that are too hard—either they'll take too long or they'll be so hard that you wouldn't get them even if you had unlimited time.

Then what? If you try to use a "school mindset" on the test, you'll keep trying to answer these questions even though you really can't do them. You'll waste a bunch of time and have to rush on other questions. As a result, you'll start to miss questions that you actually do know how to answer and your score will go down. This is the business equivalent of spending most of your annual budget by month 8... and then not having enough money left to run the business effectively for the last 4 months of the year. Not a good look.

Instead, use your business mindset to carry you through the exam. When the test finds your limit (and it will), acknowledge that! Call it a bad investment and let that problem go, ideally before you've spent very much time on it. Choose an answer, any answer, and move on.

Extend the business mindset to your studies as well. If there are certain topics that you really hate, don't study them. Seriously! Instead, on your next practice test, guess quickly and move on when one of those "bad investment opportunities" comes up. After your next practice test, you can see what your score is like and decide whether to study those topics in the future.

You might get to your goal score without ever having to master the content that you find the most annoying. Even those of us who score in the 99th percentile on the test have "guess fast on this" lists.

One caveat: You can't give up immediately on huge swaths of content. For example, don't bail on all of Reading Comprehension; that represents too great a portion of the Verbal section. You can, though, choose a subset of RC—say, science-based Inference problems.

Start orienting yourself around your business mindset today. You are *not* going to do every problem or master everything. Rather, you're going to focus on the best investment opportunities (aka, problems) for you, as you see them throughout the test. When you decide not to pursue a particular investment, pick a random answer and move on as quickly as you can—don't waste precious time on a poor investment opportunity. And feel good about the fact that you're doing exactly what you're supposed to do on the GMAT: making sound investment decisions about what to do *and* what *not* to do.

How to Organize Your Verbal Studies

"Verbal" actually means two things for the GMAT. First, verbal refers to the verbal-based skills that are tested throughout the GMAT—comprehension of complex texts, analytical reasoning around complex scenarios, and so on.

Second, verbal refers to the Verbal Reasoning (or Verbal, for short) section of the GMAT. Interestingly, a mix of quant *and* verbal skills are tested on the Data Insights (DI) section of the exam. Our *All the Quant and Data Insights* book covers all of the question types found in the DI and Quant sections, but you will also be able to use some of the verbal *skills* taught in this book when you get to the DI section of the test.

This book also covers all of the skills and strategies you'll need for the two problem types found on the Verbal section of the GMAT, Critical Reasoning (CR) and Reading Comprehension (RC).

How to Use This Book

There are three units in this book:

1. Unit One: Foundations of Verbal

2. Unit Two: Critical Reasoning

3. Unit Three: Reading Comprehension

We recommend that most people start with Units Two and Three of this book. If, while working your way through the second and third units, you realize that you need more foundational help on anything you're learning, find the corresponding chapter in Foundations of Verbal. Spend some time building your foundation in this area, then go back to the "main" CR and RC units.

If you find yourself frequently wanting to consult the Foundations Unit, then you may want to complete that entire unit before continuing with the rest of the book. And if you have never taken a standardized test before, or if you have always taken these kinds of tests in a language other than English, you may want to start with the Foundations unit.

Verbal Section Problem Types

The Verbal section of the exam contains two problem types: Critical Reasoning and Reading Comprehension.

Critical Reasoning (CR) questions test your ability to understand, analyze, critique, and infer from arguments. Reading Comprehension (RC) questions test your ability to comprehend and infer from complex narrative information.

You'll need to average about 2 minutes per question during the Verbal section, though your timing for individual questions will likely range from almost no time at all to approximately 3 minutes. The "almost no time at all" questions will be your *guess-fast* questions: questions that look way too hard/long or that you know are a big weakness of yours (aka, bad investment opportunities). On other questions—perhaps a harder question in an area of strength—you'll invest some extra time. It'll all balance out in the end.

You'll learn more about time management, as well as other test details, both in this guide and in the online resources associated with this guide. You can also test your skills using official GMAT problems that are published by the test makers in the *GMAT Official Guide* (also known as "the OG"). These problems appeared on the official GMAT in the past, so they're a fantastic resource to help you get ready for the real test. (Note: The OG is published by the official test makers. It is sold separately from the Manhattan Prep books.)

Book Purchasers: Read Me!

If you are taking a live course or complete self-study program with us, you can skip this section. Your syllabus in Manhattan Prep's online study platform will give you all of the needed assignments from all of your program resources throughout your studies.

If you have purchased books from us on Amazon or similar, then you will need to do some organization of your studies yourself. If you haven't already, create your account on the Manhattan Prep website and register your purchase of this book and any other books you may have bought from us. This will give you access to a Starter Kit syllabus, containing resources both for this book and for the test overall. Take 15 minutes right now to explore your syllabus and understand how it works.

If you purchased our *All the GMAT* book set, you will have access both to the Starter Kit syllabus and to a more extensive syllabus on our online study platform. Just register your book set on our website to unlock the *All the GMAT* syllabus and get started.

We also recommend purchasing your own copy of the most recent edition of the *GMAT Official Guide* (also known as "the OG"). The OG is published by the official maker of the GMAT and contains problems that appeared on the official GMAT in the past. It's a fantastic resource for your studies (which is why we include it in all of our live course and complete self-study programs). One more note: Don't buy any OG editions from 2022 or earlier; those were all built for the old GMAT, not for the new GMAT.

Use OG problems to train yourself under official test conditions. We recommend following the below guidelines when you devise problem sets for yourself. (If you are taking one of our courses or complete self-study programs, ignore this! You already have OG problem sets assigned in your online syllabus.)

When	What
Early in your studies	At first, try a single problem at a time: 1. Time yourself; it's perfectly fine to go up to a minute over average time for that question type. 2. If you're approaching 1 minute of *extra* time, pick an answer (any answer!); you'll have to on the real test, too, so practice that from the beginning. Then either try the problem again or decide that you'd rather guess immediately on the real test. If you try it again, don't time yourself and you can look up anything you want in your study materials. 3. Review each problem thoroughly before trying the next one.
In the middle of your studies	Add a couple of layers of complexity: 1. Try two to four problems in one straight block before stopping and analyzing the problems. Set a timer for the whole block of time and have an answer for every problem by the time the timer runs out (even if you have to guess). 2. Include some problems from lessons or assignments you completed in earlier weeks (do some new problems *and* retry some problems that you did before). These two additional layers will allow you to practice your time management and keep your skills fresh on material you studied earlier.
Later in your studies	Add some more complexity: 1. Graduate to longer sets of problems (6 for the Verbal section). 2. Mix question types—do some CR and some RC in one set. 3. Choose problems randomly out of the OG—so that even you don't know what you're about to do! After all, the real test will never tell you what kind of problem you're about to get. If you can mimic the randomness of the test, you'll train yourself to be prepared for anything.

One word of caution: Don't create problem sets that consist of many problems of the exact same type—for example, don't do four CR Strengthen questions in a row. The real test will always mix things up, so do the same with your own practice.

One last—and very important—note: Manhattan Prep's online study platform contains a host of additional resources associated with this book. These aren't "extra" or optional materials; they're integral components of your GMAT study plan.

Online, you'll find materials that explain how to manage your time during the test and what to do if you find yourself too far ahead of or behind on time. You'll also find resources to help you analyze your practice test results and figure out your study priorities going forward. You'll even find more practice problems. Register your guide today to get access to all of these materials!

UNIT ONE

Foundations of Verbal

In this unit, you will learn foundational-level concepts and skills for the verbal concepts tested on the exam. Most people can skip this unit and begin with Unit Two, but if you have never taken a standardized test before or have always taken these tests in a language other than English, consider working your way through Foundations of Verbal. You can find more guidance in the *How to Organize Your Verbal Studies* section at the beginning of this book.

In This Unit...

CR Argument Structure

In This Chapter...

- Arguments and Conclusions
- Drill 1.1—Find the Conclusion
- Building Blocks
- Drill 1.2—Identify the Building Blocks
- Common Argument Types
- Flaws in Arguments
- Drill 1.3—Match Similar Arguments
- Answers to Drill Sets

In this chapter, you will learn about the main building blocks of GMAT arguments, as well as the common types of arguments used on the test.

CHAPTER 1 CR Argument Structure

Have you ever witnessed or even taken part in the following kind of discussion?

Person A	Person B
Makes a statement of some kind.	Says something that doesn't address what Person A just said.
Responds with a random thought that popped into their head.	Confidently states an opinion as if it were a fact.
Talks in circles, leaving their true position unspoken.	Makes a mistaken assumption about what Person A wants.
Can't articulate what they really think. Winds up frustrated.	Winds up frustrated.

This sort of exchange is typical. In real life, people are generally bad at arguing effectively!

Even folks who try to be fair-minded can be fuzzy in their thinking. For instance, people will hear both sides of an issue and then say, "Well, I need more information to decide." But they can't tell you what information they need. They can't identify specific flaws in the chains of logic they've heard, so they have no idea how to fix those flaws.

It doesn't have to be this way! GMAT Critical Reasoning (CR) problems force you to really understand arguments. In the context of the GMAT, the word *argument* doesn't usually mean "a verbal scuffle or debate" (*I had an argument with my friend last night*). Rather, it means "a set of logically connected statements that put forth an assertion of some kind" (*She made the argument that we should replace the refrigerator*).

You *have* the first kind of argument, which is the verbal scuffle. In contrast, you *make* the second kind of argument, which is a case for some position.

As you study GMAT arguments—as you delve into their structure, purpose, and flaws, as well as possible cures for those flaws—you will start to notice similar arguments all around you.

Most arguments on the GMAT are flawed in some fashion. So are most arguments in the real world.

Be warned: Once your eyes are opened, there's no going back to blind acceptance of the self-serving arguments of some salesperson or politician. But that's not a bad thing, right?

In short, improving on Critical Reasoning will make you better at reasoning critically in general. That's a pretty useful side effect of your preparation for the GMAT.

1

Arguments and Conclusions

A Critical Reasoning argument looks something like this:

> To be considered a form of cardiovascular exercise, an activity must raise the heart rate and keep it elevated for at least 20 minutes. Skydiving cannot properly be considered a form of cardiovascular exercise. While skydiving certainly does elevate a person's heart rate, the skydiver only experiences freefall for 60–70 seconds, followed by 5–6 minutes under a parachute—and, of course, it is not possible to string multiple dives immediately back-to-back.

Every argument contains certain building blocks, types of information that form the complete argument.

All arguments contain **premises**. A premise is a fact or an opinion that is intended to support some claim made by the author.

Most arguments also contain **conclusions**. The conclusion is the main claim made by the author.

Together, premises and conclusions make up the **core argument**. What is the core argument about skydiving?

Premise 1: cardio = raise heart rate
AND keep high for 20+ min

Premise 2: skydiving raises heart rate
BUT fall lasts only 6–8 min

Conclusion: skydiving isn't
cardio

The conclusion of an argument is the speaker's main point or claim. Although it is often helpful to think of the conclusion at the end of the argument (as it is shown in the diagram), the conclusion may appear anywhere within the text of the argument.

When an argument does contain a conclusion (as most arguments will), it's very important for you to correctly identify it.

Drill 1.1—Find the Conclusion

Articulate the conclusion in each of the arguments. In some, you may be able to underline the conclusion in the given text. In others, you may have to rephrase the conclusion a bit or combine two pieces of information.

1. Quoting sources in your papers without attributing the quotes to those sources is forbidden on this campus. Plagiarism is strictly forbidden by our code of conduct, and quoting without attribution is a form of plagiarism.

2. The difference between a weed and a garden plant depends entirely on the opinion of the person who owns the land. Thus, it is impossible to develop a flawless garden "weed killer" that kills all types of weeds and leaves all types of garden plants unharmed. The Vytex Company's attempt to develop a perfect garden weed killer will fail.

3. An anti-smoking policy would cause a loss of revenue to the bars in Melton. Since Melton is a small town, smokers would likely just drive an extra couple of miles to bars in any of the neighboring towns, none of which have anti-smoking policies.

4. The city parks are overcrowded, leading to long wait times for athletic fields and courts and lessening citizens' enjoyment of the parks. A new park should be built at the southern tip of the city, which does not have its own park. Because the heavily populated southern end of the city lacks a park, residents regularly travel to other parts of the city to use those parks, thus leading to overcrowding.

5. Some say that Saddlebrook College provides the best value in the state. Yet this belief is simply not true: Students at the state's Tunbridge College pay less, enjoy newer buildings and smaller class sizes, and earn higher incomes after graduation.

Answers are on page 19.

Building Blocks

You've learned the first two types of Critical Reasoning building blocks:

Premise: supports the author's conclusion

Conclusion: the main claim made by the author

There are two more building blocks to learn:

Counterpoint: A counterpoint, or counterpremise, goes against the author's conclusion in some way. Some arguments contain this kind of information, but many do not.

Background: The argument also might introduce background information to provide context for the overall story.

The following exercise will help you practice finding these building blocks.

Drill 1.2—Identify the Building Blocks

Label each piece of information according to the role that it plays in the argument.

1. Company spokesperson: An investor has accused the CEO of financial impropriety, citing as evidence a $50,000 payment made to the CEO's son although no work was performed. In fact, the payment was perfectly legitimate. The son's firm provides consulting services to the company, and this was an advance payment of 10% of project fees for a new endeavor slated to start in the next month.

2. The female arkbird will lay eggs only when a suitable quantity of nesting material is available and the climate is suitably moderate. This year, unseasonable temperatures have actually increased the amount of nesting material as trees and plants die, shedding twigs and leaves. For this reason, the arkbirds in this region can be expected to lay eggs soon.

3. John Doe pleaded not guilty to the charge of embezzlement but was convicted after irrefutable evidence was found on his personal computer. It is illegal, however, to search a personal computer without the consent of the owner, so Doe's conviction will be overturned on appeal.

Answers are on page 20.

Common Argument Types

There are several patterns that the GMAT frequently uses. In this section, you will be introduced to a few common argument types. Not every argument you see on the GMAT will fit into one of these types.

Causation

Causation arguments conclude that one circumstance caused another. Take a look at the following example:

> A recent survey of senior citizens (people at least 65 years old) found that seniors who spend time caring for children under the age of five are more likely to define their health as good or excellent than those who do not spend time caring for children. Thus, to improve their health, senior citizens should be encouraged to spend time with young children.

This argument starts with the premise that two things were reported as occurring together in senior citizens (time caring for young children and good health). The conclusion implies that one of these things (caring for young children) can influence or is causing the other (good health). Why else might the two characteristics occur together?

First, the causation might actually be reversed. In general, people probably wouldn't ask someone in poor health to care for a young child. So it could be that the health status of senior citizens influences the childcare as opposed to the other way around as the conclusion posits.

Second, there might be some third factor that influences both health and childcare activities. Consider age. Younger senior citizens (those 65–70) are likely to be in better health on average than older senior citizens. Perhaps many of these younger senior citizens are still employed in the childcare industry or are more likely to have young grandchildren or other young family members.

Make sure to look out for arguments that state or imply causation. When you notice such arguments, start thinking about alternative causes.

Plans

Recall this argument (with a couple of small changes):

> The city parks are overcrowded, leading to long wait times for athletic fields and courts and lessening citizens' enjoyment of the parks. The mayor contends that a new park should be built at the southern tip of the city, which does not have its own park. Because the heavily populated southern end of the city lacks a park, residents regularly travel to other parts of the city to use those parks, thus leading to overcrowding.
>
> Which of the following, if true, most seriously undermines the mayor's plan to alleviate overcrowding at city parks?

Now, the argument is being put forth by the mayor, and the question stem explicitly lays out the goal of the plan: to alleviate overcrowding. The full plan is to build a park in an area of the city lacking a park. Residents in this part of the city will visit the new park, alleviating crowding in existing parks.

For any plan, the key point of attack is typically whether the plan will work the way that the author says it will. It's crucial to note precisely how the author states that the plan will work. Why might residents of the south still go to the old parks even after the new park is built? Could overcrowding still exist even if residents from the south go to the new park?

Trap answers will often try to go outside of the plan. For instance, a trap on this problem might revolve around building an indoor recreation center instead so that it could be used in winter. Maybe the center would attract more people and thus alleviate park overcrowding, but the question will ask you to analyze the *given* plan, not to find a way to achieve the same goal via a different plan.

In other words, don't think the way you would in the real world when someone presents you with a plan. Evaluate the exact plan as it stands.

Prediction

The conclusion of an argument is often a prediction. Consider the following example:

> In Steamtown, an average of 40% of eligible voters casts ballots in local elections. The upcoming election includes a proposal to allow the development of a mall on land that currently serves as a city park. Since many Steamtown residents are passionate about preserving the park, more than half of eligible voters will vote in the upcoming election.

The conclusion is the prediction that turnout for the upcoming election will be higher than average. This prediction is supported by the fact that many residents care about a particular issue on the ballot. However, there are many other factors that might influence voter turnout relative to other years. Are the polling locations and hours similar to those for previous elections? What if a bad storm hits on election day? Are the people who care about the park the same people who already vote in all elections?

Answers related to prediction arguments commonly focus on some other issue or intervening circumstance that could influence the prediction.

Profit

The GMAT frequently includes arguments about profits. An example follows:

> XYZ Corporation has traditionally made bicycles with steel frames. Next year, XYZ will start manufacturing bicycles with carbon fiber frames. Serious bicyclists are willing to pay a significant premium for carbon fiber frames because they are much lighter but just as durable. Thus, XYZ's profits from bicycles will increase next year.

Whenever a conclusion mentions profits, think about the profit equation: Profit = Revenue − Cost.

In this example, the conclusion states that profits will increase. The premises suggest that revenues are likely to increase because some people will pay more for bikes with carbon fiber frames. What about costs? How do the costs for materials and labor compare between carbon fiber bikes and steel bikes? GMAT arguments about profits often ignore one component of the profit equation. This forgotten component may be relevant to the answer.

Flaws in Arguments

Nearly all of the arguments on the GMAT are flawed. That is, the argument contains weak points, and the question asks you to analyze one of those weak points in some way.

You'll learn about some of these weaknesses here. In the next chapter, you'll learn about one more special kind of building block and the weaknesses associated with that building block.

1

1. Language Weaknesses

Some arguments use unjustified language. For example:

> People who jog more than 10 miles per week have a lower incidence of heart disease than people who exercise the same amount on stationary bicycles. Therefore, jogging is the best method of exercise for reducing heart disease.

The conclusion is in the final sentence: *Jogging is the best method of exercise for reducing heart disease.* The word *best* is quite extreme. Jogging is the best method ever? Better than swimming, tennis, and a million other things? Even if you prove that jogging is better in some respect than stationary bicycling, all you can say is that jogging is better than one other activity, not that it's the best.

Watch out for these extreme words: *only, never, always, cannot, certainly, obviously, inevitably, most, least, best,* and *worst.* Look for dramatic predictions and assertions: *X costs far more than Y, an immediate increase in Z,* or *a sharp decline in W.* When you see extreme language, check whether this language is justified by other information in the argument. If not, you've just found a flaw in the argument.

If you see something like this …

> Whenever there is political unrest in the world, the price of oil goes up. Thus, political unrest must be the most important influence on the price of oil.

… then think something like this:

> *Is it really the* most *important influence?*

Study Tip: Check whether extreme language is justified by the argument.

In addition to unjustified language, arguments will sometimes use false synonyms or false equivalents. For example:

> Consumers used their cell phones more this month than last month, but they talked for fewer minutes. So they must have sent more text messages this month than last month.

Used their cell phones more is not necessarily equivalent to *sent more text messages.* There are plenty of other things to do on a cell phone; they could have been playing games, surfing the web, listening to music, and so on.

Vague language can also be problematic. Recall the "people who jog" argument:

> People who jog more than 10 miles per week have a lower incidence of heart disease than people who exercise the same amount on stationary bicycles. Therefore, jogging is the best method of exercise for reducing heart disease.

What on earth does it mean to *exercise the same amount* as someone who is jogging 10 miles? Does it mean biking for the same amount of *time* or the same *distance?* The same number of calories burned? It's much faster to ride 10 miles on a stationary bike than to jog 10 miles, so if the arguer means that the distances are the same, then there is potentially another reason (besides the author's conclusion) that the joggers have less heart disease: They are exercising more hours per week. *Exercise the same amount* is vague. Question any term that's **insufficiently precise**.

2. Selection Bias

Whenever you compare two groups, make sure that the two groups are legitimately comparable. This is particularly tricky when the two groups *seem* comparable—for instance, when they are both drawn from the same population.

There are several types of selection bias. These biases are common issues in **causation** arguments.

Unrepresentative Sample

Marketers, pollsters, and social scientists of all stripes use samples. It's impossible to ask everyone in the entire population for their opinions on single- versus double-ply toilet paper, so instead you ask 100 people. You have to ensure that the sample is representative, though. In particular, you have to be wary of volunteers. For example:

> Some customers who filled out a long survey for free said that they love our company. So our customers love our company.

Isn't there a possibility that this sample of customers is disproportionately composed of people who like you? After all, they filled out a long survey for free. The potential for self-selection bias is strong here.

Survivor Bias

It is not logical to judge an entire group by concentrating only on who or what survived a process or time period while ignoring the non-survivors. It's easy to fall into this trap, though; after all, it's often hard to find out much about the people or things that didn't make it.

When you say *survive*, you might mean it literally—for instance, the population of living people over 100 years old (those who survived that long) is not representative of all people born 100 or more years ago. Those alive today are very likely different in important ways—better access to nutrition, fewer genetic maladies, etc. For example:

> A survey of living people over 100 years old showed that they have lower rates of cigarette smoking than does every other age group from 15 to 100 years old. Therefore, the rate of smoking is increasing.

Here, it is likely that those who lived to be 100 did so in part by not smoking and that plenty of people born 100 or more years ago did smoke and did not live to be 100.

Survivor bias can also involve nonliving things:

> Most ancient Greek coins made of gold and silver have been found buried in the ground. So the ancient Greeks must have buried most of their gold and silver coins.

What about the ancient Greek coins that *weren't* buried? They were probably dispersed, melted down, or otherwise destroyed. The sample of surviving coins is not representative.

Ever-Changing Pool

Many groups of people have a rotating cast of members. If a civic club voted in favor of something yesterday and against it 20 years ago, you wouldn't automatically conclude that people in the club changed their minds over time; it's pretty likely that the club includes different people than it did back then. For example:

> A petition is circulating in Capital City that opposes building a new sports center at State University on land now occupied by abandoned strip malls. Five years ago, many city residents opposed building a new State University dormitory complex, yet in a poll this year, 80% of respondents said that building the dormitory complex had been a good idea. If the people who sign the petition opposing the new sports center are polled in a few years, they will have changed their minds.

Five years ago, people opposed the new dorm, and now 80% of respondents to a poll like the dorm. Are the poll respondents the same population as the voters? Maybe the poll was conducted on or near campus; a high percentage of students in the poll would certainly skew results.

Even if the poll were representative of the city's current residents, it's not clear that they are the same residents as five years ago. Maybe some residents disliked the college's expansion plans enough to move out of town. Maybe the new dorm allowed the college to admit significantly more students, thus *diluting* the pool of people who disliked and still dislike the dorm.

If you see something like this …

> Students who joined social clubs at Hambone University and were elected officers of their clubs last year had lower grades on average than all students at Hambone over the last decade. Therefore, participation in social clubs at Hambone negatively impacts students' grades.

… then think something like this:

> *That may be true, but so what? Self-selection bias: These people wanted to prioritize socializing by joining social clubs. Survivor bias: These students were elected officers, meaning that they made it even further into socializing. Ever-changing pool: Students from last year are being compared with students over the last decade. The composition of the school may have changed over that time.*

3. Math Errors

You might not want to hear this, but even on the Verbal section of the GMAT, you can't completely get away from the Quant. A few Critical Reasoning arguments do trade on math issues. Fortunately, these issues almost never require any computation, and even in the worst case, you'll just be comparing one ratio to another.

When working with numbers on the GMAT, you'll generally be trying to find mathematically provable conclusions. Here's an example: *Alice worked fewer days last month than Bob worked, but she earned more dollars last month than Bob earned.* What can you definitely conclude? Alice must have had a higher *daily* wage (dollars per day) than Bob had.

You can't conclude that her hourly wage is higher; she may have worked a greater *total* number of hours than Bob did even though she worked fewer days. Also, notice that this conclusion is based only on inequalities and ratios. This is the way that the GMAT can avoid putting real numbers into arguments and yet still have a rigorous, airtight conclusion.

The GMAT also likes to mix up percents and real numbers. If David gets a 10% pay raise and Marie gets an 8% pay raise, who now has a higher salary? Without knowing how much the two people made before, it's impossible to tell. Don't confuse percents with actual numbers of dollars, people, etc.

Consider this argument:

> Cetadone, a new therapy for the treatment of addiction to the drug tarocaine, has been proven effective in a study centered around Regis Hospital in the western part of the state of New Portsmouth. The study involved local people suffering from an addiction to tarocaine who responded to a newspaper ad offering free treatment. Participants who received cetadone and counseling were 40% more likely to recover than were patients assigned to a control group and who received only counseling. Conventional therapies have only a 20% recovery rate. Therefore, the best way to reduce deaths from tarocaine overdose throughout all of New Portsmouth would be to fund cetadone therapy for all people addicted to tarocaine.

In this argument, 40% certainly looks like a higher number than 20%. And there are no real numbers of people here anywhere, so the argument is not confusing a percent with a real number.

However, the 20% is an actual *recovery rate for* conventional therapies.

The 40% is a *percent increase on an unknown figure*—the recovery rate of the control group. You have no way to compare this to an actual 20% recovery rate. For instance, what if the control group had a 50% recovery rate? Then the cetadone group would have a 70% recovery rate (1.4 × 50). But what if the control group had a 1% recovery rate? Then the cetadone group would have a 1.4% recovery rate, making it much less successful than conventional therapies. Be ready to test some extreme cases (high and low) to see whether the conclusion actually holds.

In short, if any numbers or numeric relationships are presented in an argument, determine whether they are being cited in a logical way. This is the exact same reasoning about percents and percent change that you will need for the Quantitative part of the exam (and, of course, the math on the actual Quant and DI sections is much harder than anything that would ever occur in Critical Reasoning), so it pays in numerous ways to have a solid knowledge of percents.

A few other standard mathematical relationships show up in Critical Reasoning as well:

Distance = Rate × Time

Profit = Revenue − Costs

Revenue = Price × Quantity

Dollars = (Dollars per Hour) × Hours

You have to know these for the Quant and DI sections of the test, of course. Ratios in general (such as *dollars per hour, miles per gallon*, etc.) are fair game. Again, you won't have to compute anything; you need to be able to follow a couple of steps to a mathematical conclusion.

4. Big Leaps in Logic

Sometimes, a conclusion makes too big of a leap in logic. For example:

> For over 100 years, the nation of Relmeer has had a mutual defense pact with the neighboring country of Gherfu. Yet last month, the government of Relmeer fell to an invasion from the United Provinces of Antocia. Thus, Gherfu is at fault for not abiding by the mutual defense pact.

Gherfu was supposed to help Relmeer, but Antocia completely defeated Relmeer anyway. Therefore, Gherfu didn't help? There is no way to tell that. Maybe Relmeer and Gherfu are small nations and the United Provinces of Antocia is a very large and powerful nation. Maybe Gherfu did absolutely everything it could. Maybe soldiers from Gherfu died valiantly in battle, trying to protect Relmeer. Here is another example:

> Amateur boxers wear headgear to protect against brain injuries from boxing. Yet, last year, three amateur boxers suffered serious brain injuries in the ring while wearing the headgear. Therefore, the headgear does not protect against brain injuries.

Well, it certainly seems true that the headgear is not 100% effective (although it would be helpful to confirm that the injured boxers were wearing the headgear correctly). However, there is a huge gap between saying that the headgear is not 100% effective (not much in life is) and saying that it *does not protect*. There are lots of things—automobile airbags, sunscreen, bulletproof vests—that do not provide 100% protection but certainly still have a protective effect.

1

Here's another example, this time with a choice of two multiple-choice answers:

> Pancreatic cancer patients as a group have only a 5% survival rate after five years. With a surgical procedure called the Whipple, followed by chemotherapy and radiation, this survival rate can be increased. Therefore, this course of treatment is the best option for all pancreatic cancer patients strong enough to undergo the surgery.
>
> What does this argument assume?
>
> (A) People who receive the Whipple operation followed by chemotherapy and radiation are likely to live longer than five years.
>
> (B) No other treatment has a better or equivalent rate of effectiveness.

Note that this argument has a significant logical flaw: It uses unjustified language. This course of treatment is the "best"? In making that conclusion, the argument assumes that other treatments must be worse. You are to take as fact that this course of treatment increases the survival rate, but what if some other course of treatment increases the rate *even more*? The author has neglected to rule out this possibility. The answer is (B).

What about incorrect choice (A)? An argument that asserts that a particular plan is the "best" one does not have to assert that that plan is likely to work—only that nothing else is *more* likely to work. In the case of a very deadly disease, sadly, even the very best treatment may not be that effective. As it turns out, the course of treatment described above currently leads to a five-year survival rate around 20%—thus, even with the "best" treatment, patients are not likely to survive five years.

One subset of a big leap in logic has to do with causation. As discussed in the prior section, when an argument **jumps to a causal relationship**, question that relationship. Why does X necessarily cause Y? Couldn't it be the other way around? Could there be some other factor influencing both observations?

Consider this argument:

> According to a recent study, cats that eat Premium Cat Food have healthier coats and shed less hair than those that do not. The higher cost of Premium Cat Food will be offset by a reduction in the need for cat grooming and house-cleaning services.

Two things are happening at the same time: Cats are eating Premium Cat Food and they are shedding less. The conclusion is that owners will save money on certain services by feeding their cats Premium Cat Food. This conclusion assumes that Premium Cat Food causes the healthier coats and a reduction in shedding. But is it necessarily the case that the cat food has these beneficial effects?

Perhaps people who can afford to purchase Premium Cat Food (and choose to do so) also provide their cats with grooming, top-notch health care, or other amenities that reduce shedding and make coats healthier. Perhaps people who spend more on cat food tend to have special breeds of cats that naturally shed less.

When changes or events occur at the same time or in sequence, don't assume that X necessarily caused Y. It could be that Y caused X. It could also be that something else entirely caused both X and Y.

Here's a summary of the argument flaws you've learned so far:

1.	Language Weaknesses	Unjustified language (e.g., an extreme word)
		False synonyms or false equivalents
2.	Selection Bias	Unrepresentative sample
		Survivor bias
		Ever-changing pool
3.	Math Errors	Conclusion not mathematically justifiable
		Percentages vs. real numbers
4.	Big Leaps in Logic	Conclusion makes huge leap. For example:

- Something good is the absolute best.
- A and B both happen, so A causes B.

1

Drill 1.3—Match Similar Arguments

Six arguments are presented below. Not all arguments are complete—some lack conclusions.

Match each argument with a partner—that is, an argument that uses the same pattern or shares the same flaw. This should result in three pairs of arguments. Articulate the pattern for each pair.

1. **Running Study:** A study concluded that running is the optimal form of exercise to effect significant changes in overall health. Study participants ran five miles per day, six days a week, for three months. At the end of the study, the participants were shown to have lost weight, reduced their cholesterol levels, and increased their cardiovascular fitness. Further, running is inexpensive and easy to do year-round in most locations.

2. **Freight Trains:** In a survey of working freight trains, engineers found that engines built before 1960 had better tolerances and higher-grade steel than engines built since 1960. Therefore, freight train engines were constructed according to higher-quality standards before 1960 than afterward.

3. **New Product:** To make a profit this quarter, Company X must increase sales of its old product while also introducing a new product that is as profitable as the old one. Whenever Company X introduces a new product, sales of the old product drop sharply.

4. **Heart Murmurs:** A veterinarian noticed more potentially fatal heart murmurs in puppies than in dogs over 15 years old. Thus, the veterinarian concluded that the diet and care given to dogs must have declined over the last 15 years.

5. **Peacekeeping Force:** For the violence in Kirkenberg to be stopped, the majority of surrounding nations must vote to send in a peacekeeping force, and the wealthy nation of Nandia must provide funding. If Nandia becomes involved in any way regarding Kirkenberg, at least half of the nations surrounding Kirkenberg will vote against intervening in Kirkenberg.

6. **Cost Cutting:** Company G determined that there were two available methods to cut production costs for its main product line: change suppliers for certain raw materials or automate certain steps in the assembly of the product. Automation will save more money than changing suppliers, so Company G will maximize its savings by automating certain steps of the assembly.

Answers are on page 21.

Answers to Drill Sets

Drill 1.1—Find the Conclusion

1. **Quoting sources in your papers without attributing the quotes to those sources is forbidden on this campus.** In order, the chain of logic could be summarized as: Quoting without attribution is plagiarism; plagiarism is forbidden; therefore, quoting without attribution is forbidden.

2. **The Vytex Company's attempt to develop a perfect garden weed killer will fail.** The chain of logic is as follows: The difference between weed and plant is based on personal opinion; therefore, it's impossible to develop a "weed killer" that kills all weeds but no plants; therefore, Vytex's attempt to develop such a product will fail. Note that there seem to be two conclusions here! The first one is sometimes called an intermediate conclusion; only the final one is considered the main conclusion.

3. **An anti-smoking policy would cause a loss of revenue to the bars in Melton.** The chain of logic is as follows: If smokers can't smoke in bars in Melton, they'll go to other bars in nearby towns; therefore, Melton's bars will lose revenue.

4. **A new park should be built at the southern tip of the city.** The chain of logic is as follows: The southern tip of the city doesn't have a park; residents in that area go to parks in other areas; those other parks are overcrowded; therefore, a new park should be built at the southern tip of the city.

5. **It is not true that Saddlebrook College provides the best value in the state.** Careful! The conclusion isn't that *Tunbridge College provides the best value in the state*—the speaker has simply pointed out that Saddlebrook can't be the best value, since another college is a better value. For instance, Saddlebrook and Tunbridge could actually be the 10th and 7th best values in the state, respectively.

   The speaker's statement of the conclusion is that *this belief is simply not true.* You have to go back to the previous sentence and substitute in what the speaker means by *this belief.* Don't go beyond what is explicitly stated in the passage.

   Be literal. Think about when you say things such as "Uncle Jay thinks he's the smartest person in our family? Even my eight-year-old is better at math than he is!" You're not arguing that your eight-year-old is the smartest person in the family—you're just pointing out that Uncle Jay can't be the best, since at least one other person is better than him.

1

Drill 1.2—Identify the Building Blocks

1. Company spokesperson:

An investor has accused the CEO of financial impropriety, citing as evidence a $50,000 payment made to the CEO's son although no work was performed.	*Counterpremise*
In fact, the payment was perfectly legitimate.	*Conclusion*
The son's firm provides consulting services to the company,	*Background*
and this was an advance payment of 10% of project fees for a new endeavor slated to start in the next month.	*Premise*

2.

The female arkbird will lay eggs only when a suitable quantity of nesting material is available and the climate is suitably moderate.	*Premise*
This year, unseasonable temperatures have actually increased the amount of nesting material as trees and plants die, shedding twigs and leaves.	*Premise*
For this reason, the arkbirds in this region can be expected to lay eggs soon.	*Conclusion*

   The most common building blocks are premises and conclusions. Many arguments, like this one, will not contain counterpremises or background information.

3.

John Doe pleaded not guilty to the charge of embezzlement but was convicted after irrefutable evidence was found on his personal computer.	*Background*
It is illegal, however, to search a personal computer without the consent of the owner,	*Premise*
so Doe's conviction will be overturned on appeal.	*Conclusion*

   At first, the fact that *irrefutable evidence* of his guilt was found may seem like a premise. The conclusion, however, is that his *conviction will be overturned*, so irrefutable evidence of his guilt doesn't support that claim. Rather, the idea that this evidence is not permissible supports the claim that his conviction will be overturned.

Drill 1.3—Match Similar Arguments

1. **#1 *Running Study* and #6 *Cost Cutting***

   Pattern: *One particular plan has a good result. Therefore, it is the best way to accomplish a certain goal.*

   Both cases use **unjustified language** in the conclusion. According to the running study, it does sound like running will help people to improve their health. There is no information to suggest, however, that this is the optimal, or best, way to do so. Running might work for some people but not others. Or tennis might be even better than running. Running is good, but there is no evidence to say that it is the best.

   The cost cutting argument is a bit trickier. If automation saves more money than changing suppliers, then doesn't that mean that automation is the better choice? Sure! But the conclusion states that, by automating certain steps, the company will *maximize* its savings. What if it *also* changes suppliers? Nothing in the argument prevents the company from taking both steps.

2. **#2 *Freight Trains* and #4 *Heart Murmurs***

   Pattern: *Right now, some things toward the end of their life cycle are better than some things toward the beginning of their life cycle. So the older things must have been better to start with.*

   The problem in both cases is **survivor bias**. In the case of the freight train engines, it is very likely that the poorly built engines from before 1960 have long since fallen apart—only the best ones are left running. So the argument is illogically comparing the *best* old engines with *all* newer engines. New engines that were badly built haven't yet had much of a chance to fall apart. In the case of the dogs, the 15-year-old dogs are probably mostly the ones who never had heart murmurs in the first place, since their littermates who did have potentially fatal heart murmurs did not live to be 15 years old, sadly.

   Just as it would be unfair to compare one university's *best* graduates with *all* of another university's graduates, it is illogical to compare a group that has been weeded out (in this case, by long periods of time) with another group that hasn't.

3. **#3 *New Product* and #5 *Peacekeeping Force***

   Pattern: *In order to solve a problem, two things must happen. If one thing happens, the other one can't. (Therefore, the solution cannot take place.)*

   The first argument presents as fact that *to make a profit this quarter, Company X must increase sales of its old product while also introducing a new product that is as profitable as the old one*. If this is true—that this is the only way to make a profit this quarter—then the next premise makes it impossible to make a profit, since *whenever Company X introduces a new product, sales of the old product drop sharply*. This is not a paradox, nor is the argument flawed. It's just that the plan won't work. This situation might be called the **self-defeating plan**.

   The peacekeeping plan is similarly doomed. For the violence to stop, two things must happen: Surrounding nations must vote to send in forces and Nandia must give money. But if Nandia gives money, the other nations won't vote to send in forces. In other words, the plan will fail.

CR Assumptions and Deconstructing Arguments

In This Chapter...

- What Is an Assumption?

- Deconstructing Arguments

- Drill 2.1—Deconstructing Arguments

- Answers to Drill Set

In this chapter, you will learn how to deconstruct GMAT arguments to identify conclusions, premises, and other important components.

CHAPTER 2 CR Assumptions and Deconstructing Arguments

What Is an Assumption?

At the end of the last chapter, you learned about a particular category of flawed argument: big leaps in logic. Big leaps can be obvious, but arguments can also make smaller and more subtle—but no less problematic—leaps.

These leaps are the result of an **assumption**. The author relies on evidence that is not explicitly stated or just asserts that something is true without providing proof.

Consider this argument:

> The impoverished nation of Beltraja has several hospitals that practice good sanitation and employ well-trained doctors. However, these doctors report that, each year, thousands of Beltrajians succumb to fatal illnesses that could have been cured with antibiotics. Therefore, a relief plan to provide regular shipments of antibiotics to Beltraja's hospitals should save lives.

This seems like a pretty decent argument. Note that the conclusion is not too extreme—the argument does not say that *all* of the people will be saved. There are some gaps, however:

> People are dying because they weren't treated with antibiotics.
>
> ↓
>
> Give the hospitals antibiotics.
>
> ↓
>
> Some of the people won't die.

In either arrowed location, what is the author assuming? For one, the author assumes that the people who died were treated at the hospitals but weren't given antibiotics for some reason. It's certainly possible that the hospitals lack an adequate supply of antibiotics, but there are other possible explanations. Perhaps it is the case that the affected Beltrajians don't have the means to travel to a hospital to be treated in the first place. The author assumes that there is only one possible (or, at least, primary) reason: a shortage of antibiotics at the hospitals.

Assumptions are the fifth, unspoken building block of arguments. The author assumes something is true without actually stating that thing or providing evidence that it is true.

About half of the question types on the GMAT revolve around the weak points of an argument, assumptions that the author is making. If you can identify the author's assumptions, then you are halfway toward answering the question correctly.

Try this one:

> Consumption of fast food contributes to obesity. If a fast food restaurant is permitted to open right next door to the local high school and to sell to students during lunchtime, the students will become obese and the school's scores on a national fitness test will decline.

List the steps leading to the conclusion (it's okay if you use a different number of "steps" than these lines and arrows imply):

_____

↓

_____

↓

_____

Here's one possible response:

> Fast food place sells to students.
>
> ↓
>
> Students become obese.
>
> ↓
>
> Students do worse on fitness test.

There are some significant assumptions in this argument.

The author assumes students will eat at this restaurant in the first place (and regularly enough to become obese). The author also assumes either that this fast food is unhealthy and will contribute to obesity or that students will generally avoid healthy items and purchase the unhealthy ones.

The author further assumes that obese people generally score lower on a national fitness test. The argument doesn't actually detail what is required on the national fitness test, let alone how a subject's weight is a factor in performance on such a test. What if doing well on the test isn't any less likely for obese people?

Changing an argument to make a "larger" claim can introduce even more assumptions. Here's the Beltraja argument again, with a few changes (in bold):

> The impoverished nation of Beltraja has several hospitals that practice good sanitation and employ well-trained doctors. However, these doctors report that **approximately 3,000 Beltrajians per year die from illnesses that could be cured** with antibiotics. Therefore, a relief plan to provide regular shipments of antibiotics to Beltraja's hospitals **will save thousands of patients per year**.

The original conclusion seemed pretty reasonable—if people are dying because of a lack of antibiotics, sending some antibiotics ought to save at least some of those people (technically, if you save just two people, you've "saved lives").

But in this new version of the argument, the original problem has been quantified—about 3,000 people are dying. The new conclusion is that you'll save *thousands*, which implies at least 2,000. Can the plan save approximately two-thirds of the people who are dying? That is a much more ambitious goal, and more evidence would help support such a big conclusion. For instance, the author is assuming that antibiotics *alone* will save at least two-thirds of these people. Perhaps there are other medical complications that would still threaten lives, even if antibiotics are made available. Or perhaps a significant percentage of these people never seek medical treatment.

Some common types of assumptions are listed below. Anything the author assumes to be true in drawing the conclusion, though, is considered an assumption, even if it does not fall into the following categories.

Assumes Shared Beliefs

Here, the arguer assumes that the listener will share certain basic beliefs—some of which are mere impressions, prejudices, and so on. Here is an example:

> Smalltown Cinema currently prohibits movie attendance by unaccompanied teenagers under age 16. If this restriction is lifted, the theater's operating expenses will increase because of an increased need for cleaning services and repairs to the facility.

Some people read this argument and do not immediately see the flaw. Restate the argument in a simpler way to clarify the argument's structure:

> IF *unaccompanied teenagers under age 16 are allowed in the theater*...
>
> THEN *the theater will have to pay for cleaning and repairs.*

What's missing in the middle of that argument? What does the arguer need to prove in order to make the argument valid?

Consider a slightly different example:

> Smalltown Cinema currently prohibits movie attendance by elderly women. If this restriction is lifted, the theater's operating expenses will increase because of an increased need for cleaning services and repairs to the facility.

Isn't the argument now kind of strange? The speaker seems to think that elderly women make a mess in theaters and break things.

The speaker has made the assumption that elderly women disproportionately mess up and damage theaters. The reason that the assumption was so easy to spot in this case was that it was *not* something most of us intuitively believe.

However, many people take it for granted that teenagers make messes and are more likely to break things. The speaker in the original argument played on a general prejudice against teenagers. Although the speaker's argument depends on the idea that "teenagers under age 16 are more likely to make theaters dirty and to damage the facilities," the speaker didn't even bother to *write* that—and certainly didn't *prove* it. Don't take anything for granted, and don't bring in outside ideas.

Here's another example:

> The Urban Apartment Towers complex has seen a number of police visits to the property recently, resulting in the police breaking up loud parties held by young residents and attended by other young people. These police visits and the reputation for loud parties are hurting the complex's reputation and ability to attract new residents. To reduce the number of police visits and improve profitability, management plans to advertise its vacant apartments in a local publication for people aged 50 and up.

What is this argument assuming but not proving? That *people aged 50 and up are less likely to have loud parties or attract police visits*. This doesn't sound like a totally unreasonable assumption, but it's an assumption nonetheless. It's the arguer's job to prove such an assumption. It's your job to notice that the arguer hasn't done so.

If you see something like this ...

> Spider silk cannot be made in a lab; it can only be harvested directly from live spiders. So it is impractical to produce spider silk on an industrial scale.

... then think something like this:

> *That assumes that you can't "farm" spiders to produce the silk. Maybe you can!*

Assumes Skill and/or Will

For people to do something, they have to be able to do it, certainly, but they also have to want to. Both skill and will are necessary.

Some arguments give you one piece but not the other. A recommendation that *everyone should exercise two hours every day* might give reasons why people should want to do so, but ignore the fact that not everyone *can* exercise that much (e.g., people who are seriously ill). Consider the following example:

> The school should offer fresh vegetables at every lunch. Children who eat fresh vegetables are healthier, and fresh vegetables are cheaper than processed food, so the budget can accommodate the change.

What's the problem here? Maybe the school can afford to offer vegetables (the skill side). The argument makes a nod toward the will side: Maybe the *parents* would want their kids to eat fresh vegetables. But what about the will of the children themselves? How many kids eat fresh vegetables voluntarily?

The *Urban Apartment Towers* argument also has a skill/will problem. Maybe over-50 people in the local area cannot afford to live in the Towers. And how badly do people over 50 want to live in an apartment complex that has a reputation for loud parties? It's the responsibility of the arguer to answer.

Assumes the Future Equals the Past

To comply with consumer protection laws in the United States, investment firms have to tell you that "past performance is no guarantee of future results." So why do materials published by mutual funds often trumpet the fact that their precious metals mutual fund exceeded its benchmark for the past three quarters?

Because they know that people fall into this logical trap. Of course, in many ways the future *will* be like the past. If you didn't assume so, life would be a lot more difficult. But this assumption goes too far. In the late 1990s, people kept plowing money into internet stocks, believing that the ride wouldn't end (or wouldn't end yet!).

Remember that the future does not have to mimic the past. In a sense, every plan and proposal is guilty of this error, since every plan and proposal is forward-looking but uses the past as evidence. But some plans are more guilty than others.

If you see something like this ...

> The price of the stock went up eight months in a row, when the market was flat. Therefore, I should buy this stock.

... then think something like this:

> *How do you know that it will keep going up? Maybe the stock has already risen too far. Maybe the increase is random. After all, if enough people flip coins, someone will flip heads eight times in a row.*

Deconstructing Arguments

Remember this argument from the previous chapter?

> To be considered a form of cardiovascular exercise, an activity must raise the heart rate and keep it elevated for at least 20 minutes. Skydiving cannot properly be considered a form of cardiovascular exercise. While skydiving certainly does elevate a person's heart rate, the skydiver only experiences freefall for 60–70 seconds, followed by 5–6 minutes under a parachute—and, of course, it is not possible to string multiple dives immediately back-to-back.

The argument gets pretty complex. It often helps to write some things down to help you map out the parts and remember the major pieces of information. Mapping the argument can also help you to understand the relationships between different parts of the argument.

Here's an example of what one student might write:

$$CE: \uparrow \text{heart rate } 20+ \min$$

$$\text{©} \quad SD \neq CE$$

$$SD \text{ too short}$$

This student used some abbreviations and symbols, but you probably have figured out what most of them mean. *CE* stands for *cardiovascular exercise* and *SD* stands for *skydiving*. The up arrow means *increase* and *20+ min* means *at least 20 minutes*. The ≠ symbol is shorthand for a common piece of information in arguments: One thing does not represent or go along with another. Finally, the © is this student's way of denoting the conclusion of the argument.

Is that the only way to map out this argument? Definitely not! Someone else might draw something like this:

$$\text{cardio} = >HR \geq 20m$$

$$\text{BUT S only } 6\text{-}7m \longrightarrow S \underline{\text{not}} \text{ cardio}$$

This student used different abbreviations of course, but she also just laid things out differently in general. Instead of writing things out line by line as she read, she read the whole argument first, then laid it out according to the logical flow of information. She writes the conclusion off to the right after the arrow to set it apart from the rest of the argument.

There are many ways to organize information from Critical Reasoning arguments. On some, you might even want to make a table or draw a picture. Your task will be to find the right style for you. Whether you use variables or abbreviations to refer to entire premises (*B = the company will go bankrupt*) or merely words (*FF = fireflies*) will depend on the complexity of the argument and your own preferences.

Keep one important principle in mind as you develop your style: abbreviate aggressively! You'll only need to use your map for about 60–90 seconds after you're done creating it. You can abbreviate down to single-letter variables and still remember what they stand for 90 seconds later!

Here are some additional examples of symbols that you could use:

$$\approx \quad \text{similar to; almost the same as happening simultaneously}$$

$$\therefore \quad \text{therefore}$$

$$[\ ] \quad \text{[assumptions]}$$

Next, arrange the pieces of the argument in a logical order, one that makes sense for you. If you prefer to write each piece of information as you read, then use symbols or arrows to indicate what leads to what (and make sure to mark the conclusion). If you prefer to read first and then write, you can reorder the information to put the conclusion last or to the right (or first, if you prefer, as long as you are consistent).

Try this argument:

> A study of 120 elderly, hospital-bound patients in the United Kingdom showed that daily consumption of Nutree, a nutritional supplement containing vitamins, fiber, and sugar, increased by an average of four months the typical life expectancy for patients of the same age and physical condition. Thus, anyone who wants to live longer should drink Nutree every day.

Here is one possibility; can you decipher the abbreviations and symbols used?

$$\text{S: old, hosp take N daily} \longrightarrow \text{+4 mo avg LE}$$

$$\therefore \text{N daily} \longrightarrow \uparrow \text{LE for all}$$

$$[\text{old vs. all?}]$$

The notetaker starts by attributing the information to a *study* (S) and then conveys the study results. N is *Nutree* and LE is *life expectancy*. It's generally a good idea to rearrange the content slightly to clarify relationships or to fit a pattern you're used to. For instance, always putting causes on the left and effects on the right is a fine habit to adopt.

The last line is not stated in the argument. The student is noticing an assumption (a bad one!): The study only followed elderly people in the hospital. Would the same results hold true for everyone? The conclusion assumes so, but this may not be valid.

Drill 2.1—Deconstructing Arguments

Try to create a map of each argument on a piece of paper. Try to brainstorm any assumptions or pinpoint any weaknesses in the argument. (Note: You saw some of these arguments earlier in this book.)

1. The difference between a weed and a garden plant depends entirely on the opinion of the person who owns the land. Thus, it is impossible to develop a flawless garden "weed killer" that kills all types of weeds and leaves all types of garden plants unharmed. The Vytex Company's attempt to develop a perfect garden weed killer will fail.

2. The city parks are overcrowded, leading to long wait times for athletic fields and courts and lessening citizens' enjoyment of the parks. A new park should be built at the southern tip of the city, which does not have its own park. Because the heavily populated southern end of the city lacks a park, residents regularly travel to other parts of the city to use those parks, thus leading to overcrowding.

3. Van Hoyt College has produced at least one Rasmussen Scholar per year for the past decade. Therefore, Van Hoyt College is a very good school.

4. Researcher: The female arkbird will lay eggs only when a suitable quantity of nesting material is available and the climate is suitably moderate. This season, the arkbirds in our local habitat will be laying eggs because unusual temperature patterns have increased the amount of nesting material preferred by the arkbird.

5. The SML-1 is a test of computer programming abilities used by Human Resources departments to make hiring decisions and assess employees. The Cyvox Corporation reported an average score of 65 out of 100 for its job applicants. At Vectorcom Company, employees achieved an average score of 83—nearly 20 points higher than Cyvox. Therefore, Vectorcom's employees are better computer programmers than Cyvox's.

Answers to Drill Set

Drill 2.1—Deconstructing Arguments

1. Vytex's Weed Killer

Weed or plant? depends owner

∴ no perfect W-K b/c OD

© ∴ V's W-K will fail

This student used the abbreviation *OD*, which stands for *opinions differ*. It's not uncommon for an argument to have some kind of debate, so you might use *deb* or *OD* (or anything else you like, as long as you're consistent!) as your standard shorthand for "there is not a consensus on this issue."

Note that there are also two sets of therefore symbols. The student used the triangle dots to show a series of conclusions, then labeled the final conclusion with the © symbol.

If it is impossible to define what a weed is, then the argument is correct that it is impossible to develop a weed killer that will kill every type of weed. The argument assumes, though, that people don't actually agree on what is a weed and what is a plant. The argument also assumes that a *perfect weed killer* must kill every last type of weed. Perhaps customers would consider a product *perfect* if it kills the most common types of weeds for a particular climate or geographic area.

2. Overcrowded Parks

P crowd   long waits

b/c S no park, ppl travel   ⟶   Build P in S

[impl: reduce crowd]

The student uses S to mean *southern tip of the city*. Notice that these notes have a horizontal orientation, with the conclusion to the right, while the notes for the first problem show a more vertical orientation. You can use whichever orientation you like, but it's a good idea to be consistent.

The author assumes that if a new park is built at the southern tip, then the residents there won't travel to other parts of the city. What if, for example, these residents are visiting relatives who live in other areas of the city? Or, what if their children play on sports teams that meet in the other parks?

Further, the argument never specifies the volume of southern residents traveling to other areas of the city; it says only that (some) residents do regularly travel to those existing parks. What if they make up only 1% of the people who use the existing parks? Reducing usage by 1% is unlikely to relieve overcrowding.

3. Van Hoyt College

$$VHC: 1 + RS/yr$$
$$\textcircled{c}\ VHC = very\ good\ school$$
$$\{\ RS = good\ ?\ \}$$

This student included a note in brackets; use brackets to denote weaknesses or assumptions that you brainstorm when reading the argument. In this case, the student is questioning whether the number of Rasmussen Scholars is actually an appropriate metric to determine that a school is a very good school. What if it is relatively easy to become a Rasmussen Scholar, but most of Van Hoyt's students still can't qualify? Or, what if the school always chooses at least one Rasmussen Scholar every year, regardless of the quality of the students?

4. Arkbirds

$$R:\ A\ needs$$
$$1)\ nesting$$
$$AND$$
$$2)\ mod\ climate\ \Big\}\ lay\ eggs$$

$$Now:\ unusual\ temp \longrightarrow nesting \longrightarrow will\ lay\ eggs$$
$$[\,what\ about\ \#2\,?\,]$$

The argument specifies that the arkbird requires two things in order to lay eggs. The first one, nesting materials, is present this season, but what about the second one? What are *unusual temperature patterns*?

The required *suitably moderate* climate is one that is relatively mild, neither too hot nor too cold. Unusual temperature patterns could be anything—they could be mild or too hot or too cold or varying wildly from day to day. It's not clear that *this season* actually fulfills the second requirement.

5. Vectorcom vs. Cyvox

$$\text{SML: test of CP skill}$$

$$\text{C appl: } 65/100$$
$$\text{V empl: } 83/100 \longrightarrow \text{V empl} > \text{C empl}$$

$$[\text{empl? or appl??}]$$

Be careful with the language on this one! Know which groups you need to compare. The argument provides data for Cyvox *applicants* and Vectorcom *employees*, then draws a conclusion about the employees of both companies. Perhaps Cyvox only hires the people who score the best on the SML-1 test. If so, it's possible that Cyvox employees actually have higher test scores, on average, than Vectorcom employees.

CR Question Types and Trap Answers

In This Chapter...

In this chapter, you will learn how to identify the different types of CR problems and how to spot common types of traps in the answers.

CHAPTER 3 CR Question Types and Trap Answers

You have spent all of the Critical Reasoning (CR) portion of this book so far discussing **arguments**. Of course, it is also crucially important to understand the question being asked about that argument.

People make a lot of mistakes when they don't pay enough attention to the question. Many times, a careless student will read an argument and pick an answer that seems to "go along" with the argument, but the answer does not do what the question specifically asks!

GMAT questions fall into a few broad categories:

- **Questions about assumptions:** These include questions that ask directly about assumptions, as well as questions that ask you to strengthen and weaken arguments.
- **Questions about evidence:** These questions might ask you to draw an inference or conclusion. Or they might ask you to resolve a discrepancy or a paradox (an apparent contradiction that may not really be contradictory).
- **Questions about structure:** These questions will sometimes have two bold statements within the argument and ask you to pick the answer that tells the role of those two statements. Alternatively, a question might ask you how one person responds to another person's argument.

Decoding the Question Stem

The **question stem** will tell you what kind of question you have been asked. It's crucial, therefore, to learn how to decode the various question stems. The most common GMAT CR question types are discussed below; you can find a deeper discussion of these and other less common question types in Unit 2 of this guide.

Here are some sample question stems for Assumption family questions:

1. The argument depends upon which of the following assumptions?

2. Which of the following, if true, most strongly supports the argument above?

3. Which of the following, if true, would most weaken the claim that Vectorcom's employees are better computer programmers than Cyvox's?

What is each question asking you to do?

1. The argument depends on which of the following assumptions?

   This question asks directly about assumptions. It is important to deconstruct the argument, finding the premises and the conclusion and, if possible, brainstorming assumptions, before reading the answer choices. If you are able to brainstorm assumptions, the task of evaluating the answer choices will be easier.

3

For the Cyvox vs. Vectorcom argument from the previous chapter, a correct assumption answer might read: "The average score for Cyvox's employees is not appreciably higher than the average score for all Cyvox applicants."

2. Which of the following, if true, most strongly supports the argument above?

This question asks you to strengthen the argument. To do so, you must know what the argument's assumptions are. The correct answer will be a new piece of information that does not have to be true, but if it is true, then the argument is strengthened.

For the Cyvox vs. Vectorcom argument, a correct Strengthen answer might read: "The average score for applicants at a particular company is typically about the same as the average score for those who are eventually hired by that company."

Notice that this choice doesn't make the argument definitely true. Strengthen answers will rarely make the argument airtight. Rather, they will introduce a new piece of information that, if true, increases the likelihood that the conclusion is valid. If average applicant scores tend to be about the same as average employee scores, then it is more likely that the argument is valid.

3. Which of the following, if true, would most weaken the claim that Vectorcom's employees are better computer programmers than Cyvox's?

This question asks you to weaken the argument. To do so, you must know what the argument's assumptions are. The correct answer will be a new piece of information that does not have to be true, but if it is true, then the argument is weakened.

For the Cyvox vs. Vectorcom argument, a correct Weaken answer might read: "The average score for applicants at a particular company is typically lower than the average score for those who are eventually hired by that company."

Notice that this choice doesn't make the argument definitely false. Weaken answers will rarely destroy the argument. Rather, they will introduce a new piece of information that, if true, increases the likelihood that the conclusion is bad. If average applicant scores tend to be lower than average employee scores, then this explains why Vectorcom would have higher employee scores than Cyvox's applicant scores, and this diminishes the advantage that the original argument seemed to assign to Vectorcom's employees.

Here are sample question stems for the two Evidence family questions, along with descriptions of what each type is asking you to do:

4. Which of the following conclusions can most properly be drawn from the information above?

This question asks you to make an inference from the facts given in the argument. The argument itself will not contain a conclusion.

The test writers are not asking you to come up with one of the flawed conclusions that the assumption-type arguments contain. Rather, they are asking you to deduce, or to conclude, something that must be true from the given information. For instance, if last month Meme Corporation both increased its price on its flagship product and sold more units of the product than it had in the prior month, then Meme Corporation's revenues from this product must be higher last month than the month before.

5. Which of the following, if true, most helps to explain the surprising finding?

This question asks you to explain some kind of contradiction or discrepancy in the information provided. For instance, Meme Corporation sold more units of a particular product this year than last year, but revenues for this product declined. They sold more but revenues went down? What could explain this strangeness? A correct answer might read: "Meme Corporation had to reduce the retail price of this product by 15% due to increased competition." Ah! Well, if they aren't making as much money on a per-product basis, then it's entirely possible for revenues to decline even if they sell more units.

In a paradox question (or a question that mentions a *contradiction* or *discrepancy*), there is always a perfectly reasonable explanation for something that looks like a contradiction or impossibility. Pay attention to the exact wording; the subtle differences are often what crack the problem open.

These five question types are among the most commonly tested on the GMAT. There are others, but you can wait to learn those when you feel you're ready to move to Unit 2 of this guide.

3

Drill 3.1—Decoding the Question Stem

For each example, determine the question type. Which words most help you to make this determination?

1. Which of the following, if true, casts the most serious doubt on the politician's argument?

2. The consultant's statements, if true, best support which of the following conclusions?

3. Which of the following, if true, most helps to explain the apparent discrepancy between increasing incidence of fatal illness and increased life expectancy among the same population?

4. The conclusion drawn above is based on the assumption that...

5. Each of the following, if true, provides some support for hiring based in part on results of the personality test described EXCEPT:

Answers are on page 48.

Trap Wrong Answers

The GMAT tries to make things tricky when you get to the answer choices. Sometimes, an incorrect answer is actually going to look *better* to you than the correct answer will look. How can you spot and avoid such traps?

First, understand how the GMAT sets up the trap in the first place. If you understand how the trap works, you are much more likely to be able to avoid it.

1. Faulty Comparisons

You were first introduced to this idea during the Language Weaknesses discussion (under Flaws in Arguments in Chapter 1). Answer choices can make faulty comparisons, too! Consider some sample answers for this argument that you've seen before:

> A study of 120 elderly, hospital-bound patients in the United Kingdom showed that daily consumption of Nutree, a nutritional supplement containing vitamins, fiber, and sugar, increased by an average of four months the typical life expectancy for patients of the same age and physical condition. Thus, anyone who wants to live longer should drink Nutree every day.
>
> The argument depends upon which of the following assumptions regarding daily consumption of Nutree?
>
> (A) It is the top method for increasing life expectancy.
>
> (B) Among the people in the study, younger patients achieved a greater increase in life expectancy than older patients.
>
> (C) The demonstrated benefits are not limited to older, institutionalized patients.

One of the answers is correct, but the other two make some type of faulty comparison.

The study tested only elderly, hospital-bound patients, but the conclusion attempts to apply to everyone. The author is assuming, then, that the study results do actually apply to other groups of people than elderly, hospital-bound patients—a match for correct answer (C).

Relative vs. absolute: Answer (A) mistakes a relative statement for an absolute. Yes, Nutree has been shown to increase life expectancy for a certain group of people; in that sense, Nutree is a benefit or a good thing. Is it the *best* way to increase life expectancy? The argument provides no information to support this extreme statement.

When the argument provides evidence that something is good or better than another thing, that doesn't necessarily make it the best or only way, nor does it mean that you definitely want to do that good thing. Likewise, evidence that something is bad or worse than another thing doesn't make it the worst, nor does it mean that you definitely don't want to do that thing. Be careful not to draw an absolute conclusion when you have been given only relative information.

Note: On Critical Reasoning, don't automatically cross off an answer just because it contains an extreme word. Think through the logic. It's entirely possible that an argument would provide support for some kind of absolute outcome; if so, then an extreme word in the answer may be just fine. Check for proof in the text!

Irrelevant comparison or distinction: Answer (B) draws a distinction that is irrelevant for the given argument. The argument never distinguishes between the older and the younger patients in the study group. In particular, the GMAT might do this when the distinction would seem to make logical sense. After all, older patients are less likely to live as long just because they are *older*. If the argument doesn't make the distinction, though, then an answer choice that makes such a distinction is a trap.

2. Misinterpret the Argument

If you misread something in the argument, then you are going to have trouble answering that question correctly. One common mistake is to bring in outside or real-world knowledge and incorrectly interpret the conclusion.

For example:

> Tuition at Low-Ranked College is $5,000 per semester. Tuition at University of High Rank is $12,000 per semester. Therefore, if I go to Low-Ranked College, I will spend less money to earn my degree.
>
> Which of the following, if true, most seriously undermines the argument?
>
> (A) I'll get a worse education at Low-Ranked College.
>
> (B) University of High Rank students make an average of $65,000 a year, while students at Low-Ranked College make an average of $32,000 a year.
>
> (C) Fees and books cost $7,800 per semester at Low-Ranked College and $600 per semester at University of High Rank.

What's the trap? Many people interpret the conclusion as something like "I should go to Low-Ranked College" or "Low-Ranked College is the better choice." The argument does not say this, however. The argument says only that *if* you go, *then* you'll spend less money to earn your degree.

The trap here is to **articulate the incorrect conclusion** to yourself. Don't bring in any real-world knowledge or baggage. Stick closely to the conclusion as written in the argument.

If you articulate the wrong conclusion here, then you might fall for trap answers (A) and (B). Both undermine the (wrong) conclusion that you should go to Low-Ranked College. Only answer (C) undermines the conclusion as given. According to this answer, you'll pay $12,800 per semester at Low-Ranked College and only $12,600 per semester at University of High Rank.

Try another:

> It is true that students who meditate at least once a week do better on the GMAT than those who never meditate. This finding does not show that meditation causes people to do better, since students who meditate are more likely than other students to have adequate time to study.
>
> Which of the following, if true, most strongly supports the argument above?
>
> (A) A person who meditates but has little time to study is more likely to give up other activities to allow more study time than a person who does not meditate and also has little time to study.
>
> (B) Among people who meditate, the more frequent the meditation, the better that person does on the test, on average.
>
> (C) Among the students who have adequate time to study, those who do not meditate do just as well on the test as those who do meditate.

In this case, the author has set up the argument to try to get you to misidentify the conclusion. What's the trap?

The author acknowledges a fact: *Students who meditate at least once a week do better on the GMAT than those who never meditate.* The tricky part is the beginning of the next sentence: *This finding does **not** show that meditation causes people to do better.*

Yes, that word is bolded for emphasis. This is the trap! Many people have already assumed that the *it is true* language means that there is a causal relationship, but the author says that there is *not* a causal relationship. Rather, according to the author, there is some other reason why these two things happen together.

If you get this conclusion wrong, then you're going to be supporting, or strengthening, the wrong argument. Indeed, trap answers (A) and (B) both support the mistaken conclusion that regular meditation causes someone to do better on the test. These are the opposite of the correct answer.

Answer (C) indicates that the key is having enough time to study in the first place. If you do, then it doesn't matter as much whether you do or do not meditate. In this scenario, perhaps people who meditate have more time on average to study because they just have more free time in general. After all, they have the time to meditate at least once a week. Therefore, answer choice (C) is correct.

Finally, did you note that incorrect answer (B) also tossed in an irrelevant comparison? The argument compares never meditating to meditating at least once a week. It doesn't distinguish between those who meditate a little and those who meditate a lot.

The wording of a question stem might also cause you to articulate the incorrect conclusion. For instance, what if the Low-Ranked College question had asked:

> Which of the following, if true, most seriously supports a claim that a degree from Low-Ranked College will not cost less than a degree from University of High Rank?

Say what? That sentence is seriously confusing! The question stem gives a different conclusion than the one in the argument: In this case, the question stem claims that a degree from Low-Ranked College will not cost less, and you're asked to support this claim. This is the same thing as undermining the original conclusion given in the argument. If you support, or undermine, the incorrect conclusion, you're going to get the question incorrect.

Another common mistake is to misinterpret the question stem, or simply to get turned around, and **answer the wrong question**. It can be easy during the stress of the test to get turned around; make sure that you write down S for Strengthen or W for Weaken (or some similar abbreviations) so that you don't mistakenly pick a Weaken answer when the question asked you to Strengthen.

3. Superficial Word Matches

Have you ever had this happen? You narrow down to two answer choices, but you don't know how to choose between them. One of them feels better, though, because many of the words in the answer choice match directly with language from the argument, while the other one doesn't match so exactly. So you pick the one that matches better . . . and later you discover that you fell into a trap.

If the GMAT made every correct answer feel like a perfect fit, then way too many people would be answering hard questions correctly. How do they get you to cross off the correct answer or at least contemplate doing so?

Try this problem out; when you're done, see if you can articulate why the correct answer is designed to sound less appealing than at least one of the incorrect answers:

> Researcher: People who study for 30 minutes a day aren't as likely to reach their goal score on the GMAT as those whose study sessions last 90 minutes a day. But those who study for more than 5 hours a day are less likely to reach their goal score on the GMAT than those who study for less than 5 hours a day. So everyone should study for more than 90 minutes a day but less than 5 hours a day.
>
> Which of the following, if true, most seriously weakens the conclusion above?
>
> (A) In some cases, daily study periods of an hour are sufficient to allow the student to achieve his or her preferred result.
>
> (B) The length or quantity of a student's study is less important than the quality of that study.
>
> (C) When studying is split among multiple sessions in a day, taking a break of 90 minutes or more between sessions can result in a failure to reach one's goal score.

Did you spot the trap or fall into it?

Let's start with trap answer (B). It might be true that quality of study is more important than quantity of study, but the argument addresses only length of study. This choice makes an irrelevant distinction between two types of study, one of which is never addressed in the argument.

The next trap answer is (C). Look at all the exact language matches between the passage and the answer choice: *sessions* [in] *a day, 90 minutes, reach* [one's] *goal score*. So what's the problem?

The 90 minutes referred to here is not the same 90 minutes referred to in the argument. In the answer, the 90 minutes represents a break, not study time. It's possible for someone to study for 15 minutes, take a 2-hour break, and then study for another 15 minutes. It's also possible for someone to study for 90 minutes, take a 90-minute break, and then study for another 90 minutes. According to the argument data, the first person studied a non-optimal length of time and the second person studied an optimal length, yet both match the language in trap answer (C): They split their studies into multiple sessions and took breaks of 90 minutes.

Why is it tempting to eliminate correct answer (A)? First, it uses some synonyms instead of direct language matches: *daily* instead of *a day*; study *periods* instead of study *sessions*; *preferred result* instead of *goal score*. All of the choice's words are valid synonyms, though: They mean the same thing as the words in the argument! Further, this choice talks about a one-hour time frame, which is not mentioned in the argument.

Logically, though, the information about this one-hour time frame does weaken the argument! If some people can reach their goal scores by studying only one hour a day, then the claim that *everyone* should study at least 90 minutes a day is weakened. By contrast, trap answer (C) doesn't fit logically, since anyone studying any length of time could take 90-minute breaks.

Dealing with the superficial word match trap is tricky, since sometimes the correct answer really does match the language of the argument. Your first line of defense is to think about the actual logic of the information and how it fits with the argument. When this doesn't work, though, and you find yourself with two answers that both seem okay, one with exact language matches and one with synonyms, take two steps:

1. Check the synonyms to make sure that they're valid based on the information given in the argument. If not, eliminate this choice.

2. If the synonyms are all valid, guess this choice, on the theory that the trap is to get someone to fall for the other answer: superficial word matches with faulty logic.

Drill 3.2—Spotting the Trap Answers

Test out what you've just learned. Give yourself approximately two minutes per question to try each of the full Critical Reasoning problems in this set. Note: You have seen some of the arguments before.

1. For the violence in Kirkenberg to be stopped, the majority of surrounding nations must vote to send in a peacekeeping force, and the wealthy nation of Nandia must provide funding. If Nandia becomes involved in any way regarding Kirkenberg, at least half of the nations surrounding Kirkenberg will vote against intervening in Kirkenberg.

    The claims above most strongly support which of the following conclusions?

    (A) Nandia is the wealthiest nation in the region surrounding Kirkenberg.

    (B) Violence in Kirkenberg is likely to result in unrest in other countries in the region.

    (C) It is unlikely that the violence in Kirkenberg will be stopped.

    (D) Most nations surrounding Kirkenberg oppose the current leadership in Nandia.

    (E) The peacekeeping forces would not have sufficient equipment without financial support from Nandia.

2. The Urban Apartment Towers complex has seen a number of police visits to the property recently, resulting in the police breaking up loud parties held by young residents and attended by other young people. These circumstances are hurting the complex's reputation and ability to attract new residents. To reduce the number of police visits and improve profitability, management plans to advertise its vacant apartments in a local publication for people aged 50 and up.

    Which of the following, if true, would cast the most doubt regarding the effectiveness of the management's plan?

    (A) No recent police visits to Urban Apartment Towers have been to the apartments of residents over the age of 50.

    (B) A substantially cheaper apartment complex may be built in a neighboring town.

    (C) Residents over the age of 50 are more likely to call police in circumstances in which young people would not call.

    (D) A nearby condominium complex of similar size had far fewer police visits last year than Urban Apartment Towers.

    (E) People over 50 are much more likely than young people to host parties with fewer than 10 guests.

3. Lexton University began offering Biology 101 courses online as well as in a traditional classroom setting. Students in all sections of the course were given the same final exam. On average, the students in the online sections received higher scores on the final exam than students in the traditional classroom-based sections. Therefore, the students in the online sections learned more about biology than did students in the classroom-based sections.

    The argument above is based on which of the following assumptions?

    (A) Final exam scores accurately represent how much students learned about biology.

    (B) Most current Lexton students report that they would be interested in taking some but not all of their courses online.

    (C) Students from Burbain College who took only online accounting courses scored better on the accounting licensing exam than students who took only traditional classroom-based accounting courses.

    (D) Lexton University should begin offering other introductory courses online.

    (E) In post-course surveys, the students enrolled in the online sections reported studying an average of two more hours per week than students in the classroom-based sections.

4. A plastics factory next to Hullson River dumps its waste, which contains a certain toxin, directly into the river. The amount of waste the factory dumps into the river is directly proportional to the amount of plastic the factory produces. This year, the factory produced 50% more plastic than last year. Yet measurements taken 50 yards downstream of the waste dump site show that concentrations of the toxin were significantly lower than they were at the same site last year.

    Which of the following, if true, does the most to explain the surprising finding?

    (A) The factory is considering adopting a production technique that would drastically reduce the amount of the toxin produced.

    (B) Unseasonably heavy rains have increased the volume of water in Hullson River by 75%.

    (C) In studies, high concentrations of the toxin in water have been shown to inhibit certain species of fish from laying eggs.

    (D) When the plastic factory produces more plastic, the concentration of the toxin within the waste dumped into the river increases.

    (E) Another factory, located upstream from the plastics factory, produces waste containing a different toxin and dumps that waste into the river.

5. In Mountain Village, the frequency of bears entering residential neighborhoods has recently increased due to a shortage of food in the forest in which the bears live. In order to track the locations that the bears visit, Mountain Village has set up a special phone number that residents are asked to call if they see a bear in a residential neighborhood.

Which of the following, if true, most strongly supports the claim that the plan will have its intended effect?

(A) A neighboring town decreased bear entries into residential neighborhoods by installing trash cans with specially designed lids that bears cannot open.

(B) The new phone number that residents are asked to call has not been widely publicized.

(C) Bears generally pose no threat to humans although they may behave aggressively toward small domestic animals.

(D) Residents have been educated as to how to scare the bears away without making them more aggressive.

(E) Bears generally enter residential neighborhoods during the daytime hours when many residents are outside.

Answers are on pages 48–52

Answers to Drill Sets

Drill 3.1—Decoding the Question Stem

1. **Weaken** (*cast doubt* is a synonym for weaken).

2. **Inference.** Careful! The word *support* makes this seem like a Strengthen question. Note what you're supporting though: one of *the following conclusions*. Where are those conclusions located? In the answer choices! You'll need to infer, or deduce, what must be true from the information given in the argument.

3. **Explain a discrepancy.** Pick the answer that resolves the discrepancy by providing a reasonable explanation for what looked, at first, like a contradiction.

4. **Assumption.** The question asks you to find something that the author assumes in drawing his conclusion in the argument above.

5. **Strengthen (EXCEPT).** This is a tricky one. In this case, the word *support* does signal a Strengthen question because the question itself tells you the conclusion to support (you should base part of your hiring decision on this personality test). If a question asks you to support a conclusion given in the argument or question stem, then it is a Strengthen question. If a question asks you to support a conclusion given in the answer choices, then it is an Inference question.

   In addition, this is an EXCEPT question. Four of the answers will strengthen the conclusion; these four answers are all incorrect. One answer will not strengthen the conclusion. This answer will not necessarily weaken the conclusion; it might do nothing at all to the conclusion. This answer is the correct one.

Drill 3.2—Spotting the Trap Answers

1. **(C) It is unlikely that the violence in Kirkenberg will be stopped:** You saw this argument before.

   The question asks you to support a conclusion found in the answer choices, so this is an Inference problem.

   Sketch out what you know:

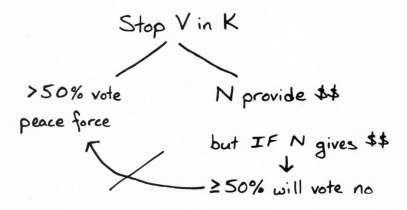

In order for the violence to stop, two things must happen: 1) At least 50% of surrounding nations have to vote to send in a peacekeeping force, *and* 2) Nandia has to provide funding. But if Nandia does actually provide that funding, then *at least half* of the other nations will vote against sending in the peacekeeping force.

What must be true, given this information? On the one hand, Kirkenberg needs funding from Nandia. On the other, if it gets that funding, then it won't have 50% or greater support from the surrounding nations for the peacekeeping force. Things don't look good for Kirkenberg. Answer **(C)** is correct: It looks pretty unlikely that the violence in Kirkenberg can be stopped.

Answer (A) goes too far with the word *wealthiest*. Nandia is described only as *wealthy*, not the *wealthiest*. Answer (B) goes beyond the scope of the argument; no information is provided as to what may happen in other countries.

Answers (D) and (E) both introduce information that goes beyond what the argument discusses. On Inference questions, stick tightly to the information presented. Don't bring in outside information. Answer (D) talks about the *current leadership* and answer (E) talks about *equipment*, neither of which is addressed in the argument.

2.   **(C) Residents over the age of 50 are more likely to call police in circumstances in which young people would not call:** You saw this argument in a previous chapter.

The question asks you to *cast doubt* on the plan, or weaken the argument.

> Young: loud parties, police
>
> hurting UAT
>
> Plan: target 50+ yrs ⟶ ↓ police, ↑ profit

What is the plan? There have been a bunch of loud parties held and attended by young people and the police have been called. The complex is getting a bad reputation and having trouble attracting new residents. The plan is to *advertise to people aged 50 and up* in order to *reduce the number of police visits and improve profitability*. What assumptions is the author making, and how might these assumptions weaken the argument?

The author assumes older people won't also have loud parties; however, maybe people over 50 have the loudest parties of all. That would certainly weaken the argument. The author also assumes older people are going to want to move into a complex with a bad reputation for loud parties and police visits. The part about profitability is also a big leap: Why will having older residents improve profitability?

If older people do move in, and they are also more likely to call the police over various issues, as answer **(C)** states, then bringing in older residents makes it less likely that management's plan to reduce the number of police visits is going to work.

If answer (A) is true, it might actually *strengthen* the assumption that older people don't have loud parties. Answer (B) doesn't address the management's plan for Urban Apartment Towers specifically.

Answer (D) is a faulty comparison: The size might be similar, but the residents' ages might be far different, the layout of the complex might be different enough to minimize noise, and so on.

Answer (E) matches a lot of the language from the argument, but the meaning of those words is off. Plus, if anything, this might actually strengthen the argument by showing that older people typically have smaller parties (though you'd also have to assume that smaller parties are quieter parties, which isn't a given).

3. **(A) Final exam scores accurately represent how much students learned about biology:** This is a brand-new argument.

The question asks you to identify an assumption made by the author.

Bio 101: online or trad   Ⓒ

                                 → online learned more

online exam > trad exam

              [maybe already knew more?]

LU offers the same class both online and in a traditional classroom. On the final exam, the online students did better than the others. The argument concludes that the online students learned more during the course. What is the author assuming?

She assumes that a higher final exam score actually means they learned more during the course. Maybe, for some reason, those students knew more about biology before the class started. Maybe they're better at taking tests in general. Maybe they cheated!

Answer **(A)** matches the assumption.

Answers (B) and (D) don't address the actual events that occurred. Note that (D) follows from the conclusion: If it really is the case that people learn better online, then maybe it would be a good idea for Lexton to offer more online classes. The question didn't ask this, though; the question asked you to find an assumption used to draw the conclusion.

Answer (C) is an irrelevant comparison. While data from another college showing that students learned more from an online course might help the argument, note that this choice does not actually say the online Burbain students learned more in their accounting course. The choice shows the same data that Lexton presented: Certain students did better on an exam, but who knows why they did better?

Answer (E) sounds good. If the online students studied two more hours per week, then it makes sense that they did better. But this is a trap; the choice is too specific. Remember, the question asked: What is the author assuming to be true? The author does not have to assume that the students studied an average of two hours more, specifically. They could have studied one hour more on average or three hours more on average, or any other number. The online students could even have studied less if they studied more efficiently!

4.   **(B) Unseasonably heavy rains have increased the volume of water in Hullson River by 75%:** This is another new argument.

The question asks you to explain a *surprising finding*. This is an Explain a Discrepancy question.

waste (with A) ⟶ river

> plastic = > waste; +50% plastic this yr

BUT conc of A much lower?? How?

The plastics factory dumps waste, including a specific toxin, straight into the river. It produced more plastic this year so, according to the argument, it should also be dumping more waste. But measurements show that there's a lot less of the toxin in the river this year than last year. How come?

The argument doesn't say that the amount of the toxin A produced is directly proportional to the waste produced. Maybe the factory did have more waste but it changed something in its manufacturing process (or something else) and that reduced how much of the toxin was produced? Or maybe the equipment used to measure the toxin levels changed or is faulty somehow?

It turns out to be another explanation entirely. Answer **(B)** indicates that it's been raining a lot, which significantly increased the amount of water in the river. The argument says that the concentration levels were measured, or the percentage of the toxin in the water. But if the water volume is much higher, then the *concentration* levels could go down even if there's just as much (or more!) of the toxin in the water this year as last year. If you add a teaspoon of salt to a cup of water, that water is going to taste a lot saltier than if you added a teaspoon of salt to a gallon of water.

Answer (A) might explain a *future* reduction in the toxin, but the argument is discussing what has already happened. Answers (C) and (E) are irrelevant; you need to explain the surprising info about the original toxin, not something about fish laying eggs or anything about a different toxin.

Answer (D) might look good because it matches a lot of the language from the passage, but be careful! It is actually the opposite of what you need. If it's the case that more production of plastic leads to more of the toxin, then the finding that the concentrations have decreased is even more surprising. Your task is not to show why something is surprising. Your task is to explain, or to resolve, that discrepancy.

5.   **(E) Bears generally enter residential neighborhoods during the daytime hours when many residents are outside:** This is another new argument.

The question asks you to strengthen the plan. What is that plan?

↓ food ⟶ ↑ bears in nbrhd

Plan: call phone # ⟶ track location

Because of a food shortage, a lot more bears are coming into the neighborhoods (abbreviation: *nbrhd*). The village is asking people to call in when they see a bear so that the village can track the location of the bears.

What is the author assuming? First, the author assumes that people will actually see the bears. What if the bears hide among the trees and bushes or only come out at night? Second, the author assumes that people will pick up the phone and call. Perhaps the residents just don't care.

Answer **(E)** fits one of the assumptions: If the bears come during the daytime hours and residents are often outside at that time, then it's more likely that they'll actually see the bears.

Answer (A) goes after the wrong conclusion. The village isn't trying to stop the bears from coming (at least not yet). The stated goal is just to track the location of the bears. Answer (D) is similarly tempting: If you run into a bear, it would definitely be helpful to know how to scare it off! This still isn't the goal of the plan, though.

Answer (B) weakens the argument; if people don't know the number, how can they call, even if they see a bear?

Answer (C) might explain why the village wants to track the bears' locations, but it does not address whether the plan will work.

3

Putting It All Together on CR

In This Chapter...

In this chapter, you will practice everything you have learned so far about CR.

CHAPTER 4 Putting It All Together on CR

It's time to test your new skills using a full drill!

This set is designed both to test you on what you've learned and to stretch your brain a bit. You learned about some of the question types in the preceding chapters. Others are types you haven't learned about yet! Do your best, and consider this your introduction to the next level of CR study.

In Unit 2 of this guide, you will learn about the full set of CR problem types, including strategies for deconstructing complicated arguments, eliminating trap answers, and identifying tricky correct answers.

Drill 4.1—Critical Reasoning "Hints"

The following drill contains 10 Critical Reasoning problems, representing a variety of question types.

Every problem is followed by one or more hints. If you don't feel that you need a hint, then go ahead and answer the question without looking at the hints.

If you do want a hint, read them one at a time. If you don't need them all, don't use them all! Read only as much as you need to have an idea of what to do next.

1. President of Teachers' Union: **Many people are convinced that declining test scores in our district are the fault of teachers.** Yet our school district has recently seen a large influx of enrolling students who do not speak any English at all. Nearby districts that have seen a similar influx of students who do not speak English have all experienced much larger drops in test scores. It is a testament to the skill and dedication of our teachers that test scores in our district have dropped so little.

    The bold statement in the argument plays which of the following roles?

    (A) It is the main conclusion of the argument.

    (B) It is a finding that the argument seeks to explain.

    (C) It introduces an explanation that the argument seeks to refute.

    (D) It provides support for the main conclusion of the argument.

    (E) It is a judgment that the argument corroborates.

    HINT #1: Try to answer this question in your own words before you read the answer choices. In order to do so, it will help to diagram.

    HINT #2: Try to label each piece of information using the CR building block categories.

    HINT #3: What is the conclusion? How does the boldface information relate to the conclusion?

2. The drug Nephoprene is the only drug proven to help certain harmful medical conditions, but it also has serious side effects. Doctors are responsible for weighing the benefits of a drug against the possible harm to the patient from side effects, and most doctors have chosen not to prescribe Nephoprene even to patients who would experience benefits.

The considerations given best serve as part of an argument that

(A)   Nephoprene will not cure patients

(B)   most doctors have determined that the side effects of Nephoprene outweigh the benefit

(C)   patients who want to take Nephoprene are not able to obtain prescriptions for it

(D)   not all patients with medical conditions that can be helped by Nephoprene will actually experience benefits when taking it

(E)   most drugs have some side effects, whether mild or more serious

HINT #1: *The considerations given best serve as part of an argument that* indicates that the answer choices contain an argument. The word *argument* is a synonym for *conclusion*.

HINT #2: If the answers contain conclusions, then the question is an Inference question.

HINT #3: On Inference questions, your task is to find an answer that must be true based on the information from the argument.

3. A candidate for governor has suggested repealing the state law requiring cigarette advertisers to print a warning label about the dangers of smoking on every cigarette pack. He suggests a new law requiring cigarette manufacturers to publish recent data and studies about the dangers of smoking on websites that the manufacturers will create for this purpose. The candidate argues that the plan will provide consumers with more detailed information so that they may make better decisions about smoking.

The argument assumes which of the following?

(A)   It is harder to break an addiction to alcohol than to cigarettes.

(B)   Consumers are willing and able to visit the websites and evaluate the data and studies presented.

(C)   Competing candidates for governor have not introduced the same or a superior plan relating to cigarette warnings.

(D)   Most people are not able to break their addictions to cigarettes.

(E)   Smoking will become more popular if this plan is not enacted.

HINT #1: This is an Assumption question.

HINT #2: Your task on Assumption questions is to find something that fills the gap between the author's premises and the author's conclusion. What is the author assuming to be true in drawing his conclusion?

HINT #3: This argument is a plan. In general, the author assumes the plan will work as stated. What are the weak points in the plan?

4

4. Researchers have noted that panda bears that have given birth to live offspring live longer in the wild. Therefore, these researchers have concluded that giving birth to live offspring increases a panda's lifespan.

    The argument makes which of the following assumptions?

    (A) Pandas that have given birth to live offspring will not be killed by predators.

    (B) Since male pandas cannot give birth, female pandas live longer than male pandas.

    (C) Pandas that are already likely to live longer are not more likely to give birth to live offspring.

    (D) Female pandas are not likely to die while giving birth.

    (E) Pandas that have given birth to multiple live offspring are likely to live even longer than pandas that have given birth to only a single live offspring.

    HINT #1: This is an Assumption question.

    HINT #2: Your task on Assumption questions is to find something that fills the gap between the author's premises and the author's conclusion. What is the author assuming to be true in drawing this conclusion?

    HINT #3: In the sequence of events, what causes what?

5. Newspaper editorial: It is important that penalties for adults dealing drugs on school grounds remain extremely severe. If the penalties became less severe, more students would become addicted to drugs.

    Which of the following is an assumption that supports drawing the conclusion above from the reason given for that conclusion?

    (A) Drug dealers are already being deterred from drug dealing on school grounds due to the penalties currently in place.

    (B) Drug use is harmful to the academic careers of students.

    (C) Drug dealing on school grounds is punished more harshly than drug dealing off school grounds.

    (D) Those who deal drugs on school grounds are not employees at those schools.

    (E) There is a significant chance that some of those addicted to drugs will ultimately die from drug-related causes.

    HINT #1: This is an Assumption question.

    HINT #2: Your task on Assumption questions is to find something that fills the gap between the author's premises and the author's conclusion. Can you brainstorm anything that the author is assuming to be true?

    HINT #3: This argument is a plan. In general, the author assumes the plan will work as stated. What are the weak points in the plan?

6. In the last 10 years, usage of pay phones in Bridgeport has dropped by 90%. Since cell phone usage is much higher among middle- and upper-income residents of Bridgeport than among lower-income residents, the Bridgeport City Council has decided to remove pay phones from middle- and upper-income neighborhoods, while retaining those in lower-income neighborhoods. The council's reasoning is that this plan will respond appropriately to demand for pay phones and thereby inconvenience very few people.

    Which of the following, if true, would most strongly support the claim that the plan to retain pay phones only in lower-income neighborhoods will have the intended effect?

    (A) In certain areas, pay phone usage has dropped only 50%–60% over the past 10 years.

    (B) Middle-income residents are more likely to use pay phones than high-income residents.

    (C) Some lower-income residents do use cell phones.

    (D) People who need a pay phone are most likely to use one within two miles of their home.

    (E) Eliminating pay phones would save the city money.

    HINT #1: This is a Strengthen question.

    HINT #2: Your goal on Strengthen questions is to find a new piece of information that, if true, would make the conclusion at least a little more likely to be valid.

    HINT #3: Can you brainstorm any assumptions before looking at the answer choices?

7. The Orange Corporation is conducting market research in preparation for the launch of its new device, the 3-D eSlate. Thus far, in Orange's market research, two groups have emerged as likely buyers of the eSlate: medical professionals and people making more than $250,000 a year. Since the number of medical professionals in the target market plus the number of people making more than $250,000 a year in the target market is over 20 million people, and since Orange typically achieves a sales rate of 25% or more in its target markets, Orange will sell over 5 million units of the eSlate.

    Which of the following, if true, would most weaken the author's conclusion?

    (A) Nearly 45% of medical professionals in the target market have already purchased a similar product from a competitor.

    (B) The eSlate has many more uses for education professionals than for medical professionals.

    (C) Many people with astigmatism and other vision problems will have trouble using the 3-D features of the eSlate.

    (D) Many medical professionals make more than $250,000 a year.

    (E) People who make more than $250,000 a year buy more electronic devices than people who make less than $250,000 a year.

    HINT #1: This is a Weaken question.

    HINT #2: Your task is to find a new piece of information that, if true, will make the argument a little less likely to be valid. You do not need to destroy the argument.

    HINT #3: What is the argument assuming? What do the numbers tell you and what *don't* they tell you?

8.   A study of full-time employees in Langlia revealed that female workers take more days off from work due to illness than do male workers. The same study also revealed that female workers are more likely than male workers to go in to work when they are sick.

Which of the following conclusions can most properly be drawn from the information above?

(A)   Langlian employers prefer that sick employees stay home so as to avoid infecting others.

(B)   Childbearing and related medical conditions are responsible for the greater number of sick days taken by Langlian female workers.

(C)   In Langlia, both male and female workers sometimes call in sick when they are actually healthy.

(D)   In Langlia, female workers are sick on more work days than male workers.

(E)   Female workers in Langlia are more conscientious about their jobs than are male workers.

HINT #1: This is an Inference question.

HINT #2: The correct answer to an Inference question will be something that must be true given the information in the argument.

9.   This year, the Rocktown school district offered a free summer enrichment program called "History Rocks" to its rising fourth-grade students. Therefore, fourth graders in the Rocktown school district will score better this year on American history tests.

Each of the following, if true, would strengthen the author's conclusion EXCEPT:

(A)   "History Rocks" focuses entirely on American history.

(B)   The majority of the district's rising fourth graders attended the program.

(C)   For the past five years, Rocktown students have scored lower, on average, on American history tests than have students in neighboring towns.

(D)   The material on fourth-grade history tests in Rocktown is substantially similar to the material being covered in the enrichment program.

(E)   It has been proven that students retain knowledge better when learning one subject at a time, as is the case in the "History Rocks" program.

HINT #1: This is a bit of a weird question type: It's asking you what does *not* strengthen the conclusion. What kind of answer would fit the bill?

HINT #2: The four incorrect answers should strengthen the conclusion. The correct answer should either weaken it or do nothing to it.

10. Over the past three decades, the number of hospital beds available for inpatient psychiatric treatment in the United States has declined from 4 per 1,000 population to 1.3 per 1,000 population. Over the same period in Japan, beds increased from 1 per 1,000 population to 2.9 per 1,000 population. Also during this period, annual mortality rates for persons with mental disorders have risen substantially in the United States, while declining in Japan.

   Which of the following, if true, would cast the most serious doubt on the conclusion that the reduction in hospital beds is principally responsible for the increase in mortality in the United States?

   (A) The number of hospital beds available for inpatient psychiatric treatment in Canada has declined over the past three decades, with no increase in mortality.

   (B) Due to advances in medical care and training over the past three decades, outpatient treatment is more effective than inpatient treatment for many mental disorders.

   (C) The incidence of mental disorders in Japan has been decreasing, even as the country has increased the number of beds available for inpatient psychiatric treatment.

   (D) Over the past three decades, Japan has offered state-sponsored health insurance to all citizens, while the United States has not.

   (E) Over the past three decades, the incidence of mental disorders that are more likely to end in death has risen in the United States and declined in Japan.

   HINT #1: This is a Weaken question.

   HINT #2: Your task on Weaken questions is to find an answer that makes the argument less likely to be valid.

   HINT #3: When the question stem contains specific information about the argument, that information typically either is the conclusion or is referring to the conclusion.

Answers are on pages 61–67

Critical Reasoning Next Steps

Congratulations! You're done with Foundations of Critical Reasoning. It's time to jump to the main Critical Reasoning chapters in Unit 2 of this book.

The next unit includes more specific methods of deconstructing arguments and ways to eliminate tricky incorrect answers. In conjunction with our book, we also recommending using the *GMAT Official Guide* books, which contain real GMAT questions from past exams.

Answers to Drill Set

Drill 4.1—Critical Reasoning "Hints"

1. **(C) It introduces an explanation that the argument seeks to refute:**

$$\downarrow \text{scores} \longrightarrow \text{T fault}$$

$$\text{P: BUT} >> \text{S can't speak E}$$

$$\text{sim schools: } \downarrow\downarrow \text{ scores}$$

$$\copyright \text{ our T: drop is less!}$$

This question type was not presented earlier in the guide, but it asks about the building blocks that you learned about in Chapter 1.

When the question asks you to "describe the role" of a particular boldface statement, first find the conclusion of the argument. Then, see how the boldface statement relates to that conclusion.

The president of the union claims that, in fact, the test results are good. Other districts with similar student bodies had even larger drops in test scores. How does the boldface statement relate to this claim?

The boldface statement claims that the declining test scores are a problem and the fault of the teachers; this goes against the president's claim. The correct answer, then, is not (A), (D), or (E), which all support the conclusion.

Between (B) and (C), the key is whether the argument is trying to *explain* or *refute* the boldface information. Since the argument actively goes against what the boldface statement claims, the correct answer is **(C)**.

2. **(B) Most doctors have determined that the side effects of Nephoprene outweigh the benefits:**

$$\text{N} = \text{helpful but bad SE}$$

$$\text{most D: no N, even when helps}$$

The wording of the question stem indicates that the answer choices contain an *argument*, or conclusion. If the answer choices contain a conclusion, then this is an Inference question. On Inference questions, your task is to find something that must be true according to the information given in the argument.

The argument establishes that Nephoprene is the *only* drug that can help certain medical conditions. If doctors are responsible for weighing the benefits against the side effects, and most decide not to prescribe Nephoprene, even though it's the only available drug for certain conditions, then these doctors must have decided that the benefits were not worth the side effects. Answer **(B)** is a match.

Choice (A) is a good trap: If Nephoprene did cure patients, then wouldn't the doctors prescribe it even if it had bad side effects? Not necessarily. What if the side effect is to cause a heart attack that may kill the patient?

Answer (C) is too extreme; the argument says only that *most* doctors don't prescribe Nephoprene, not that it's impossible for any patient to get a prescription.

Answers (D) and (E) are probably true about drugs in general, but this particular argument does not provide evidence to support either answer.

3. **(B) Consumers are willing and able to visit the websites and evaluate the data and studies presented:**

C: stop warning on pack

move to web

© > d+l ⟶ better decision

[too much d+l ?]

On Assumption questions, your task is to find the answer that plugs the gap between one of the premises and the conclusion. What is this author assuming to be true but not stating outright?

In this case, the argument makes many assumptions:

That people make smoking decisions rationally (not based on addiction or other personal preferences)

That people will visit the website

That people will be able to understand the information presented on the website

Answer **(B)** matches with the second and third assumptions listed above. Answers (A) and (C) both make irrelevant distinctions; alcohol addiction is not at issue, nor are competing plans from other candidates.

Answer (D) is a potential reason why the plan might not help people to break the addiction, but this is not what the question asked! Make sure you're answering the correct question. Answer (E) is out of scope; the general popularity of smoking is not addressed.

4. **(C) Pandas that are already likely to live longer are not more likely to give birth to live offspring:**

wild P live baby, live longer

∴ live baby ⟶ live longer

[causation?]

On Assumption questions, your task is to find the answer that reflects something the author assumes to be true in order to draw her conclusion.

The author assumes that one thing causes another: that giving birth to live offspring causes the panda to live longer. Perhaps it's the case that the pandas who are healthier in the first place are more likely both to give birth to live offspring and to live longer.

Answer **(C)** correctly articulates the author's assumption, though the negative language is tricky. The author assumes that pandas that are likely to live longer in general are *not* also more likely to give birth to live offspring. This has to be assumed in order to conclude that giving birth to live offspring causes a panda to live longer.

Answers (A) and (D) explain why these female pandas live as long as or longer than other female pandas, but since it is a fact that pandas that have given birth to live offspring live longer, these answers don't really have an impact on the argument.

Answer (B) refers to male pandas, but the argument is only about female pandas; this distinction is irrelevant.

Answer (E) might be a good answer if you were asked to strengthen the conclusion, but this information about multiple vs. single births is an irrelevant comparison. The conclusion doesn't hinge upon the number of live births, just whether the panda has given live birth at all.

5. **(A) Drug dealers are already being deterred from drug dealing on school grounds due to the penalties currently in place:**

$$\downarrow \text{pen} \longrightarrow \uparrow \text{addict S}$$

$$\therefore \text{keep severe pen}$$

$$[\text{when not at school ?}]$$

On Assumption questions, your task is to find the answer that reflects something the author assumes to be true in order to draw his or her conclusion. Here are some assumptions in the argument:

The students will take the drugs.

The students have money to buy the drugs.

At least some students who take the drugs will become addicted.

Drug dealers are aware of and deterred by different levels of penalties in different situations.

Answer **(A)** is a very close match with the last idea. The argument certainly does assume that drug dealers care about what the penalties are—it assumes that the current high penalties are keeping drug dealers away and that lower penalties would increase their activities.

Answers (B) and (E) are reasonable to believe, but the argument says nothing about academic work or death.

Answer (C) has a similar problem. The argument addresses only drug dealing on school grounds; comparing this situation to drug dealing off of school grounds is irrelevant.

The argument does not make any assumptions about who is dealing the drugs, so answer (D) is out of scope.

6. **(D) People who need a pay phone are most likely to use one within two miles of their home:**

B: PP use ↓ 90%   remove PP M+U
                                        keep PP L
M+U cell >> L cell   ⟶   (meet demand)

On Strengthen questions, your job is to find something that would make the argument more likely to be valid. The correct answer does not have to make the argument definitely true.

What does the author assume in drawing the conclusion that dropping pay phones from middle- and upper-income neighborhoods while leaving them in lower-income neighborhoods will be the best way to meet *demand* and *inconvenience very few people*?

First, the author assumes that there is some correlation between cell phone usage and pay phone usage. Those who don't use cell phones as much, the reasoning goes, are more likely to use pay phones. (Note the vagueness of the phrase *cell phone usage*. Are lower-income residents less likely to have phones at all? Or do they just use their phones less?)

The author also assumes that people are most likely to want to use pay phones in their own neighborhoods (as opposed to, say, traveling to an area with lousy cell phone reception, where a pay phone might be someone's only option!).

Answer **(D)** matches the assumption that the lower-income residents are using pay phones close to home.

Answer (A) is tempting but it's a trap. The choice doesn't indicate *where* these statistics apply! If usage has dropped 90% overall but only 50%–60% in upper-income neighborhoods, then the conclusion is actually weakened.

Answer (B) makes an irrelevant distinction—in order to evaluate this argument, you don't need any data splitting the upper- and middle-income groups from each other.

The argument doesn't assume that no lower-income residents use cell phones; it only requires that their usage is lower. Answer (C) is incorrect.

Answer (E) addresses the wrong conclusion! The question is not whether the plan is a good idea in general or whether the city should implement the plan. Rather, the conclusion states that following the plan will meet demand and avoid inconveniencing people; these considerations have nothing to do with whether the city will save money.

7. **(D) Many medical professionals make more than $250,000 a year:**

1) MP

2) > $250k/y   1+2 > 20m ppl

© if ¼ buy ⟶ > 5m units sold

[math right?]

On Weaken questions, your job is to find an answer that will make the argument at least somewhat less likely to be valid. The correct answer will not usually invalidate the argument completely.

Did you discover any assumptions in the argument, particularly with respect to those numbers?

The company is targeting two markets: medical professionals and people who make more than $250,000 a year. Do those two groups have any overlap? For example, what if 1 million medical professionals also make more than $250,000 a year? How were they counted?

Since the argument simply adds up to the two numbers, it counts these people twice. In the worst-case scenario, imagine that there are 10 million medical professionals who make more than $250,000 a year. So there are only 10 million people total, not 20 million.

The concluding calculation is based on the assumption that there are 20 million people in the target markets. If there are fewer than 20 million people, then a *25% or greater* sales rate may not result in 5 million units sold.

Answer **(D)** addresses this weakness in the argument. If it is true that there is overlap between the two groups, then Orange is less likely to hit 5 million units in sales.

Answers (A) and (E) introduce some numbers; evaluate how they would impact the argument. If nearly 45% have already purchased a similar product, then perhaps not as many people are left to buy Orange's new product. But the company is only depending on a *25% or greater* sales rate, so there are still plenty of customers left (and the fact that so many medical professionals have bought a similar product seems to indicate a certain amount of demand).

Answer (E) makes an irrelevant distinction. The argument is concerned only with those who make more than $250,000 a year.

Answer (B) also makes an irrelevant comparison; the argument does not address the market for education professionals.

Without knowing what percentage of the population is affected by *astigmatism and other vision problems*, it's impossible to assess the impact of choice (C) on the argument. The company is only targeting a *25% or greater* sales rate. Further, the choice says only that people would have trouble using certain features; this does not mean that they would not buy the product at all.

8. **(D) In Langlia, female workers are sick on more work days than male workers:**

W sick days > M

W work sick > M

This is an Inference question; it is asking you to deduce something that must be true from the information given in the argument.

If women in Langlia take more sick days *and* are more likely to go to work when they are sick, then they must be sick on more work days in general than men are. Answer **(D)** is a match.

Answer (A) is reasonable to believe in the real world, but the argument contains no information about the preferences of employers. Likewise, the argument provides no information about the conscientiousness of employees, so answer (E) is also wrong.

Answer (B) goes too far. While childbearing and related medical conditions might be one cause of the difference between women and men in Langlia, the argument provides no information as to why women take more sick days than men.

Answer (C) also goes too far. The argument restricts itself to days taken off *due to illness*, not days taken off when the sun is shining or someone would rather go to the movies.

9. **(C) For the past five years, Rocktown students have scored lower, on average, on American history tests than have students in neighboring towns:**

free HR class to 4th graders ⟶ 4th will ↑ score on AH tests

This EXCEPT question is a variation on a regular Strengthen question. The four incorrect answers will strengthen the argument. The correct answer will either weaken the argument or do nothing at all to it—but the correct answer will *not* strengthen the argument.

There are a great many assumptions in this argument. The argument assumes that students will actually sign up for and attend the free class. It assumes that the material in "History Rocks" is the same kind of material tested on American history tests (maybe "History Rocks" teaches the history of Ancient Greece, for instance), and that the students will remember what they learned long enough to score well on tests during the upcoming school year.

Choices (A) and (D) strengthen by filling the gap related to whether "History Rocks" teaches the same kind of material tested on American history tests.

Choice (B) strengthens by filling the gap related to whether students will actually sign up for and attend the free class.

Choice (E) strengthens by filling the gap related to whether students will remember what they learned long enough to score well on tests during the upcoming school year.

Choice **(C)** provides information that might explain why Rocktown wants to offer the free summer program, but this information does not address whether the plan will work as intended. As such, it neither strengthens nor weakens the plan; it doesn't address the plan at all.

10. **(E) Over the past three decades, the incidence of mental disorders that are more likely to end in death has risen in the United States and declined in Japan:**

US

bed ↓ from 4 to 1.3

↑↑ die

Japan

bed ↑ from 1 to 2.9

↓ die

Ⓒ ↓ bed → ↑ die

The question asks you to cast doubt on, or weaken, the conclusion that the reduction in hospital beds for inpatient psychiatric treatment in the United States is the primary cause for the increase in mortality among this population.

Did you notice where the conclusion to this argument was stated? It was actually in the question, not the main body of the argument. The GMAT sometimes structures arguments in this manner, so don't be surprised to find a conclusion as part of the question.

In order to weaken the idea that the reduction in beds is the cause, you could find another plausible cause for the increase in mortality rate. There are many possible alternatives: an increase in poverty or illegal drug use, a change in treatment plans or health insurance policies, and so on.

Note that, though the body of the argument addresses both the United States and Japan, the conclusion is limited specifically to the United States. Expect a trap or two in the answer choices revolving around Japan.

Answer (A) goes outside the scope of the argument by discussing Canada. While it might be true that Canada and the United States are similar in various ways, data about Canada does not weaken the conclusion about the United States.

Likewise, answer (B) brings up the idea of outpatient treatment, but the argument specifically refers to inpatient treatment. Further, this choice might explain why the number of inpatient hospital beds has declined, but it does not address the mortality issue.

Answer (C) is the Japan trap. The conclusion relates specifically to the situation in the United States. The knowledge that the incidence of mental disorders in Japan has been decreasing does not apply to the claim about the United States.

Answer (D) is tempting. Perhaps mortality is higher in the United States because not as many people have access to health insurance? Here's the catch: This lack of access has existed over the entire three-decade period. So why did the United States have an increase in mortality during this period?

Choice **(E)** is the correct answer. If certain types of mental disorders that are more likely to result in death are on the rise in the United States, but not in Japan, then that provides an alternative reason why the United States had an increase in mortality rates. The number of beds might have had nothing to do with it.

How to Read on RC

In This Chapter...

- Reading Comprehension

- Why GMAT Reading Comprehension Is Hard
  (*Don't Skip This Intro!*)

- Find the Simple Story

- A Balanced Read

- Practicing a Balanced Read

In this chapter, you will learn how to comprehend dense text effectively even when reading very quickly.

CHAPTER 5 How to Read on RC

Reading Comprehension

Reading Comprehension (RC) passages on the GMAT are typically one to five paragraphs in length and appear on the left-hand side of the screen, while one question at a time appears on the right-hand side.

If the passage is long, you will be able to scroll up and down the left-hand side of the screen while the right-hand side remains static. A typical passage is accompanied by three or four questions. Since you can see only one question at a time, you won't know until you answer the third question whether a fourth one will appear. This is how the screen will be laid out:

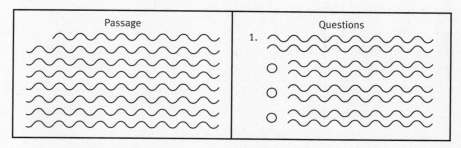

The passages are excerpts from longer works, generally in the fields of business, history, science, and social science. Since the passages have been greatly shortened and adapted, they sometimes seem to begin abruptly; the passages lack the background information or interesting introduction you are accustomed to in much of your reading.

Some of the questions ask about specific details in the passage, while others ask about the main idea, the structure of the passage, or the author's purpose in including certain information. Still other questions ask you to make inferences—in fact, you may be asked to infer on both Reading Comprehension and Critical Reasoning.

Some people think that you can't improve on RC—after all, you've known how to read for 20 or more years at this point, right?

These people are completely wrong! It is absolutely possible to improve a great deal on RC, if you are willing to do the work.

Time to get started!

Why GMAT Reading Comprehension Is Hard
(*Don't Skip This Intro!*)

Why is it hard to read a passage and answer questions about it? After all, you're reading this book right now, right? Obviously, you can read just fine. And, on the GMAT, you're allowed to look back at the passage anytime you want. So why does anyone get *anything* wrong?

There are several answers to that question. One is that GMAT reading passages are a lot harder to read than this book and your time is quite limited. Some people respond to these circumstances by rushing through the reading so much that they gain little more than a superficial understanding of the passage. Some of the trap answer choices you will encounter are set up for just this circumstance.

Others will read as they were taught to do in school: slowly and thoroughly, while taking extensive notes along the way. This is great for comprehension but won't work on the GMAT because you are not given much time. You'll have to rush on the questions or rush later in the Verbal section, either of which will lead to careless mistakes.

So what do you need to do? Learn how to read in a balanced way. Read carefully enough to learn the main ideas and the main contrasts, or changes of direction, in a passage, while setting aside much of the nitty-gritty detail—until you are asked a question about it.

You may be thinking: Well, if I have to learn it later, I'd rather just read it all carefully right now. Here's the beauty of the GMAT: You *don't* have to learn it all later. You will be asked just three or four questions for each passage. You will literally be able to ignore certain details and examples forever, because you won't be asked about every detail in the passage.

Things can (and will!) go wrong at the level of the question, too. For instance, consider this question:

> What is the function of the second paragraph in relation to the rest of the passage?

That's a pretty specific question, but someone who is rushing or not reading carefully might interpret the question too loosely.

For example, you are likely to pick an incorrect answer if you interpret the question as "What's going on with paragraph 2?" This is because some of the incorrect answers may, in fact, be *true*. To be clear: *Some of the incorrect answers in GMAT Reading Comprehension are 100% true facts.* But they are facts that, for instance, do not explain the role of the second paragraph in relation to the rest of the passage. An answer choice can be true and yet not answer the particular question asked.

In the next several chapters, you'll learn how to read on the GMAT and how to answer the different kinds of questions you'll be asked.

Find the Simple Story

Quick! Your boss is about to go into a conference call with her boss. The subject: what your department has accomplished in the past 12 months. You have five minutes to prepare your boss for this call. What do you do?

You don't have much time, obviously, so you're going to have to summarize pretty heavily. Plus, your boss doesn't have a lot of time to learn a bunch of detailed facts. You're going to have to put together the **simple story** for your boss (and hers!).

You work at a biotech firm; here's an excerpt from the introduction of a paper your division recently published, reflecting what you've done for the past 12 months:

> The previously made observation that the most rare variants in the human genome are also the most responsible for disease is supported by this new study that demonstrates that more common genome variants are less likely to be found in functional regions of the genome, and the functional regions are those that are actually expressed, such as in the form of disease.

Wow. That's a mouthful. Strip out the technical detail: What's the basic story?

prev idea: rare variants → ↑ disease

new study: supports

The basic story is twofold:

1. Originally, *rare variants* of the genome (whatever that is) were thought to be most responsible for causing disease.

2. The new study supports that original idea. Hooray!

How? Why? You don't care. Not right now, anyway. You've got the main idea; if you get a question about how, exactly, the new study supports the original theory, you can come back to that part of the sentence and try to understand it better. (And if you don't get such a question, you can ignore that detail forever.)

In order to find the simple story, you're going to need to figure out several things:

- What is the main point of each paragraph?
- What major contrasts, or changes of direction, exist?
- What is the main idea of the entire passage?

Following is information on how to develop these ideas during your first read-through of the passage.

A Balanced Read

Follow these steps to conduct a balanced read of a passage, gathering the main ideas while not getting too tangled up in the details:

1. Get oriented. Read the first couple of sentences carefully and write down the main idea of that first paragraph.

2. Find the main ideas of the remaining paragraphs. Pay particular attention to any language that signals foreshadowing, contrast, or a change of direction.

3. Know *why* the details are there but not *what* they say at anything more than a basic level.

4. Articulate the simple story. When you're done with the first read-through, you want to know the main point of the entire passage, as well as the major twists and turns of the story.

You'll have to do all of the above in about one and a half to two minutes! In other words, you'll need to learn this process well so that you can read efficiently and not get bogged down in details.

Here is how to effectively execute each of the four steps.

Step 1: Get Oriented

Read the first two or three sentences of the first paragraph carefully. They will set the context for the entire story. If the first paragraph is on the shorter side, read the entire thing carefully.

Start to make your map of the passage: Jot down a few notes to summarize what the first paragraph conveys. You can write as you read, or you can wait to write until you've finished the paragraph—different people prefer different approaches. Either way, do take the time to articulate explicitly to yourself the point of the first paragraph, even if you only jot down a couple of words as a reminder.

Focus on the main ideas. Don't try to learn the details!

Now you might begin to understand how you can do all of this in just one and a half to two minutes: You aren't actually going to pay a ton of attention to the annoying details.

How do I find the main point of the whole passage?

Ultimately, you want to be able to articulate the simple story. The heart of that story is the main point of the entire passage. This main point could be located anywhere, but it is most often located in the first paragraph or the beginning of the second paragraph.

Step 2: Find the Main Idea of the Remaining Paragraphs

Whoever wrote the passage had some reason for including each paragraph. Your task is to figure out what that reason is. Ask yourself:

What is the main idea of each paragraph?

Why is it included in the passage?

For the most part, the first sentence or two of the paragraph will help you to answer these questions. After that, you're going to start to get into detail, which you're mostly going to ignore. (See Step 3 for more on how to handle detail.)

Do, though, look for language that signals summaries or conclusions (*therefore* . . .) or changes of direction (*however* . . .). You can turn your brain back on and pay attention when you see that kind of big-picture language.

As before, jot down a few words to help you remember the main idea of the paragraph, as well as any major conclusions or contrasts that you think may be important.

Step 3: Minimize the Details

Don't spend time trying to memorize, or even understand, examples, technical discussions, or other detailed information. Instead, focus on why the detailed information is there. Ask yourself:

Why is this detail here?

Is it an example to illustrate the main idea of the paragraph?

Is it evidence to support a contention the author is making?

Does the detail explain how some theory works?

5

Other than that, don't try to understand what all of the detail means. Seriously! Each passage contains more detail than you will be asked about in the questions, so why bother trying to learn things that you're never going to need?

Instead, you'll come back to the particular details you need once you're offered a question that depends on that detail. You'll learn how to do that in a later chapter.

Step 4: Articulate the Simple Story

By the end of your read-through, you will probably be able to articulate the simple story of the passage. In order to do this, you will have to accomplish two tasks:

1. Articulate the main point of the passage.

    Why did the author bother to sit down and write this passage in the first place? She had some thesis that she was trying to establish.

    Perhaps there was an old way of explaining some phenomenon, but new research has uncovered a better explanation. Perhaps there are two competing business principles or processes, each of which has its positive points, but neither of them is perfect. Perhaps the author wants to contend that a series of historical events occurred for a particular reason.

    In general, the main point is not a simple recitation of facts. The author is interested in discussing not just *what* happened but *why* it may have happened (or, possibly, what the future implications might be).

2. Find the main contrasts, or changes of direction, in the story.

    Every passage has at least one contrast or change of direction; this kind of information makes for good questions! Contrasting information also underpins the story the passage is trying to tell.

    Common change of direction signals include such words and phrases as *however, but, yet, unexpectedly, it was once thought, now,* and *more recent research shows*.

Remember the biotech company's discovery from earlier in the chapter? Perhaps the full simple story is something like this:

> The original theory was that the more rare variants of the genome were more likely to lead to disease. Our recent research shows that more common variants are less likely to lead to disease, which indirectly supports the original theory. Direct support, however, is better than indirect support, so more research should be done in the coming year to try to more directly support the original hypothesis.

The passage would have far more technical detail of course, but you're not going to get all caught up in it. You're going to pick out the simple story that your boss can tell her boss to make the case that your department should be given more research funds for the coming year.

Practicing a Balanced Read

That's a lot to remember. Time to put it into practice!

First, create a "cheat sheet" for yourself, including your major goals and the steps that you want to follow. Then, test out the process by reading the following passage and taking some notes.

Try to stick to the roughly two-minute time frame you want to use on the real test. If your reading speed is just not fast enough right now, that's okay; give yourself an extra minute or so. Do *not*, though, use extra time to try to understand thoroughly, memorize, or take notes on every last detail in the passage! Stick to your goal: Find the simple story.

During salary negotiations, some career advisors recommend that the job seeker allow the company to make the initial salary offer. Proponents of this approach assert that

5   making an initial offer that is too high or too low can hurt a party's position. For example, if a job seeker initially requests a lower salary than the employer was prepared to provide, then the end result is likely to be a lower final

10   salary offer than might have been attained had the candidate allowed the company to start the negotiations. Thus, the party that initially does not name a salary is in a better position to protect its interests even while

15   allowing the opposing side to feel more in control of the negotiations.

Critics of this approach emphasize the importance of anchors, cognitive focal points that direct any given negotiation. Under the

20   anchoring principle, the initial offer becomes the number to which all other numbers are compared. The party who makes the initial offer is able to define the range of the negotiation and thereby has more significant

25   influence over the final deal. In order to avoid undermining their own interests, job seekers would purposely start negotiations at a higher-than-expected anchor point, but not a point so high that the company in question

30   balks at negotiating entirely.

Harvard Law School's Program on Negotiation suggests one further step: establish an anchor without making an explicit offer. A candidate might mention, for instance,

35   that a colleague recently accepted a similar position at a specified salary or that the average salary for people with similar qualifications falls within a particular range. Such anchoring tactics may diminish the

40   sometimes adversarial effect of a direct offer.

How did it go? Below is an example of what a strong GMAT test-taker might think and map out while reading this passage:

Lines 1–6:

Hmm. Some *advisors say the person should let the company make the initial offer—but not all? And* proponents *are recommending this? I wonder whether the passage is also going to talk about what opponents think. This may be some foreshadowing. I think I'll read a little farther before I write anything down.*

Lines 6–16:

Okay, there's at least one good reason for the individual to let the company make the offer: if you unknowingly start too low, then the company's likely to offer you less than it otherwise might have. In that case, you're better off waiting to see what the company offers first.

I still think they're going to talk about a different point of view ... [glancing at the beginning of paragraph 2] ... yep, critics! Okay, so I'm going to make a little table to map out the main points here.

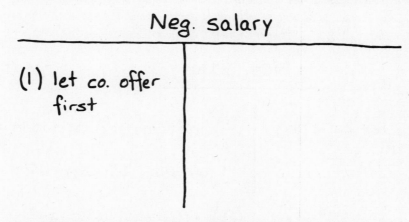

(Note: The number shows the paragraph in which that info is found.)

Lines 17–22:

Anchors are ... cognitive focal points? [Reads it again.] Nope, I have no idea what that means. Okay, don't get hung up on that. Keep going. The second sentence makes more sense. The initial number is an anchor because all of the future numbers get compared to the initial number. And apparently that means you get more influence over the final deal.

Lines 22–30:

Oh, interesting. So the final deal will probably be within some range of the initial starting point. If so, and if you can set that initial starting point, then I can see how you'd have more influence over the final deal. But what if you start too low, like the first paragraph said?

Ah, I see. You purposely start out at the higher end, maybe more than you know they'll pay. But at least you're getting them to start from a higher point. Yeah, if I were negotiating a salary, I'd definitely rather start higher and negotiate down a bit than start too low and leave money on the table.

Neg. salary

(1) let co. offer first	(2) indiv offer first and high
	end up ↑↑ overall?

Okay, one more paragraph to go. Is there a third theory?

Lines 31–40:

No, they're still talking about the second theory. Apparently, making a direct offer might come across as adversarial, but you might be able to get around that by citing statistics about the salary for similar positions (vs. just making a direct offer yourself). Harvard Law School says so!

Neg. salary

(1) let co. offer first	(2) indiv offer first and high
	end up ↑↑ overall?
	(3) cite similar stats

So what's the overall story here?

There are two different theories for negotiating a salary. First, the job seeker should let the company make the first offer so that the job seeker doesn't inadvertently go too low. Second, the job seeker should make the first offer and make it on the high side, anchoring the subsequent negotiations around this higher number. The job seeker might start by citing statistics for similar positions to solidify the anchor.

It sounds like the second theory offers more upside and a stronger negotiating position, as long as you don't mistakenly offer too low a salary to start.

During the test, you can't write that all out—there's not enough time! Further, you don't want to just copy large blocks of text from the passage because you may not understand what you are writing. Try to summarize the main ideas in your own words. With enough practice, you'll become proficient at articulating the story to yourself, without having to write everything down.

There was a major difference in the way that the test-taker handled paragraph 1 versus paragraph 2. She understood paragraph 1 immediately, so well that she was able to free up some brain cells to speculate about what might be coming next.

By contrast, she got hung up on the first sentence of the second paragraph. She wasn't sure what that whole *cognitive focal point* thing was, but she kept going to the second sentence and that helped her understand what this new theory was about. Then, notice that she was again able to start thinking about the bigger picture when she got to the detail: Her thoughts and notes didn't even mention the idea of making an offer that is high *but not so high* as to stop negotiations.

Rather, she connected the overall idea of making an initial high offer to the contrasting recommendation in the previous paragraph: Don't make the initial offer at all! She even thought about how this would apply if she were negotiating an offer herself; putting yourself into the Reading Comprehension passage or Critical Reasoning argument is a great way to wrap your brain around the complexities under discussion.

Finally, she tried to anticipate what might be coming in the third paragraph but she wasn't right. That's okay. It's still a good exercise to try to anticipate. If you're right, you'll feel vindicated and will remember the information better; if you're wrong, you'll be curious to see what the next paragraph really is talking about … and you'll remember the information better. Either way, you win!

5

Ready for another one? Try this passage; it's longer, so on the real test, you'd want to take about three minutes. (Again, you can give yourself some extra time now, earlier in the learning process, but do *not* use that extra time to get into detail that you should be skimming for now.)

In 1901, divers exploring the remains of a shipwreck off the coast of Greece discovered a contraption believed to have been used by Ancient Greeks to predict solar eclipses. The
5 Antikythera Mechanism was composed of a fixed-ring dial representing the 12 months of the Egyptian calendar and an inner ring representing the 12 zodiac signs. Inside, a complex assembly of bronze gears
10 mechanically replicated the irregular motions of the Moon caused by its elliptical orbit around the Earth through the use of two gear-wheels, one of which was slightly off-center, connected by a pin. Regarded as the
15 world's first analog computer, the Antikythera Mechanism involved remarkably intricate physics considering that, only 300 years earlier, the Ancient Greeks still believed the world was flat. Accurately predicting lunar and
20 solar eclipses, as well as solar, lunar, and planetary positions, it predated similar technology by 1,000 years. The timing and nature of its existence remains one of science's great puzzles to this day. How and by
25 whom was it created?

Today, scientists understand much more about the complexities of the orbital revolutions that cause solar eclipses to occur; for instance, the Earth's orbit around the Sun
30 is also elliptical such that, depending on the time of year, the Earth is gradually traveling nearer to or farther from the Sun. Further, since the plane of the Moon's revolution around the Earth is not the same as the plane
35 of the Earth's revolution around the Sun, all calculations predicting a solar eclipse must be completed in three dimensions. While in modern times the use of satellites, telescopes, and other high-tech equipment has greatly
40 enhanced our capacity for such calculations, when the Antikythera Mechanism was created, the sole source of information available to scientists was observation of the night sky. It is thus not surprising that, under certain
45 circumstances, the device is inaccurate by up to 38 degrees; what is astonishing is that the device is remarkably accurate over a wide range of conditions.

Recent analysis dating the device to 205 BC,
50 earlier than previously thought, suggests that the eclipse prediction mechanism was based not on Greek trigonometry but on Babylonian arithmetical methods borrowed by the Greeks. This conjecture makes plausible Cicero's claim
55 that Archimedes created the mechanism, as Greek trigonometry was nonexistent in 205 BC.

What did you think? The second passage is longer than the first one, of course. It also has more technical detail. Were you able to push through and ignore detail that was too hard to grasp right away? Or, did you get hung up at certain points, enough that your understanding of the overall passage was negatively impacted? This is what you're going to learn to do better right now.

Let's go back to the strong-at-RC test-taker and see how she would think her way through this passage.

Lines 1–4:

Shipwreck—cool. A hundred years ago. A contraption believed to have been used to predict solar eclipses. *Something technical and they're not 100% sure what it was for, but they think it was for predicting an eclipse (Moon covering Sun).*

Lines 4–22:

Calling that thing AM. Showed the 12 months and the zodiac signs. Complex inside showed the Moon's orbit around the Earth. Remarkably intricate—*okay, so it was impressive, maybe ahead of its time? Yes: AM was accurate and it* predated similar technology by 1,000 years.

Lines 22–25:

Puzzle: who made it and how? But it's still a puzzle to this day, *so what's the rest of the passage about? A new theory about who and how? Speculation?*

(1) AM found, spec: anc Grk, predict solar eclipse?
        AM= sophis, not sure how made or who

Note: *Spec* is short for speculation. The passage says the AM was *believed* to have been used by ancient Greeks. *Sophis* is short for sophisticated.

Lines 26–28:

Now scientists know a lot more about calculating eclipses; this is highlighting how amazing it was that the Ancient Greeks were able to figure this stuff out.

Lines 28–37:

Ugh, lots of detail about how solar eclipses work. Skimming, skimming . . .

(1) AM found, spec: anc Grk, predict solar eclipse?
        AM= sophis, not sure how made or who
(2) Now: DTL eclipse

Note: *DTL* is this test-taker's shorthand for "the passage has lots of detail about this topic, if I need to come back to it later."

Lines 37–48:

Oh, here we go. Today, there are lots of tools to help calculate this stuff, but when AM was made, all they had was what they observed in the sky. It's pretty amazing that it's as accurate as it is.

(1) AM found, spec: anc Grk, predict solar eclipse?

     AM= sophis, not sure how made or who

(2) Now: DTL eclipse

     AM= surpris acc.

Lines 49–57:

Hmm, now they think AM was made even earlier than they previously thought. Maybe it was created by Arch? Evidence based on math. Speculating, but still no answers about who made it and how.

(1) AM found, spec: anc Grk, predict solar eclipse?

     AM= sophis, not sure how made or who

(2) Now: DTL eclipse

     AM= surpris acc.

(3) C: made by Arch(?)

     evid given (math)

Note: *Evid given* is this test-taker's shorthand for "the passage provides specific evidence to support this claim or contention."

Simple story:

AM created by Ancient Greeks to predict solar eclipses. Mystery: Who made it and how could they do this relatively accurately when all they had was observation of the night sky? Remarkably sophisticated given what they had to work with. Para 2 gets into lots of detail about how to predict an eclipse. But Para 3 only speculates about when it was created and by whom, and we still don't know how they made it, so the mystery hasn't actually been resolved.

Did you notice how much of the technical detail the test-taker skimmed right over, particularly in paragraphs 2 and 3?

This is where you don't want to let yourself get hung up and distracted from your goal: Find the simple story.

It's going to take a lot of training to get yourself to the point that you are comfortable just leaving that detail for later. At first, you're going to feel that something is wrong, that you can't possibly understand everything because you're not learning that detail right now. And you're right—you aren't going to understand everything thoroughly. That's not your goal.

Remember, the passage will give you more detail than you actually need in order to answer the questions. You only want to bother learning the details that you need, so don't waste precious time and mental energy learning something when you aren't even sure yet whether you'll get a question about it.

Speaking of questions, it's time to move to the next chapter, where you'll tackle General questions, including Main Idea questions.

RC Main Ideas and General Questions

In This Chapter...

In this chapter, you will learn how to identify the main idea of a passage and how to answer General RC question types.

CHAPTER 6 RC Main Ideas and General Questions

What is a Main Idea?

In order to be able to articulate the simple story, you have to understand the main idea that a passage is trying to convey. But what does a main idea look like on the GMAT, and how can you be sure you've found it?

GMAT main ideas are not quite the same as real-world main ideas.

Non-GMAT reading passages—including news articles, editorials, and academic papers—often have pretty straightforward main ideas, such as:

- Here's how bees pollinate certain plants.
- There are several different methods for seeding a cotton field (and here are the options).
- The city council should not approve the permit for a new shopping mall (and here are some reasons why).

A GMAT main idea is not likely to take the form "Here are some facts." A GMAT passage always has a point: The author is trying to make the case for a specific thesis. In the last chapter, the second passage asserted that the Antikythera Mechanism is still a mystery to this day, and the author spent the rest of the passage supporting this thesis.

Nor is a GMAT passage likely to say "I believe this conclusion, and here are my reasons." GMAT main ideas are more nuanced. Even when a writer is arguing "for" something, she will typically present multiple points of view. It might not be that obvious that the author prefers one of the views. In the negotiation passage from the last chapter, the author never stated a preference for one theory but did provide a lot of supporting evidence as to why the anchoring theory may be better.

Find the Point

Most of the time, the **point** will fall into one of a few categories:

1. A change (Here's a situation—but now there's a new theory/explanation/set of circumstances.)
2. A twist (Here's something that seems straightforward—but it's not what you think!)
3. A judgment call (Here are two options—and now I'm going to tell you which one is better!)

From now on, the point will refer to the overarching main idea of an entire passage. Individual paragraphs may also have their own main ideas.

Many passages take the form "The [noun] was doing something, but now it's doing something else," or "A group of people thought something for a particular reason, but now the reason is wrong, so maybe the thing they were thinking isn't really true (but we need more information to find out)." Some GMAT points do give opinions, but the opinion will usually be contrasted against a view presented in the first paragraph ("A certain group of people have traditionally thought *X*—but actually, *Y*!").

Where to Look

The point is often articulated in a single, discrete sentence in the passage, though sometimes it may be spread over a couple of sentences. It is most often found in the first paragraph or the beginning of the second paragraph (though it could technically be anywhere in the passage). Of course, you need to read the first paragraph to understand that the second paragraph is presenting a *change*, *twist*, or *judgment call*. Often, the first paragraph sets up an idea or situation, and then the second paragraph provides a contrast that gives you the point.

Often, the first sentence or two will provide background information or set context, but sometimes the opening sentence will give you the point. For instance, if the first line begins "A stunning new theory has changed everything we thought we knew about the rotation of the Earth around the Sun," then that's almost certainly the main idea right there. It's pretty likely that the passage will tell you a little bit about what people have traditionally thought, before returning to explaining that stunning new theory.

While you are reading through a GMAT passage for the first time, imagine a small voice in the back of your mind saying something like, "Facts facts facts facts facts! *But what*?!" (Imagine that in a silly voice. *Facts facts facts facts facts!* The facts are not the main idea—keep looking!)

Try that out in the following exercise.

6

Drill 6.1—Find the Point

As you read, jot down notes to help you find the point of each passage and the main idea of each individual paragraph. If appropriate, identify whether the passage has a change, a twist, or a judgment call.

Passage 1: Freelancing

As the proportion of Australian workers who are self-employed has boomed in the past decade, the topic of wealth creation for freelancers has become much
5 more prevalent in business magazines. A standard maxim among such publications is that a sole proprietor is best off treating her business as a much larger enterprise with a set of core departments, including
10 but not limited to executive, production, human resources, marketing, and finance functions. In effect, the freelancer would devote time and attention to each "department" in order to optimize her
15 chances of success, and would, unaided, create content, advertising campaigns, contracts, and quarterly budgets.

Most freelancers, however, presently operate in the creative realm,
20 encompassing not only traditional arts such as photography and writing but also more technical services such as computer programming and software engineering. Such creative forms of labor demand
25 highly specialized skills. For the creative freelancer, then, whose most valued asset is labor, conceptualizing one's business in such a fashion risks the dilution of the company's most important resource:
30 the freelancer's skills. Distributing one's labor across platforms is a zero-sum game that may yield positive results in some scenarios but not necessarily all. A photographer who spends his
35 time developing a marketing plan may consequently jeopardize his public image by failing to devote sufficient effort to expanding his portfolio via new and high-value artwork. Moreover, because "word
40 of mouth" is typically considered the most powerful means of marketing in a creative industry, the potential benefits of such a trade-off are far from certain.

Now, use your notes to answer the following:

The point of the passage:

_____

_____

_____

_____

The main idea of paragraph 1:

_____

_____

_____

_____

The main idea of paragraph 2:

_____

_____

_____

_____

Passage 2: Polymers

Synthetic polymers are man-made polymers colloquially referred to as "plastics." These polymers can be classified in many ways, perhaps the most useful
5 regarding how they respond to heat. For example, thermosets are permanently set plastics; they do not melt, even when subjected to high temperatures. Thermoplastics, however, become
10 malleable when heated and can be remolded as they are cooled. As a result, thermoplastics can be recycled more easily than thermosets and are used in the manufacture of toys, water bottles,
15 and other goods that are typically used for limited time periods and subsequently discarded. Thermosets are more difficult to recycle and are often used as adhesives or sealants in high-wear settings,
20 circumstances in which the less malleable nature of the material is a distinct advantage, despite the inability to recycle at a later date.

Thermoplastics can be further
25 differentiated as amorphous or semi-crystalline. While both amorphous and semi-crystalline thermoplastics melt when heated, amorphous thermoplastics soften gradually in response to heat
30 while semi-crystalline thermoplastics remain solid until a precise melting point. Semi-crystalline thermoplastics tend to be tougher, suitable for weight-bearing goods such as folding chairs, whereas
35 amorphous thermoplastics are more common for products that break apart easily, such as packing peanuts.

The contrasting molecular structures of the various plastics underpin the way in
40 which each responds to heat. Thermoset polymers are chemically "cured," involving the formation of chemical bonds and resulting in rigid three-dimensional molecular structures. Unlike thermosets,
45 thermoplastics are two-dimensional chains connected by intermolecular forces. In amorphous thermoplastics, the molecules are randomly ordered, resembling a jumble of yarn, while semi-
50 crystalline thermoplastics feature ordered molecular "crystals."

6

Now, use your notes to answer the following:

The point of the passage:

_____

_____

_____

_____

The main idea of paragraph 1:

_____

_____

_____

The main idea of paragraph 2:

_____

_____

_____

The main idea of paragraph 3:

_____

_____

_____

_____

Answers are on pages 97–99.

General Questions

General questions test your understanding of the overall point and the simple story. General questions fall into one of two main categories:

1. Primary Purpose: What is the point of the passage?

2. Paragraph: What is the purpose of a specific paragraph?

Try this Primary Purpose question for the Freelancing passage.

As the proportion of Australian workers who are self-employed has boomed in the past decade, the topic of wealth creation for freelancers has become much
5 more prevalent in business magazines. A standard maxim among such publications is that a sole proprietor is best off treating her business as a much larger enterprise with a set of core departments, including
10 but not limited to executive, production, human resources, marketing, and finance functions. In effect, the freelancer would devote time and attention to each "department" in order to optimize her
15 chances of success, and would, unaided, create content, advertising campaigns, contracts, and quarterly budgets.

Most freelancers, however, presently operate in the creative realm,
20 encompassing not only traditional arts such as photography and writing but also more technical services such as computer programming and software engineering. Such creative forms of labor demand
25 highly specialized skills. For the creative freelancer, then, whose most valued asset is labor, conceptualizing one's business in such a fashion risks the dilution of the company's most important resource:
30 the freelancer's skills. Distributing one's labor across platforms is a zero-sum game that may yield positive results in some scenarios but not necessarily all. A photographer who spends his
35 time developing a marketing plan may consequently jeopardize his public image by failing to devote sufficient effort to expanding his portfolio via new and high-value artwork. Moreover, because "word
40 of mouth" is typically considered the most powerful means of marketing in a creative industry, the potential benefits of such a trade-off are far from certain.

The primary purpose of the passage is to

(A) describe a current debate taking place among authors of a certain type of literature

(B) attack a particular theory as fundamentally untenable

(C) explain the prevalent theory of a particular business area

(D) discuss how one principle of business may not be optimal in all cases

(E) contrast two views with respect to a particular business area

6

How did that go? Before you keep reading, look over your work for a moment. What was hard about the problem? Did your understanding of the point go along with the correct answer? What was tempting about some of the incorrect answers?

When a new question pops up on the screen, your first task is to figure out what kind of question it is. In this case, the language *primary purpose* indicates that this is a Primary Purpose, or Main Idea, question.

Next, you want to reread or remember whatever information you have about the main idea and articulate in your own words what you think the answer should say.

If you've gotten a good grasp of the simple story from your read-through, then you likely won't have to go back to the passage to reread anything for Main Idea questions. For the Freelancing passage, the point is something like "Some people think freelancers should run themselves like a business, but this could be detrimental for those working in creative fields."

Finally, you're ready to go find a match in the answer choices. Look for something that goes along with the idea you've articulated to yourself. Here's how a strong Reading Comprehension test-taker might think through the five answers on this problem:

	Answer Choice	Reader's Thoughts
(A)	describe a current debate taking place among authors of a certain type of literature	*The first paragraph does say that business magazines recommend that people run themselves like businesses. But the contrasting paragraph doesn't say anything about the magazines. It sounds like the author's opinion, not a debate among magazine writers. Eliminate.*
(B)	attack a particular theory as fundamentally untenable	*Too strong. The author says only that the theory might not apply to a certain type of freelancer. Eliminate.*
(C)	explain the prevalent theory of a particular business area	Prevalent *means dominant or the most widespread. Maybe the "act like a business" theory is dominant, but this choice entirely misses the contrasting point of view. Eliminate.*
(D)	discuss how one principle of business may not be optimal in all cases	*Yes, this is it. There is this theory, or principle, but it could turn out to be bad for certain people. I think this is it, but I'm going to check the last one to make sure.*
(E)	contrast two views with respect to a particular business area	*Oh, this one's tricky. My first thought was that this one is right, too, but now that I'm rereading it…it doesn't say quite the right thing. It's not about a particular business area. That would mean, hey, we're only talking about photographers. Rather, the first group has a theory it thinks applies to everyone, and the author is pointing out that it might not apply to people working in creative fields (emphasis on the plural—many fields!). Eliminate.*

The correct answer is (D).

Congratulations! You just used the 4-step RC process to answer your first question. Here's a summary of the process:

Step 1: Identify the question.

Step 2: Find the support.

Step 3: Predict an answer.

Step 4: Eliminate and find a match.

In the coming chapters, you'll learn more about how to use the process for the different question types found on Reading Comprehension. Now, test out your newfound skills on some more problems.

Drill 6.2—Answer the General Questions

For each passage, answer the General question provided. Practice using the 4-step process to answer the question.

Passage 1: Anchoring

During salary negotiations, some career advisors recommend that the job seeker allow the company to make the initial salary offer. Proponents of this approach
5 assert that making an initial offer that is too high or too low can hurt a party's position. For example, if a job seeker initially requests a lower salary than the employer was prepared to provide, then
10 the end result is likely to be a lower final salary offer than might have been attained had the candidate allowed the company to start the negotiations. Thus, the party that initially does not name a salary is in a
15 better position to protect its interests even while allowing the opposing side to feel more in control of the negotiations.

Critics of this approach emphasize the importance of anchors, cognitive focal
20 points that direct any given negotiation. Under the anchoring principle, the initial offer becomes the number to which all other numbers are compared. The party who makes the initial offer is able to define
25 the range of the negotiation and thereby has more significant influence over the final deal. In order to avoid undermining their own interests, job seekers would purposely start negotiations at a higher-
30 than-expected anchor point, but not a point so high that the company in question balks at negotiating entirely.

Harvard Law School's Program on Negotiation suggests one further step:
35 establish an anchor without making an explicit offer. A candidate might mention, for instance, that a colleague recently accepted a similar position at a specified salary or that the average salary for
40 people with similar qualifications falls within a particular range. Such anchoring tactics may diminish the sometimes adversarial effect of a direct offer.

1. Which of the following best describes the purpose of the third paragraph of the passage?

(A) To argue that Harvard Law School's principle is the best of the principles discussed

(B) To conclude that following the anchoring principle is more likely to result in a higher starting salary

(C) To suggest that diminishing any potential adversarial effects should be the primary concern of the candidate

(D) To offer a counterexample to the principle discussed in the prior paragraph

(E) To provide additional guidance regarding the operation of the anchoring principle

Passage 2: Polymers

Synthetic polymers are man-made polymers colloquially referred to as "plastics." These polymers can be classified in many ways, perhaps the most useful
5 regarding how they respond to heat. For example, thermosets are permanently set plastics; they do not melt, even when subjected to high temperatures. Thermoplastics, however, become
10 malleable when heated and can be remolded as they are cooled. As a result, thermoplastics can be recycled more easily than thermosets and are used in the manufacture of toys, water bottles,
15 and other goods that are typically used for limited time periods and subsequently discarded. Thermosets are more difficult to recycle and are often used as adhesives or sealants in high-wear settings,
20 circumstances in which the less malleable nature of the material is a distinct advantage, despite the inability to recycle at a later date.

Thermoplastics can be further
25 differentiated as amorphous or semi-crystalline. While both amorphous and semi-crystalline thermoplastics melt when heated, amorphous thermoplastics soften gradually in response to heat
30 while semi-crystalline thermoplastics remain solid until a precise melting point. Semi-crystalline thermoplastics tend to be tougher, suitable for weight-bearing goods such as folding chairs, whereas
35 amorphous thermoplastics are more common for products that break apart easily, such as packing peanuts.

The contrasting molecular structures of the various plastics underpin the way in
40 which each responds to heat. Thermoset polymers are chemically "cured," involving the formation of chemical bonds and resulting in rigid three-dimensional molecular structures. Unlike thermosets,
45 thermoplastics are two-dimensional chains connected by intermolecular forces. In amorphous thermoplastics, the molecules are randomly ordered, resembling a jumble of yarn, while semi-
50 crystalline thermoplastics feature ordered molecular "crystals."

2.   The passage is primarily concerned with

(A) providing examples of real-world uses for various related substances

(B) contrasting the chemical compositions of various substances

(C) presenting a useful basis for classifying a set of related substances

(D) assessing the pros and cons of recycling various types of substances

(E) outlining the primary categories of a set of related substances and proposing uses for each category

6

Passage 3: Greek Wreck

In 1901, divers exploring the remains of a shipwreck off the coast of Greece discovered a contraption believed to have been used by Ancient Greeks to
5 predict solar eclipses. The Antikythera Mechanism was composed of a fixed-ring dial representing the 12 months of the Egyptian calendar and an inner ring representing the 12 zodiac signs.

10 Inside, a complex assembly of bronze gears mechanically replicated the irregular motions of the Moon caused by its elliptical orbit around the Earth through the use of two gear-wheels, one of which
15 was slightly off-center, connected by a pin. Regarded as the world's first analog computer, the Antikythera Mechanism involved remarkably intricate physics considering that, only 300 years earlier,
20 the Ancient Greeks still believed the world was flat. Accurately predicting lunar and solar eclipses, as well as solar, lunar, and planetary positions, it predated similar technology by 1,000 years. The timing
25 and nature of its existence remains one of science's great puzzles to this day. How and by whom was it created?

Today, scientists understand much more about the complexities of the orbital
30 revolutions that cause solar eclipses to occur; for instance, the Earth's orbit around the Sun is also elliptical such that, depending on the time of year, the Earth is gradually traveling nearer to or
35 farther from the Sun. Further, since the plane of the Moon's revolution around the Earth is not the same as the plane of the Earth's revolution around the Sun, all calculations predicting a solar eclipse
40 must be completed in three dimensions. While in modern times the use of satellites, telescopes, and other high-tech equipment has greatly enhanced our capacity for such calculations, when the
45 Antikythera Mechanism was created, the sole source of information available to scientists was observation of the night sky. It is thus not surprising that, under certain circumstances, the device is inaccurate by
50 up to 38 degrees; what is astonishing is that the device is remarkably accurate over a wide range of conditions.

Recent analysis dating the device to 205 BC, earlier than previously thought,
55 suggests that the eclipse prediction mechanism was based not on Greek trigonometry but on Babylonian arithmetical methods borrowed by the Greeks. This conjecture makes plausible
60 Cicero's claim that Archimedes created the mechanism, as Greek trigonometry was nonexistent in 205 BC.

3. Which of the following best describes the relationship of the second paragraph to the passage as a whole?

(A) It provides evidence to support the main idea introduced earlier in the passage.

(B) It presents a hypothesis that is rejected in the final paragraph of the passage.

(C) It offers an example of a theory proposed in the first paragraph of the passage.

(D) It suggests a solution to a problem described earlier in the passage.

(E) It draws a parallel between two phenomena discussed in the passage.

Answers are on pages 99–103.

Answers to Drill Sets

Drill 6.1—Find the Point

The answers below show one possible way to map out the passage and articulate the point and main ideas; your wording won't match exactly, of course. Ask yourself: Was I able to paraphrase in order to state the point concisely? Did I understand the purpose of each paragraph? Do I know the type of detail found in each paragraph?

Passage 1: Freelancing

(1) Bus Pub: FL should run as business w/ dep'ts, etc.

(2) auth: BUT creative FL might be hurt by this

The point: While some freelancers might benefit from treating themselves as complete businesses, freelancers working in creative fields may find that this approach hurts them (because they're better off spending more time creating whatever they make).

Main idea of paragraph 1: A *standard maxim* says that freelancers should treat themselves like businesses, with multiple departments that they "run" as a larger company would.

Main idea of paragraph 2: BUT (twist!) freelancers working in creative fields might find this harmful rather than helpful; they may need to keep creating stuff in order to sustain their businesses.

When a passage tells you that something is a *standard maxim* or attributes something to conventional wisdom, there's a pretty good chance that the passage is about to give you a twist: "Here's what most people think (or what people used to think), but (twist!) here's how you should really be thinking about it now."

Passage 2: Polymers

In the map on the next page, the test-taker indented paragraph 2 because the content is a subset of just the *thermoplastics* category from the first paragraph. Also, notice that, for the third paragraph, the test-taker either started to get bored or decided that the paragraph was too technical. She just wrote *DTL* to signal that more detail about the chemical structure can be found by going back into the third paragraph. This is a great strategy to use when the passage gets too technical.

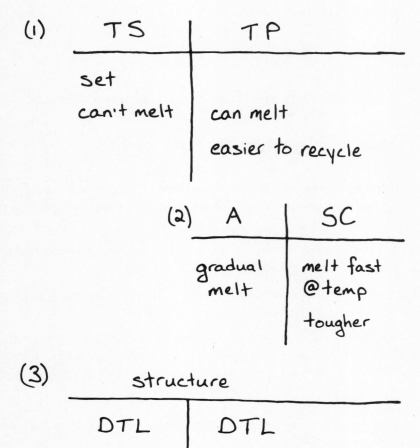

(1) man-made Poly = plastic

★ most useful: classify by heat

(1)

TS	TP
set can't melt	can melt easier to recycle

(2)

A	SC
gradual melt	melt fast @ temp tougher

(3) structure

DTL	DTL

The point: The most useful way to classify man-made plastics is based on how they respond to heat.

Main idea of paragraph 1: Same as the point. (Support: two types of plastics respond differently to heat.)

Main idea of paragraph 2: One of the two types from the previous paragraph can be split into two subgroups based on…you guessed it…how they respond to heat.

Main idea of paragraph 3: The heat thing is based on the fact that these different kinds of plastic have different molecular structures. (Ignore the word *molecular* as much as possible! They have different structures.)

The point of this passage is tough to spot, even though it's right in the second sentence. When the point is given to you early, you often can't be sure that it is the point until you get through more of the passage. In this case, the technical detail is distracting, too, so how are you going to pick up that the second sentence is, in fact, the point?

The key words are these: *perhaps the most useful*. The polymers can be classified in many ways? That's just a fact. *Perhaps the most useful* way is based on how they respond to heat? That's an opinion or a claim, and claims make for a good point.

Drill 6.2—Answer the General Questions

1. **Anchoring: (E) To provide additional guidance regarding the operation of the anchoring principle**

   Step 1: Identify the question.

   The language *purpose of the third paragraph* in the question stem indicates that this is a Paragraph question.

   Step 2: Find the support.

   Review your notes on the third paragraph or glance back at the first sentence or two of the paragraph.

   Step 3: Predict an answer.

   The paragraph *suggests one further step* to what was discussed in the prior paragraph. In other words, the paragraph is elaborating on the anchoring principle. The correct answer should convey this idea.

6

Step 4: Eliminate and find a match.

Answer Choice	Explanation
(A) To argue that Harvard Law School's principle is the best of the principles discussed	Paragraph 3 discusses a particular tactic for the anchoring principle; it does not discuss a separate principle. Further, the passage does not say that this tactic is the *best* of any tactic.
(B) To conclude that following the anchoring principle is more likely to result in a higher starting salary	The second paragraph might be interpreted as arguing this for the anchoring principle, but the third paragraph does not do this (nor does the passage as a whole *conclude* this).
(C) To suggest that diminishing any potential adversarial effects should be the primary concern of the candidate	The paragraph suggests that this is or should be one concern of a job candidate, but it provides no information that it should be the *primary* concern.
(D) To offer a counterexample to the principle discussed in the prior paragraph	This choice directly contradicts the passage. The third paragraph *supports* the second paragraph. The third paragraph provides a refinement, or *further step*, that can be taken with the anchoring principle introduced in the second paragraph.
(E) To provide additional guidance regarding the operation of the anchoring principle	CORRECT. The third paragraph describes an additional way in which the anchoring principle can be used effectively.

Notice that one of the trap answers (arguably) describes a paragraph of the passage, but not the paragraph that the question asks about. This is a common trap on Paragraph questions.

Also keep an eye out for answer choices that directly contradict what the passage says. Someone reading too quickly could easily reverse the information mentally. This is one reason it is so important to predict the answer in your own words before going to the choices!

2. **Polymers: (C) presenting a useful basis for classifying a set of related substances**

Step 1: Identify the question.

The language *primarily concerned with* in the question stem indicates that this is a Primary Purpose, or Main Idea, question.

Step 2: Find the support.

Ideally, you will have determined the main idea during your read-through of the passage; if you need to refresh your memory, return to your map.

Step 3: Predict an answer.

On Main Idea questions, Steps 2 and 3 are often compressed into one. The point of the passage is something like *probably the best way to classify man-made plastics is based on how they respond to heat.*

Step 4: Eliminate and find a match.

Answer Choice	Explanation
(A) providing examples of real-world uses for various related substances	They do give some real-world uses, but that's not the main point. The examples are there to support the contention about classifying based on reaction to heat.
(B) contrasting the chemical compositions of various substances	The third paragraph does talk about this a bit, but it's not the overall point, which should connect to the whole passage.
(C) presenting a useful basis for classifying a set of related substances	CORRECT. This matches the point. The *related substances* are the various kinds of plastics, and the *useful basis for classifying* these plastics is the way they respond to heat.
(D) assessing the pros and cons of recycling various types of substances	This information is mentioned only as part of the passage detail; it is not the main point.
(E) outlining the primary categories of a set of related substances and proposing uses for each category	So close! This one looks good right up until the word *proposing*. The author doesn't propose anything related to usage of the plastic; rather, the author mentions what they are already used to build.

Notice that several of the incorrect answers mention details that are present in the passage; in other words, they represent true information from the passage. They just don't represent the *main idea*, which should relate to and encompass the passage as a whole. In the future, watch out for traps that do reflect something the passage said but don't answer the specific question asked.

The other trap answer is very close to correct but takes things one step too far with the word *proposing*. Watch out for trap answers that are 90% right but mess things up via just one or two incorrect words.

3. **Greek Wreck: (A) It provides evidence to support the main idea introduced earlier in the passage.**

Step 1: Identify the question.

The language *the relationship of the second paragraph to the passage as a whole* in the question stem indicates that this is a Paragraph question. Your task is to determine what role this paragraph plays in the overall simple story.

Step 2: Find the support.

Review your notes on the second paragraph, paying attention to how it relates to the other paragraphs. Or, glance back at the second paragraph, as well as several lines immediately before and after it.

Step 3: Predict an answer.

One test-taker's map of this passage might look like this:

(1) AM found, spec: anc Grk, predict solar eclipse?

    AM= sophis, not sure how made or who

(2) Now: DTL eclipse

    AM= surpris acc.

(3) C: made by Arch(?)

    evid given (math)

The point is something like "We still don't know who made AM or how it was made, but it was surprisingly accurate at predicting solar eclipses." The first paragraph introduces the point. The second paragraph talks about how very complex eclipses are, underscoring the surprising fact that the AM is pretty accurate given that whoever made it didn't have any of the sophisticated equipment that is available today.

The second paragraph, then, is providing additional information to support the claim made in the first paragraph (that AM is surprisingly accurate given how old it is).

Step 4: Eliminate and find a match.

Answer Choice	Explanation
(A) It provides evidence to support the main idea introduced earlier in the passage.	CORRECT. This matches what the second paragraph does.
(B) It presents a hypothesis that is rejected in the final paragraph of the passage.	Whoops! Time to look at the third paragraph, too. That paragraph talks more about who might have invented AM. The third paragraph isn't rejecting anything from the second paragraph, so this choice can't be right.
(C) It offers an example of a theory proposed in the first paragraph of the passage.	This one's closer. The first paragraph, though, didn't propose a theory as to who made this thing or how it was made; it just says that we still don't know.
(D) It suggests a solution to a problem described earlier in the passage.	The first paragraph could be described as a discussion of a problem. But the second paragraph does not propose a solution to that conundrum. (The third paragraph could be described this way.)
(E) It draws a parallel between two phenomena discussed in the passage.	Drawing a parallel would be making a connection between two separate phenomena, or events. The passage does not discuss two such events. Further, the second paragraph elaborates on the point discussed in the first paragraph, so answer (A) is a better match.

When there are several paragraphs, you may begin Steps 2 and 3 by reviewing only the paragraph with the point and the paragraph about which the question asks. When you get to the answers, though, you might realize that you also need to look at another paragraph, as the wording of answer (B) required. If you like, you can look at all paragraphs first. Alternatively, you can delay reviewing all paragraphs until you know for sure that an answer choice requires you to do so.

Answer (D) exemplifies a common trap on Paragraph questions: This answer choice describes a different paragraph in the passage. This information is true; it just doesn't answer the question asked.

RC Specific Questions

In This Chapter...

In this chapter, you will learn how to identify and answer the different types of RC questions that ask about specific details of the passage.

CHAPTER 7 RC Specific Questions

Specific questions require you to get into the detail of the passage. The questions can ask you to perform different kinds of analyses. In this chapter, you'll learn about the three most common Specific question types and you'll have a chance to practice your new skills.

Specific Detail Questions

Specific Detail questions ask you to find and "regurgitate" specific facts from the passage. That sounds kind of gross! It's not as bad as it sounds: Your task is to find a specific piece of information in the passage and then find the answer choice that most accurately matches that piece of information. Many people like this particular type of Reading Comprehension (RC) question best because it really can be just like repeating back what someone has already told you.

Try out this short passage and question.

In the early 1940s, women's participation in the U.S. labor market changed dramatically as a result of the labor shortages resulting from the drafting of men
5   to fight in World War II. Although persistent and institutionalized discrimination had discouraged women from paid work during the 1930s, the wartime government used patriotic propaganda to encourage women
10 to work in defense industries. While women's employment was still viewed as an extraordinary measure for extraordinary times—and the female worker as merely filling in for a soldier to whom the job
15 "properly" belonged—gender barriers were lowered somewhat during this period, and pay began to equalize. Despite these moves toward women's participation in the workforce, however, shifting forces in the
20 post-war labor market meant that fewer American women worked outside the home in 1952 than in 1942.

According to the passage, which of the following was true of working women in the United States during World War II?

(F) As soon as soldiers returned home from the war, women were happy to give up their paid jobs and return to the home.

(G) Women exhibited extraordinary levels of skills relative to what was expected of them.

(H) Wages for women were closer to the typical wages paid to males than had been the case in earlier decades.

(I) Gender barriers were lowered, resulting in greater educational opportunities for women.

(J) Women were better suited than men to certain tasks needed in the defense industries.

1930s: W ≠ hold jobs

WWII 1940s: M → war, W → jobs

(P) *good for W: discrim ↓, pay more =*

BUT 1952 W work < 1942

The point: Discrimination decreased and pay became more equal when more women joined the workforce during World War II, but 10 years later, fewer women were working outside the home.

Step 1: Identify the Question

The language *according to the passage* indicates that this is a Specific Detail question. The question stem further indicates that you are looking for information about working women in the United States during World War II. (Note: You may already know that World War II took place from 1939 to 1945. If not, the first sentence of the passage indicates that the war was going on in the early 1940s.)

Step 2: Find the Support

The 1940s time frame was mostly detailed in the middle of the passage. The information about the 1930s (that women were discouraged from working) was pre-war and the information about 1952 was post-war.

Find the relevant text and, in order to get full context, start reading two to three lines before the "meat" of the text. Here's the relevant text (lines 5–17) for the wartime period:

> Although persistent and institutionalized discrimination had discouraged women from paid work during the 1930s, the wartime government used patriotic propaganda to encourage women to work in defense industries. While women's employment was still viewed as an extraordinary measure for extraordinary times—and the female worker as merely filling in for a soldier to whom the job "properly" belonged—gender barriers were lowered somewhat during this period, and pay began to equalize.

Step 3: Predict an Answer

So what was true? The government encouraged women to work. They were still viewed as filling in, not the real workers. But gender barriers were lowered a bit and pay got a little bit more equal.

Step 4: Eliminate and Find a Match

(A) Based on the last sentence of the paragraph, it sounds like the women did eventually give up their jobs, but nothing indicates that they did so happily, nor does the passage indicate that this occurred *as soon as* the men returned home. Eliminate.

(B) The passage does use the word *extraordinary*, but in a different context. The fact that women were doing what was usually "man's work" was viewed as *extraordinary*, or very unusual. The passage does not indicate how competent the women were at their jobs. Eliminate.

(C) Yes! This matches the language *pay began to equalize*. It was not as equal before (*in earlier decades*), and it began to become more equal during the wartime 1940s.

(D) This answer choice starts out well, but then veers into issues not discussed in the passage. The passage says that *gender barriers were lowered*, but educational opportunities are never mentioned. Eliminate.

(E) The passage does not indicate anything about the competence or skills of women in the workforce in the 1940s. Eliminate.

The correct answer is (C).

Step Summary

For Specific Detail questions, your four steps are as follows:

Step 1: Identify the Question

According to the passage . . .

The passage mentions which of the following . . .

Step 2: Find the Support

Don't rely on your memory, and don't even rely on your handwritten passage map exclusively. Use your passage map to figure out where you need to go in the original source passage.

Step 3: Predict an Answer

Read the text that you identified as important, and try to answer the question in your own words.

Step 4: Eliminate and Find a Match

Cross off any answer choices that are far from what you predicted or that contradict what the passage actually said. If you have more than one answer left, check the remaining choices against the relevant text from the passage.

Inference Questions

Inference questions are quite different from Specific Detail questions. When the GMAT asks you to infer something, it is not asking you to repeat back something that the passage already told you. Rather, the GMAT is asking you to draw a conclusion that must be true based on the information given in the passage. For example, what can you infer from this sentence?

As opposed to typical artifacts from the period, the newly named Rozzi Urn depicts a battle scene.

A valid GMAT inference might be:

> Typical artifacts from the period in question do not depict battle scenes.

You might be thinking, "Duh. That's what the first sentence just said." But it isn't, not quite. The inference "flips" the given information into something new that absolutely must be true based on the original information. That's what you're looking to do on the GMAT: Take a little baby step away from the given information to get to something that must be true.

On the GMAT, you will get into trouble if you infer the way that most people infer in the real world. In the real world, if someone tells you that *cats make the best pets*, you'd probably think that this person has a cat, or used to have a cat, or maybe wants to get a cat. However, none of these things has to be true. On the GMAT, a valid inference *must be able to be proved true* based on some information from the passage. (For instance, it must be true that this person doesn't think that dogs make equally good pets.)

Advanced Tip: On Inference questions, the following are indicators of a WRONG answer:

- Answers that are *probably* true (but not definitely)
- Answers that require additional assumptions (such as about what people might have been thinking when they did something or about what will happen in the future)

By the way, not every Inference question uses the word *infer*. Many questions use words such as *suggest* or *imply*. All of these questions will be treated the same way: Find the relevant information in the passage and pick something that MUST be true based on that information.

7

Drill 7.1—What Can You Infer?

Determine what else must be true for each statement given. If you get stuck, try "flipping" the information.

1. Toads, unlike frogs, lack teeth and spend most of their time on land.

2. Irish-American groups pressed for a more accurate treatment of the Irish Potato Famine in textbooks used in American schools.

3. The company's household products division was responsible for 40% of its profits in 2010. The balance of its profits came from its beauty products, baby care, and health products divisions, with 25% of the balance coming from the baby care division.

4. Unlike most skinks, the crocodile skink of Papua New Guinea is nocturnal or crepuscular (active in the early mornings and at dusk).

5. In 1980, Canadian expenditures on these measures were only slightly lower than U.S. expenditures on these same measures. Throughout the 1980s and early 1990s, the Canadian expenditures increased by a constant rate of 2% per year and the U.S. expenditures by a constant rate of 3% per year.

6. In 2008, Ecuador became the first nation in the world to pass a constitution codifying the rights of nature.

7. Because of monumental shifts in the social behavior studied by the researcher in the 1970s, the researcher's methodology has proved to be of more lasting value than her results.

Answers are on page 126.

GMAT Inferences

Now that you've had some practice drawing GMAT inferences, try this full question.

In the early 1940s, women's participation in the U.S. labor market changed dramatically as a result of the labor shortages resulting from the drafting of men to fight in World War II.

5 Although persistent and institutionalized discrimination had discouraged women from paid work during the 1930s, the wartime government used patriotic propaganda to encourage women to work in defense

10 industries. While women's employment was still viewed as an extraordinary measure for extraordinary times—and the female worker as merely filling in for a soldier to whom the job "properly" belonged—gender barriers were

15 lowered somewhat during this period, and pay began to equalize. Despite these moves toward women's participation in the workforce, however, shifting forces in the post-war labor market meant that fewer

20 American women worked outside the home in 1952 than in 1942.

Which of the following can be inferred regarding women's employment during the period discussed in the passage?

(A) Discrimination against women in the work-place increased between 1942 and 1952.

(B) Women's job qualifications decreased during the period 1942–1952.

(C) The end of World War II caused many men to come home and take back jobs they had once held.

(D) Increased economic prosperity in the 1950s meant women didn't have to work.

(E) More women worked outside the home in 1942 than 10 years later.

1930s: W ≠ hold jobs

WWII 1940s: M → war, W → jobs

ⓟ good for W: discrim ↓, pay more =

BUT 1952 W work < 1942

The point: Some good came of more women joining the workforce during World War II, but this good regressed after the war ended. (Note: This is worded a bit differently than it was earlier; different people will word the point in somewhat different ways!)

MEMORIZE IT!

If a passage tells you that something happened, and an Inference answer choice gives a *possible reason* why that thing happened, then that choice is incorrect! Do not assign causes for factual events given in the passage.

Step 1: Identify the Question

The word *inferred* indicates that this is an Inference question. The question stem further indicates that you need to infer something about *women's employment*.

MEMORIZE IT!

Do not pick an answer that is merely "consistent with" something you were told in the passage. The correct answer must be able to be proven true from the passage.

Step 2: Find the Support

Most of the passage is about the topic of women's employment, so remind yourself of the major time frames:

> …*discrimination discouraged women from paid work during the 1930s*

> …*wartime government…encourage[d] women to work*

> …*fewer women worked outside the home in 1952 than in 1942*

Note: The passage contains additional detail about wartime employment; if none of the answers match on your first pass, you can narrow down and review the more specific details about the 1940s.

Step 3: Predict an Answer

The correct answer should "flip" what the passage says. If women were discouraged from working in the 1930s but encouraged in the 1940s, then there was a change in behavior or attitudes toward women working. If fewer women worked outside the home in 1952, then more worked outside the home in 1942.

Step 4: Eliminate and Find a Match

(A) *Discrimination* was mentioned for the 1930s, not 1942 or 1952. Eliminate.

(B) The passage indicates that fewer women worked outside the home in 1952 than in 1942, but it does not say *why*. One possibility might have to do with job qualifications, but this does not have to be true. Eliminate.

(C) This sounds pretty good—that's probably what happened when the war ended. Leave this choice in.

(D) The passage doesn't mention anything about economic prosperity. Eliminate.

(E) This is exactly what Step 3 says: More women worked outside the home in 1942! But what about answer (C)?

It turns out that answer (C) is a big trap. While it certainly sounds reasonable to assume that a lot of men came back from World War II and took their old jobs back, the passage doesn't provide the information needed to make this inference. What if most of the soldiers died or were too injured to resume their old jobs? What if they came back and wanted to take new jobs, not resume their old ones? The passage does state that fewer women worked outside the home by 1952, but it does not provide information to infer that soldiers specifically took back their old jobs.

The correct answer is (E).

For Inference questions, your four steps are as follows:

Step 1: Identify the Question

It can be inferred...

The author implies...

The passage suggests...

Step 2: Find the Support

As with all Specific questions, don't rely on your memory. Use your little handwritten map of the passage to figure out where you need to go in the passage.

Step 3: Predict an Answer

Read the text that you identified as important, and try to answer the question in your own words. If you're not sure how to flip the language, just identify the relevant text on which the inference should be based.

Step 4: Eliminate and Find a Match

Cross off any answer choices that could be true but do not have to be true (as well as any that can't be true, of course!). The correct answer must be able to be proven from the text of the passage.

Specific Purpose Questions

Specific Purpose questions ask you *why* the author mentions a specific piece of information. (For this reason, these questions are also sometimes called Why questions.)

It's important to recognize when the author is asking you *why* vs. *what*. The answers to the questions "What are you studying?" and "Why are you studying it?" are quite different! To see an illustration of how a Why question works, try out the problem below.

In the early 1940s, women's participation in the U.S. labor market changed dramatically as a result of the labor shortages resulting from the drafting of men to fight in World War II.
5   Although persistent and institutionalized discrimination had discouraged women from paid work during the 1930s, the wartime government used patriotic propaganda to encourage women to work in defense
10   industries. While women's employment was still viewed as an extraordinary measure for extraordinary times—and the female worker as merely filling in for a soldier to whom the job "properly" belonged—gender barriers were
15   lowered somewhat during this period, and pay began to equalize. Despite these moves toward women's participation in the workforce, however, shifting forces in the post-war labor market meant that fewer
20   American women worked outside the home in 1952 than in 1942.

The author mentions *the female worker as merely filling in for a soldier to whom the job "properly" belonged* primarily in order to

(A) argue that women should not have taken jobs away from soldiers

(B) assert that women were generally less competent than men to do the jobs in question

(C) establish that persistent and institutionalized discrimination still predominated in the workplace

(D) acknowledge that the changes brought about for female workers during this time period were not universally positive

(E) explain why gender barriers were lowered somewhat during the period in question

1930s: W ≠ hold jobs

WWII 1940s: M → war, W → jobs

(P) good for W: discrim ↓, pay more =

BUT 1952 W work < 1942

The point: Some good came of more women joining the workforce during World War II, but this good regressed after the war ended.

You know the drill now! Use the 4-step process to answer the question.

Step 1: Identify the Question

The words *in order to* indicate that this is a Specific Purpose, or Why, question. Why did the author include the specific line quoted in the question stem?

Step 2: Find the Support

On Why questions, you'll need to make sure you have the full context. The sentence or two preceding the quoted text will typically tell you why the author introduced that text, so start a bit before the quoted text, in this case lines 5–17:

> "Although persistent and institutionalized discrimination had discouraged women from paid work during the 1930s, the wartime government used patriotic propaganda to encourage women to work in defense industries. While women's employment was still viewed as an extraordinary measure for extraordinary times—and the female worker as merely filling in for a soldier to whom the job "properly" belonged—gender barriers were lowered somewhat during this period, and pay began to equalize."

Step 3: Predict an Answer

Before the war, women experienced a lot of discrimination. Then, the government started encouraging women to work. The *while* start to the next sentence indicates a twist: The fact that women were working was still viewed as something they wouldn't (or even shouldn't) be doing if the men hadn't gone off to war, but some things did get better for women.

The author is showing the two sides of the coin. The country needed women to work, and the fact that so many did helped to lower gender barriers, but many people still felt that the situation was, or should be, only temporary.

7

Step 4: Eliminate and Find a Match

(A) The men were off at war; they were literally unavailable to take the jobs. The government encouraged the women to fill in. Eliminate.

(B) The passage mentions nothing about the competency of either men or women. Eliminate.

(C) While it is likely true that discrimination still existed, the author didn't include these words in order to address that issue. Rather, the author is acknowledging that the changes brought about by the war, while a step forward for women, were not entirely positive. Eliminate.

(D) Yes! Why does the author talk about this negative aspect? It's an introduction to the two positive changes cited later in the sentence (gender barriers lowered, pay more equalized). The author is using this text to acknowledge that the changes, while generally good ones, did not fix the overall issues experienced by women in the labor force.

(E) Just the opposite, in fact! The lowering of gender barriers was a positive for women. The fact that they were still viewed as filling in for men to whom the jobs "properly" belonged is a negative. Eliminate.

The correct answer is (D).

For Specific Purpose (or Why) questions, your four steps are as follows:

Step 1: Identify the Question

in order to…

serves primarily to…

Step 2: Find the Support

Don't rely on your memory. Use your little handwritten map of the passage to figure out where you need to go in the passage. Make sure to start a sentence or two before the specific text cited, as the setup for a Why answer often occurs just before the cited information is given in the passage.

Step 3: Predict an Answer

Read the text that you identified as important, and try to answer the question in your own words.

Step 4: Eliminate and Find a Match

Cross off any answer choices that are far from what you predicted or that contradict what the passage actually said. If you have more than one answer left, check the remaining choices against the relevant text from the passage.

Congratulations! You've made it through the three most common Specific question types tested on Reading Comprehension passages. Make your own summary sheet that indicates the 4-step process for each question type (you can just copy what's here, but you'll remember better if you write it in your own words). Test out your newly acquired skills in the following drill set.

Drill 7.2—Try Full Passages

First, grab your phone or another timer: You're going to time yourself while working on these drills! Each passage has a suggested time limit given; you may work a little more quickly or a little more slowly than this suggested time limit.

Before answering the questions, articulate the point to yourself, as well as the purpose of each paragraph. Use the 4-step process to answer the questions.

Ready? Go!

Passage 1: Supernovae (6.5 minutes)

A supernova is a brief stellar explosion so luminous that it can outshine an entire galaxy. While the explosion itself typically lasts less than 15 seconds, the light emitted by the
5 supernova can take weeks or months to fade from view. During that time, a supernova can emit an amount of energy equivalent to the amount of energy the Sun is expected to radiate over its entire lifespan; the heat thus
10 generated can create heavy elements, such as mercury, gold, and silver. Although supernovae explode frequently, few of them are visible to the naked eye from the Earth.

For millennia, humans have recorded
15 supernova sightings; speculation about the origin and meaning of the phenomenon helped to develop modern models of scientific thought. Tycho Brahe was the first to postulate that the source of the explosion
20 must be very far away from the Earth. After the sighting of a new supernova in 1604, Galileo sought to explain the phenomenon and built upon Tycho's theory in a series of lectures widely attended by the public in
25 Padua, Italy. The lectures not only sought to explain the origin of the "star" (some posited that perhaps it was merely "vapour near the Earth"), but also seriously undermined the views of most philosophers and scientists at
30 the time that the heavens were unchangeable. This idea was foundational to the geocentric worldview underpinned by a central and all-important Earth, around which other celestial bodies revolved. Galileo's
35 observations of the 1604 supernova helped to promote a heliocentric worldview, in which the planets (including the Earth) revolved around the Sun.

1. The primary purpose of the passage is to

   (A) explain the origins and history of supernovae

   (B) describe a shift in thought as a result of a natural event

   (C) juxtapose two opposing views about supernovae

   (D) establish the validity of a theory jointly held by two prominent scientists

   (E) illustrate how the scientific process works

2. The passage suggests that which of the following is true of the heliocentric model of the galaxy?

   (A) Tycho and other scientists agreed with Galileo that it was superior to the geocentric view.

   (B) It held that the Earth was the all-important center of the galaxy.

   (C) It was proved true based on data gathered from the 1604 supernova event.

   (D) It was later superseded by the geocentric worldview.

   (E) Prior to 1604, it was not the predominant theory describing the relationship between the planets and the Sun.

7

3. The passage mentions which of the following as a result of the supernova of 1604?

   (A) The supernova created and dispersed the heavy elements out of which the Earth and everything on it is made.

   (B) Tycho and Galileo worked together to promote the heliocentric worldview.

   (C) The public was interested in hearing lectures about the phenomenon.

   (D) Galileo's lectures were opposed by most philosophers and scientists.

   (E) Those who thought the supernova was "vapour" were proved wrong.

Passage 2: Freelancing (6.5 minutes)

As the proportion of Australian workers who are self-employed has boomed in the past decade, the topic of wealth creation for freelancers has become much more prevalent
5 in business magazines. A standard maxim among such publications is that a sole proprietor is best off treating her business as a much larger enterprise with a set of core departments, including but not limited to
10 executive, production, human resources, marketing, and finance functions. In effect, the freelancer would devote time and attention to each "department" in order to optimize her chances of success, and would,
15 unaided, create content, advertising campaigns, contracts, and quarterly budgets.

Most freelancers, however, presently operate in the creative realm, encompassing not only traditional arts such as photography
20 and writing but also more technical services such as computer programming and software engineering. Such creative forms of labor demand highly specialized skills. For the creative freelancer, then, whose most valued
25 asset is labor, conceptualizing one's business in such a fashion risks the dilution of the company's most important resource: the freelancer's skills. Distributing one's labor across platforms is a zero-sum game that may
30 yield positive results in some scenarios but not necessarily all. A photographer who spends his time developing a marketing plan may consequently jeopardize his public image by failing to devote sufficient effort to
35 expanding his portfolio via new and high-value artwork. Moreover, because "word of mouth" is typically considered the most powerful means of marketing in a creative industry, the potential benefits of such a trade-off are far
40 from certain.

4. According to the passage, which of the following statements about the present-day freelancer population in Australia is true?

(A) It is increasingly preoccupied with the question of how to create more wealth.

(B) The majority of the freelancer population is composed of creative professionals.

(C) Most freelancers are artists.

(D) Many freelancers see themselves as structurally identical to larger corporations.

(E) It has redefined the priorities of the publishing industry.

5. It can be inferred from the passage that the author believes word-of-mouth marketing

(A) is more prevalent in photography than in other industries

(B) is a form of marketing that requires no work on the freelancer's part

(C) calls into question the utility of a particular business model

(D) lends credence to a photographer's choice to develop a marketing plan

(E) underscores the importance of rejecting a widely held view

6. The author of the passage mentions the photographer (in line 31) primarily in order to

(A) provide an example of an instance in which the principle being discussed could be problematic

(B) suggest that, for this category of worker, the principle being discussed is rarely useful

(C) promote the idea that photography should be viewed as an exception to a general rule

(D) illustrate that marketing decisions are unique in that they should be considered based upon context

(E) remind readers that artistic integrity is more important than marketing for a true artist

7

This page intentionally left blank

Passage 3: Cargo Cults (8.5 minutes)

Cargo cults are religious movements that have appeared in isolated tribal societies following interaction with technologically advanced cultures. Such cults arose in earnest
5 in the years following World War II, as members of tribal societies came into contact with radios, televisions, guns, airplanes, and other "cargo" brought to Melanesian islands as part of the Allied war effort. Members of
10 native societies, having little knowledge of Western manufacturing, found soldiers' explanations of the cargo's provenance unconvincing. Some concluded that the "cargo" had come about through spiritual
15 means, created by the deities and ancestors of the native people, and that the foreigners had attracted the cargo to themselves through trickery, or through an error made by the deities and ancestors. Cargo cults arose for
20 the purpose of attracting material wealth back to its "rightful owners" via religious rituals that sought to mimic the actions of the foreigners in order to attract cargo. On the island of Tanna in Vanuatu, cult members constructed
25 elaborate airstrips and control towers intended to attract airplanes; soldiers in re-created U.S. Army uniforms conducted parade ground drills with wooden rifles.

Members of cargo cults commit the fallacy
30 of confusing a *necessary* condition with a *sufficient* one. It is true that an airstrip and a control tower are necessary for executing a safe landing of an airplane; they are not, however, sufficient to attract an airplane in
35 the first place. Thus, the term "cargo cult" has arisen as an idiom to describe those who mimic the superficial appearance of a procedure without understanding the underlying purpose, meaning, or functioning
40 of that procedure.

In the book *Surely You're Joking, Mr. Feynman!*, physicist Richard Feynman dedicates a chapter to "cargo cult science," the appearance of real science without an
45 understanding of the underlying workings of real science. For example, through meticulous experimentation, a researcher named Young discovered that laboratory rats were using the sounds made by a maze's floorboards to
50 memorize positions within the maze, thus invalidating experimental results. When the maze was put on a floor of sand, this cue was removed, and future experiments were more valid. However, some scientists—cargo cult
55 scientists—went on running rats through a maze without the sand, publishing their results and going about the motions of science without, as Feynman argues, actually doing science.

7. The primary purpose of the passage is to

(A) offer a suggestion for improving the results of scientific experiments

(B) explain the origin and wider adaptation of a particular term

(C) demonstrate that cargo cults mistakenly confuse preceding events with causal events

(D) argue that it is important for scientists to take into account the research of other scientists in their fields

(E) establish that the cargo cult members' mistakes in logic could be remedied through the scientific method

8. The passage suggests that some residents of Tanna concluded that they were the "rightful owners" (line 21) of the cargo because

(A) they didn't believe the reasons given for the goods' actual origins

(B) they believed all possessions were created by deities

(C) they believed they were owed a debt by their ancestors

(D) military forces had given them the cargo

(E) guns and airplanes were unknown to them prior to World War II

9.   The author introduces the example of the researcher named Young (lines 47–54) in order to

   (A)   demonstrate the difference between a necessary cause and a sufficient one

   (B)   explore the contributions to science made by Feynman and his students

   (C)   establish that members of cargo cults cannot also be members of the scientific research community

   (D)   argue that the scientific method is not the only means by which to conduct a scientific experiment

   (E)   illustrate how some scientists might not be conducting rigorous scientific research

10.   According to the passage, the similarity between cargo cult members and practitioners of cargo cult science can most appropriately be described in which of the following ways?

   (A)   Both use inappropriate equipment to try to force a phenomenon to occur.

   (B)   Both refuse to accept the principles of the scientific method.

   (C)   Both adhere to certain processes without fully understanding how those processes function.

   (D)   Both believe that forces outside of their control may impact their lives or research.

   (E)   Both would benefit from enhanced scientific education.

Passage 4: Anchoring (6.5 minutes)

During salary negotiations, some career advisors recommend that the job seeker allow the company to make the initial salary offer. Proponents of this approach assert that
5 making an initial offer that is too high or too low can hurt a party's position. For example, if a job seeker initially requests a lower salary than the employer was prepared to provide, then the end result is likely to be a lower final
10 salary offer than might have been attained had the candidate allowed the company to start the negotiations. Thus, the party that initially does not name a salary is in a better position to protect its interests even while
15 allowing the opposing side to feel more in control of the negotiations.

Critics of this approach emphasize the importance of anchors, cognitive focal points that direct any given negotiation. Under the
20 anchoring principle, the initial offer becomes the number to which all other numbers are compared. The party who makes the initial offer is able to define the range of the negotiation and thereby has more significant
25 influence over the final deal. In order to avoid undermining their own interests, job seekers would purposely start negotiations at a higher-than-expected anchor point, but not a point so high that the company in question
30 balks at negotiating entirely.

Harvard Law School's Program on Negotiation suggests one further step: establish an anchor without making an explicit offer. A candidate might mention, for instance,
35 that a colleague recently accepted a similar position at a specified salary or that the average salary for people with similar qualifications falls within a particular range. Such anchoring tactics may diminish the
40 sometimes adversarial effect of a direct offer.

11. According to the passage, the proponents of the two theories differ in that

(A) one group believes that remaining silent is the better way to negotiate, while the other group believes that active conversations are necessary

(B) one group believes that its theory will lead to the best possible salary outcome for the job seeker, while the other group believes that its theory will lead to the best possible salary outcome for the company

(C) one group believes that a high anchoring point should be set, while the other group believes that a low anchoring point should be set

(D) one group believes that the party to make the starting offer has the stronger negotiating position, while the other group believes that the party to make the starting offer has the weaker negotiating position

(E) one group believes that an adversarial negotiating approach is preferable, while the other group believes that a non-adversarial approach is preferable

12. The passage suggests that, when following the anchoring principle, a job candidate who begins negotiations by offering a modest salary level will likely end up with

(A) a lower salary offer than he would have secured if he had made an initial offer that was extremely low

(B) a salary similar to that of someone who allowed the company to set the initial anchor point

(C) a lower salary than he would have secured if he had offered a higher starting level

(D) a higher salary than he would have secured if he had offered a higher starting level

(E) a higher salary than he would have secured if he had allowed the company to make the initial offer

7

13. The author cites the Program on Negotiation (lines 31–34) in order to

    (A) establish that a reputable institution supports one negotiation method over another

    (B) acknowledge a controversy associated with a particular negotiation method

    (C) demonstrate that a single negotiation method is not sufficient for all possible situations

    (D) assert that one negotiation method is markedly superior to another

    (E) introduce an additional tactic for use with a specific negotiation method

Answers are on pages 127–143.

Answers to Drill Sets

Drill 7.1—What Can You Infer?

1. Since toads are presented as *unlike frogs* in a specific way, it must be true that frogs have teeth and do not spend most of their time on land. (If you said "frogs spend most of their time in the water," then you were using outside information—for all you know from the sentence, frogs spend most of their time in the air.)

2. If Irish-American groups *pressed for a more accurate treatment*, they must have thought that the treatment of the Irish Potato Famine in textbooks used in American schools was not accurate enough.

3. *The balance* means "the rest" or "the remainder." So if household products accounted for 40% of its profits and baby products for 25% *of the balance*, then baby products accounted for 25% of the leftover 60%. One-fourth of 60% is 15%. Thus, household accounted for 40% and baby for 15%, for a total of 55%, so the other two divisions, beauty and health, combined for 45%.

4. The clue is *unlike most skinks*. Since the crocodile skink is active at night (*nocturnal*) or in the early morning or at dusk, pretty much the only time that leaves for the regular skinks is daytime. Thus, most skinks are active in the daytime. (If you've never heard of a skink, don't worry—almost no one has. No previous knowledge of skinks is required here.)

5. The Canadian expenditures were lower in 1980 and then grew at a slower rate than the already higher American expenditures. Throughout the given time period of the 1980s and early 1990s, then, U.S. expenditures were consistently higher (or Canadian expenditures were consistently lower).

   Think a little more about #5. Since you know for sure that American expenditures throughout the period were always higher and also grew at a faster rate, you could also infer some fairly random-sounding (but not really random) facts, such as:

   > Canadian expenditures in 1987 were lower than American expenditures in 1989.

   That sounds out of scope, but actually, that statement must be true based on the original information—if American expenditures are higher throughout the entire period, and the gap between the American and Canadian expenditures widens every year, then you can safely conclude that American expenditures were always greater than Canadian expenditures from the same year or an earlier year.

6. If Ecuador was the first nation to pass this particular type of constitution, then you can infer that, prior to 2008, no country had passed this type of constitution. You could even infer something that might sound too specific at first: As of 2001, Germany did not codify the rights of nature.

7. It might be helpful to paraphrase the original argument before making an inference. The argument is saying something like: Since a lot has changed since the 1970s, the researcher's methodology is still valuable, but the actual results are not as valuable.

   What can you infer from that? Her results are out of date.

Drill 7.2—Try Full Passages

Passage 1: Supernovae

Main point: A particular type of phenomenon (supernova) helped some scientists to support a new model (the Earth revolves around the Sun).

Paragraph 1: Supernovae expend a huge amount of energy and some can be seen from the Earth.

Paragraph 2: Supernovae ended up being part of the support for a new heliocentric worldview (the Earth revolves around the Sun, not the other way around).

Passage map:

(1) SN: explode, really bright
         DTL

(2) SN spec → modern sci thought
     TB 1st: SN really far away
     1604 G: origin, undermine P
           G: Earth revolves around sun

1. **(B) describe a shift in thought as a result of a natural event:**

Step 1: Identify the question.

The words *primary purpose* indicate that this is a Primary Purpose question.

Step 2: Find the support.

Ideally, you will have determined the main idea during your read-through of the passage; if you need to refresh your memory, return to your map.

Step 3: Predict an answer.

The point of the passage: A particular type of phenomenon (supernova) helped some scientists to support a new model (the Earth revolves around the Sun).

Step 4: Eliminate and find a match.

	Answer Choice	Explanation
(A)	explain the origins and history of supernovae	The first paragraph does explain what supernovae are. The origins are not explored, however, nor does this choice account for the message in the second paragraph.
(B)	describe a shift in thought as a result of a natural event	CORRECT. Some scientists used supernovae as one piece of evidence in support of a new scientific model.
(C)	juxtapose two opposing views about supernovae	The passage does discuss two opposing views (geocentric vs. heliocentric), but these are not views *about supernovae.*
(D)	establish the validity of a theory jointly held by two prominent scientists	The passage does not indicate that Galileo and Tycho's theory is now valid. (Be careful not to bring in your own outside knowledge!)
(E)	illustrate how the scientific process works	This choice is too broad. One could argue that the scientific process was in use, but the purpose of the passage is much more specific.

2. **(E) Prior to 1604, it was not the predominant theory describing the relationship between the planets and the Sun:**

Step 1: Identify the question.

The word *suggests* indicates that this is an Inference question.

Step 2: Find the support.

The question asks about the heliocentric model; this is first referenced later in lines 25–38 of the second paragraph:

> The lectures not only sought to explain the origin of the "star" (some posited that perhaps it was merely "vapour near the Earth"), but also seriously undermined the views of most philosophers and scientists at the time that the heavens were unchangeable. This idea was foundational to the geocentric worldview underpinned by a central and all-important Earth, around which other celestial bodies revolved. Galileo's observations of the 1604 supernova helped to promote a heliocentric worldview, in which the planets (including the Earth) revolved around the Sun.

Step 3: Predict an answer.

At the time, *most philosophers and scientists* believed in something called the *geocentric* view. But *Galileo's observations of the supernova helped to promote a heliocentric* view. The heliocentric view, then, was relatively new, and Galileo did not agree with most of the others.

Step 4: Eliminate and find a match.

Answer Choice	Explanation
(A) Tycho and other scientists agreed with Galileo that it was superior to the geocentric view.	The argument indicates only that Galileo built upon Tycho's supernovae theory, not that Tycho agreed with the heliocentric worldview. Further, no other scientists are also cited as agreeing with Galileo.
(B) It held that the Earth was the all-important center of the galaxy.	The geocentric view holds this, not the heliocentric view.
(C) It was proved true based on data gathered from the 1604 supernova event.	The passage does not indicate that the heliocentric model was proved true at any point.
(D) It was later superseded by the geocentric worldview.	At the time, *most philosophers and scientists* believed the geocentric view; the heliocentric view is presented as new or gaining in importance, after the geocentric view.
(E) Prior to 1604, it was not the predominant theory describing the relationship between the planets and the Sun.	CORRECT. Since *most philosophers and scientists* believed in the geocentric worldview prior to Galileo's lectures, it must be the case that the heliocentric view was not the predominant theory prior to those lectures.

3. **(C) The public was interested in hearing lectures about the phenomenon:**

Step 1: Identify the question.

The language *mentions which of the following* indicates that this is a Specific Detail question.

Step 2: Find the support.

What happened as a result of the 1604 supernova? Lines 20–30 talk about this:

> After the sighting of a new supernova in 1604, Galileo sought to explain the phenomenon and built upon Tycho's theory in a series of lectures widely attended by the public in Padua, Italy. The lectures not only sought to explain the origin of the "star" (some posited that perhaps it was merely "vapour near the Earth"), but also seriously undermined the views of most philosophers and scientists at the time that the heavens were unchangeable.

Step 3: Predict an answer.

Multiple things occurred as a result of the 1604 supernova. Start with the first one or two and check the answers for a match. If that doesn't work, read a little farther and check the answers again.

Galileo gave some lectures to the public. He tried to explain where the supernova came from. He also ended up undermining what most scientists at the time thought.

Step 4: Eliminate and find a match.

Answer Choice	Explanation
(A) The supernova created and dispersed the heavy elements out of which the Earth and everything on it is made.	The first paragraph does mention that a supernova can create heavy elements, but the Earth must already have existed when the 1604 supernova, specifically, was observed (by people living on the Earth!).
(B) Tycho and Galileo worked together to promote the heliocentric worldview.	The passage indicates only that Galileo built on some of Tycho's earlier work, not that the two worked together.
(C) The public was interested in hearing lectures about the phenomenon.	CORRECT. The passage indicates that Galileo's lectures on the supernova were *widely attended by the public*.
(D) Galileo's lectures were opposed by most philosophers and scientists.	Galileo's theory did undermine the theory followed by most of his peers, but the passage does not indicate that his peers opposed what he had to say.
(E) Those who thought the supernova was "vapour" were proved wrong.	The vapour idea was one hypothesis; the passage does not indicate that the 1604 supernova or Galileo's lectures outright disproved this (or any other) hypothesis.

Note that the detail mentioned in the correct answer was so minor that you might not have called it out specifically when reviewing the passage. That's okay. As long as you have just reread the two or three pertinent sentences, either you will be able to recall those kinds of seemingly more minor details or you will be able to recheck the text quickly since you have just identified the relevant couple of sentences.

7

Passage 2: Freelancing

Main point: The "freelancer as a company" idea might work for some businesses, but freelancers should be careful that they're not actually harming their businesses, especially those working in creative fields.

Paragraph 1: Business magazines say that a freelancer should still have all the "departments" that a larger company would have.

Paragraph 2: The author thinks this won't always work, especially for those in the creative realm. If creative freelancers take too much time away from actually creating stuff, then the overall business may be hurt.

Passage map:

(1) Bus Pub: FL should run as business w/ dep'ts, etc.

(2) auth: BUT creative FL might be hurt by this

4.   (B) **The majority of the freelancer population is composed of creative professionals:**

Step 1: Identify the question.

The language *according to the passage* indicates that this is a Specific Detail question.

Step 2: Find the support.

The passage mentions Australian freelancers in the very first sentence (lines 1–5):

> As the proportion of Australian workers who are self-employed has boomed in the past decade, the topic of wealth creation for freelancers has become much more prevalent in business magazines.

The passage adds additional information about this population at the beginning of the second paragraph (lines 17–22):

> Most freelancers, however, presently operate in the creative realm, encompassing not only traditional arts such as photography and writing but also more technical services such as computer programming and software engineering.

Step 3: Predict an answer.

In Australia, a higher proportion of self-employed workers are freelancers today than 10 years ago, and most of them work in creative fields.

7

Step 4: Eliminate and find a match.

Answer Choice	Explanation
(A) It is increasingly preoccupied with the question of how to create more wealth.	The passage says that business magazines are talking about this more, not that freelancers are becoming preoccupied with the topic.
(B) The majority of the freelancer population is composed of creative professionals.	CORRECT. The first sentence of the second paragraph indicates this.
(C) Most freelancers are artists.	This is a tricky answer! *Operating in the creative realm* does not necessarily mean that someone is an artist. The title of artist is more narrow than the idea of working in the creative realm in general.
(D) Many freelancers see themselves as structurally identical to larger corporations.	The passage does not indicate that this is the case.
(E) It has redefined the priorities of the publishing industry.	While the passage does say that business magazines are writing more about wealth creation for freelancers, no information is provided to say that the priorities of the publishing industry have been redefined.

5. **(C) calls into question the utility of a particular business model:**

Step 1: Identify the question.

The word *inferred* indicates that this is an Inference question.

Step 2: Find the support.

Word-of-mouth marketing is mentioned at the end of the passage in lines 31–40:

> A photographer who spends his time developing a marketing plan may consequently jeopardize his public image by failing to devote sufficient effort to expanding his portfolio via new and high-value artwork. Moreover, because "word of mouth" is typically considered the most powerful means of marketing in a creative industry, the potential benefits of such a trade-off are far from certain.

Step 3: Predict an answer.

As a photographer contributes to his portfolio, he may gain much wider reach via word-of-mouth marketing. Taking time away from the portfolio to write up a marketing plan might actually hurt this photographer's business. So the author believes that word-of-mouth marketing could be valuable enough, in some cases, to negate the idea that a freelancer should run himself as a complete business.

7

Step 4: Eliminate and find a match.

Answer Choice	Explanation
(A) is more prevalent in photography than in other industries	The photographer is just one example; the author doesn't compare photography to other industries.
(B) is a form of marketing that requires no work on the freelancer's part	No, expanding the portfolio is work!
(C) calls into question the utility of a particular business model	CORRECT. The author uses this as an example of why the "run as a business" theory might not be useful for all freelancers.
(D) lends credence to a photographer's choice to develop a marketing plan	If anything, the opposite! If he's developing a marketing plan, he might have to take time away from building his portfolio, which would have potentially helped expand his word of mouth.
(E) underscores the importance of rejecting a widely held view	This choice goes too far. The author doesn't completely reject the theory; rather, the author points out that it would not necessarily be the right path for everyone.

6.   **(A) provide an example of an instance in which the principle being discussed could be problematic:**

Step 1: Identify the question.

The language *primarily in order to* indicates that this is a Specific Purpose, or Why, question.

Step 2: Find the support.

The photographer is first mentioned later in the second paragraph. Start a sentence or two before, as the answer to a Why question often hinges on the information just prior (lines 23–36):

> For the creative freelancer, then, whose most valued asset is labor, conceptualizing one's business in such a fashion risks the dilution of the company's most important resource: the freelancer's skills. Distributing one's labor across platforms is a zero-sum game that may yield positive results in some scenarios but not necessarily all. A photographer who spends his time developing a marketing plan may consequently jeopardize his public image by failing to devote sufficient effort to expanding his portfolio via new and high-value artwork.

Step 3: Predict an answer.

The photographer is an example to illustrate how someone could risk the dilution of [his] skills and to establish that the "run as a business" plan might not work in all scenarios.

7

Step 4: Eliminate and find a match.

Answer Choice	Explanation
(A) provide an example of an instance in which the principle being discussed could be problematic	CORRECT. This is exactly why the example of the photographer is introduced.
(B) suggest that, for this category of worker, the principle being discussed is rarely useful	The passage specifically states that the *principle may yield positive results in some scenarios but not necessarily all*. This language does not match the usage *rarely useful*.
(C) promote the idea that photography should be viewed as an exception to a general rule	The author does not use photography as an exception to the rule. Rather, the author uses this example to illustrate her main point.
(D) illustrate that marketing decisions are unique in that they should be considered based upon context	This choice is confusingly worded. Luckily, you can use just the first half to answer: *marketing decisions are unique*. The passage does not indicate this.
(E) remind readers that artistic integrity is more important than marketing for a true artist	Some people may believe this, but the passage does not indicate this.

7

Passage 3: Cargo Cults

Main point: A particular phenomenon (cargo cult) has evolved into a general term that can apply to other groups (including modern groups), not just isolated tribes.

Paragraph 1: WWII: Technologically advanced groups brought technology to isolated tribal societies who thought the technology was spiritual in nature. They developed cargo cults that tried to "attract" the technology back to them.

Paragraph 2: Cargo cult is now a term to describe anyone who superficially mimics something without really understanding what's going on.

Paragraph 3: Feynman wrote about a scientific example of cargo cult science dealing with lab rats.

Passage map:

① tribe interact Western → CC
　gods created equip
　get it back via rituals

② CC = stepping thru motions
　　　not really understanding

③ F: "CC science" same def as
　　ex: Young, rats

7. **(B) explain the origin and wider adaptation of a particular term:**

Step 1: Identify the question.

This is a Primary Purpose question.

Step 2: Find the support.

Ideally, you will have determined the main idea during your read-through of the passage; if you need to refresh your memory, return to your map.

Step 3: Predict an answer.

The main point, as articulated earlier, is:

> A particular phenomenon (cargo cult) has evolved into a general term that can apply to other groups (including modern groups), not just isolated tribes.

Step 4: Eliminate and find a match.

Answer Choice	Explanation
(A) offer a suggestion for improving the results of scientific experiments	While you might surmise that Feynman's suggestion is "don't be a cargo cult scientist," the point of the overall passage doesn't rest on scientific experiments.
(B) explain the origin and wider adaptation of a particular term	CORRECT. This matches the main point.
(C) demonstrate that cargo cults mistakenly confuse preceding events with causal events	This choice is confusing. The examples given in the first paragraph do go along with this idea. The broader point, however, is that the term cargo cult itself has expanded in usage and meaning.
(D) argue that it is important for scientists to take into account the research of other scientists in their fields	Most people would agree with this, but it is not the main point of this particular passage.
(E) establish that the cargo cult members' mistakes in logic could be remedied through the scientific method	This is a mash-up of some ideas in the passage. The cargo cult members are making logical mistakes, but the passage doesn't focus on employing the scientific method to fix these mistakes. (This could apply to the scientists in paragraph 3, but not to the tribal members in paragraph 1.)

8. **(A) they didn't believe the reasons given for the goods' actual origins:**

Step 1: Identify the question.

The word *suggests* indicates that this is an Inference question.

Step 2: Find the support.

The question references specific lines. As always, start a sentence or two before the actual reference, in this case lines 9–23:

> Members of native societies, having little knowledge of Western manufacturing, found soldiers' explanations of the cargo's provenance unconvincing. Some concluded that the "cargo" had come about through spiritual means, created by the deities and ancestors of the native people, and that the foreigners had attracted the cargo to themselves through trickery, or through an error made by the deities and ancestors. Cargo cults arose for the purpose of attracting material wealth back to its "rightful owners" via religious rituals that sought to mimic the actions of the foreigners in order to attract cargo.

Step 3: Predict an answer.

In the absence of what they considered a convincing explanation, some tribe members came up with their own explanation: Their own deities (gods) and ancestors made this stuff but were *tricked* by the foreigners…so the foreigners are not the rightful owners. Therefore, the tribe members must be the rightful owners (according to their reasoning).

Step 4: Eliminate and find a match.

Answer Choice	Explanation
(A) they didn't believe the reasons given for the goods' actual origins	CORRECT. They found the soldiers' explanations *unconvincing*. In other words, they didn't believe the (true!) reasons given, so they eventually came up with their own explanation.
(B) they believed all possessions were created by deities	The word *all* is too extreme. The cargo in question was believed to be made by deities or ancestors, but no reference is made to *all possessions*.
(C) they believed they were owed a debt by their ancestors	The passage does say that they believed the cargo to be created by deities and ancestors, but it says nothing about the ancestors specifically owing them a debt.
(D) military forces had given them the cargo	If the military had given them the cargo, then they would not have needed to *attract [it]* back to themselves.
(E) guns and airplanes were unknown to them prior to World War II	The passage says that they had *little knowledge of manufacturing*, but does not provide evidence to infer that these objects were completely *unknown* to the islanders.

9. **(E) illustrate how some scientists might not be conducting rigorous scientific research:**

Step 1: Identify the question.

The *in order to* language indicates that this is a Specific Purpose question. Why did the author introduce the example of Young?

Step 2: Find the support.

Support can be found in lines 42–59:

> . . . physicist Richard Feynman dedicates a chapter to "cargo cult science," the appearance of real science without an understanding of the underlying workings of real science. For example, through meticulous experimentation, a researcher named Young discovered that laboratory rats were using the sounds made by a maze's floorboards to memorize positions within the maze, thus invalidating experimental results. When the maze was put on a floor of sand, this cue was removed, and future experiments were more valid. However, some scientists—cargo cult scientists—went on running rats through a maze without the sand, publishing their results and going about the motions of science without, as Feynman argues, actually doing science.

Step 3: Predict an answer.

Young supports Feynman's contention that some (other) scientists are going through the motions of science without actually conducting good science.

7

Step 4: Eliminate and find a match.

	Answer Choice	Explanation
(A)	demonstrate the difference between a necessary cause and a sufficient one	Paragraph 2, not paragraph 3, mentions the concept of necessary and sufficient.
(B)	explore the contributions to science made by Feynman and his students	The passage doesn't indicate that Young was Feynman's student or that Feynman had anything to do with Young's experiment.
(C)	establish that members of cargo cults cannot also be members of the scientific research community	Though it's true that the islanders probably aren't also members of the scientific research community, the passage doesn't say that such a crossover is impossible. In fact, Feynman contends that certain scientists are basically members of a scientific cargo cult.
(D)	argue that the scientific method is not the only means by which to conduct a scientific experiment	While this may be true in the real world, the passage doesn't introduce Young's experiment for this reason.
(E)	illustrate how some scientists might not be conducting rigorous scientific research	CORRECT. The other scientists did not take Young's research findings into account; they just kept performing bad experiments.

10.   **(C) Both adhere to certain processes without fully understanding how those processes function:**

Step 1: Identify the question.

The language *according to the passage* signals that this is a Specific Detail question.

Step 2: Find the support.

The question asks for a similarity between the islanders in paragraph 1 and the cargo cult scientists in paragraph 3. The answer should have something to do with the definition of cargo cults, which can be found in lines 35–40 of paragraph 2:

> Thus, the term "cargo cult" has arisen as an idiom to describe those who mimic the superficial appearance of a procedure without understanding the underlying purpose, meaning, or functioning of that procedure.

Step 3: Predict an answer.

People in both groups are operating with only a superficial understanding of the situation at hand.

Step 4: Eliminate and find a match.

	Answer Choice	Explanation
(A)	Both use inappropriate equipment to try to force a phenomenon to occur.	The islanders do this, but the scientists do not.
(B)	Both refuse to accept the principles of the scientific method.	The scientific method is not mentioned with relation to the islanders. (It also isn't accurate to say that the scientists refuse to accept the principles of the scientific method; rather, they appear not to understand those principles.)
(C)	Both adhere to certain processes without fully understanding how those processes function.	CORRECT. This matches the way in which the term *cargo cult* is used.
(D)	Both believe that forces outside of their control may impact their lives or research.	If anything, the opposite is true. The islanders think things are within their control; otherwise, they would not take steps to try to attract the cargo to themselves.
(E)	Both would benefit from enhanced scientific education.	This may be true for the scientists, but the topic of scientific education is irrelevant for the islanders.

Passage 4: Anchoring

Main point: Two camps: 1) Let the other side start so that you don't start too low by accident, and 2) you start with a higher offer to set the anchoring point for remaining negotiations. The second option addresses the concerns of the first.

Paragraph 1: Negotiation approach: Let the other side go first so that you don't underbid.

Paragraph 2: Alternative strategy: Go first to set the anchor point for future negotiations. Start on the high side.

Paragraph 3: Harvard supports #2: Start by giving a stat for someone else or an average.

Passage map:

Neg. salary

(1) let co. offer first

(2) indiv offer first and high

end up ↑↑ overall?

(3) cite similar stats

11. **(D) one group believes that the party to make the starting offer has the stronger negotiating position, while the other group believes that the party to make the starting offer has the weaker negotiating position:**

Step 1: Identify the question.

According to the passage indicates that this is a Specific Detail question.

Step 2: Find the support.

Return to your notes summary for this question. The first paragraph summarizes the position of the first group and the second and third paragraphs summarize the position of the second group.

Step 3: Predict an answer.

One group thinks that the job seeker should let the company offer first. The other group thinks that the job seeker should offer first and should specifically offer a salary at the high end of an acceptable range.

Step 4: Eliminate and find a match.

Answer Choice	Explanation
(A) one group believes that remaining silent is the better way to negotiate, while the other group believes that active conversations are necessary	The first paragraph does mention a party that declines to make the initial offer, but only at first. If one side never speaks, it's impossible to negotiate! The passage doesn't indicate that either side supports remaining silent throughout the negotiation.
(B) one group believes that its theory will lead to the best possible salary outcome for the job seeker, while the other group believes that its theory will lead to the best possible salary outcome for the company	Both groups think that their theory will help the *job seeker*.
(C) one group believes that a high anchoring point should be set, while the other group believes that a low anchoring point should be set	One group does believe in setting a high anchoring point, but the other does not believe in setting a low anchoring point.
(D) one group believes that the party to make the starting offer has the stronger negotiating position, while the other group believes that the party to make the starting offer has the weaker negotiating position	CORRECT. The anchoring group does believe that the party making the opening offer is in the stronger position. The other group does believe that making the opening offer puts that party in a weaker position.
(E) one group believes that an adversarial negotiating approach is preferable, while the other group believes that a non-adversarial approach is preferable	The passage does not say that either group believes in an adversarial approach to negotiations.

12. **(C) a lower salary than he would have secured if he had offered a higher starting level:**

Step 1: Identify the question.

The word *suggests* indicates that this is an Inference question.

Step 2: Find the support.

Support can be found in lines 19–30:

> Under the anchoring principle, the initial offer becomes the number to which all other numbers are compared. The party who makes the initial offer is able to define the range of the negotiation and thereby has more significant influence over the final deal. In order to avoid undermining their own interests, job seekers would purposely start negotiations at a higher-than-expected anchor point, but not a point so high that the company in question balks at negotiating entirely.

Step 3: Predict an answer.

The anchoring strategy is to figure out a reasonable salary range and then start the negotiation by offering something at the high end (but still reasonable/within range). According to the theory, the job seeker will end up with a better salary in the end because he will have established a high anchor point around which future counteroffers will be based.

So what might happen if someone offers only a modest salary level to start? This scenario is basically what the proponents of the first theory fear: If you start too low, you are more likely to end up with a lower salary than you might otherwise have gotten (after all, the company is unlikely to make a counteroffer that is higher than what you initially propose!).

Step 4: Eliminate and find a match.

Answer Choice	Explanation
(A) a lower salary offer than he would have secured if he had made an initial offer that was extremely low	*Extremely low* is lower than *modest* (which is low but not extremely so). Thus, the modest initial offer would anchor at a higher point and would likely lead to a higher salary in the end than an extremely low initial offer would.
(B) a salary similar to that of someone who allowed the company to set the initial anchor point	According to the anchoring principle, making a modest offer initially will set a low anchor for the negotiations and will likely lead to a lower outcome. Allowing the company to make the initial offer runs the risk of establishing a low anchor as well, because the company wants to offer as little as it can to secure the candidate. However, the passage offers no way to compare these two effects.
(C) a lower salary than he would have secured if he had offered a higher starting level	CORRECT. The anchoring principle says that if you start with a higher offer, you'll be more likely to end up with a higher salary in the end. If you start with a more modest salary, then, you'll be likely to end up with a lower offer instead.
(D) a higher salary than he would have secured if he had offered a higher starting level	The anchoring principle says the opposite: If the initial offer is too modest, then he will likely end up with a *lower* offer.
(E) a higher salary than he would have secured if he had allowed the company to make the initial offer	The anchoring principle is theorized to work to the candidate's benefit when he starts with a high offer, not a modest offer. It is not clear from the passage whether setting a modest anchor would result in a higher salary than allowing the company to make the initial offer.

7

13. **(E) introduce an additional tactic for use with a specific negotiation method:**

Step 1: Identify the question.

The *in order to* language indicates that this is a Specific Purpose question.

Step 2: Find the support.

Because the citation is at the beginning of a paragraph and this is a Why question, remind yourself of the purpose of the prior paragraph. The second half of paragraph 2 (lines 19–30) introduces the anchoring principle and explains how it works. Continue by reading text referred to in the question.

> Harvard Law School's Program on Negotiation suggests one further step: establish an anchor without making an explicit offer. A candidate might mention, for instance, that a colleague recently accepted a similar position at a specified salary, or that the average salary for people with similar qualifications falls within a particular range. Such anchoring tactics diminish the sometimes adversarial effect of a direct offer.

Step 3: Predict an answer.

The third paragraph introduces *one further step* to follow when using the anchoring principle. The information, then, elaborates on the principle introduced in the previous paragraph.

Step 4: Eliminate and find a match.

Answer Choice	Explanation
(A) establish that a reputable institution supports one negotiation method over another	The passage doesn't indicate that Harvard's Program on Negotiation prefers one method to the other.
(B) acknowledge a controversy associated with a particular negotiation method	Although the *sometimes adversarial effect* might be viewed as a potential *controversy*, a controversy associated with a negotiation method would be a debate about its efficacy or its side effects. The fact that a direct offer sometimes has an adversarial effect is not presented as a controversy itself.
(C) demonstrate that a single negotiation method is not sufficient for all possible situations	This choice may be true in the real world, but the passage itself does not say this. Moreover, in this context, the word *demonstrate* is a synonym of *prove*; you would need a level of mathematical certainty to demonstrate, or prove, this.
(D) assert that one negotiation method is markedly superior to another	The information from the Program on Negotiation does not in any way denigrate (or even mention!) the other method (i.e., letting the other party make the first offer).
(E) introduce an additional tactic for use with a specific negotiation method	CORRECT. The given information does represent an additional tactic that can be used with one of the methods presented in the passage: namely, being the first to set an anchor in salary negotiations.

How to Get Better at RC

In This Chapter...

In this chapter, you will learn effective methods for continuing to study and practice RC. You'll also have a chance to practice everything you've learned so far about RC.

CHAPTER 8 How to Get Better at RC

Improving Your Reading in General

Learning to become a better reader takes time and practice; if you are not planning to take the GMAT for six months or longer, then you have the time to become a better (and faster!) reader in preparation for the GMAT, business school, and life in general.

The following article was first published on Manhattan Prep's GMAT blog; it has been updated exclusively for *GMAT All the Verbal*.

How to Improve Your Reading Skills for Reading Comprehension

If you don't already read university-level material (in English) every day, then today is the day to start! But it's not enough just to read this material. You'll need to make sure that you are also learning how to comprehend and analyze the complex ideas found in this kind of writing.

How? You're about to learn!

Reading Passages on the GMAT

Reading on the GMAT is not exactly like reading in the real world (when was the last time someone gave you just three minutes to read something?), but it can mimic certain work situations. You typically have more to do than you have time to do it carefully, so you have to prioritize, and GMAT reading is no different.

GMAT reading passages are also typically more dense than the kinds of things you're reading on a daily basis, so you're going to need to seek out more academically focused material with which to practice.

Non-GMAT Reading Sources

Those who are learning English and aren't planning to take the GMAT for at least six months to a year may want to begin with business and science articles in newspapers such as *The Wall Street Journal* or magazines such as *The Economist*. These sources are a bit too "casual" and easy to read compared to most GMAT material, but they can provide you with a good way to build foundational skills.

Sources that are closer to "GMAT-speak" include:

- *Scientific American* for the harder science passages
- *The University of Chicago Magazine* (particularly feature articles)
- *Harvard Magazine* (particularly research articles)

Look for article titles or summaries that sound decently challenging to you.

How to Read from Non-GMAT Sources

So how can you learn GMAT-specific lessons from these non-GMAT reading sources? (Note: The recommendations below are geared toward helping you prepare for the GMAT; we would recommend somewhat different strategies if you were looking for pure comprehension without artificial time limits.)

First, GMAT reading material rarely provides a long introductory section or much of a conclusion, but those features are quite common in news and magazine articles. Skip the first paragraph or two (possibly several), and dive in somewhere in the middle. Read approximately three to five paragraphs (you want about 200–350 words), and give yourself a time limit: 1.5 minutes for a shorter length and 2 minutes for a longer one.

Don't expect to get 100% comprehension from what you read initially; after all, you aren't actually paying close attention to the full text. Don't give yourself extra time; stop when that buzzer buzzes. Part of your task is to become comfortable with reading quickly and actually *not* fully comprehending what you just read.

Then try to articulate the following:

- The main point of each individual paragraph
- The main idea of the entire article (or at least of this section of the article) without having to go back to the introductory paragraph; don't expect to get it exactly right, since you aren't actually reading the entire article.
- "Judgment" language (opinions, hypotheses, comparisons)
- Changes in direction in the text that you read: *however* language, two differing points of view, etc.

Then, go read more and gauge your accuracy. Read a couple of additional paragraphs. Does that change your answers to the exercises above? How? Why? Read a bit more and do the same. Finally, read the entire article.

When you start to feel more comfortable with this type of reading, add another layer of complexity: What might they ask you about the details of the article? What can you infer for GMAT purposes? (That is, what is not stated but must be true based upon information given in the article?) Do you understand the detail well enough that you could summarize it for someone else, possibly using easier language?

Content

To start, you might read articles that cover all kinds of content. GMAT Reading Comprehension (RC) passages come in one of four main categories: Physical Sciences, Biological Sciences, Social Sciences, and Business. As you study, ask yourself: Is your RC ability the same regardless of the type of content? Or do you tend to struggle more with certain kinds of content? If the latter is true, then start doing some more non-GMAT reading in those areas.

What do you do when you hit a particular sentence that makes you think, "What in the world does that mean?" Examine the nearby text, looking for context that can help you to decipher the meaning.

For example, do you remember this text from the Cargo Cult passage?

> Members of cargo cults commit the fallacy of confusing a necessary condition with a sufficient one. It is true that an airstrip and a control tower are necessary for executing a safe landing of an airplane; they are not, however, sufficient to attract an airplane in the first place.

What in the world is that *necessary* vs. *sufficient* stuff all about? Hey, the sentence right after offers an example! Use the example to understand the original point.

The tribe members would build an airstrip, thinking that that would "make" planes arrive and land. If a plane does want to land there, then you do need to have some kind of airstrip. But just having the airstrip doesn't guarantee that a plane is going to show up. The airstrip is *necessary* for a plane to land, but the airstrip is not *sufficient* to guarantee that a plane will land. That's what that abstract first sentence means.

Most of the time, when an RC passage offers a complex sentence, one of two things will happen. If the sentence is trying to convey a bigger idea, then the passage will offer an example or some other information to help you comprehend that big idea. If the sentence is about some outlandish or really technical detail, on the other hand, then you may not ever need to figure it out because you may not get a question about that detail. (And if you do, the passage will often offer additional explanation or an example to help you.)

Takeaways

1. If you want to be a better reader, practice reading from non-GMAT sources. If necessary, build up from "lighter" sources, such as *The Wall Street Journal* and *The Economist*, to more GMAT-like material, such as scientific and university magazines.

2. Answer certain questions about the material that you read: What's the overall point? What's the purpose of each paragraph? What are the main judgments made? What changes of direction exist?

3. If any specific content areas tend to give you trouble, practice those areas more. Learn to look for other clues in the text that will help you to comprehend the tough sentence or information.

How to Study from the Official Guide

You will definitely want to use the *GMAT Official Guide* (OG) to study Reading Comprehension (as well as the other sections of the exam). The OG contains real test questions from past official GMAT tests.

If you pick up a physical copy of the OG, there are some differences to take into account while studying, since you'll take the exam itself on a computer. On the RC section, the differences are even more pronounced:

The *Official Guide*	The Real GMAT (a Computer-Adaptive Test (CAT))
You can write in the book.	You can't write on the screen.
There are 3–9 questions per passage (usually 5–7).	There are 3–4 questions per passage.
Questions are at all levels of difficulty.	Questions adapt to your level of ability.
You can see all the questions at once.	You can only see one question at a time.
You can skip questions and go back to previous questions.	As on all of the GMAT, you cannot go back to review until you reach the end of that section.
You must time yourself.	A clock on the screen counts down.

8

Perhaps the most obvious difference between the *Official Guide* and the real exam is the number of questions per passage. The *Official Guide* gives as many as nine questions for a single passage, but on a computer-adaptive test, you would see only the three or four questions that have been selected for your level of performance (based on how well you've been doing on the Verbal section in general).

You want to make your *Official Guide* practice as much like the real GMAT as possible. Therefore, next are some instructions for studying from the *Official Guide*.

First, **treat the book like a computer screen**. Prop it up vertically. It's pretty annoying to read that way, isn't it? You're going to have to look up to read and down to write on a separate piece of paper...just as you will on the real exam. Start practicing that way now.

Next, **plan to do only three or four questions**, not all of the questions given. The more you do, the more of an advantage you have because you already know so much more about the passage. If there are more than four questions, try doing just the even questions first. In a couple of months, you can try the passage again, this time doing the odd questions.

Answer each question before moving to another. Because you can see all of the questions at once, it's tempting to jump around. Don't. Also, if you suddenly realize that you made a mistake on an earlier question, don't go back and look at that problem again now. Make your practice experience mimic what will happen on the real test.

Finally, **time yourself**. Give yourself about 1.5 to 2 minutes to read (depending on length, complexity, and your reading speed). Plan to average about 1.5 minutes per question (though General questions should take closer to 1 minute). Add up that time and give yourself one block of time for the particular passage and three or four questions you're about to do.

On the real GMAT, you will first see a passage and just one question on the screen. If you wish, you can read that question (it is recommended to preview the question stem only, not read all the answer choices) before you read the passage. Note that, on the real exam, you will not see the other questions, so do not preview any others before reading the passage.

Once you finish a passage...you're not actually done! You're going to learn how to get better by analyzing the passage and questions. Read on to learn how!

Advanced Tip: When reviewing the problem that you've done, imagine that, on every question, you have to argue with four other people, each of whom insists that one of the other answers is correct. Articulate aloud how you would convince each of those people why that other answer is, in fact, wrong.

How to Diagnose Problems in Your Reading Comprehension Process

Once you've completed a set of RC questions, compare your understanding of the passage now with what you understood before you answered any of the questions. Do you still think the point is the same? Or, do you have a better understanding now of the point the passage was really trying to make? Did you change your mind about the purpose of any of the paragraphs or any of the judgments or changes in direction going on in the passage?

If your later understanding of the main ideas is much stronger, then reread the passage now to try to figure out what you missed on your first read-through that you want to pay attention to on future first read-throughs. Did you rush too much and skim or skip over important parts of the main messages? Did you get too sucked into certain details and lose sight of the big picture? Adjust your reading process accordingly.

Next, take a look at the questions. Analyze each one based on the 4-step process. Did you:

- Correctly identify the question type? If not, what type of question is it and how will you know next time?

- Find the proper support in the passage? If not, why not? Did you misread or misunderstand the question? Did you get confused about some of the details in the passage? Did you forget or decide to skip this step entirely? How will you fix these problems for next time?

- Articulate an answer in your own words? If you did but your answer was inaccurate, see whether you can articulate a better answer now (including why it's a better answer!). If you couldn't do so, figure out why. It may be that this question was too hard to do so.

- Know what kind of characteristics the correct answer should have, based on the question type? For instance, on an Inference question, did you think about making sure that the answer was something that must be true? If not, figure out how you should verify your thinking for the correct answer next time.

- Spot and eliminate trap answers? What traps did you fall into (or almost fall into) and why? How will you avoid those types of traps in the future?

When people study, they typically feel great when answering questions correctly and disappointed when they get something wrong. But if you're answering everything correctly, then you are not actually challenging yourself and learning how to get better! Your goal is to improve, right? So when you get something wrong, change your mindset: Get a little bit excited, because you are about to learn how to get a better score on the GMAT!

How to Plan Your Study Sessions

Don't do more than one passage in a row; review and analyze your work between passages so that you can apply the lessons and get even better next time.

A good study session for Reading Comprehension might consist of the following:

- Make 5–10 new flash cards from the online Vocabulary and RC Idioms list (found in your Manhattan Prep account) and quiz yourself on your existing flash cards.

- Read one to two non-GMAT articles using the instructions from the previous section.

- Do one passage according to the instructions above, including analyzing all of your work afterwards.

- Quiz yourself on your new flash cards, as well as your flash cards from previous sessions.

Practice RC several times a week, but make sure to mix in study sessions for other question types (Verbal, Quant, and Data Insights). You'll learn better if you keep cycling back around to different topics and question types.

8

Next Steps

Congratulations! You are almost done with the Reading Comprehension section of this book! You just have one last task: a problem set that will test you on everything that you've just learned.

As you complete the problem set below, follow all of the steps of the RC process:

1. Find the main point and the purpose of each paragraph.

2. Create a passage map to keep track of the location of this information.

3. Use the 4-step process to answer each question:

   Step 1: Identify the question.

   Step 2: Find the support.

   Step 3: Predict an answer.

   Step 4: Eliminate and find a match.

When you're done, analyze your work and articulate to yourself what you want to do differently next time in order to get better. Then, try another passage and do it all over again.

This page intentionally left blank

8

Put It All Together: Four Full GMAT Passages and Questions

Complete each passage, together with its questions. Each passage has a suggested time limit, though you may work a little more quickly or slowly than average. Don't rush so much that you make careless mistakes, and don't take so much extra time that your performance on other questions in a test section would be negatively impacted.

Choose the best answer choice for the following questions.

Questions 1–4 refer to the following stimulus.

Passage 1: Greek Wreck (9 minutes)

In 1901, divers exploring the remains of a shipwreck off the coast of Greece discovered a contraption believed to have been used by Ancient Greeks to
5 predict solar eclipses. The Antikythera Mechanism was composed of a fixed-ring dial representing the 12 months of the Egyptian calendar and an inner ring representing the 12 zodiac signs.
10 Inside, a complex assembly of bronze gears mechanically replicated the irregular motions of the Moon caused by its elliptical orbit around the Earth through the use of two gear-wheels, one of which
15 was slightly off-center, connected by a pin. Regarded as the world's first analog computer, the Antikythera Mechanism involved remarkably intricate physics considering that, only 300 years earlier,
20 the Ancient Greeks still believed the world was flat. Accurately predicting lunar and solar eclipses, as well as solar, lunar, and planetary positions, it predated similar technology by 1,000 years. The timing
25 and nature of its existence remains one of science's great puzzles to this day. How and by whom was it created?
      Today, scientists understand much more about the complexities of the orbital
30 revolutions that cause solar eclipses to occur; for instance, the Earth's orbit around the Sun is also elliptical such that, depending on the time of year, the Earth is gradually traveling nearer to or
35 farther from the Sun. Further, since the plane of the Moon's revolution around the Earth is not the same as the plane of the Earth's revolution around the Sun, all calculations predicting a solar eclipse
40 must be completed in three dimensions. While in modern times the use of

satellites, telescopes, and other high-tech equipment has greatly enhanced our capacity for such calculations, when the
45 Antikythera Mechanism was created, the sole source of information available to scientists was observation of the night sky. It is thus not surprising that, under certain circumstances, the device is inaccurate by
50 up to 38 degrees; what is astonishing is that the device is remarkably accurate over a wide range of conditions.
      Recent analysis dating the device to 205 BC, earlier than previously thought,
55 suggests that the eclipse prediction mechanism was based not on Greek trigonometry but on Babylonian arithmetical methods borrowed by the Greeks. This conjecture makes plausible
60 Cicero's claim that Archimedes created the mechanism, as Greek trigonometry was nonexistent in 205 BC.

1. It can be inferred from the third paragraph that

    (A) the Ancient Greeks were more sophisticated than most people believe

    (B) Babylonian arithmetical methods predate Greek trigonometry

    (C) the greatest thinker in Ancient Greece was Archimedes

    (D) information obtainable by modern-day telescopes was also available in Ancient Greece

    (E) the Antikythera Mechanism was more likely to accurately predict a solar eclipse than modern-day technology

8

2. According to the passage, which of the following statements about the Antikythera Mechanism is true?

    (A) It was created by Archimedes.

    (B) It is 1,000 years old.

    (C) It was created in the 1900s.

    (D) It was the world's first digital computer.

    (E) It could be 38 degrees inaccurate.

3. According to the passage, which of the following is true about the orbit of the Earth around the Sun?

    (A) It renders predicting solar eclipses impossible without a telescope.

    (B) It is explainable using Greek trigonometry.

    (C) It is, unlike the Moon's orbit around the Earth, elliptical.

    (D) It is, like the Moon's orbit around the Earth, elliptical.

    (E) It is in the same plane as the Moon's orbit around the Earth.

4. The passage suggests which of the following about models that predict solar eclipses?

    (A) Until the last century, it was impossible to create models that would accurately predict solar eclipses.

    (B) When it was discovered in 1901, the Antikythera Mechanism was the only model available to predict solar eclipses.

    (C) The Antikythera Mechanism is not the only model that attempts to predict solar eclipses.

    (D) The calendar months and the zodiac signs are both important for tracking the irregular motions of the Moon.

    (E) The unpredictability of such models makes them suitable only as curiosities or antiques.

Questions 5–7 refer to the following stimulus.

Passage 2: Polymers (6.5 minutes)

Synthetic polymers are man-made polymers colloquially referred to as "plastics." These polymers can be classified in many ways, perhaps the most useful
5 regarding how they respond to heat. For example, thermosets are permanently set plastics; they do not melt, even when subjected to high temperatures. Thermoplastics, however, become
10 malleable when heated and can be remolded as they are cooled. As a result, thermoplastics can be recycled more easily than thermosets and are used in the manufacture of toys, water bottles,
15 and other goods that are typically used for limited time periods and subsequently discarded. Thermosets are more difficult to recycle and are often used as adhesives or sealants in high-wear settings,
20 circumstances in which the less malleable nature of the material is a distinct advantage, despite the inability to recycle at a later date.

Thermoplastics can be further
25 differentiated as amorphous or semi-crystalline. While both amorphous and semi-crystalline thermoplastics melt when heated, amorphous thermoplastics soften gradually in response to heat
30 while semi-crystalline thermoplastics remain solid until a precise melting point. Semi-crystalline thermoplastics tend to be tougher, suitable for weight-bearing goods such as folding chairs, whereas
35 amorphous thermoplastics are more common for products that break apart easily, such as packing peanuts. The contrasting molecular structures of the various plastics underpin the way in
40 which each responds to heat. Thermoset polymers are chemically "cured," involving the formation of chemical bonds and resulting in rigid three-dimensional molecular structures. Unlike thermosets,
45 thermoplastics are two-dimensional chains connected by intermolecular forces. In amorphous thermoplastics, the molecules are randomly ordered, resembling a jumble of yarn, while semi-
50 crystalline thermoplastics feature ordered molecular "crystals."

5. According to the passage, semi-crystalline thermoplastic polymers differ from thermoset polymers in which of the following ways?

(A) Semi-crystalline thermoplastic polymers melt at a specific temperature, whereas thermoset polymers soften gradually in response to heat.

(B) Semi-crystalline thermoplastic polymers melt at a specific temperature, whereas thermoset polymers do not melt even when subjected to high temperatures.

(C) Semi-crystalline thermoplastic polymers soften gradually in response to heat, whereas thermoset polymers melt at a specific temperature.

(D) Semi-crystalline thermoplastic polymers soften gradually in response to heat, whereas thermoset polymers do not melt even when subjected to high temperatures.

(E) Semi-crystalline thermoplastic polymers do not melt even when subjected to high temperatures, whereas thermoset polymers melt at a specific temperature.

6. The passage implies which of the following about the recycling of synthetic polymers?

(A) The molecular structure of a synthetic polymer at least partially determines whether the polymer can be recycled.

(B) Semi-crystalline thermoplastic polymers can be recycled more easily than amorphous thermoplastic polymers can be.

(C) Thermosets would be easier to recycle if manufacturers would choose less malleable starting materials.

(D) Polymers are more difficult to recycle in general than are other substances.

(E) The "curing" process allows the final product to be more easily recycled in the future.

8

7. Which of the following plastic products best exemplifies an amorphous thermoplastic polymer as it is presented in the passage (lines 28–29)?

    (A) The caulking that seals ceramic tiles on an outdoor swimming pool

    (B) A stepladder that can bear a weight of up to 250 pounds

    (C) A toy water gun that remains solid until it is heated to a precise temperature

    (D) A sheet of insulation intended to withstand drastic temperatures

    (E) A yogurt container that gradually melts when exposed to increasing temperatures

Questions 8–11 refer to the following stimulus.

Passage 3: Language (7.5 minutes)

Jakobson argues that languages differ primarily in what they must convey rather than what they may convey. He asserts that, accordingly, if language shapes how
5 we think, it does so by determining what speakers are *obligated* to think about rather than what they are *allowed* to think about. This view is both a departure from the behaviorist stance that all thought
10 is inherently linguistic (and that there is therefore no distinction) and a rejection of the pure "mould theories" advanced by Whorf, which argue that all thought is shaped by language. Rather, Jakobson
15 suggests, some thoughts are shaped by language and some are not.

The Aboriginal tongue Guugu Yimithirr, as an illustration, lacks coordinates related to the self, such as "in front of," "behind,"
20 "left of," and "right of," and instead relies strictly on geographic coordinates—east, west, south, and north. Native Guugu Yimithirr speakers are able to identify which direction is north without a
25 compass, while native English speakers do not typically develop this intuitive sense of cardinal direction. Whorf would argue that this difference is merely one of myriad ways in which linguistic patterns
30 codify our thoughts, but Jakobson would more specifically point to the requisite aspects of Guugu Yimithirr that are lacking in English. In other words, Guugu Yimithirr speakers are forced to consider
35 cardinal direction, while English speakers are free to consider it or not. Studying how languages constrain us, Jakobson believes, could lead to new discoveries in regard to how we think. For instance, a
40 language in which common terms denote gender ("him") imposes information on listeners, whereas one in which gender is irrelevant ("they") leaves more open to interpretation.

8. The author of the passage is primarily concerned with

(A) contrasting multiple theories in a discipline

(B) discussing a particular theory and its implications

(C) presenting a new theory that supplants the previously dominant theory

(D) examining the origins of an academic position

(E) reconciling two historically opposed views

9. According to the passage, which of the following statements best describes mould theories of language?

(A) Some thoughts are shaped by language and some are not.

(B) There is no difference between thought and language.

(C) Languages differ primarily in their restrictiveness.

(D) Language influences all thought.

(E) Thought influences all language.

10. The passage suggests that which of the following is more restrictive for a speaker?

(A) Directions that reflect personal orientation, as compared to those that rely only on cardinal keys

(B) Pronouns in which gender is embedded, in contrast to pronouns that are gender-neutral

(C) Pronouns that are gender-neutral, as opposed to pronouns for which gender is inherent

(D) Mould theories compared to behaviorist theories

(E) Jakobson's view in comparison to Whorf's view

8

11. With respect to the relationship of language to thought, the passage indicates that Jakobson believes that

    (A) language shapes some thoughts

    (B) most thoughts are shaped by language

    (C) if thoughts are shaped by language, language must be shaped by thoughts

    (D) the two are not interrelated

    (E) linguistic patterns codify all thought

8

Questions 12–16 refer to the following stimulus.

Passage 4: Switzerland (9 minutes)

Note: This passage has five related questions. On the real test, you will be given no more than four questions per passage. Your time limit here reflects the fact that the more questions you have, the faster it should be to answer the later questions (because you know more by then!).

Switzerland has three official national languages (French, Italian, and German) and two major religions (Catholicism and Protestantism). This level of diversity has
5 often led to conflict and even violence in other countries, but Switzerland has maintained a peaceful coexistence since its establishment as a federal state in 1848. What could explain this unusual
10 stability? A new study examines well-defined topographical and political boundaries separating groups and draws some surprising conclusions. In Switzerland, landscape elements tend to separate linguistic groups,
15 while political cantons, which are similar to states or provinces, tend to separate religious groups. The study suggests that these physical or geographical barriers allow for partial autonomy among disparate groups
20 within a single country and thus foster peace.

The study considered the effect of physical separations, such as those caused by lakes and mountain ranges,
25 determining the scale of these boundaries via an edge detection algorithm that calculates topographical heights. Where a sharp contrast in height, such as a cliff, also continued for a significant distance,
30 the researchers designated a physical boundary between groups. Throughout the regions separated by these types of boundaries, a quiet reign of peace has persisted for nearly two centuries. Where
35 such boundaries do not exist, however, politically or linguistically mixed cantons are more prevalent and violence is more common. One such canton, Jura, has both a history of conflict and a porous
40 mountain range that does not fully separate linguistic groups.

Some researchers hypothesized that political boundaries might encourage stability in places where physical
45 boundaries are absent. However, existing evidence suggests that political

boundaries might not be sufficient to discourage violence. For example, Jura was formed in 1979 in response to sustained
50 attacks between a local German-speaking Protestant population and another French-speaking Catholic population. The new canton created an autonomous political region for the French-speaking Catholic
55 population, though the French-speaking Protestant region chose to remain affiliated with the German-speaking Protestants in the existing canton of Bern, valuing similar religion over
60 similar language. Because of remaining linguistic differences, conflict in the region continued. A proposal to combine the French-speaking Protestant areas with the French-speaking Catholic areas is currently
65 being considered, despite little evidence that any boundaries except physical ones effectively temper violence.

12. In the passage, the author is primarily interested in

(A) suggesting a modification to a flawed theory

(B) initiating a debate about the true cause of a historical conflict

(C) introducing a theory that seeks to answer a particular question

(D) arguing that one method for addressing a question is preferable to another

(E) explaining the development of an established theory

8

13. According to the passage, which the following is true about physical boundaries between populations within the same country?

    (A) They are the only proven method for fostering peace.

    (B) They allow distinct groups to live more autonomously and peacefully than might otherwise be the case.

    (C) They can be the result of natural or man-made landscape elements.

    (D) They are less effective than political boundaries in maintaining peace in a region.

    (E) They are more easily overcome with the advent of modern technology and transportation.

14. The author of the passage discusses the history of the canton Jura in order to

    (A) prove definitively that physical boundaries are the key to maintaining peace among disparate political and religious groups

    (B) remind readers that it is extremely difficult to sustain peace in all regions of a country

    (C) speculate about how Switzerland might finally resolve the ongoing conflicts in the region

    (D) provide an example of a canton in which the lack of physical boundaries appears to exacerbate differences of opinion among the populace

    (E) suggest that there are alternative methods to reduce conflict among warring groups when physical boundaries are not present

15. Which of the following is true of the study of topographical boundaries discussed in the passage?

    (A) It considered the length as well as the height of natural boundaries.

    (B) It was conducted by French and German researchers.

    (C) It did not take into account man-made physical boundaries.

    (D) It concluded that physical boundaries are necessary in order to ensure a certain level of peace among the population.

    (E) It rated mountains as more effective barriers than lakes.

16. It can be inferred from the passage that Switzerland's political boundaries

    (A) are responsible for its remarkable history of peaceful coexistence among diverse groups

    (B) are typically based upon natural geographic boundaries

    (C) lead to more conflict in French- and German-speaking areas than in Italian-speaking areas

    (D) are capable of being changed

    (E) should be based upon language similarities, not religious similarities

8

Put It All Together: Answers

Passage 1: Greek Wreck

Main point: The Antikythera Mechanism pretty accurately predicts solar eclipses. It's unclear who invented it and how.

Paragraph 1: The Antikythera Mechanism for predicting solar eclipses is a mystery: Who made it and how did they make it?

Paragraph 2: Modern understanding of the factors involved makes it even more surprising that the ancient mechanism was as accurate as it was.

Paragraph 3: Archimedes might have created it in 205 BC.

Passage map:

(1) AM found, spec: anc Grk, predict solar eclipse?
　　AM= sophis, not sure how made or who

(2) Now: DTL eclipse
　　AM= surpris acc.

(3) C: made by Arch(?)
　　evid given (math)

Note: *DTL* stands for detail, signaling that a certain part of the passage contains more detail about a particular topic.

1. **(B) Babylonian arithmetical methods predate Greek trigonometry:**

Step 1: Identify the question.

The word *inferred* in the question stem indicates that this is an Inference question.

Step 2: Find the support.

Support can be found in lines 53–62:

> Recent analysis dating the device to 205 BC, earlier than previously thought, suggests that the eclipse prediction mechanism was based not on Greek trigonometry but on Babylonian arithmetical methods borrowed by the Greeks. This conjecture makes plausible Cicero's claim that Archimedes created the mechanism, as Greek trigonometry was nonexistent in 205 BC.

Step 3: Predict an answer.

What can be inferred? The device was once thought to have been created later than 205 BC. If they now think that it was based on Babylonian arithmetical methods, then those methods must have been in existence already in 205 BC.

Step 4: Eliminate and find a match.

Answer Choice	Explanation
(A) the Ancient Greeks were more sophisticated than most people believe	The paragraph doesn't address what most people believe about how sophisticated the Ancient Greeks were.
(B) Babylonian arithmetical methods predate Greek trigonometry	CORRECT. This matches the predicted answer: the Babylonian methods were already in existence by 205 BC. The passage states that Greek trigonometry was *nonexistent in 205 BC*, so the Babylonian math predated the Greek math.
(C) the greatest thinker in Ancient Greece was Archimedes	The paragraph indicates only that Cicero thinks Archimedes may have created the mechanism; it does not mention other *thinkers*.
(D) information obtainable by modern-day telescopes was also available in Ancient Greece	The third paragraph does not indicate this; in fact, the second paragraph appears to contradict it.
(E) the Antikythera Mechanism was more likely to accurately predict a solar eclipse than modern-day technology	The third paragraph does not indicate this; if anything, the second paragraph implies the opposite.

2. **(E) It could be 38 degrees inaccurate:**

Step 1: Identify the question.

According to the passage indicates that this is a Specific Detail question. What is true of the Antikythera Mechanism? The passage includes several facts.

Step 2: Find the support.

Details can be found throughout the passage:

> ...was composed of a fixed-ring dial representing the 12 months of the Egyptian calendar and an inner ring representing the 12 zodiac signs. (lines 6–9)

> Regarded as the world's first analog computer, the Antikythera Mechanism involved remarkably intricate physics...(lines 16–18)

> ...under certain circumstances, the device is inaccurate by up to 38 degrees. (lines 48–50)

> Recent analysis dating the device to 205 BC...(lines 53–54)

Step 3: Predict an answer.

The correct answer should match one of the descriptive facts given about the Antikythera Mechanism.

Step 4: Eliminate and find a match.

Answer Choice	Explanation
(A) It was created by Archimedes.	Cicero claims this; the passage indicates, however, that the creator is still not definitively known.
(B) It is 1,000 years old.	It *predated similar technology by 1,000 years*, but it is believed to have been created in 205 BC, more than 2,000 years ago.
(C) It was created in the 1900s.	It was discovered in 1901; it was created much earlier.
(D) It was the world's first digital computer.	The first paragraph indicates that it was considered the world's first *analog* computer.
(E) It could be 38 degrees inaccurate.	CORRECT. This information is found in the last sentence of the second paragraph, lines 49–50.

3. **(D) It is, like the Moon's orbit around the Earth, elliptical:**

Step 1: Identify the question.

According to the passage indicates that this is a Specific Detail question.

Step 2: Find the support.

Support can be found in the second paragraph:

> . . . the Earth's orbit around the Sun is also elliptical such that, depending on the time of year, the Earth is gradually traveling nearer to or farther from the Sun. (lines 31–35)

Step 3: Predict an answer.

The orbit is elliptical, which seems to mean that the Earth is sometimes closer to the Sun and sometimes farther away.

8

Step 4: Eliminate and find a match.

Answer Choice	Explanation
(A) It renders predicting solar eclipses impossible without a telescope.	The passage indicates that the Antikythera Mechanism was relatively reliable even without telescopes.
(B) It is explainable using Greek trigonometry.	The third paragraph discusses trigonometry in relation to the Antikythera Mechanism (and, further, says that it was probably *not* used).
(C) It is, unlike the Moon's orbit around the Earth, elliptical.	The Earth's orbit is elliptical... what about the Moon's? Check the passage. Paragraph 1:... *the irregular motions of the Moon caused by its elliptical orbit around the Earth* (lines 11–13). The Moon's orbit is also elliptical.
(D) It is, like the Moon's orbit around the Earth, elliptical.	CORRECT. The orbits of the Earth and of the Moon are both elliptical.
(E) It is in the same plane as the Moon's orbit around the Earth.	The second paragraph indicates that the opposite is true: the two planes are not the same.

At times, while reviewing answer choices, you will have to return to the passage to confirm some detail or add some information. In this case, the question stem did not mention the Moon's orbit, but answers (C) and (D) did. When that happens, return to Step 2 and find the necessary proof in the passage.

4. **(C) The Antikythera Mechanism is not the only model that attempts to predict solar eclipses:**

Step 1: Identify the question.

The word *suggests* indicates that this is an Inference question. The question asks about models that predict solar eclipses in general, not just the Antikythera Mechanism in particular, so expect the correct answer to be based on broader information about such devices.

Step 2: Find the support.

Support can be found in the first and second paragraphs:

> Accurately predicting lunar and solar eclipses, as well as solar, lunar, and planetary positions, it predated similar technology by 1,000 years. (lines 21–24)

> While in modern times the use of satellites, telescopes, and other high-tech equipment has greatly enhanced our capacity for such calculations, when the Antikythera Mechanism was created, the sole source of information available to scientists was observation of the night sky. (lines 41–47)

Step 3: Predict an answer.

The correct answer should convey something that must be true about solar eclipse prediction models in general.

Step 4: Eliminate and find a match.

Answer Choice	Explanation
(A) Until the last century, it was impossible to create models that would accurately predict solar eclipses.	The Antikythera Mechanism is described as fairly accurate, and it was created approximately 2,000 years ago.
(B) When it was discovered in 1901, the Antikythera Mechanism was the only model available to predict solar eclipses.	The passage indicates only that this was the earliest known model, not that it is or was the only one at the time of its discovery.
(C) The Antikythera Mechanism is not the only model that attempts to predict solar eclipses.	CORRECT. The first paragraph says that the Antikythera Mechanism *predated similar technology by 1,000 years* (lines 23–24). In other words, at least one additional type of solar eclipse model was made.
(D) The calendar months and the zodiac signs are both important for tracking the irregular motions of the Moon.	This is mentioned only in relation to the Antikythera Mechanism specifically.
(E) The unpredictability of such models makes them suitable only as curiosities or antiques.	The Antikythera Mechanism is described as relatively accurate, not unpredictable. Further, *such models* is too broad; ancient models might be considered antiques, but the question stem could refer to any models that predict solar eclipses, including modern ones.

Passage 2: Polymers

Main point: The most useful way (perhaps) to classify plastics is based on how they respond to heat.

Paragraph 1: The most useful way (perhaps) to classify plastics is based on how they respond to heat.

Paragraph 2: One type, thermoplastics, can be broken into two subgroups with their own characteristics relative to heat.

Paragraph 3: The different molecular structures determine how each one responds to heat.

Passage map:

(1) man-made Poly = plastic

★ most useful: classify by heat

(1)

TS	TP
set can't melt	can melt easier to recycle

(2)

A	SC
gradual melt	melt fast @temp tougher

(3)

structure	
DTL	DTL

Note: *DTL* stands for detail, signaling that a certain part of the passage contains more detail about a particular topic.

5.   **(B) Semi-crystalline thermoplastic polymers melt at a specific temperature, whereas thermoset polymers do not melt even when subjected to high temperatures:**

Step 1: Identify the question.

According to the passage indicates that this is a Specific Detail question. The question asks specifically about the difference between thermoplastics and thermosets.

The passage further subcategorizes the thermoplastics; will you need to look at the subcategories in order to answer the question? Glance at the answer choices to see. Yes!

Step 2: Find the support.

Support can be found in the first and second paragraphs:

> For example, thermosets are permanently set plastics; they do not melt, even when subjected to high temperatures. Thermoplastics, however, become malleable when heated and can be remolded as they are cooled. (lines 5–11)

> …amorphous thermoplastics soften gradually in response to heat while semi-crystalline thermoplastics remain solid until a precise melting point. (lines 28–31)

Step 3: Predict an answer.

Thermosets don't melt; thermoplastics do. Amorphous ones soften gradually while semi-crystalline ones stay set until hitting a certain temperature.

Step 4: Eliminate and find a match.

Answer Choice		Explanation
(A)	Semi-crystalline thermoplastic polymers melt at a specific temperature, whereas thermoset polymers soften gradually in response to heat.	The description of semi-crystalline is true, but the second half describes amorphous thermoplastics, not thermosets.
(B)	semi-crystalline thermoplastic polymers melt at a specific temperature, whereas thermoset polymers do not melt even when subjected to high temperatures.	CORRECT. Both descriptions match what the passage says.
(C)	semi-crystalline thermoplastic polymers soften gradually in response to heat, whereas thermoset polymers melt at a specific temperature.	The first portion describes amorphous plastics, not semi-crystalline. The second portion describes semi-crystalline plastics, not thermosets.
(D)	semi-crystalline thermoplastic polymers soften gradually in response to heat, whereas thermoset polymers do not melt even when subjected to high temperatures.	The first portion describes amorphous plastics, not semi-crystalline. The description of thermosets is true.
(E)	semi-crystalline thermoplastic polymers do not melt even when subjected to high temperatures, whereas thermoset polymers melt at a specific temperature.	The definitions are reversed; the first portion describes thermosets, and the second portion describes semi-crystalline plastics.

8

6. **(A) The molecular structure of a synthetic polymer at least partially determines whether the polymer can be recycled:**

Step 1: Identify the question.

The word *implies* indicates that this is an Inference question. Recycling is mentioned in the first paragraph.

Step 2: Find the support.

Support can be found in the first paragraph:

> As a result, thermoplastics can be recycled more easily than thermosets. . . Thermosets are more difficult to recycle. . . (lines 11–23)

Step 3: Predict an answer.

The passage directly states that thermoplastics are easier to recycle than thermosets, so what is the inference? The information seems to imply that the rigidity of the material determines how easy or hard it is to recycle.

Step 4: Eliminate and find a match.

Answer Choice	Explanation
(A) The molecular structure of a synthetic polymer at least partially determines whether the polymer can be recycled.	CORRECT. The ability to recycle is based, at least in part, on each type's response to heat. The third paragraph indicates that the molecular structure determines (*underpins*) the way in which each responds to heat.
(B) semi-crystalline thermoplastic polymers can be recycled more easily than amorphous thermoplastic polymers can be.	Read carefully! If anything, the passage implies that the reverse would be true. Semi-crystalline plastics are more rigid than amorphous plastics. The only explicit comparison about the capability to be recycled is between thermosets and thermoplastics, not the two types of thermoplastics.
(C) Thermosets would be easier to recycle if manufacturers would choose less malleable starting materials.	Another trap! The passage does mention malleability in relation to thermosets: *the less malleable nature of the material is a distinct advantage, despite the inability to recycle at a later date* (lines 20–23). If anything, the passage implies that more malleable starting materials would make the materials easier to recycle.
(D) Polymers are more difficult to recycle in general than are other substances.	The passage does not discuss other materials.
(E) The "curing" process allows the final product to be more easily recycled in the future.	The "curing" process is mentioned in relation to thermosets, which are more *difficult* to recycle.

This is a tough problem. Many people would have to go through the answers twice on this one because the evidence on which to base the inference requires you to combine two pieces of information from different parts of the passage. These kinds of *synthesis* problems are among the hardest on the test.

7. **(E) A yogurt container that gradually melts when exposed to increasing temperatures:**

Step 1: Identify the question.

Surprise! This is an uncommon type that was not introduced earlier in this guide. You'll recognize these in the future because they ask you to extrapolate beyond the passage. In this case, you need to come up with a real-life example of an amorphous thermoplastic—something that fits the description of this type of plastic.

Step 2: Find the support.

Support can be found in lines 26–37 of the second paragraph:

> While both amorphous and semi-crystalline thermoplastics melt when heated, amorphous thermo-plastics soften gradually in response to heat. . . amorphous thermoplastics are more common for products that break apart easily, such as packing peanuts.

Step 3: Predict an answer.

The product should be something that melts gradually or relatively steadily when heated and/or a product designed to break apart easily.

Step 4: Eliminate and find a match.

	Answer Choice	Explanation
(A)	The caulking that seals ceramic tiles on an outdoor swimming pool	The first paragraph indicates that thermosets, not amorphous thermoplastics, are used as *sealants in high-wear settings* (line 19).
(B)	A stepladder that can bear a weight of up to 250 pounds	The second paragraph indicates that semi-crystalline thermoplastics, not amorphous thermoplastics, are *suitable for weight-bearing goods* (lines 33–34).
(C)	A toy water gun that remains solid until it is heated to a precise temperature	The second paragraph indicates that semi-crystalline thermoplastics melt in this way, not amorphous thermoplastics.
(D)	A sheet of insulation intended to withstand drastic temperatures	Thermosets would be able to withstand drastic tempera-tures; amorphous thermoplastics melt when exposed to heat.
(E)	A yogurt container that gradually melts when exposed to increasing temperatures	CORRECT. Amorphous thermoplastics melt gradually when exposed to heat.

8

Passage 3: Language

Main point: In contrast to some other theorists, Jakobson thinks that language shapes some thoughts but not others.

Paragraph 1: Jakobson differs from some other theorists. He thinks that languages shape how we think based upon what we're obligated to think about: *Some thoughts are shaped by language and some are not* (lines 15–16).

Paragraph 2: Guugu Yimithirr example: Jakobson has a certain interpretation, in contrast to Whorf's interpretation.

Passage map:

1. J: what language MUST convey vs. MAY convey

   language → some thoughts (not all)

   ≠ behaviorist, W's mould (L → all T)

2. unlike E, G uses NSEW and G ppl just know

   G forces direction, E doesn't

   J: studying constraints → how we think?

Note: The "does not equal" symbol signals that Jakobson's views disagree with the views shown on this line of the map. The question mark at the end of the last line signals that Jakobson believes the one *could* lead to the other, not that it definitely does. You may choose to use longer abbreviations than the single letters used here, but don't take the time to write out the full names of people, languages, etc.

8. **(B) discussing a particular theory and its implications:**

Step 1: Identify the question.

Primarily concerned with signals that this is a Primary Purpose question.

Step 2: Find the support.

Ideally, you will have determined the main idea during your read-through of the passage; if you need to refresh your memory, return to your map.

Step 3: Predict an answer.

On Primary Purpose questions, use your map and your understanding of the main point to articulate an answer. The passage is focused primarily on what Jakobson thinks, though it does mention that his views don't go along with those of two other positions (the behaviorist views and Whorf's mould theories). The other views are presented primarily as a contrast to Jakobson's views.

Step 4: Eliminate and find a match.

	Answer Choice	Explanation
(A)	contrasting multiple theories in a discipline	The passage does mention two alternative opinions in one sentence in the first paragraph, but the primary focus is on Jakobson's theory.
(B)	discussing a particular theory and its implications	CORRECT. The passage primarily discusses Jakobson's point of view, describing it in the first paragraph and illustrating it via the Guugu Yimithirr example in the second paragraph. The passage concludes by mentioning broader implications at the end of the second paragraph.
(C)	presenting a new theory that supplants the previously dominant theory	The passage doesn't indicate that either of the earlier theories was dominant, nor does it indicate that Jakobson's theory is the new dominant theory.
(D)	examining the origins of an academic position	The passage doesn't address how Jakobson came to develop his theory in the first place.
(E)	reconciling two historically opposed views	The passage does not reconcile the opposing points of view. No information indicates that the groups have come to agreement.

9. **(D) Language influences all thought:**

Step 1: Identify the question.

According to the passage indicates that this is a Specific Detail question. The mould theories were mentioned in the first paragraph.

Step 2: Find the support.

Support can be found in lines 4–14 of the first paragraph:

> . . . if language shapes how we think, it does so by determining what speakers are obligated to think about rather than what they are allowed to think about. This view is both a departure from the behaviorist stance that all thought is inherently linguistic (and that there is therefore no distinction) and a rejection of the pure "mould theories" advanced by Whorf, which argue that all thought is shaped by language.

Step 3: Predict an answer.

Jakobson's theory goes against the mould theories. The mould theories argue that all thought is shaped by language.

8

Step 4: Eliminate and find a match.

Answer Choice	Explanation
(A) Some thoughts are shaped by language and some are not.	Jakobson believe this; this is not part of Whorf's mould theories.
(B) There is no difference between thought and language.	The behaviorist position promotes this view, not the mould theories.
(C) Languages differ primarily in their restrictiveness.	Jakobson believe this; this is not part of Whorf's mould theories.
(D) Language influences all thought.	CORRECT. This is how the passage describes the mould theories: *all thought is shaped by language* (lines 13–14). In other words, language shapes (or influences) all thought.
(E) Thought influences all language.	This is the opposite of the description of the mould theories, which says that *all thought is shaped by language* (lines 13–14), not that all thought shapes or influences language.

10.   **(B) Pronouns in which gender is embedded, in contrast to pronouns that are gender-neutral:**

Step 1: Identify the question.

The word *suggests* indicates that this is an Inference question. The phrase *more restrictive* might lead you to consider the constraints imposed by a language.

Step 2: Find the support.

Support can be found in lines 33–44 at the end of the passage:

> . . . Guugu Yimithirr speakers are forced to consider cardinal direction, while English speakers are free to consider it or not. Studying how languages constrain us, Jakobson believes, could lead to new discoveries in regard to how we think. For instance, a language in which common terms denote gender ("him") imposes information on listeners, whereas one in which gender is irrelevant ("they") leaves more open to interpretation.

Step 3: Predict an answer.

Since Guugu Yimithirr doesn't contain certain descriptive words, the speakers are forced to use north, south, east, and west. That's restrictive. Also, if more specific information is required or built in (such as gender), that's more restrictive.

Step 4: Eliminate and find a match.

Answer Choice	Explanation
(A) Directions that reflect personal orientation as compared to those that rely only on cardinal keys	This choice is the opposite of what the question asks. The cardinal directions are described as more restrictive, because the speakers cannot use personal orientation.
(B) Pronouns in which gender is embedded, in contrast to pronouns that are gender–neutral	CORRECT. This matches one of the restrictive examples given in the passage.
(C) Pronouns that are gender-neutral, as opposed to pronouns for which gender is inherent	The passage states the opposite: The gendered pronouns are more restrictive than the gender-neutral pronouns.
(D) Mould theories compared to behaviorist theories	The restrictiveness of language is not mentioned in relation to the competing theories.
(E) Jakobson's view in comparison to Whorf's view	The restrictiveness of language is not mentioned in relation to the competing theories.

11. **(A) language shapes some thoughts:**

Step 1: Identify the question.

The language *the passage indicates* signals that this is a Specific Detail question.

Step 2: Find the support.

Support can be found in the first paragraph:

> . . . if language shapes how we think, it does so by determining what speakers are obligated to think about rather than what they are allowed to think about. (lines 4–8)

> . . . some thoughts are shaped by language and some are not. (lines 15–16)

Step 3: Predict an answer.

According to Jakobson, it isn't the case that language always shapes how we think. Sometimes it does and sometimes it doesn't.

Step 4: Eliminate and find a match.

Answer Choice	Explanation
(A) language shapes some thoughts	CORRECT. This matches the last sentence of the first paragraph.
(B) most thoughts are shaped by language	The passage indicates only that Jakobson thinks that *some* thoughts are shaped by language, not *most*.
(C) if thoughts are shaped by language, language must be shaped by thoughts	This choice is trying to mix up confusing language from the passage. Jakobson asserts only that some thoughts are shaped by language and some thoughts are not.
(D) the two are not interrelated	Jakobson does believe that the two are interrelated at least some of the time.
(E) linguistic patterns codify all thought	This reflects Whorf's point of view, not Jakobson's.

8

Passage 4: Switzerland (9.5 minutes)

Main point: Physical boundaries separating groups with significant differences (e.g., language, religion) can help to maintain peace.

Paragraph 1: A study suggests that Switzerland is unusually peaceful despite being very diverse (religion and language) because physical or geographical barriers keep groups separated.

Paragraph 2: In areas with significant physical barriers, things have been peaceful. In areas without these boundaries, there's been a lot of conflict.

Paragraph 3: Some hypothesized that political boundaries might reduce conflict, but the evidence shows otherwise.

Passage map:

1) S: 3 Ls, 2 Rs
   usually conflict, but not in S. Why?
   Study: phys barriers may explain

2) Study: DTL
   signif. phys barrier: peaceful
   no barrier: > conflict (eg, J)

3) political boundary work too?
   not really
   eg J

Note: *DTL* stands for detail; you can use this abbreviation to signal that a paragraph contains a lot of detail that you might want to return to later (if you're asked a question about that detail). Other abbreviations may not be exactly the way you would write them; just make sure that you aren't taking too much time to write out more detail than you need.

12. **(C) introducing a theory that seeks to answer a particular question:**

Step 1: Identify the question.

The language *primarily interested in* signals that this is a Primary Purpose question.

Step 2: Find the support.

Ideally, you will have determined the main idea during your read-through of the passage; if you need to refresh your memory, return to your map.

Step 3: Predict an answer.

A study indicates that physical or geographic barriers may be what help diverse areas to maintain peace.

Step 4: Eliminate and find a match.

Answer Choice	Explanation
(A) suggesting a modification to a flawed theory	The passage discusses a new theory, not an existing one that was then altered.
(B) initiating a debate about the true cause of a historical conflict	The passage does talk about an area that has experienced conflict historically, but there is not a debate about the specific cause of a specific conflict.
(C) introducing a theory that seeks to answer a particular question	CORRECT. The first paragraph asks a question, *What could explain this unusual stability?* (lines 9–10), and introduces a theory that seeks to answer that question.
(D) arguing that one method for addressing a question is preferable to another	The rejected political boundaries theory might be considered a second method, but it can't be said that one is *preferable* to the other. Rather, the political boundaries theory was introduced as a potential alternative when no physical boundaries exist.
(E) explaining the development of an established theory	The passage does not indicate that the geographic boundaries theory is established; in fact, it describes the study as *new*.

8

13. **(B) They allow distinct groups to live more autonomously and peacefully than might otherwise be the case:**

Step 1: Identify the question.

According to the passage indicates that this is a Specific Detail question.

Step 2: Find the support.

Support can be found in the first and second paragraphs:

> The study suggests that these physical or geographical barriers allow for partial autonomy among disparate groups within a single country and thus foster peace. (lines 17–21)

> Throughout the regions separated by these types of boundaries, a quiet reign of peace has persisted for nearly two centuries. (lines 31–34)

Step 3: Predict an answer.

The passage indicates that physical barriers help keep the peace.

Step 4: Eliminate and find a match.

Answer Choice	Explanation
(A) They are the only proven method for fostering peace.	The passage discusses only one other possible method (political boundaries) for fostering peace. It does not indicate that physical boundaries are the only available method.
(B) They allow distinct groups to live more autonomously and peacefully than might otherwise be the case.	CORRECT. This matches the language from the passage.
(C) They can be the result of natural or man–made landscape elements.	Be careful not to bring in outside knowledge! The passage only mentions natural barriers as examples of *physical boundaries*. You do not know whether *man-made* landscape elements would work in the same way as natural elements (such as cliffs), or in fact whether the author would consider man-made features *physical boundaries* at all. (This is not to say that the author is excluding man-made features; you simply do not know how man-made features are treated.)
(D) They are less effective than political boundaries in maintaining peace in a region.	The passage says the opposite: They are more effective than political boundaries in maintaining peace.
(E) They are more easily overcome with the advent of modern technology and transportation.	This choice is a trap for someone who is rushing or getting tired and not reading carefully. *Barriers* sound like they may need to be *overcome*, but the passage does not discuss this; rather, the barriers are seen as a positive.

8

14.   **(D) provide an example of a canton in which the lack of physical boundaries appears to exacerbate differences of opinion among the populace:**

Step 1: Identify the question.

The language *in order to* indicates that this is a Specific Purpose, or Why, question. Remember to read a bit before you try to figure out why the author introduced the topic of Jura.

Step 2: Find the support.

Support can be found in lines 34–41 at the end of the second paragraph:

> Where such boundaries do not exist, however, politically or linguistically mixed cantons are more prevalent and violence is more common. One such canton, Jura, has both a history of conflict and a porous mountain range that does not fully separate linguistic groups.

Step 3: Predict an answer.

Jura doesn't have physical boundaries, and it has experienced lots of conflict. This supports the theory that physical boundaries help keep the peace.

Note: The third paragraph has some more detail about Jura, but you may be able to understand the main idea after the first example. If the information in the second paragraph isn't enough to narrow down to one answer, then return to the third paragraph.

Step 4: Eliminate and find a match.

Answer Choice	Explanation
(A) prove definitively that physical boundaries are the key to maintaining peace among disparate political and religious groups	The example supports the theory but does not prove it true definitively.
(B) remind readers that it is extremely difficult to sustain peace in all regions of a country	Although it is likely true that peace is difficult to sustain everywhere, this is not why the author introduces the example. Rather, the author is further supporting the physical barrier theory.
(C) speculate about how Switzerland might finally resolve the ongoing conflicts in the region	The passage does not indicate any effective solutions; in fact, the final example given at the end of the third paragraph is dismissed as unlikely to be effective.
(D) provide an example of a canton in which the lack of physical boundaries appears to exacerbate differences of opinion among the populace	CORRECT. Jura is used specifically as an example to support the physical barrier theory.
(E) suggest that there are alternative methods to reduce conflict among warring groups when physical boundaries are not present	Jura has had lots of conflict, not reduced conflict. The political barrier theory is unlikely to be effective, according to the passage.

8

15. **(A) It considered the length as well as the height of natural boundaries:**

Step 1: Identify the question.

What *is true of* something discussed in the passage? This language signals a Specific Detail question. *Topographical* is mentioned in the first and second paragraphs.

Step 2: Find the support.

Support can be found in the first and second paragraphs:

> A new study examines well-defined topographical and political boundaries separating groups and draws some surprising conclusions. (lines 10–13)

> The study considered the effect of physical separations, such as those caused by lakes and mountain ranges, determining the scale of these boundaries via an edge detection algorithm that calculates topographical heights. Where a sharp contrast in height, such as a cliff, also continued for a significant distance, the researchers designated a physical boundary between groups. (lines 22–31)

Step 3: Predict an answer.

The study used an algorithm to calculate height differences. They also considered the length of the boundary. If the barrier had some defined combination of length and height differences, it was called a physical barrier.

Step 4: Eliminate and find a match.

Answer Choice	Explanation
(A) It considered the length as well as the height of natural boundaries.	CORRECT. This matches the language of the passage.
(B) It was conducted by French and German researchers.	The passage does not indicate who conducted the study.
(C) It did not take into account man-made physical boundaries.	The only examples mentioned are natural (e.g., *cliffs*), but that does not mean that man-made barriers were actually excluded from or ignored by the research. It's possible that they were included but just not mentioned in the passage.
(D) It concluded that physical boundaries are necessary in order to ensure a certain level of peace among the population.	The study claimed only that physical boundaries could help maintain peace, not that such boundaries are necessary to maintain peace.
(E) It rated mountains as more effective barriers than lakes.	Though the passage does mention using both height and length when designating something a barrier, it does not actually indicate which types of barriers the study considered most effective.

8

16.   **(D) are capable of being changed:**

Step 1: Identify the question.

The language *inferred* indicates that this is an Inference question. The first and third paragraphs discuss Switzerland's political boundaries.

Step 2: Find the support.

Support can be found in the first and third paragraphs:

> In Switzerland, landscape elements tend to separate linguistic groups while political cantons, which are similar to states or provinces, tend to separate religious groups. (lines 13–17)

> Jura was formed in 1979. . . The new canton created an autonomous political region for the French-speaking Catholic population. . . Because of remaining linguistic differences, conflict in the region continued. A proposal to combine the French-speaking Protestant areas with the French-speaking Catholic areas is currently being considered, despite little evidence that any boundaries except physical ones effectively temper violence. (lines 48–67)

Step 3: Predict an answer.

Political cantons are typically separated by religion. The separation in Jura didn't actually fix things, though, and they're thinking about combining based on language instead, even though trying to set political boundaries hasn't been shown to be effective.

Step 4: Eliminate and find a match.

Answer Choice	Explanation
(A) are responsible for its remarkable history of peaceful coexistence among diverse groups	The passage suggests that *geographical boundaries* are responsible for maintaining the peace, not *political boundaries*.
(B) are typically based upon natural geographic boundaries	The passage discusses *political boundaries* as separate from *geographical boundaries*.
(C) lead to more conflict in French- and German-speaking areas than in Italian-speaking areas	The passage doesn't provide any specific information about Italian-speaking areas.
(D) are capable of being changed	CORRECT. As noted in the third paragraph, the boundaries were changed at least once, in 1979 with the creation of Jura, and the Swiss are considering another proposal to change them again.
(E) should be based upon language similarities, not religious similarities	The passage indicates that *political* boundaries don't seem to work, no matter what they're based on.

Critical Reasoning

In this unit, you will learn a process for deconstructing arguments in order to understand how the information fits together logically. You will also learn how to recognize the different Critical Reasoning question types, what kind of analysis to do for each specific type, and how to avoid trap answers.

In This Unit...

Argument Structure

In This Chapter...

In this chapter, you will learn how to deconstruct arguments into their core components, or building blocks. You'll also learn how to recognize certain common types of arguments that will be discussed throughout the rest of this unit.

CHAPTER 9 Argument Structure

Here is an example of a typical GMAT argument in a Critical Reasoning (CR) problem:

> The expansion of the runways at the Bay City Airport will allow larger planes to use the airport. These new planes will create a lot of noise, a nuisance for residents who live near the airport. However, many of the residents in this neighborhood work in construction, and the contract to expand the runways has been awarded to a local construction company. Thus, the expansion of the runways will lead to an increased quality of life for the residents of this neighborhood.

In order to solve CR problems effectively and efficiently, you need to pay close attention to the specific information given for that problem, while keeping in mind how to reason through a problem of that type.

For every question, begin by understanding what you are *given*:

What is this author actually arguing?

What are the pieces of this argument?

How do they fit together?

Think about these questions in relation to the argument above before you keep reading.

On the GMAT:

1. All arguments contain at least one **Premise**. A premise is information used by the author to support some claim or conclusion. That information may be a fact or an opinion. In the example above, sentence 3 is a premise because it helps to support the author's conclusion.

2. Most (though not all) arguments contain a **Conclusion**, the primary claim the author is trying to prove or the outcome of a plan that someone is proposing. In the runway expansion example, sentence 4 is a conclusion.

3. Many arguments (though not all) contain **Background** information, which provides context to allow you to understand the basic situation. The information is true but does not either support or go against the conclusion. In the runway argument, sentence 1 provides background.

4. Some arguments contain a **Counterpoint** or counterpremise—a piece of information that goes against the author's conclusion. In the example above, sentence 2 represents a counterpoint because it goes against the author's conclusion.

5. Many arguments rely on at least one **Assumption**—something that is not stated in the argument but that the author *must believe to be true* in order to draw the given conclusion. Without the assumption, the argument fails. By definition, you will not be able to identify an assumption in the text of the argument because it is unstated. In the runway expansion argument, one assumption is that the construction jobs are more important to quality of life than the nuisance and noise of the increase in flights.

Collectively, these categories represent the **Building Blocks** of an argument. How do you know which sentences fall into which categories? Try to articulate your own thought process for the runway expansion argument, then take a look at the decision process of this fictional student:

Argument	Reader's Thoughts
The expansion of the runways at the Bay City Airport will allow larger planes to use the airport.	*Hmm. This is a fact. It could be a* **premise** *or it could just be background. I'm not sure yet.*
These new planes will create a lot of noise, a nuisance for residents who live near the airport.	*Now they're moving into claim territory. Something negative will come from this project. Why are they telling me this? I can't figure that out until I know the conclusion.*
However, many of the residents in this neighborhood work in construction, and the contract to expand the runways has been awarded to a local construction company.	*The word* however *indicates a contrast between sentences 2 and 3. What's the contrast? The noise is a negative consequence of the expansion, while winning a work contract is a positive consequence. Looks like I've got a* **premise** *and a* **counterpoint** *in these two sentences, but I don't know which one is which yet.*
Thus, the expansion of the runways will lead to an increased quality of life for the residents of this neighborhood.	*The word* thus *usually indicates a* **conclusion**. *Yes, this does seem like a conclusion—this project will have a certain outcome (better quality of life in this neighborhood), and I can now see how the previous two sentences fit into this conclusion. Sentence 3 is a* **premise** *because it provides one way in which the quality of life might be better for these people (they might make more money), and sentence 2 is a* **counterpoint** *because it tells me a negative consequence.*
After reading the argument: What is the author assuming?	*The author presents a cost of the plan (noise) and a benefit (construction jobs). In order for the expansion to increase quality of life, the author* **assumes** *that the benefit outweighs the cost.*

Notice how many times the reader thought, "I'm not sure yet" (or something along those lines). That will happen frequently while reading an argument. You're gathering information and trying to understand what each piece might be, but you won't really know how everything fits together until you know what the conclusion is—and that might not be until the end of the argument. Here's the argument again, with each sentence labeled:

Background

Counterpoint

The expansion of the runways at the Bay City Airport will allow larger planes to use the airport. These new planes will create a lot of noise, a nuisance for residents who live near the airport. However, many of the residents in this neighborhood work in construction, and the contract to expand the runways has been awarded to a local construction company. Thus, the expansion of the runways will lead to an increased quality of life for the residents of this neighborhood.

Premise

Conclusion

The Core

The premise (or premises) and conclusion represent the **Core** of the argument. Remember that not all arguments will have a conclusion, but all will have at least one premise, so you will always have at least a partial core. The core represents what the author is trying to tell you or prove to you.

In this problem, the core consists of these two pieces:

However, many of the residents in this neighborhood work in construction, and the contract to expand the runways has been awarded to a local construction company.

Thus, the expansion of the runways will lead to an increased quality of life for the residents of this neighborhood.

Premise: provides one piece of evidence toward the conclusion

Conclusion: the claim supported by the given evidence

The argument is not airtight. For example, do you know for sure that residents of the neighborhood work for the local construction company that won the contract? If they don't, then perhaps residents won't benefit after all. As you'll see later in this book, that kind of reasoning will help when you get to the question-answering stage.

Building Blocks of an Argument

Here are the **building blocks** discussed so far:

Premise

- Is part of the **core** of the argument; present in every argument.
- Supports the author's conclusion.
- Can be a fact or an opinion; can be a description, historical information, data, or a comparison of things.
- Is often signaled by words or phrases such as *because of, since, due to,* or *as a result of.*

Conclusion

- Is part of the **core** of an argument; present in most arguments.
- Represents the author's main opinion or claim; can be in the form of a prediction, a judgment of quality or merit, a statement of causality, or the outcome of a plan.
- Is supported by at least one **premise**.
- Is often signaled by words such as *therefore, thus, so,* or *consequently* (although harder arguments might use such a word elsewhere in the argument in an attempt to confuse you).

Background

- Is not part of the **core**; not always present.
- Provides context to help understand the **core**; similar to premises but less important to the argument itself.
- Is almost always fact-based; can be in almost any form: historical information, data, descriptions of plans or ideas, definitions of words or concepts, and so on.

9

Counterpoint

- Is not part of the **core**; only present occasionally.
- Opposes or goes against the author's **conclusion** in some way.
- Introduces multiple opportunities for traps: believing that the **conclusion** is the opposite of what it is, mistakenly thinking that a **counterpoint** is a **premise** (and vice versa), and so on.
- Is often signaled by a transition word such as *although*, *though*, *however*, *yet*, and *but* (recognize, though, that the counterpoint may come before such words).

Assumption

- Is not part of the **core**; is not written down in the argument.
- Is something that the author must believe is true in order to draw the given **conclusion**.

Argument Structure

The runway expansion argument used all four of the building blocks in this order:

Background–Counterpoint–Premise–Conclusion

The GMAT can vary the types of building blocks used in a particular argument, and it can also vary the order of those building blocks. Most arguments on the GMAT will contain at least one premise and one conclusion; you will see some arguments later on that contain only premises. If you can categorize the building blocks given in any particular argument, you're one step closer to answering the question correctly.

Pop Quiz

It's time to test your skills. You have three tasks. First, read the argument and try to identify the role of each sentence or major piece of information (note that one sentence could contain two different pieces of information). Use that information to jot down the premise(s) and conclusion. Second, try to articulate in your own words *how* the premise(s) support the conclusion. Third, identify any assumptions that must be true to draw the given conclusion.

1. Budget Fitness will grow its membership base by 10% in the next six months. Budget Fitness has recently crafted a clever ad campaign that it plans to air on several local radio stations.

2. Last year, the Hudson Family Farm was not profitable. However, the farm will be profitable this year. The farm operators have planted cotton, rather than corn, in several fields. Because cotton prices are expected to rise dramatically this year, the farm can expect larger revenues from cotton sales than it previously earned from corn.

Answers are on page 193.

Signal Words

Certain words can provide valuable clues as to whether you've got a conclusion, a premise, or a counterpoint. If an argument says, "Adnan will earn a high test score because he has studied hard," the word *because* signals a cause-and-effect relationship. One thing (he has studied hard) is supposed to lead to another (he will earn a high score on the test). The premise here is the cause that follows the *because*, and the conclusion is the claimed result.

Finish the following exchange:

>Sam: Can I borrow your car?

>Marie: Even though you don't have a driver's license...

What is Marie likely to say next? She has acknowledged a reason that she should *not* let Sam borrow her car, but her sentence implies that she's about to let him borrow it anyway. (Not very wise, Marie!)

What if the conversation had gone this way?

>Sam: Can I borrow your car?

>Marie: I like you, Sam. However, you don't have a driver's license, so...

This time, Marie's not falling for Sam's charming smile! She's about to deny him access to her car.

What's the difference? How do you know that, in the first case, Marie seems willing to lend Sam her car, while, in the second case, she isn't going to do so?

Signal words! The term *even though* signals an acknowledgment of or a concession to an opposing point of view. Even though it's true that Sam doesn't have a driver's license, Marie will still let him borrow her car. The contrast word *however*, on the other hand, flips a switch: Marie may like Sam, but she's not about to let him use her car when he doesn't even have a driver's license.

You can use these kinds of language clues to help you classify information in arguments:

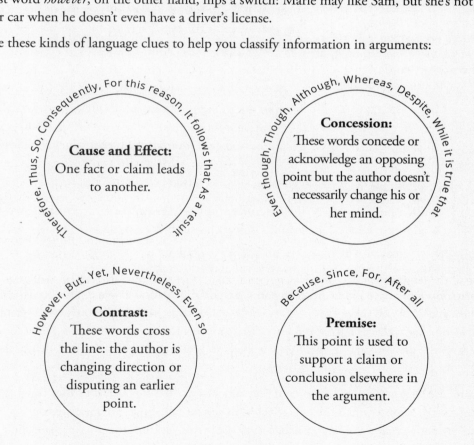

You likely know most or all of these words already, but you might not have consciously considered why they're used in certain contexts. Start paying attention! These signal words will make your job easier during the test.

Intermediate Conclusions and the Therefore Test

You have one more building block to learn in this chapter. Read and deconstruct the argument below:

> The owner of a small publishing company plans to lease a new office space that has floor-to-ceiling windows and no internal walls, arguing that the new space will enhance worker productivity. The owner cites a recent study showing that workers exposed to natural light throughout the day tended to report, on average, a higher level of job satisfaction than did those who worked in office spaces that used fluorescent lighting. Thus, the owner concluded, exposure to natural light has a positive effect on workers' job satisfaction.

The owner of a small publishing company plans to lease a new office space that has floor-to-ceiling windows and no internal walls,	*This is likely to be background information because it introduces a plan to do something but no actual claim (yet). The argument is probably about the plan, or a result of the plan.*
arguing that the new space will enhance worker productivity.	*This might be the conclusion because it describes the predicted future benefit of the company's plan.*
The owner cites a recent study showing that workers exposed to natural light throughout the day tended to report, on average, a higher level of job satisfaction than did those who worked in office spaces that used fluorescent lighting.	*This seems to be a premise in support of that conclusion. The workers will be more productive because the new space will provide exposure to natural light through the floor-to-ceiling windows.*
Thus, the owner concluded, exposure to natural light has a positive effect on workers' job satisfaction.	*Hmm, this is strange. This appears to be the conclusion as well. It uses the word* thus, *it represents an explanation for the study's results, and it even says that* the owner concluded *this!*

This is a tough one! In this case, you have *two* claims that could be conclusions. Now what?

This brings you to another building block, the **Intermediate Conclusion** (also known as the secondary conclusion). What is an intermediate conclusion? Look at this simpler example:

> The burglar is clumsy and often makes a lot of noise while robbing homes. As a result, he is likely to get caught. Thus, in the near future, he will probably end up in jail.

The first sentence is a basic premise: It indicates some factual information about the robber. The second sentence is a claim made based upon that premise: *Because* he makes noise, he is likely to get caught. This is a conclusion—but, wait, there's a third sentence! That third sentence also contains a claim, and this claim follows from the previous claim: *Because* he is likely to get caught, there is a good chance he will end up in jail.

Essentially, a premise supports a conclusion, and that conclusion then supports a further conclusion. If you place the events in logical order, then the first conclusion can be called the intermediate conclusion. The second conclusion can be called the final conclusion to distinguish it from the intermediate conclusion. Alternatively, you might reserve the word *conclusion* for the final conclusion and call the intermediate conclusion another premise—just recognize that it's a claim that is supported by other premises, and that in turn supports the (final) conclusion.

Either way, how do you figure out which is which? Use the **Therefore Test**. Call the two claims A (he's likely to get caught) and B (he will probably end up in jail). Plug the two claims into two sentences using *because* and *therefore*, and ask yourself which one is true:

> BECAUSE A (he's likely to get caught), THEREFORE B (he will probably end up in jail).

> OR

> BECAUSE B (he will probably end up in jail), THEREFORE A (he's likely to get caught).

(Using both *because* and *therefore* may seem like overkill, but it ensures that you keep the roles straight!) Which sentence makes more sense to you? The first scenario makes sense, but the second one doesn't. The fact that he will probably end up in jail should follow the *therefore*, so it is the final, real conclusion. The fact that he's likely to get caught follows the *because*, so it is only an intermediate conclusion.

In the burglar passage above, the three pieces were presented in logical progression: **premise–intermediate conclusion–final conclusion**. Arguments won't always follow this logical order, however; they might mix up the order and toss in additional information.

Try the Therefore Test with the job satisfaction argument. You have two possible conclusions:

1. (A) ... arguing that the new space will enhance worker productivity.

2. (B) Thus, the owner concluded, exposure to natural light has a positive effect on workers' job satisfaction.

Which scenario makes more sense?

> BECAUSE the new space will enhance worker productivity, THEREFORE exposure to natural light has a positive effect on workers' job satisfaction.

> OR

> BECAUSE exposure to natural light has a positive effect on workers' job satisfaction, THEREFORE the new space will enhance worker productivity.

The second scenario makes more sense, so B is the intermediate conclusion and A is the final conclusion.

As is typical of arguments with an intermediate conclusion, the premise supports the intermediate conclusion, which then supports the final conclusion:

A study found a correlation between natural lighting and job satisfaction. The owner concludes that exposure to natural light causes better job satisfaction. The owner then concludes that the new, light-filled space will enhance productivity.

Here's the original argument again:

> The owner of a small publishing company plans to lease a new office space that has floor-to-ceiling windows and no internal walls, arguing that the new space will enhance worker productivity. The owner cites a recent study showing that workers exposed to natural light throughout the day tended to report, on average, a higher level of job satisfaction than did those who worked in office spaces that used fluorescent lighting. Thus, the owner concluded, exposure to natural light has a positive effect on workers' job satisfaction.

The argument begins with **background** information, then goes straight into the final **conclusion**. Next, you're given a **premise** followed by an intermediate conclusion.

As the previous argument demonstrates, the logical structure of a GMAT argument can get a little complicated. If there is more than one logical step, make sure that your understanding is firm before you attempt to answer the question.

Common Argument Types

GMAT arguments cover a variety of topics from business to biology to traffic patterns of cities. Although the topics are varied, many arguments feature similar logic. Some of the most common argument types are presented in this section.

Approach all arguments on the GMAT as a skeptical reader. As you read, consider the "what if" questions you would want to ask the author when evaluating whether you believe the author's conclusion. In the discussion of argument types that follow, some of the issues and questions that are most relevant for each type are provided.

Causation

In causation arguments, circumstances are presented. The conclusion proposes a particular cause for that set of circumstances.

> In October, a local news station completed a redesign of its website. In November, the number of articles read on the website increased by 50%. Thus, the redesigned website clearly attracted more users or encouraged users to read more articles per visit.

For causation arguments, correct answer choices often relate to potential other causes for the observed result. In this case, the conclusion states that the redesign is responsible for the increase in articles read; you would want to consider what else might have caused the increase. For example, what if the news station provided extensive coverage of an important local election taking place in November?

Plan

A plan proposes a course of action to achieve a specific goal. In a plan, the conclusion is the goal of the plan. The words *in order to* or simply *to* frequently precede the goal of the plan.

> Metropolis has experienced an increase in the amount of trash in its city parks. In order to reduce the amount of litter in the parks, Metropolis plans to double the number of trash cans in each city park.

A plan must work as expected to achieve its aim. A plan may fail if the steps of the plan don't work as anticipated or there are unexpected costs or hindrances not discussed in the original argument. In this case, the plan seeks to limit people from littering in the park by making trash cans more accessible. What if the litter in the park is actually blowing into the park from the surrounding streets and sidewalks?

Prediction

Sometimes arguments conclude with a prediction of a future event.

> Rainfall totals were higher this year than they were last year in Eastown. Since wheat farmers rely on rain to irrigate their fields, yields of wheat per acre in Eastown will be higher than last year's yields.

In order for a prediction to come true, no other circumstances can intervene that might work against the prediction. In this case, the argument discusses only precipitation. How have temperatures this year affected wheat growth?

Profit

When arguments discuss profit, the conclusion often states that profits will increase or decrease—in other words, profit arguments are frequently a subcategory of predictions. You are expected to know that Profit = Revenue − Cost. Often, arguments will discuss only one element of profit (either revenues or costs), whereas the answer choices will focus on the other component.

Not every argument will fit into one of these categories, and sometimes the lines between categories get blurry. You might read an argument that seems like a plan to increase profit. Don't stress if you are not sure how to classify an argument; instead, think of the classification as another tool that can help you understand the argument and lead you toward the right answer. In subsequent chapters, you will learn what to expect in answer choices for each type of argument for different question types.

Answers to Pop Quiz

1.	Budget Fitness will grow its membership base by 10% in the next six months.	*This is a prediction about the future, so it is a claim, not a fact. This is a good candidate to be the conclusion.*
	Budget Fitness has recently crafted a clever ad campaign that it plans to air on several local radio stations.	*Budget Fitness already crafted the campaign—this is a fact. It is also a fact that the company currently "plans" to air the campaign (though whether it will actually air is uncertain, since that is a future event). This information supports the claim in the first sentence, so it is a premise.*

(Task 1) The order of the parts is **conclusion–premise**. If you rewrite it as premise → conclusion, then you have something like this:

> BF has ad to air on radio → BF will grow members 10% in 6 mos

(Task 2) The author claims that the gym *will* increase its membership in the future *because* the company will launch an ad campaign. Presumably, the company thinks that this campaign will help attract new customers.

(Task 3) The argument assumes that the ad campaign will be effective in attracting new customers. (Note: There are often many assumptions contained in a given argument and many ways to word similar assumptions. The answer provided is just one example.)

9

2.	Last year, the Hudson Family Farm was not profitable.	*This is a fact; it already occurred in the past. This may be background info, a premise, or a counterpoint.*
	However, the farm will be profitable this year.	*The word* however *indicates a change in direction. This prediction is the opposite of what happened last year. This future prediction is a good candidate to be the conclusion, in which case the previous sentence would be a counterpoint.*
	The farm operators have planted cotton, rather than corn, in several fields.	*This is a fact. Hmm, why does it matter which crop the farm is planting?*
	Because cotton prices are expected to rise dramatically this year, the farm can expect larger revenues from cotton sales than it previously earned from corn.	*Okay, planting cotton will lead to more revenue than was earned last year. The author is using this information to support his conclusion in sentence 2.*

(Task 1) The order of the parts is **counterpoint–conclusion–premise–premise**. Reordering as premises → conclusion, you get this:

> Cotton prices will be higher and the farm is planting cotton. → The farm will be profitable this year.

You might have been unsure about the third sentence. Does it really support the conclusion (**premise**) or does it just describe the situation (**background**)? Don't worry too much about this distinction. There are frequently sentences that could be classified either way. Your classification of this type of information is unlikely to influence your ability to answer the question correctly as long as you correctly identify the conclusion.

(Task 2) The argument predicts that an unprofitable farm *will* become profitable *because* a change in crops will result in higher revenues.

(Task 3) What about costs? The premise states that revenues will be higher, but revenues and profits are not the same thing. The author assumes the costs associated with cotton are not high enough to cancel out the increased revenues.

Argument Structure Cheat Sheet

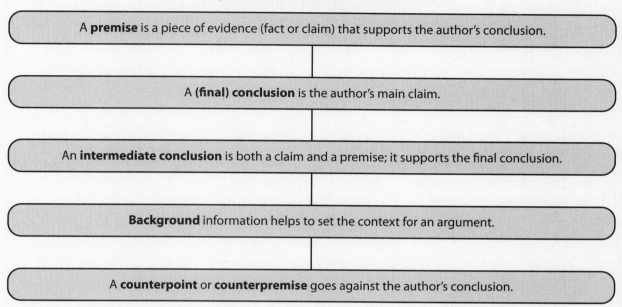

Argument Structure Cheat Sheet

A **premise** is a piece of evidence (fact or claim) that supports the author's conclusion.

A **(final) conclusion** is the author's main claim.

An **intermediate conclusion** is both a claim and a premise; it supports the final conclusion.

Background information helps to set the context for an argument.

A **counterpoint** or **counterpremise** goes against the author's conclusion.

These building blocks will help you to understand the structure of an argument and answer the question.

When there is more than one conclusion or claim, use the Therefore Test to find the final conclusion. One of these two scenarios will work: either "*Because A is true, therefore B is true*" or "*Because B is true, therefore A is true.*" The claim that follows the *therefore* in the working scenario is the final, real conclusion.

Problem Set

Identify the role of each sentence or major piece of information.

1. The school library currently depends heavily on donated books, which are often out of date or in poor condition. In order to encourage more students to use the library, the school administration has designated $10,000 of next year's budget to be used solely for the purchase of new books.

2. A program instituted by a state government to raise money allows homeowners to prepay their future property taxes at the current rate. Even if the government were to raise the tax rate in a subsequent year, any prepaid taxes would allow the homeowner to maintain taxes at the lower rate, lowering the overall property tax burden over time. For this reason, homeowners should participate in the program.

3. Tay-Sachs disease, a usually fatal genetic condition caused by the buildup of gangliocides in nerve cells, occurs more frequently among Ashkenazi Jews than among the general population. The age of onset is typically six months and generally results in death by the age of four.

4. The average level of physical fitness among students at North High School is likely to decline over the next few years. Due to recent changes in the way that the school calculates students' grades, earning a high grade in a physical education class will no longer improve a student's grade point average. Therefore, students who would otherwise have taken optional gym classes will be more likely to choose other electives in which earning a high grade is worth more points.

Determine whether each sentence or major piece of information is **part of the main argument** (a conclusion or premise) or **part of a counterargument** (a counterpoint). Then, determine what role the information plays in the main argument or counterargument: Is it a **conclusion** or a **premise**?

5. Some critics have argued that the price of food and drink at Ultralux, a restaurant, is too high for the quality offered. However, Ultralux features a beautiful interior and comfortable seating. Research has shown that consumers actually perceive food and drink as being of higher quality when they are consumed in such a setting. Thus, the food and drink at Ultralux are reasonably priced.

6. When compared to non-exercisers, people who exercise regularly also spend more time sitting or lying down in each 24-hour period. Because the risk of cancer and heart disease is higher among people who are more sedentary, doctors often recommend that their patients engage in regular physical exercise. However, since people who exercise are in fact often more sedentary than those who do not, this recommendation is counterproductive.

Solutions

1. | The school library currently depends heavily on donated books, which are often out of date or in poor condition. | **Background.** *This is a statement of fact. It doesn't directly support the conclusion, which is that more students will use the library in the future. Instead, it helps to explain why a particular plan was chosen (rather than supporting the conclusion that the plan will work).* |
|---|---|
| In order to encourage more students to use the library, | **Conclusion.** *This argument describes a plan. When an argument describes a plan, the outcome of the plan is the conclusion of the argument.* |
| the school administration has designated $10,000 of next year's budget to be used solely for the purchase of new books. | **Premise.** *This statement explains why more students will use the library. Any statement that helps explain why the conclusion is true is a premise, since it supports the conclusion.* |

2. | A program instituted by a state government to raise money allows homeowners to prepay their future property taxes at the current rate. | **Background.** *This is a statement of fact. It isn't a premise, because it doesn't support the idea that homeowners should participate in the program—it just tells you what the program is.* |
|---|---|
| Even if the government were to raise the tax rate in a subsequent year, | **Counterpoint.** *In this part of the argument, the author is bringing up a potential complication: The government might raise taxes after someone has already prepaid. Since this is something that might complicate the plan, it's a potential counterpoint.* |
| any prepaid taxes would allow the homeowner to maintain taxes at the lower rate, lowering the overall property tax burden over time. | **Premise.** *The author now resolves the potential complication. By showing that the counterpoint isn't actually a major issue (in fact, it's a reason why someone would* want *to pre-pay!), the author supports the main argument.* |
| For this reason, homeowners should participate in the program. | **Conclusion.** *This is what the author wants to convince you of. Notice that it has a* because…therefore *relationship with the rest of the argument: Because homeowners would have a lower tax burden, they should therefore participate in the program.* |

3. | Tay-Sachs disease, a usually fatal genetic condition caused by the buildup of gangliocides in nerve cells, occurs more frequently among Ashkenazi Jews than among the general population. | **Premise (or Background).** *This is a tricky one. There actually isn't a conclusion in this argument! Normally, the key to spotting premises is to find statements that support the conclusion. But if there isn't a conclusion, that won't work. You'd probably see this "argument" in an Inference problem, which we'll look at later. For now, if you see an argument that doesn't have a conclusion, treat all of the statements in it like premises.* |
|---|---|
| The age of onset is typically six months and generally results in death by the age of four. | **Premise (or Background).** *Like the sentence above, this is a statement of fact, so it can't be a conclusion. This "argument" just consists of two facts and doesn't draw a conclusion from either of them. You'd only see this in an Inference problem, which we'll learn about later on. For now, think of both of these sentences as premises.* |

4.	The average level of physical fitness among students at North High School is likely to decline over the next few years.	*Conclusion.* *When you first read this, it may not be obvious that it's the main conclusion. You can't necessarily spot the conclusion until you've read the entire argument. This is the main conclusion because everything else in the argument supports it. For instance, the fact that students will take fewer gym classes supports the belief that students will become less physically fit.*
	Due to recent changes in the way that the school calculates students' grades, earning a high grade in a physical education class will no longer improve a student's grade point average.	*Premise.* *This is a statement of fact, so it can't be a conclusion. It supports the intermediate conclusion (in the next sentence), by explaining why students will take fewer gym classes.*
	Therefore, students who would otherwise have taken optional gym classes will be more likely to choose other electives in which earning a high grade is worth more points.	*Intermediate conclusion.* *This sentence starts with* therefore, *and it's supported by the premise in the previous sentence. Don't be fooled! It isn't the main conclusion, because it supports the conclusion in the first sentence. If a statement is supported by part of the argument, but supports another part of the argument, it's an intermediate conclusion.*

5.	Some critics have argued that the price of food and drink at Ultralux, a restaurant, is too high for the quality offered.	*Counterargument.* *This is the conclusion drawn by the critics, who the author of the argument disagrees with.*
	However, Ultralux features a beautiful interior and comfortable seating.	*Main argument.* *This is one of the author's premises. It supports the point the author is making, which is that Ultralux actually isn't overpriced.*
	Research has shown that consumers actually perceive food and drink as being of higher quality when they are consumed in such a setting.	*Main argument.* *This is another one of the author's premises. It helps to explain why the author believes that Ultralux has fair prices.*
	Thus, the food and drink at Ultralux are reasonably priced.	*Main argument.* *This is the author's conclusion: It's the main point that the author's evidence supports.*

9

6.	When compared to non-exercisers, people who exercise regularly also spend more time sitting or lying down in each 24-hour period.	***Main argument.*** *It isn't obvious right away that this is part of the main argument. It's a fact, not an opinion, so it won't be the conclusion. Keep reading until you find the author's conclusion, which states that recommending exercise is counterproductive. Since this statement supports that conclusion, this is one of the author's premises.*
	Because the risk of cancer and heart disease is higher among people who are more sedentary,	***Counterargument.*** *This is the reasoning used by doctors, who the author disagrees with. It supports the doctors' conclusion, so it's being used as a premise.*
	doctors often recommend that their patients engage in regular physical exercise.	***Counterargument.*** *This is the doctors' recommendation. If an argument offers a recommendation and supports that recommendation with evidence, the recommendation itself is the conclusion. The author disagrees with this conclusion, so in this argument, this is a counterpoint.*
	However, since people who exercise are in fact often more sedentary than those who do not,	***Main argument.*** *This is basically the same thing that the author said in the first sentence! It's just restated to make it clear that sitting or lying down equates to being sedentary. Just like the first sentence, this is a premise belonging to the author.*
	this recommendation is counterproductive.	***Main argument.*** *This is what the author wants to convince you of! It's her conclusion. She disagrees with the doctors; her two premises explain why she disagrees.*

9

Methodology

In This Chapter...

In this chapter, you will learn a 4-step process for use on all Critical Reasoning questions. The process will help you to identify the different question types, do the analysis required to reach the correct answer, and avoid trap answers.

CHAPTER 10 Methodology

In the previous chapter, you learned about argument building blocks and examined how to *deconstruct* an argument in order to understand how the pieces of information are related. These tasks represent the first two steps of the overall 4-step approach for any Critical Reasoning problem.

Before diving into the 4-step process, let's discuss what you *don't* want to do. While you have a lot of flexibility in how you work your way through the problem, there are some approaches that are downright bad, such as this one:

1. Read the argument pretty quickly, don't write anything down, don't understand the big picture.

2. Read the question.

3. Realize you need to read the argument again in order to answer; reread the argument.

4. Reread the question.

5. Examine the answers, eliminating one or several.

6. Read the argument for the third time.

7. Eliminate another answer.

8. Start checking each remaining answer against the argument and rereading the argument.

9. Repeat until one answer is left.

What's the problem? That's incredibly inefficient! If you've ever taken any standardized test before, you know that these tests have serious time pressure. The GMAT is no exception. In fact, you need to average about two minutes per CR question. So what do you do instead?

Use Manhattan Prep's 4-step approach for all CR questions:

Step 1: Identify the question.

Step 2: Deconstruct the argument.

Step 3: State the goal.

Step 4: Work from wrong to right.

Step 1: Identify the Question

Most arguments are followed by a question (you'll learn about one exception later). The wording of the question stem allows you to identify which type of question you're about to answer. You will need to employ different kinds of reasoning for different types of questions, so you want to know, right from the start, what kind of question you have.

There are three broad categories of Critical Reasoning questions: the **Structure-Based Family**, the **Assumption-Based Family**, and the **Evidence-Based Family**. Each of these families contains a few distinct question types. In later chapters, you'll learn how to identify all of the question types.

The Structure–Based Family

These questions ask you to determine something based upon the building blocks of the argument. What pieces are included in the argument and how do they fit together?

Question Type	Sample Question Phrasing	Goal
Describe the Role	In the argument given, the two boldface portions play which of the following roles?	Identify the roles (building blocks) of the boldface portions of the argument.
Describe the Argument	In the passage, the mayor challenges the council member's argument by doing which of the following?	Describe how a certain piece of information affects the argument.

The Assumption–Based Family

These questions all depend upon an understanding of the **assumptions** made by the author to reach a certain conclusion. As discussed earlier, an assumption is something that the author *does not state* in the argument, but something that the author *must believe to be true* in order to draw the given conclusion. Without the assumption, the argument fails.

You'll learn much more about assumptions in future chapters; for now, take a look at this short example:

> Pedro received a higher score than Dan did on a recent algebra test. Therefore, Pedro is better at math than Dan.

You may have identified one or more logical jumps that the author had to make to get from the premise (higher score on an algebra test) to the conclusion (better at math). Assumptions fill these gaps in logic; they are what must be true for the conclusion to hold. Below are a couple examples of assumptions in this argument:

> Assumption: Scores on the algebra test are representative of overall math ability.

> Assumption: Dan and Pedro took the test under similar conditions (e.g., they were given the same amount of time).

If you were to insert an assumption into the argument, it would make the argument better:

> Pedro received a higher score than Dan did on a recent algebra test. Scores on the algebra test are representative of overall math ability. Therefore, Pedro is better at math than Dan.

An assumption should plug a hole in the argument. Most arguments on the GMAT rely on multiple assumptions, so inserting one assumption doesn't make the argument airtight. The assumption will be necessary to the argument; that is, if the assumption *isn't* true, the argument breaks down.

There are five types of Assumption Family questions, as shown below, which will be covered further in subsequent chapters:

Question Type	Sample Question Phrasing	Goal
Find the Assumption	The argument depends on which of the following assumptions?	Identify an unstated assumption.
Strengthen the Argument	Which of the following, if true, provides the most support for the argument above?	Identify a new piece of information that strengthens the author's argument.
Weaken the Argument	Which of the following, if true, most seriously weakens the argument?	Identify a new piece of information that weakens the author's argument.
Evaluate the Argument	Which of the following must be studied in order to evaluate the argument above?	Identify a piece of information that would help to determine the soundness of the argument.
Find the Flaw	Which of the following indicates a flaw in the reasoning above?	Identify something illogical in the argument.

The Evidence–Based Family

These arguments all lack conclusions; they consist entirely of premises. They also won't include any assumptions. You're asked to find something that *must be true* or something that *resolves a discrepancy* in order to answer the question. You'll learn more about both of these question types later in the book.

Question Type	Sample Question Phrasing	Goal
Inference	Which of the following can be logically concluded from the passage above?	Identify something that must be true based on the given information.
Explain a Discrepancy	Which of the following, if true, most helps to explain the surprising finding?	Identify a new piece of information that resolves some apparent paradox in the argument.

This book also discusses a variation called Fill in the Blank. This variation is not a different question type; rather, it's a different way of presenting other question types.

As you go through each of the families and their question types, you will learn what kind of language signals specific question types—and so you'll know how to identify the question, the first step in the process.

Step 2: Deconstruct the Argument

Now that you've identified the family and question type, you can use that information to deconstruct the argument. You began to learn how to do this in the prior chapter when you labeled arguments using the building block components.

At this stage, many people take a few light notes. If Critical Reasoning is already a strength for you and you don't write anything, then you may not need to start. If, on the other hand, you want to improve CR significantly, then making an argument map will likely be one of your necessary strategies.

10

Revisit the first argument from the last chapter. As you deconstruct the argument, jot down an abbreviated map of the argument.

> The expansion of the runways at the Bay City Airport will allow larger planes to use the airport. These new planes will create a lot of noise, a nuisance for residents who live near the airport. However, many of the residents in this neighborhood work in construction, and the contract to expand the runways has been awarded to a local construction company. Thus, the expansion of the runways will lead to an increased quality of life for the residents of this neighborhood.

Here's one method of note-taking, idea by idea:

BC ↑ rnwy → ↑ P → > noise

BUT res work in constr [so work for them?]

Ⓒ plan → better life for res

This map may seem cryptic by itself, but remember, you will always have access to the argument on your screen. You do not have to answer the question using only your notes. In fact, if you are taking too many notes, it can be helpful to imagine that you cannot use those notes to answer the question. The process of creating them is what matters.

Avoid writing down full sentences. Try to abbreviate dramatically, even reducing whole words to single letters on the fly, as was done above:

BC = Bay City Airport

↑ = expansion, larger

rnwy = runway

→ = therefore

> = more

P = planes

res = residents

constr = construction

If these abbreviations are too cryptic for you, of course, make them longer. But if you practice, you'll be amazed by how much you can abbreviate. Some of your abbreviations will be one-off creations; others you'll use all the time (e.g., a right arrow to mean *therefore*). The goal as you create these notes is not to record every detail of the argument, but rather to help your brain understand the argument in real time. An effective map will summarize the core of the argument, including the premises and the conclusion. Now that you've delineated the parts of the argument for yourself, you'll be in a better position to answer the question.

Here are a few tips for effective note-taking on the fly. First, most people would probably start by writing down only the information from the first sentence:

BC ↑ rnwy → ↑ P

Then, as you continue reading, you might realize that the second sentence follows from the first: Those bigger planes then cause more noise. As a result, you might choose to continue writing on the same line, even though the additional information is given in a separate sentence. In this fashion, you are linking together the parts of the argument.

10

Second, did you note the question in the brackets: *[so work for them?]* Why is that there? The argument says that many residents work in construction. It also says a local company was awarded the contract to do the work. Did you notice anything missing? The argument never actually said that the residents of this neighborhood work for the local construction company. That might be something to think about as you try to answer the question. Feel free to jot down any thoughts you have about the argument, in particular its holes, as you go. Just be sure to bracket those thoughts, so that you don't ever think they're part of the argument itself.

Not everyone writes this much; some people don't write anything at all. Throughout the examples in this book, you will see samples of sentence-by-sentence notes for a variety of arguments. Practice to determine what works best for you. At first, you might write down too much and get bogged down. Keep practicing for at least a few weeks; as you gain skill, you'll discover how quickly you can take useful, highly abbreviated notes.

Step 3: State the Goal

This is a crucial step: What exactly are you trying to do when you answer this question? What's your goal? At this stage, you know what kind of question you have, you (hopefully) understand the argument and how it fits together, and you know the conclusion (if there is one). What's next?

In stating your goal, consider how the question type applies to the specific argument. Each question type requires a certain kind of reasoning and demands certain characteristics from the correct answer. For example, imagine that the question for the Bay City Airport argument asked:

> Which of the following most strengthens the argument?

This is a **Strengthen the Argument** question; on these questions, you are looking for a new piece of information that makes the conclusion more likely to be true. You'll learn what to look for in correct answers for each question type as you work through this guide. What do you think of the following goal statements for the Bay City Airport argument?

- Which answer makes the conclusion more likely?

- Which answer makes it more likely that the runway expansion will improve quality of life in the neighborhood?

The first statement is too general; all it does is reiterate the general goal on Strengthen the Argument questions, and it provides no information about the conclusion you are trying to strengthen. The second, on the other hand, brings together the general goal with the specific conclusion of the argument. A more specific goal statement makes it easier to differentiate between answers that are related to the conclusion versus those that are not.

After you have stated your goal, spend a little time thinking about any issues you see in the argument. Are there any logical flaws? Are there other factors that are important to the conclusion but that the author has not mentioned? You may not identify issues on all arguments, but a little brainstorming can help as you move on to step 4.

Step 4: Work from Wrong to Right

Finally, the answer choices! On GMAT Verbal in general, you're asked to find the "best" answer. You're going to use a 2-step process to do so:

1. First, look through all five answers and eliminate as many "definitely wrong" answers as you can. Do *not* try to decide which is the *right* answer right now. Instead, concentrate on eliminating *wrong* answers.

2. If you have only one answer left after this first pass, great; you're done. If you have two or more answers left, then compare those remaining answers.

Why do you want to attack the answers this way, "working from wrong to right"? By definition, finding the *best* answer is a comparison; if you spot a tempting wrong answer, you might not be able to spot what is wrong with it until you've read the right answer. It's most efficient to dump all of the "No way!" answers as fast as you can, and then directly compare the remaining, more tempting answers. Of course, there will always be only one right answer, but your final choice will be made easier if you have already eliminated the bad wrong answers.

Finally, remember one last tip for Verbal questions: When you've narrowed it down to two answers, compare those two answers just once more. Then pick and move on. Going back and forth multiple times is a waste of time—either you know it after comparing the first time or you don't.

When you work from wrong to right, it's critical to keep track of your thinking on your scrap paper. In the testing center, the scrap pad is not erasable, so you need to decide how to write down ABCDE and how to notate your thoughts.

Decision 1: How do I write down ABCDE?

Option 1	Pros	Cons
Write ABCDE for each question.	Can write on/cross off each letter; can keep letters right next to map about argument.	Have to write 23 separate times as you proceed through the Verbal section.

This option might look like this, if the first question is Weaken the Argument (noted with a W) and the second question is Strengthen the Argument (noted with an S):

```
W    A B̸ C D̸ E

notes
notes



S    A B C̸ D E

notes
notes
```

Option 2	Pros	Cons
Write ABCDE at the top of the page, then move to a new line for each question.	Only have to write once for each page (several times for entire test).	Have to keep track "below" each letter; map might not be right next to answer tracking row.

This option might look like the diagram below, in which the first question is Weaken and the second question is Strengthen. In testing centers, the scrap pad you'll be given is graph paper, so there will already be lines built in to separate the five answer choices.

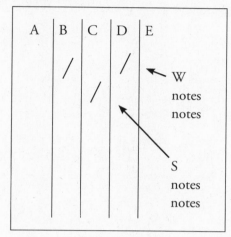

If you take the test online, you will provide your own dry-erase board for your scratch work—in other words, you *can* erase as you go. In this case, write ABCDE down once, then keep track of your answer choice eliminations immediately below each letter. When you're done with that problem, erase just your notations, leaving the ABCDE to use for the next problem.

Decision 2: What symbols will I use to keep track of my thoughts?

You need four symbols. You can use any symbols you prefer as long as you consistently use the same symbols:

Ⅹ or /	Definitely wrong
~	Maybe
?	I have no idea.
o	This is it!

10

Try using the 4-step process on an actual problem:

> Many companies use automated telephone services: Callers hear a machine-generated voice and are able to select options using the numbers on the telephone keypad. Research shows that callers are more patient when the machine-generated voice is that of a woman. Thus, smaller companies that cannot afford an automated service should consider hiring women, rather than men, to interact with customers by phone.
>
> Which of the following, if true, would be most damaging to the conclusion above?
>
> (A) Automated telephone services are becoming cheaper and cheaper every year.
>
> (B) Patient customers tend to order more products and return fewer products than impatient customers.
>
> (C) A separate study indicated that the extra patience exhibited by callers is limited to interactions with an automated system.
>
> (D) Some customers prefer automated systems to talking with a live person.
>
> (E) On average, callers are only slightly more patient when interacting with a female voice, rather than a male voice, in an automated telephone system.

How did you do with each step? Did you identify the question type? Do you feel comfortable with your map, and did you identify the conclusion (if there is one)? Did you remember to state the goal (briefly) before looking at the answers? Did you use the 2-step process to assess the answer choices, working from wrong to right?

Here's how someone might work through the problem above, step-by-step. The table displays text from the problem, the student's thoughts, and the relevant notes on scrap paper:

Step 1: Identify the Question

Argument	Thoughts	Paper
Which of the following, if true, would be most damaging to the conclusion above?	Most damaging to the conclusion *means this is a Weaken. I need to find the conclusion, and I need to think about what flaws or gaps might exist in the argument.*	W A B C D E

Step 2: Deconstruct the Argument

Argument	Thoughts	Paper
Many companies use automated telephone services:	*Sounds like background, but I'll jot down a note anyway.*	auto phone
Callers hear a machine-generated voice and are able to select options using the numbers on the telephone keypad.	*This is describing what an automated phone system is; I probably don't need to write that down.*	
Research shows that callers are more patient when the machine-generated voice is that of a woman.	*This is a fact, not a claim, so it has to be either a premise or counter-premise. It's probably a premise, since there's only one sentence left.*	Res: female = ↑ patience
Thus, smaller companies that cannot afford an automated service should consider hiring women, rather than men, to interact with customers by phone.	*This is the only claim, so it's the conclusion. Now I can go back and add a ⓒ to the conclusion in my map and a + to the premise.*	Small co's → use women phone

The final map might look something like this:

W   A B C D E

auto phone

+ Res: female = ↑ patience

ⓒ Small co's → use women phone

Your map might look very different from the map above. That's perfectly fine as long as your map conveys to you the basic flow of information clearly and concisely as you put it together. Remember, the map is most useful as you make it, not as you look at it later.

Step 3: State the Goal

The question is a Weaken question, so briefly restate the main reasoning and conclusion of the argument. Once you have stated your specific goal, do a little brainstorming about any concerns you have with the argument.

Small companies should hire women to answer the phones, because callers are more patient when hearing automated female voices.

How would I weaken this specific argument? What would make it less likely that companies should hire women to answer phones?

Hmm. The evidence is about automated female voices, while the conclusion is about real women. Is there any kind of disconnect there?

Step 4: Work from Wrong to Right

Now, attack the answers!

Argument	Thoughts	Paper
(A) Automated telephone services are becoming cheaper and cheaper every year.	*The conclusion discusses what companies should do when they can't afford automated services. This choice addresses those who can buy the service, so it's irrelevant to the argument.*	~~A~~
(B) Patient customers tend to order more products and return fewer products than impatient customers.	*This is a good reason for the company to do whatever it can to keep its customers in a patient mood. If anything, that would strengthen the argument.*	~~B~~
(C) A separate study indicated that the extra patience exhibited by callers is limited to interactions with an automated system.	*Hmm. This highlights a distinction between automated and live voices... Does that distinction have anything to do with the argument? Well, the conclusion only talks about hiring actual people, but it looks like all of the evidence is about automated systems. That could be a problem for the argument. Keep this one in.*	C ~
(D) Some customers prefer automated systems to talking with a live person.	*This argument is about only those companies that can't afford the system and are using real people. Nope, this isn't it.*	~~D~~
(E) On average, callers are only slightly more patient when interacting with a female voice, rather than a male voice, in an automated telephone system.	*This one seems to be telling me there isn't a huge difference between hearing male and female voices—but there is still a small positive effect for female voices. If anything, this strengthens the argument; after all, as a small business owner, I'll take any necessary steps that will get me more business! I've crossed off four answers, so (C) is the correct answer.*	~~E~~

At the end, the answer choice letters on your paper would look like this:

~~A~~ ~~B~~ Ⓒ ~~D~~ ~~E~~

Drill 10.1—Identify the Question

Warm up by matching each Critical Reasoning question stem to the type of question it's asking:

1. Which of the following indicates a vulnerability of the argument above?

2. Which of the following, if true, most strongly suggests that the plan will fail to achieve its desired outcome?

3. In the argument given, the boldfaced portion plays which of the following roles?

4. In the passage above, the biologist responds to the journalist's claim by doing which of the following?

5. Which of the following, if true, would best explain the garden snail's paradoxical behavior?

6. Which of the following conclusions is most strongly supported by the statements given?

7. Which of the following would be most useful to research in order to assess the likelihood that the teacher's claim is correct?

8. Which of the following, if true, would provide the strongest justification for the mayor's conclusion?

9. Which of the following is an assumption on which the school board's argument depends?

(A) Describe the Role	(D) Strengthen the Argument	(G) Find the Flaw
(B) Describe the Argument	(E) Weaken the Argument	(H) Inference
(C) Find the Assumption	(F) Evaluate the Argument	(I) Explain a Discrepancy

Answers to Drill Set

Drill 10.1—Identify the Question

1. **(G):** The right answer to a Find the Flaw problem will point out, in general terms, a vulnerability or logical problem with the argument.

2. **(E):** If an argument describes a plan, the outcome of the plan is the conclusion of the argument. Weakening the argument means showing that the plan might fail.

3. **(A):** Describe the Role problems are the only problems in which parts of the argument appear in bold.

4. **(B):** A Describe the Argument problem asks you to describe the logic of someone's argument in more general terms.

5. **(I):** Explain a Discrepancy problems often refer to a surprise, paradox, or unusual finding in the question stem. Your task is to explain why it occurred.

6. **(H):** This question stem implies that the conclusion will be in the answer choices, not in the argument itself. This makes it an Inference problem. Be careful not to confuse this with a Strengthen the Argument question, which might also use the word *support*!

7. **(F):** Evaluate the Argument questions ask you to find the most useful question to ask or topic to research.

8. **(D):** Providing a justification for an argument is the same as Strengthening the Argument.

9. **(C):** Find the Assumption questions will ask you to find an assumption made by the author or something upon which the argument relies.

Methodology Cheat Sheet

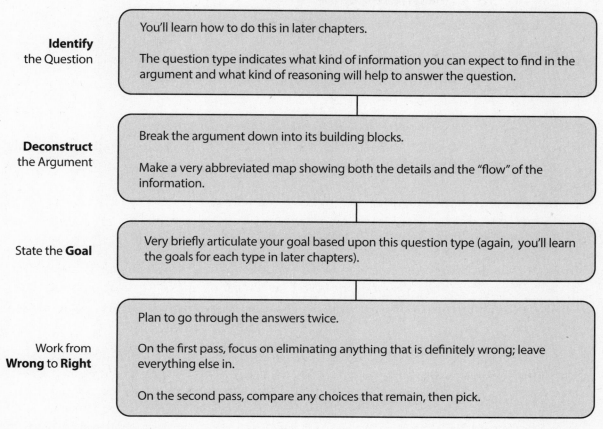

Methodology Cheat Sheet

Identify
the Question

You'll learn how to do this in later chapters.

The question type indicates what kind of information you can expect to find in the argument and what kind of reasoning will help to answer the question.

Deconstruct
the Argument

Break the argument down into its building blocks.

Make a very abbreviated map showing both the details and the "flow" of the information.

State the **Goal**

Very briefly articulate your goal based upon this question type (again, you'll learn the goals for each type in later chapters).

Work from
Wrong to **Right**

Plan to go through the answers twice.

On the first pass, focus on eliminating anything that is definitely wrong; leave everything else in.

On the second pass, compare any choices that remain, then pick.

Know how you're going to keep track of your answers on your scrap paper. First, decide whether to have a separate ABCDE grid for each problem or whether to use the "write once per page" method described earlier in the chapter. Second, make sure you have four consistent symbols for these four labels:

1. Definitely wrong

2. Maybe

3. I have no idea.

4. This is it!

Problem Set

Map each argument on your paper, identifying the conclusion (if one exists) and the premise(s).

1. The overwhelming majority of advertisers prefer not to have their products associated with controversial content. In order to increase its advertising revenue, a large blogging platform plans to stop placing advertisements on blogs that deal with controversial topics, thus attracting advertisers who would otherwise be reluctant to advertise on the platform.

2. A series of research studies has reported that flaxseed oil can have a beneficial effect in reducing tumor growth in mice, particularly the kind of tumor found in human postmenopausal breast cancer. Thus, flaxseed oil should be recommended as an addition to the diets of all postmenopausal women.

3. During the past 30 years, the percentage of the population that smokes cigarettes has consistently declined. During the same time period, however, the number of lung cancer deaths attributed to smoking cigarettes has increased.

4. The Chinese white dolphin is a territorial animal that rarely strays far from its habitat in the Pearl River Delta. In recent years, increasing industrial and agricultural runoff to the delta's waters has caused many white dolphins to perish before they reach breeding age. Unless legislation is enacted to ensure there is no further decline in the delta's water quality, the Chinese white dolphin will become extinct.

5. Most doctors recommend consuming alcohol only in moderation, since the excessive intake of alcohol has been linked to several diseases of the liver. Drinking alcohol is no more dangerous for the liver, however, than abstaining from alcohol entirely. Last year, more nondrinkers than drinkers were diagnosed with liver failure.

6. To increase the productivity of the country's workforce, the government should introduce new food guidelines that recommend a vegetarian diet. A study of thousands of men and women revealed that those who stick to a vegetarian diet have IQs that are approximately five points higher than those who regularly eat meat. The vegetarians were also more likely to have earned advanced degrees and hold high-paying jobs.

10

This page intentionally left blank

Solutions

Note: The sample maps shown below represent one style of map. Just make sure that your map is legible and concise and that it conveys the main points in a way that makes sense to you.

1.

Argument	Thoughts	Paper
The overwhelming majority of advertisers prefer not to have their products associated with controversial content.	*This is a fact. It could be background. Or, if it supports the conclusion, it's a premise.*	Adv: controv = bad
In order to increase its advertising revenue,	*Somebody is trying to increase revenue. That sounds like a goal. When the argument describes a plan, I can think of the goal of that plan as the conclusion.*	© Adv rev ↑
a large blogging platform plans to stop placing advertisements on blogs that deal with controversial topics,	*This is a premise describing how the goal will be achieved.*	Plan: no ads on controv blogs
thus attracting advertisers who would otherwise be reluctant to advertise on the platform.	*This is the result of the previous premise, and it supports the conclusion. This is an intermediate conclusion.*	Plan: no ads on controv blogs → more adv

The structure of this argument is **premise–conclusion–premise–intermediate conclusion**.

2.

Argument	Thoughts	Paper
A series of research studies has reported that flaxseed oil can have a beneficial effect in reducing tumor growth in mice, particularly the kind of tumor found in human postmenopausal breast cancer.	*This is a fact. It's either background or a premise.*	Res: flax helps ↓ tumor mice esp postmen b-cancer
Thus, flaxseed oil should be recommended as an addition to the diets of all postmenopausal women.	*Definitely the conclusion.*	© Postmen women shd take flax

The structure of this argument is **premise–conclusion**.

3.

Argument	Thoughts	Paper
During the past 30 years, the percentage of the population that smokes cigarettes has consistently declined.	*This is a fact. It's either background or a premise.*	30y: % pop smoke cig ↓ steady
During the same time period, however, the number of lung cancer deaths attributed to smoking cigarettes has increased.	*Another fact, so another premise. There isn't a conclusion.*	Same time: lung canc dead from cig ↑

The structure of this argument is **premise–premise**. Remember, not all GMAT arguments contain conclusions.

4.

Argument	Thoughts	Paper
The Chinese white dolphin is a territorial animal that rarely strays far from its habitat in the Pearl River Delta.	*This is a fact. It's either background or a premise.*	Dolphin stays in delta
In recent years, increasing industrial and agricultural runoff to the delta's waters has caused many white dolphins to perish before they reach breeding age.	*This is also a fact—either background or premise.*	Recent: ind + ag in delta → dolphin dies b4 breed
Unless legislation is enacted to ensure there is no further decline in the delta's water quality, the Chinese white dolphin will become extinct.	*And here's the conclusion.* [Note: H2O here is an abbreviation for water, based on the chemical formula H_2O.]	IF govt doesn't fix H2O → dolphin extinct

The structure of this argument is **premise–premise–conclusion**.

5.

Argument	Thoughts	Paper
Most doctors recommend consuming alcohol only in moderation, since the excessive intake of alcohol has been linked to several diseases of the liver.	*This is a fact. It's either background or a premise.*	Drs rec ↓ alc bc ↑ alc → liver dis
Drinking alcohol is no more dangerous for the liver, however, than abstaining from alcohol entirely.	*Oh, this has the word however! The last sentence was a counterpremise, and this one sounds like the conclusion.*	Ⓒ Drink not worse than abstain
Last year, more nondrinkers than drinkers were diagnosed with liver failure.	*This supports the previous sentence; it's a premise. (It also seems pretty flawed. What **percentage** of nondrinkers vs. drinkers had liver disease?)*	Last yr: more nondrink had liv dis

The structure of this argument is **counterpremise–conclusion–premise**.

6.

Argument	Thoughts	Paper
To increase the productivity of the country's workforce, the government should introduce new food guidelines that recommend a vegetarian diet.	*This is definitely a claim. It sounds like a conclusion, though I don't know for sure yet.*	Govt shd rec veg to ↑ wrkr prod
A study of thousands of men and women revealed that those who stick to a vegetarian diet have IQs that are approximately five points higher than those who regularly eat meat.	*This is a fact—the results of a study. It also supports the claim above, so it's a premise.*	Study: veg ↑ IQ than non-veg
The vegetarians were also more likely to have earned advanced degrees and hold high-paying jobs.	*This is another premise supporting the first sentence.*	Veg > better schl + high pay

The structure of this argument is **conclusion–premise–premise**.

Tip: When first learning this method, many people write too much. As part of your review, ask yourself, "Did I write this down in the most effective way? Did my map make sense? Did I write down something that I could have skipped, or did I use too many words when I could have abbreviated more?" If you were really off the mark, write out the map again in a more ideal way—and articulate to yourself why this new way is better than the old way.

10

The Assumption Family: Find the Assumption

In This Chapter...

In this chapter, you will learn the role that assumptions play in arguments and how to answer the first of five question types that all rely on assumptions somehow.

CHAPTER 11 The Assumption Family: Find the Assumption

Assumptions are the key to the largest family of questions, the Assumption Family; all five question types in this family contain arguments that involve at least one assumption made by the author. (The *author* refers to the hypothetical person who is "arguing" the argument and believes that argument to be valid.)

How Assumptions Work

An assumption is something that *the author must believe to be true* in order to draw a certain conclusion; however, the author *does not state* the assumption in the argument. The assumption itself might not necessarily be true in the real world; rather, the *author* believes that it is true in order to make the argument.

For example, what does the author of the following argument assume must be true?

> No athletes under the age of 14 can qualify for Country Y's Olympic team. Therefore, Adrienne can't qualify for Country Y's Olympic team.

therefore

No athlete under 14 can qualify
for Olymp from Y.

(premise)

Adrienne can't qual for Y's
Olymp team.

(conclusion)

The author assumes that this premise applies to Adrienne—in other words, that she is an athlete from Country Y and that she is under the age of 14. There may be other reasons she would not qualify for the Olympic team (perhaps her sport is not included), but if she can't qualify *for this reason*, then it must be because she is otherwise qualified (that is, she is an athlete from Country Y) but is too young.

The diagram above represents the **core** of the argument. The core consists of the conclusion and the main premise or premises that lead to that conclusion, as well as the unstated *assumption(s)*. You need assumptions as much as you need any other piece of the argument to make the whole thing work. After all, if Adrienne were *not* under 14, then the argument above would make no sense.

Assumptions fill at least part of a gap in the argument; the gap is represented by the arrow in the diagram above. If you insert a valid assumption into the argument, it makes the argument much better:

> No athletes under the age of 14 can qualify for Country Y's Olympic team. *Adrienne is an athlete from Country Y who is under the age of 14.* Therefore, Adrienne can't compete for Country Y's Olympic team.

11

No athlete under 14 can qualify
for Olymp from Y.

(premise)

therefore

Adrienne can't qual for Y's
Olymp team.

(conclusion)

*Adrienne is an athlete from Country Y
who is under the age of 14.*

(assumption)

The argument above has a single obvious assumption that fills the gap on its own. Most GMAT arguments contain multiple assumptions, none of which individually fill the gap. Any one assumption will not automatically make the argument airtight, but it will make the argument more likely to be true, and the argument will depend on each of those assumptions. Take any assumption away and the argument collapses.

In order to train yourself to notice the presence of assumptions, think of someone with whom you enjoy having intellectual debates. Whenever you talk to this person, your brain is already on the offensive. "Really? I'm not so sure about that. You've failed to consider…" Pretend this person is the one making the argument to you. How would you try to pick it apart? You'll be attacking assumptions.

Okay, are you ready? Brainstorm some assumptions for the following argument:

> Thomas's football team lost in the championship game last year. The same two teams are playing in the championship game again this year, and the players on Thomas's team have improved. Therefore, Thomas's team will win the championship game this year.

Picture that person with whom you debate; what would you say? Maybe something like this: "You're just *assuming* that Thomas's team has improved enough to be competitive with last year's winning team! You're also assuming that last year's winning team has *not* improved enough to keep themselves clearly ahead of Thomas's team!" As you brainstorm, however, remember that on the GMAT, you never have to come up with any assumption in a vacuum. After all, the test is multiple choice! If you are asked to find an assumption, one of the choices will be a valid assumption and the other four choices will not be. So, while it's worth reading critically to poke holes in weak arguments, don't spend too much time thinking up assumptions on your own.

Here are a couple of important strategies for dealing with assumptions on the test:

Do		Don't
Notice gaps and articulate assumptions you can think of relatively easily.	**but**	Don't spend more than about 20 seconds brainstorming up front.
Look for your brainstormed assumptions in the answers.	**but**	Don't eliminate answers just because they don't match any of your brainstormed assumptions.
Choose an answer that the author must believe to be true in order to draw the conclusion.	**but**	Don't hold out for something that makes the conclusion "perfect" or definitely true.

Try inserting a brainstormed assumption into the football argument to see how it works:

> Thomas's football team lost in the championship game last year. The same two teams are playing in the championship game again this year, and the players on Thomas's team have improved enough to be competitive with the defending champion team. Therefore, Thomas's team will win the championship game this year.

If the author is going to claim that the improvement will lead to a victory for Thomas's team, then it is *necessary* for the author to believe that this improvement was enough to put that team at least at the same level as the defending champion team. Otherwise, it wouldn't make sense to say that, because these players have improved, they will win this year.

It is still not a foregone conclusion that Thomas's team will definitely win, even though the author clearly believes so. There are too many other potential factors involved; the author is making many assumptions, not just one. It is only necessary to find one assumption, though; it is not necessary to make the argument foolproof.

Drill 11.1—Brainstorm Assumptions

Brainstorm at least one assumption that must be true. If you like, you can draw out the argument core.

1. Over 30% of students at an elementary school failed the state reading test last year. In order to reduce the failure rate, the school plans to offer free reading tutoring after school.

2. The employees of Quick Corp's accounting department consistently show a significant jump in productivity in the two weeks before taking vacation. Clearly, the knowledge that they are about to go on vacation motivates the employees to be more productive.

3. Mayor: The Acme Factory has developed a new manufacturing process that uses chemical Q, the residue of which is toxic to babies. In order to protect our children, we need to pass a law banning the use of this chemical.

Answers to Drill Set

Drill 11.1—Brainstorm Assumptions

Possible assumptions are noted in italics below the arrow. You may brainstorm different assumptions from the ones shown. Other assumptions are acceptable as long as they represent something that MUST be true in order to make the given argument.

1.

therefore

Offer free tutoring   Reduce reading test failure

Students will go. Tutoring will help pass.

The author argues that offering free after-school tutoring will reduce the failure rate on the test. The plan must work as expected for that conclusion to hold. Students, especially those who are likely to fail the test, must actually attend the tutoring sessions. Also, the tutoring must help students pass the test. If, for example, the tutoring focused on material that was not on the test, it might not make much difference for failure rates.

2.

therefore

2 wks b4 vaca:
h ↑ prod

emp choose >> prod
b4 vaca

*They didn't plan vacation to
occur right after a big deadline
or other busy time.*

The author concludes that employees decide to be more productive *because* they'll be taking vacation soon; this is a **causation** argument. Perhaps it's the case, instead, that the employees choose to take vacation right after they know they'll be *forced* to work harder for some other reason. For example, maybe everyone in the accounting department takes vacation right after the annual financial report is due. The author is assuming that *other* causes of the jump in productivity don't apply in this case.

3.

therefore

Acme using Q,
toxic baby

to protect kids,
ban Q

*If Acme uses Q, then kids will
somehow come into contact
with Q.*

The mayor assumes that the use of chemical Q in the production process will somehow eventually expose babies to the chemical residue. Maybe the chemical is used only for something that never comes into contact with the final product and will never come into contact with kids.

Assumption Family Questions

There are five types of Assumption questions. The first major type, Find the Assumption, is covered in this chapter. In the next chapter, you'll learn about the next two major types: Strengthen the Argument and Weaken the Argument. Later, you'll be introduced to the two remaining types in the Assumption Family: Evaluate the Argument and Find the Flaw.

Each type of question has its own key characteristics and goals, but some characteristics are common to all five types. There will always be a conclusion, so you definitely want to look for it. In addition, *while* you read, try to notice any gaps, indicating assumptions, that jump out at you (but don't take much longer than you normally take to read the argument itself).

Find the Assumption Questions

Find the Assumption (FA) questions ask you to, well, find an assumption that the author must believe to be true in order to make the argument. If the correct answer were *not* true, the argument would not be valid.

Your task is to figure out which answer choice represents something that must hold true according to the author. Note one especially tricky aspect of these problems: The assumption itself might only be true in the mind of the author. You might think, "Well, is that really true in the real world? I don't think that has to be true." Don't ask that question! The only issue is whether the *author* must believe it to be true in order to arrive at the conclusion. If the argument is "Planets are wonderful; therefore, Pluto is wonderful," then the assumption is that Pluto is a planet (whether you still think it is or not).

Identifying the Question

These questions are usually easy to identify, because the question stem will use some form of the noun *assumption* or the verb *to assume*. Occasionally, the question may ask for a new premise or a new piece of information that is required or necessary to draw the conclusion. Here are a couple of examples:

> Which of the following is an *assumption* on which the argument depends?

> Which of the following is *required* for the mayor's plan to succeed?

Try this sample argument:

> When news periodicals begin forecasting a recession, people tend to spend less money on nonessential purchases. Therefore, the perceived threat of a future recession decreases the willingness of people to purchase products that they regard as optional or luxury goods.

> Which of the following is an assumption on which the argument depends?

Do the first couple of steps before looking at the answer choices:

Step 1: Identify the Question

Which of the following is an assumption on which the argument depends?	*The question stem uses the word* assumption, *so it is the Assumption type. Write* FA *on the scrap paper and then the answer choice letters.*	FA A B C D E

Step 2: Deconstruct the Argument

When news periodicals begin forecasting a recession, people tend to spend less money on nonessential purchases.	*This sounds like a premise, though I suppose it could be a conclusion. The news periodicals predict a recession, and then people spend less money.*	Periodicals forecast recess → ppl spend ↓ $ non-ess
Therefore, the perceived threat of a future recession decreases the willingness of people to purchase products that they regard as optional or luxury goods.	*This is the conclusion. The premise above tells what people do—spend less money. The conclusion tries to claim* why *they do it—a perceived future threat.*	Ⓒ Perceived threat → ppl spend ↓ $ lux
	What is the author assuming? That people are actually reading or hearing about the forecasts. That the recession hasn't already started and that's why people are spending less money—maybe the periodicals are just slow in *forecasting something that has already started. Also, the author assumes that* nonessential *and* luxury *mean the same thing.*	

Did you come up with any other assumptions? The key is to get your brain thinking about these things, but there are almost always multiple possible assumptions; you may not brainstorm the exact one that will show up in the answers.

Step 3: State the Goal

When you state your goal, you want to think about how the question type should be applied to the argument you just read. To do this, it can be helpful to articulate the core to yourself. You don't necessarily need to write/draw it out unless you want to.

therefore

Periodicals forecast: recess! ↓ spend non-ess Perceived threat → spend lux $ ↓

People reading/hearing info from periodicals. Threat only perceived today; recession hasn't already started.

State your goal. What has to be true for the forecasts of a recession to result in decreased spending on luxury goods?

Take a look at the full problem now:

> When news periodicals begin forecasting a recession, people tend to spend less money on nonessential purchases. Therefore, the perceived threat of a future recession decreases the willingness of people to purchase products that they regard as optional or luxury goods.
>
> Which of the following is an assumption on which the argument depends?
>
> (A) People do not always agree as to which goods should be considered luxury goods.
>
> (B) Many more people read news periodicals today than five years ago.
>
> (C) Most people do not regularly read news periodicals.
>
> (D) Decreased spending on nonessential goods does not prompt news periodicals to forecast a recession.
>
> (E) At least some of the biggest spenders prior to the recession were those who curtailed their spending after the recession began.

Step 4: Work from Wrong to Right

As you move to the answer choices, look for the assumptions you brainstormed but also be flexible; you might not have thought of the assumption in the correct answer, or the assumption you thought of may be phrased differently than you imagined. On FA questions, traps often involve an answer that is not tied to the conclusion, an answer that makes the argument weaker, not stronger, or an answer that makes an irrelevant distinction or comparison. (Note: You'll learn more about trap answers later in the chapter.)

11

(A) People do not always agree as to which goods should be considered luxury goods.	*I can believe that this is true in the real world, but this is irrelevant to the conclusion. The argument is not based upon whether people agree as to how to classify certain goods.*	~~A~~
(B) Many more people read news periodicals today than five years ago.	*This sounds a little bit like one of my brainstormed assumptions—the argument assumes that people are actually reading those periodicals. I'm not so sure about the more today than five years ago part, though. You don't absolutely have to believe that in order to draw that conclusion. I'll keep it in for now, but maybe I'll find something better.*	B̰
(C) Most people do not regularly read news periodicals.	*This is also about reading the periodicals . . . but it's the opposite of what I want! The argument needs to assume that people DO read the periodicals; if they don't, then how can they be influenced by what the periodicals forecast?*	~~C~~
(D) Decreased spending on nonessential goods does not prompt news periodicals to forecast a recession.	*Let's see. This choice is saying that the drop in spending is not itself causing the forecasts. That's good, because the argument is that the causality runs the other way: The forecasts cause the drop in spending. This one is looking better than answer (B). I can cross off (B) now.*	D̰
(E) At least some of the biggest spenders prior to the recession were those who curtailed their spending after the recession began.	*Hmm. This one sounds good, too. Maybe if some of the biggest spenders keep spending during the recession, then the overall amount of money being spent won't go down that much . . . although the argument doesn't really seem to depend on how much it goes down. Oh, wait: This says after the recession began—but the conclusion is about a perceived threat of a future recession. Nice trap!*	~~E~~

~~A~~   B̰   ~~C~~   Ⓓ   ~~E~~

There were a couple of good brainstormed assumptions, but none that matched the exact assumption contained in the correct answer, (D). That's okay; be prepared to be flexible!

Note that answer choice (C) contained an "opposite" answer: It weakened the conclusion rather than making it stronger.

The Negation Technique

On harder questions, you might find yourself stuck between two answer choices. To unstick yourself, try the **Negation Technique**.

On Find the Assumption questions, the correct answer will be something that the author must believe to be true in order to make the argument. As a result, if you were to turn the correct answer around to make the opposite point, then the author's argument should be harmed. Negating the correct answer should weaken the author's conclusion.

Try it out on the *News Periodicals* problem from above. Say that you narrowed the answers to (B) and (D):

> (B)   Many more people read news periodicals today than five years ago.
>
> (D)   Decreased spending on nonessential goods does not prompt news periodicals to forecast a recession.

Recall the argument itself as mapped out above:

> Periodicals forecast recess → ppl spend ↓ $ non-ess
>
> Perceived threat → ppl spend ↓ $ lux

The author argues that when the periodicals forecast a recession, people perceive a future threat, and so people choose to spend less money on luxury goods.

What if answer choice (B) were *not* true? It would say something like:

> (B)   The same number or fewer people read news periodicals today than five years ago.

Does this weaken the author's conclusion? Not really. While the argument does assume that at least some people are reading news periodicals, it doesn't discuss what used to happen five years ago, nor does it hinge on any sort of change over time.

Try negating answer (D):

> (D)   Decreased spending on nonessential goods DOES prompt news periodicals to forecast a recession.

Hmm. If spending goes down and then the news periodicals react by forecasting a recession...then the author has it backwards! The news periodicals aren't causing a behavior change in consumers. Rather, they're reacting to something the consumers are already doing. Thus, the argument no longer works. Negating this answer breaks down the author's argument, so this choice is the right answer.

A word of warning: Don't use this technique on every answer choice or you'll be in danger of spending too much time. However, when you're stuck, the Negation Technique can be a big help. And if *that* doesn't work, as always, you know what to do: Guess and move on.

Right Answers

For Find the Assumption questions, the right answer is necessary to the conclusion. Generally, you will not see a lot of new language or new ideas different from what was in the argument; the exception is assumptions that exclude another possibility. Take a look at this argument you saw in a previous chapter:

11

Metropolis has experienced an increase in the amount of trash in its city parks. In order to reduce the amount of litter in the parks, Metropolis plans to double the number of trash cans in each city park.

Which of the following is an assumption on which the argument depends?

(A) Trash will not blow into the park from the streets and sidewalks surrounding the park.

(B) Some people still choose to litter even if there is a trash receptacle within 20 feet of their location.

This argument is a plan: put more trash cans in parks to reduce litter. You are looking for an assumption: What is necessary for the increase in trash cans to reduce litter in the parks?

Answer (A) might have given you pause because it introduces something not discussed in the argument: trash from the surrounding streets and sidewalks. But answer (A) is actually excluding the possibility. The plan presented can only reduce litter coming from inside the park because that is where there will be more trash cans. Answer (A) is the correct answer and an example of an assumption that excludes a possibility, and thus may have new ideas or language. If you were wondering, answer (B) actually makes the argument worse, suggesting people may still litter even with more trash cans.

Below are some common assumptions for different argument types. Note that some arguments will have unique assumptions that do not match the categories described:

- **Causation:** In an argument that concludes that X causes Y, assumptions often exclude reverse causation (Y causes X) or outside causes (Z causes both X and Y).

- **Plan:** In a plan, an assumption may validate that the steps of the plan will work as expected or exclude a previously unmentioned detriment to the plan (see park litter example above).

- **Prediction:** In order for a prediction to come true, you have to assume that no other future events beyond those mentioned in the argument will intervene.

- **Profit:** For profit to move in the direction predicted by the argument, there cannot be some other factor that outweighs the predicted outcome. For example, a conclusion that states profit will increase assumes there is not some hidden cost that exceeds the benefit.

Common Trap Answers

On many Find the Assumption questions, a trap answer won't actually address the conclusion. Because the question specifically asks you to find an assumption necessary to draw that conclusion, an answer that has **No Tie to the Conclusion** must be wrong. Answer (A) from the *News Periodicals* problem is a good example: *People do not always agree as to which goods should be considered luxury goods.* The conclusion of that argument is about what causes a person to spend less money on a luxury good—regardless of how that specific person classifies luxury goods. The conclusion does not depend upon whether different people would agree to classify the same item as a luxury good. One person might decide to cut out caviar while someone else decides to cut out Netflix; they're both cutting back on luxuries, even though they have different ideas of what that means.

Trap answers can also use **Reverse Logic**, as in answer choice (C). Reverse logic does the opposite of what you want; in this case, answer (C) actually makes the argument worse, but an assumption should make the argument stronger.

Answers (B) and (E) are examples of another trap: making an **Irrelevant Distinction or Comparison**. The argument does not hinge upon whether people read more now than they did five years ago. Nor does it depend upon the highest spending consumers doing something different from the rest of consumers. Rather, all consumers are lumped together in the argument.

Find the Assumption Cheat Sheet

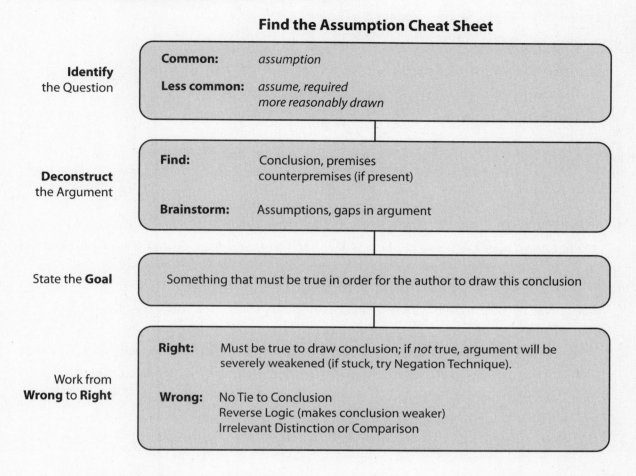

Take a picture of this page and keep it with the review sheets you're creating as you study. Better yet, use this page as a guide to create your own review sheet—you'll remember the material better if you write it down yourself. Where appropriate, put it in your own words and you'll remember it even better.

Problem Set

Answer each question using the 4-step Critical Reasoning process.

1.   **Identify the question.**

2.   **Deconstruct the argument:** Find the conclusion and map the argument on your paper.

3.   **State the goal:** What will the right answer need to do?

4.   **Work from wrong to right:** Eliminate four wrong answers. Watch out for common wrong answer types.

Before you review each problem, try to identify as many **No Tie**, **Reverse Logic**, and **Irrelevant Distinction** wrong answers as you can. There will be at least one common wrong answer type in each problem, and probably more!

1.   *MTC and Asthma*

Methyltetrachloride (MTC) is a chemical found in some pesticides, glues, and sealants. Exposure to MTC can cause people to develop asthma. In order to halve the nation's asthma rate, the government plans to ban all products containing MTC.

The government's plan to halve the nation's asthma rate relies on which of the following assumptions?

(A)   Exposure to MTC is responsible for no less than half of the nation's asthma cases.

(B)   Products containing MTC are not necessary to the prosperity of the American economy.

(C)   Asthma has reached epidemic proportions.

(D)   After MTC is used in an area, residual amounts of the chemical can be detected months or years later.

(E)   Dust mites and pet dander can also cause asthma.

2.   *Oil and Ethanol*

Country N's oil production is not currently sufficient to meet its domestic demand. In order to sharply reduce its dependence on foreign sources of oil, Country N recently began requiring all automobiles produced in the country to use a blend of gasoline and ethanol, rather than gasoline alone. Country N produces enough ethanol from agricultural by-products to make up for the gap between its domestic oil production and its current demand for energy.

Which of the following must be assumed in order to conclude that Country N will succeed in its plan to reduce its dependence on foreign oil?

(A)   Electric power is not a superior alternative to ethanol in supplementing automobile gasoline consumption.

(B)   In Country N, domestic production of ethanol is increasing more quickly than domestic oil production.

(C)   Ethanol is suitable for the heating of homes and other applications aside from automobiles.

(D)   In Country N, oil consumption is not increasing at a substantially higher rate than domestic oil and ethanol production.

(E)   Ethanol is as efficient as gasoline in terms of mileage per gallon when used as fuel for automobiles.

3. *Exchange Student*

   Student Advisor: One of our exchange students faced multiple arguments with her parents over the course of the past year. Not surprisingly, her grade point average (GPA) over the same period showed a steep decline. This is just one example of a general truth: Problematic family relationships can cause significant academic difficulties for our students.

   Which of the following is required for the student advisor to conclude that problematic family relationships can cause academic difficulties?

   (A) Last year, the exchange student reduced the amount of time spent on academic work, resulting in a lower GPA.

   (B) The decline in the GPA of the exchange student was not the reason for the student's arguments with her parents.

   (C) School GPA is an accurate measure of a student's intellectual ability.

   (D) The student's GPA is lower than the average GPA for exchange students at the university.

   (E) Fluctuations in academic performance are typical for many students.

4. *Genetics*

   Two genes, BRCA1 and BRCA2, are linked to hereditary breast cancer. Genetic testing, which can detect these genes, is increasing in both accuracy and prevalence. The test is also less painful and invasive than a mammogram, which is typically used to detect early signs of breast cancer. Therefore, we can expect the percentage of women who undergo mammograms each year to decrease.

   Which of the following is an assumption on which the argument depends?

   (A) Some women who are tested for BRCA1 and BRCA2 will choose not to undergo a mammogram.

   (B) The percentage of women undergoing mammograms each year has remained consistent over the last decade.

   (C) Aside from BRCA1 and BRCA2, there are no other genes that are strongly linked to breast cancer.

   (D) Doctors will continue to recommend regular mammograms for all women at risk of breast cancer, regardless of the results of genetic testing.

   (E) A significant percentage of cases of breast cancer are linked to BRCA1 or BRCA2.

Solutions

1. MTC and Asthma: The correct answer is (A). Try to spot any **No Tie to the Conclusion**, **Reverse Logic**, or **Irrelevant Distinction or Comparison** wrong answers before you keep reading!

Step 1: Identify the Question

The government's plan to halve the nation's asthma rate relies on which of the following assumptions?	*Asks for the* assumption; *this is a Find the Assumption question.*	FA A B C D E

Step 2: Deconstruct the Argument

Methyltetrachloride (MTC) is a chemical found in some pesticides, glues, and sealants.	*This is just a fact—background or maybe a premise.*	MTC = chem
Exposure to MTC can cause people to develop asthma.	*Another fact but it's specifically a bad fact. This is likely a premise.*	Can → asthma
In order to halve the nation's asthma rate, the government plans to ban all products containing MTC.	*Okay, the government has a plan to ban MTC, and the result will be (they claim) that the asthma rate will be cut in half. There are no numbers or anything to support that. Are a lot of people exposed now? What percentage of those who develop asthma were exposed? Etc.*	© Gov plan: ban MTC to ½ asthma rate

Step 3: State the Goal

The government claims that it can halve the asthma rate by banning MTC, but it gives absolutely no evidence or numbers to support halving *the rate.*

I need to find an answer that supports the idea that they can halve the asthma rate—maybe that a very large percentage of people who develop asthma were exposed to MTC or something like that.

Step 4: Work from Wrong to Right

(A) Exposure to MTC is responsible for no less than half of the nation's asthma cases.	*This sounds similar to what I said. Let's see. If MTC actually is responsible for at least half of asthma cases, then getting rid of it would get rid of all those cases as well. This one looks pretty good.*	A ∼
(B) Products containing MTC are not necessary to the prosperity of the American economy.	***No tie.*** *This is a deceptive wrong answer. It says that these products aren't economically important, but the conclusion isn't about economics! The conclusion talks about whether the plan will halve the asthma rate, regardless of the economic effects.*	~~B~~
(C) Asthma has reached epidemic proportions.	***No tie.*** *This answer choice explains why we might want to reduce the asthma rate. But it doesn't address the specific plan at all.*	~~C~~
(D) After MTC is used in an area, residual amounts of the chemical can be detected months or years later.	***Reverse logic.*** *This actually weakens the government's proposal. Since MTC sticks around long after the chemicals are actually used, banning the chemicals now may not reduce the asthma rate.*	~~D~~
(E) Dust mites and pet dander can also cause asthma.	***Irrelevant distinction.*** *Sure, there are other things that can cause asthma. But the argument isn't about these things—it's specifically about MTC. The fact that other things can also cause asthma doesn't change anything about the MTC situation.*	~~E~~

2. Oil and Ethanol: The correct answer is (**D**). Try to spot any **No Tie to the Conclusion, Reverse Logic**, or **Irrelevant Distinction or Comparison** wrong answers before you keep reading!

Step 1: Identify the Question

Which of the following must be assumed in order to conclude that Country N will succeed in its plan to reduce its dependence on foreign oil?	*Contains the phrase* must be assumed—*this is a Find the Assumption question.*	FA A B C D E

Step 2: Deconstruct the Argument

Country N's oil production is not currently sufficient to meet its domestic demand.	*They produce oil but can't make enough for their own needs. That must mean they have to import some oil.*	N oil prod < dom demand
In order to sharply reduce its dependence on foreign sources of oil, Country N recently began requiring all automobiles produced in the country to use a blend of gasoline and ethanol, rather than gasoline alone.	*They're requiring cars to use a combo of gas and ethanol, and they think that'll lead to having to use less foreign oil.*	To ↓ for. oil, N reqs ethanol in cars
Country N produces enough ethanol from agricultural by-products to make up for the gap between its domestic oil production and its current demand for energy.	*Okay, so they do make enough ethanol PLUS oil combined to satisfy their own needs currently. What about gas? And what if demand changes in future?*	N eth + oil = curr demand

Step 3: State the Goal

Country N thinks it can sharply reduce the amount of foreign oil it needs if it starts making people own cars that use ethanol. Will the plan really work that way? They're assuming people really will start to use the ethanol. They're also assuming they'll continue to produce enough oil and ethanol in the future.

I need to find an answer that must be true in order to allow the author to draw the conclusion above.

Step 4: Work from Wrong to Right

(A) Electric power is not a superior alternative to ethanol in supplementing automobile gasoline consumption.	**Irrelevant distinction.** *Comparing ethanol to electric power doesn't tell me anything useful about ethanol, which is what I really care about. We're supposed to find something that goes with the plan stated in the argument, and that plan mentions nothing about electric power.*	~~A~~
(B) In Country N, domestic production of ethanol is increasing more quickly than domestic oil production.	*If this is true, then switching stuff to ethanol seems like a good call. Does it have to be true in order to draw the conclusion? What if the two were increasing at the same rate? That would be fine, actually. This doesn't have to be true—so it isn't a necessary assumption.*	~~B~~
(C) Ethanol is suitable for the heating of homes and other applications aside from automobiles.	**Irrelevant distinction.** *The argument only talks about a plan to have cars start using ethanol. Whether the plan will also work for homes doesn't have anything to do with cars.*	~~C~~
(D) In Country N, gasoline consumption is not increasing at a substantially higher rate than domestic oil and ethanol production.	*Hmm. The argument is assuming in general that the ethanol + oil production can keep up with the country's demand. So, yes, the author would have to assume that gas consumption isn't increasing at a much faster rate than production.* *Let's try negating this one: If gas consumption were increasing at a much higher rate, what would happen? Oh, they might have to get more from foreign sources—bingo! Negating this does weaken the conclusion.*	D̰
(E) Ethanol is as efficient as gasoline in terms of mileage per gallon when used as fuel for automobiles.	**No tie.** *The conclusion isn't about gas mileage, it's about reducing foreign oil dependency. There isn't necessarily a link between those two things. Maybe people will use more ethanol than gas if it's less efficient, but maybe they won't.*	~~E~~

~~A~~   ~~B~~   ~~C~~   Ⓓ   ~~E~~

3. Exchange Student: The correct answer is **(B)**. Try to spot any **No Tie to the Conclusion**, **Reverse Logic**, or **Irrelevant Distinction or Comparison** wrong answers before you keep reading!

Step 1: Identify the Question

Which of the following is required for the student advisor to claim that problematic family relationships can cause academic difficulties?	*This is an unusual question stem. It doesn't include the word assumption, but it does include a synonymous idea: What is required to draw the conclusion? This is an assumption question.*	FA A B C D E

Step 2: Deconstruct the Argument

Student Advisor: One of our exchange students faced multiple arguments with her parents over the course of the past year.	*This is a fact—background or a premise.*	Advisor: student had args w parents
Not surprisingly, her grade point average (GPA) over the same period showed a steep decline.	*Not only did the student's GPA go down, but the advisor says* not surprisingly. *Sounds like the advisor is going to conclude a causal relationship.*	GPA ↓↓
This is just one example of a general truth: Problematic family relationships can cause significant academic difficulties for our students.	*Here we go: The advisor claims that this student's family problems* caused *the academic problems. Maybe there was a different cause.*	↓ © Fam probs → acad probs

Step 3: State the Goal

I need to find an answer that the author must believe to be true in order to draw this conclusion. The only thing I can think of right now is very general: If the advisor is assuming the family problems were what caused the academic problems, then the advisor is also assuming there wasn't something else causing the academic problems.

Step 4: Work from Wrong to Right

(A) Last year, the exchange student reduced the amount of time spent on academic work, resulting in a lower GPA.	**Reverse logic.** *This actually works against the advisor's conclusion. It suggests a different reason that the student's grades decreased. If this different reason is correct, then the advisor's reasoning is incorrect. An assumption always has to support the conclusion and can't work against it.*	~~A~~
(B) The decline in the GPA of the exchange student was not the reason for the student's arguments with her parents.	*Let's see. This is kind of what I said before—there is not a different cause for the decline of her GPA.* *Let's try negating this. If the student's GPA went down first and then her parents got mad at her for that reason, then you can't claim that the family problems caused the lower GPA. The advisor's argument would fall apart. This choice looks good.*	B̰
(C) School GPA is an accurate measure of a student's intellectual ability.	**No tie.** *The conclusion has nothing to do with intellectual ability! It discusses academic difficulties and their relationship to GPA and does not draw any comparison to the student's intellectual ability.*	~~C~~
(D) The student's GPA is lower than the average GPA for exchange students at the university.	**Irrelevant distinction.** *The argument deals with a decrease in a single exchange student's GPA. It isn't necessary to compare that student to other students in order to explain the decrease in her own GPA.*	~~D~~
(E) Fluctuations in academic performance are typical for many students.	**Reverse logic.** *This actually works against the advisor's conclusion. The advisor argues that the problematic family relationship caused the student's difficulties. However, this answer choice suggests that the student's GPA decrease was actually due to random fluctuation. An assumption will never work against the conclusion.*	~~E~~

~~A~~   (B̰)   ~~C~~   ~~D~~   ~~E~~

4. Genetics: The correct answer is (**A**).

Step 1: Identify the Question

Which of the following is an assumption on which the argument depends?	*The word* assumption *indicates that this is a Find the Assumption question.*	FA A B C D E

Step 2: Deconstruct the Argument

Two genes, BRCA1 and BRCA2, are linked to hereditary breast cancer.	*A fact about genes and cancer.*	2 genes linked to b-cancer
Genetic testing, which can detect these genes, is increasing in both accuracy and prevalence.	*We're getting better at testing for these genes, and we're doing it more often.*	testing: acc & freq ↑
The test is also less painful and invasive than a mammogram, which is typically used to detect early signs of breast cancer.	*Now the argument is comparing this testing to an alternative test for breast cancer. Looks like the genetic test has some advantages, although I still don't know if it's as good at detecting cancer.*	genetic test vs mammo.: less pain, less invasive
Therefore, we can expect the percentage of women who undergo mammograms each year to decrease.	*Here's the conclusion: It's a prediction about the future. Since genetic testing has these advantages, a smaller percentage of women will have mammograms in the future.*	© mammo. % ↓

Step 3: State the Goal

The author claims that the percentage of women who have mammograms will decrease. I know that mammograms have some disadvantages compared to genetic testing, but the author is making a big assumption in concluding that fewer people will actually have them! The right answer is something that must be true in order for the author to reach this conclusion.

Step 4: Work from Wrong to Right

(A) Some women who are tested for BRCA1 and BRCA2 will choose not to undergo a mammogram.	*If at least some women get tested and then don't have a mammogram, then that would help to reduce the percentage of mammograms. But does this have to be true? Actually, I think it does. For fewer women to have mammograms, at least some women must be changing their minds about having one.*	A̰
(B) The percentage of women undergoing mammograms each year has remained consistent over the last decade.	**No tie.** *The conclusion deals with what will happen in the immediate future: The percentage of women undergoing mammograms each year will decrease. This answer choice describes something that happened in the past. I don't know whether the past and the future are related here.*	B̶
(C) Aside from BRCA1 and BRCA2, there are no other genes that are strongly linked to breast cancer.	**Irrelevant distinction.** *Comparing those two genes to a third gene doesn't tell me anything about the mammogram situation. The argument is only about the results of genetic testing for those two genes, not about breast cancer more broadly.*	C̶
(D) Doctors will continue to recommend regular mammograms for all women at risk of breast cancer, regardless of the results of genetic testing.	**Reverse logic.** *If anything, this suggests that the prevalence of mammograms will stay the same, since genetic testing won't change doctors' recommendations. An assumption always has to support the conclusion.*	D̶
(E) A significant percentage of cases of breast cancer are linked to BRCA1 or BRCA2.	**No tie.** *This doesn't tell me anything about who will undergo a mammogram. If I assume that women who discover that they have this gene will choose not to have a mammogram, this might cause a decline in the number of mammograms. But I'd have to make my own assumptions in order to use that reasoning and that isn't allowed.*	E̶

The Assumption Family: Strengthen and Weaken

In This Chapter...

In this chapter, you will learn how to recognize and answer the second and third of the five question types in the Assumption Family: Strengthen and Weaken.

CHAPTER 12   The Assumption Family: Strengthen and Weaken

In the previous chapter, you learned about the first major question type in the Assumption Family: Find the Assumption. If you haven't read the previous chapter yet, please do so before reading this chapter.

To recap briefly:

- Assumptions are something an author must believe to be true in order to draw the conclusion. These assumptions are not stated explicitly in the argument.
- All assumption arguments will contain a "core": a conclusion and the major premise or premises that lead to it.
- All assumption arguments will include at least one (and probably more than one) unstated assumption.

This chapter addresses the next two Assumption Family question types: **Strengthen the Argument** and **Weaken the Argument**. Like Find the Assumption, these two types are commonly tested on the GMAT. They also hinge upon identifying an assumption.

Strengthen and Weaken: The Basics

Both Strengthen and Weaken questions ask you to find a *new* piece of information that, if added to the existing argument, will make the conclusion either more likely to be true (strengthen) or less likely to be true (weaken).

In the case of Strengthen, the new piece of information will typically provide evidence to support an assumption. In the case of Weaken, the new piece of info will attack an assumption: It will serve as evidence that the assumption is invalid.

How does this work? Let's look at one of the arguments from the last chapter again:

> Thomas's football team lost in the championship game last year. The same two teams are playing in the championship game again this year, and the players on Thomas's team have improved. Therefore, Thomas's team will win the championship game this year.

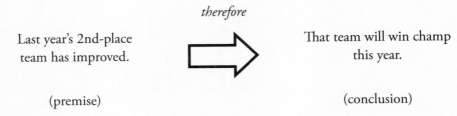

therefore

Last year's 2nd-place team has improved.

That team will win champ this year.

(premise)

(conclusion)

If you were asked a Find the Assumption question, the answer might be something like this: Thomas's team has improved enough to be competitive with the defending champions. In order for the author to draw this conclusion, that point must be assumed. If Thomas's team hasn't improved enough to be (at minimum) competitive with last year's first-place team, then it wouldn't make any sense to say that *because* they have improved, they will win this year.

If you're asked a Strengthen question, how does the answer change? A Strengthen answer provides some new piece of information that does not have to be true, but *if it is true*, that information does make the conclusion more likely to be valid. For example:

> The star quarterback on the defending champion team will miss the game due to an injury.

Must it be true that the star quarterback will miss the game in order for the author to believe that Thomas's team will win? No. If that information *is* true, though, then the conclusion is more likely to be true. Thomas's team is more likely to win if a star player on the opposing team can't play.

What happens if you're asked a Weaken question? Similarly, a Weaken answer provides a new piece of information that does not have to be true, but *if it is true*, then the conclusion is a bit less likely to be valid. For example:

> The players on the defending champion team train more than the players on any other team.

That specific fact does not have to be true in order for you to doubt the claim that Thomas's team will win—there are lots of reasons to doubt the claim—but *if it is true* that the defending champion team trains more than all of the other teams, then the author's conclusion just got weaker.

Note that Strengthen and Weaken question stems include the words *if true* or an equivalent variation. In other words, you are explicitly told to accept the information in the answer as true.

Finally, there are three possible ways that an answer choice could affect the argument on both Strengthen and Weaken questions: The answer *strengthens* the argument, the answer *weakens* the argument, or the answer *does nothing* to the argument. One of your tasks will be to classify each answer choice into one of these three buckets.

Strengthen the Argument Questions

Strengthen questions ask you to find a *new* piece of information that, if added to the existing argument, will make the argument somewhat more likely to be true.

Most often, Strengthen questions will contain some form of the words *strengthen* or *support*, as well as the phrase *if true*. Here are some typical examples:

> Which of the following, if true, most strengthens the argument above?

> Which of the following, if true, most strongly supports the mayor's claim?

Strengthen questions will sometimes use synonyms in place of the strengthen/support language. These synonyms may do the following:

- Provide the best basis *or* the best reason for
- Provide justification for
- Provide evidence in favor of (a plan or a conclusion)

Strengthen questions may occasionally lack the exact phrase *if true*, but some other wording will provide a similar meaning. That wording might be something quite similar, such as *if feasible* (in reference to a plan). Alternatively, the wording might indicate that the answer can be *effectively achieved* or *successfully accomplished* (indicating that the information would become true).

Try this short example:

> At QuestCorp, many employees have quit recently and taken jobs with a competitor. Shortly before the employees quit, QuestCorp lost its largest client. Clearly, the employees were no longer confident in QuestCorp's long-term viability.
>
> Which of the following, if true, most strengthens the claim that concerns about QuestCorp's viability caused the employees to quit?
>
> (A) Employees at QuestCorp's main competitor recently received a large and well-publicized raise.
>
> (B) QuestCorp's largest client accounted for 40% of sales and nearly 60% of the company's profits.
>
> (C) Many prospective hires who have interviewed with QuestCorp ultimately accepted jobs with other companies.

The question stem indicates that this is a Strengthen question. Deconstruct the argument. The core might be:

therefore

lost client,
ppl quit

(premise)

quit b/c concern
about success

(conclusion)

Remember, you can write the core down or you can just articulate the core to yourself mentally. Whichever path works best for you is fine.

Make sure that you understand what the argument is trying to say. The author claims that, because the company lost its largest client, some employees lost confidence in the company, so they quit. The author assumes that losing that client will be a significant blow to the company. What if the company has many clients and the largest client only represented a very small fraction of the business? The author also assumes there aren't other reasons why employees quit.

State your goal: How would you strengthen this particular conclusion?

This is a Strengthen question, so I have to find some evidence that supports the claim that people quit specifically because they lost confidence in the company after it lost its largest client.

(A) Employees at QuestCorp's main competitor recently received a large and well-publicized raise.	*Wouldn't that make QuestCorp's employees jealous—maybe they'd expect more money? That'd make it more likely that they quit because of pay issues rather than a loss of confidence in the company. If anything, this weakens the conclusion; I want a Strengthen answer.*	~~A~~
(B) QuestCorp's largest client accounted for 40% of sales and nearly 60% of the company's profits.	*Ouch. Then losing this client would be a pretty serious blow to the company. This is a fact that helps make the conclusion a little more likely; I'll keep it in.*	B ~
(C) Many prospective hires who have interviewed with Quest-Corp ultimately accepted jobs with other companies.	*Hmm. Prospective hires are not employees. I was asked to strengthen the part about employees losing confidence in the company. I could speculate that maybe something is wrong with QuestCorp if people take other jobs ... but the answer doesn't even tell me why these people took other jobs. Maybe QuestCorp rejected them!*	~~C~~

~~A~~   (B)   ~~C~~

The correct answer is (B).

Answer choice (A) represents one common trap on Strengthen questions: The answer does the opposite of what you want. That is, it weakens the conclusion rather than strengthening it.

Answer choice (C) represents another common trap: The answer addresses (and sometimes even strengthens) something other than what you were asked to address. In this case, the answer does seem to imply that there's something not so great about QuestCorp, but it discusses the wrong group of people (prospective hires) and doesn't actually provide any information that allows you to assess what they think of QuestCorp's viability. (Again, that last part doesn't matter in the end, because it's already talking about the wrong group of people.)

Putting It All Together

Try a full problem now:

> Donut Chain, wishing to increase the profitability of its new store, will place a coupon in the local newspaper offering a free donut with a cup of coffee at its grand opening. Donut Chain calculates that the cost of the advertisement and the free donuts will be more than compensated for by the new business generated through the promotion.
>
> Which of the following, if true, most strengthens the prediction that Donut Chain's promotion will increase the new store's profitability?
>
> (A) Donut Chain has a loyal following in much of the country.
> (B) Donut Chain has found that the vast majority of new visitors to its stores become regular customers.
> (C) One donut at Donut Chain costs less than a cup of coffee.
> (D) Most of the copies of the coupon in the local newspaper will not be redeemed for free donuts.
> (E) Donut Chain's stores are generally very profitable.

Step 1: Identify the Question

Which of the following, if true, most strengthens the prediction that Donut Chain's promotion will increase the new store's profitability?	*The language* if true *and* most strengthens the prediction that... *indicates that this is a Strengthen the Argument question. Also, the question stem tells me the conclusion I need to address: The plan will lead to better profitability.*	S A B C D E © promo → ↑ prof

Step 2: Deconstruct the Argument

Donut Chain, wishing to increase the profitability of its new store, will place a coupon in the local newspaper offering a free donut with a cup of coffee at its grand opening.	*Donut Chain thinks that giving away a free donut will lead to increased profitability.*	promo = free coupon
Donut Chain calculates that the cost of the advertisement and the free donuts will be more than compensated for by the new business generated through the promotion.	*It costs $ to place the ad and give away free donuts, but Donut Chain thinks it'll get enough new business to offset those costs. Still, does that lead to better profitability?*	$ spent < $ new biz
(brainstorm assumptions)	*The argument isn't 100% clear that the profitability part is the conclusion, but the question stem also said so. The author is assuming that giving away a free donut once will lead to increased revenues over time (what if they never come back?), and that will then lead to increased profits (more revenues don't necessarily equal more profits).*	

Step 3: State the Goal

I need to strengthen the claim that a particular plan is going to lead to increased profitability. The plan is to distribute coupons to give away free donuts.

I need to find an answer that makes it a little more likely that this plan will lead to more profits.

Step 4: Work from Wrong to Right

(A) Donut Chain has a loyal following in much of the country.	*This is good for Donut Chain. Does that mean it will increase profitability though? No. It's already an established fact. Plus, it only says that Donut Chain enjoys a loyal following in much of the country, not necessarily where the new store is located.*	A̶
(B) Donut Chain has found that the vast majority of new visitors to its stores become regular customers.	*So if Donut Chain can get people to visit once, they'll usually keep coming back. That sounds pretty good for Donut Chain's plan, which is all about getting people to visit the first time for that free donut.*	B ~
(C) One donut at Donut Chain costs less than a cup of coffee.	*This tells me nothing about profits or revenues or how much they could sell or anything, really. This doesn't address the argument.*	C̶
(D) Most of the copies of the coupon in the local newspaper will not be redeemed for free donuts.	*If this happens, then Donut Chain's plan is really unlikely to work—it spends money on the ads, but never gets the new customers to come in. That weakens the conclusion.*	D̶
(E) Donut Chain's stores are generally very profitable.	*It's good that Donut Chain stores are usually profitable; that means this new one is likely to be profitable, too. The conclusion, though, specifically talks about increasing the store's profitability—and the question specifically asks whether this plan will accomplish that goal. This choice looks tempting at first, but it doesn't address whether this plan will increase profitability.*	E̶

A̶ (B) C̶ D̶ E̶

Where's The Conclusion?

In the Donut Chain argument above, you might have noticed the question provided additional information about the conclusion (that the coupon would increase profitability). Read this argument and question, and try to find the conclusion:

> Average customer wait times at the registry of motor vehicles (RMV) in Starton have increased by 30 minutes in the last year. The RMV recently developed a smartphone application that allows customers to view current wait times and predicted wait times later in the day.
>
> Which of the following, if true, most strengthens the claim that the smartphone application will decrease average wait times at the RMV?

The question asks you to support the claim that the app will decrease wait times. So that claim is the conclusion of the argument. But is that conclusion ever in the argument? No: The first statement says that wait times are a problem, but the possibility of reducing them is not in the argument.

Be aware that sometimes the conclusion of the argument is never stated in the argument but is instead found in the question. When you do step 1, look out for language in the question about a specific claim or prediction you are trying to support (or refute, depending on the argument type). Sometimes the GMAT hides the conclusion in the question, most frequently on Strengthen, Weaken, and Evaluate the Argument questions.

Right Answers

On Strengthen questions, right answers need to provide additional information that makes the conclusion more likely. Do not eliminate an answer just because you see a new word or idea; consider whether the answer is logically connected to the conclusion.

In the Donut Chain example, the right answer talked about *regular customers*. Although regular customers are not mentioned in the argument, such customers have a link to profitability and thus are relevant to strengthening the conclusion.

Common Trap Answers

One of the most common traps is the Reverse Logic answer: The question asks you to strengthen, but a trap answer choice weakens the conclusion instead. You saw an example of this with answer choice (D) in the Donut Chain problem. These can be especially tricky if you misread the conclusion or otherwise get turned around while evaluating the argument.

Most of the wrong answers will have no tie to the argument—they will neither strengthen nor weaken the argument. Some of these will be more obviously wrong, but these answers can also be quite tricky. A No Tie trap might address something in a premise without actually affecting the conclusion; answer choice (E) in the Donut Chain problem is a good example. Notice that it says something positive about Donut Chain, but not anything that addresses the specific chain of logic in the argument.

Strengthen Variant: Fill in the Blank

Contrary to popular belief, **Fill in the Blank (FitB) questions** are not actually a separate question type; rather, any of the existing question types can be presented in FitB format. In practice, most FitB questions are Strengthen questions; occasionally, they are Inference or Find the Assumption questions.

Look at an example:

> Which of the following most logically completes the argument below?
>
> XYZ Industries sells both a premium line of televisions and a basic line. The higher-end line sells at a 20% premium over the basic line and accounts for about half of the company's revenues. The company has announced that it will stop producing premium televisions and sell only the basic line in the future. This plan will help to improve profitability, since _____.

Right away, you'll notice that there is no question stem after the argument—but there is a question above. The location of the question stem (and the blank at the end of the argument) indicates that you have the FitB structure. But which type of question is it?

The clue to help you identify the question will be just before the blank. In the vast majority of these problems, the word *since* or *because* will be just before the blank, in which case you have a Strengthen question.

The author claims that *this plan will help to improve profitability*. As with any Strengthen question, your task is to find an answer that will make this claim more likely to be true.

For the example above, for instance, a correct answer might read:

> premium televisions cost 40% more to produce and market than do basic televisions

If the company charges 20% more for a premium television, but has to pay 40% more to produce and market it, then it's more likely that the company makes less money on premium televisions than it does on basic ones. (This is not an absolute slam dunk, but that's okay. You just have to make the argument more likely to be valid.) Given this, the plan to drop the premium televisions and sell only the basic ones is more likely to improve profitability, strengthening the author's case.

On some FitB questions, the correct answer reinforces or even restates a premise already given in the argument. Most of the time, though, the correct answer will introduce a new premise, as with regular Strengthen questions. Either way, the result will be the same: The answer will make the author's argument at least a little more likely to be true.

Negatively Worded Claims

Many FitB questions introduce a negatively worded twist. Take a look at this variation on the original argument:

> Which of the following most logically completes the argument below?
>
> XYZ Industries sells both a premium line of televisions and a basic line. The higher-end line sells at a 20% premium but also costs 40% more to produce and market. Producing more televisions from the basic line, however, will not necessarily help to improve profitability, since _____ .

This is still a Strengthen question because the word *since* is just before the underline. The conclusion is that last sentence: A particular plan will *not* necessarily help to improve profitability. Why? Consider this possible correct answer:

> the market for basic televisions is shrinking

In other words, producing more TVs doesn't necessarily mean the company can *sell* more TVs, and it would have to sell them in order to make money. If the market for basic TVs is shrinking, then producing more of those TVs won't necessarily be beneficial for the company's profitability.

If you see *since* _____ in a FitB question, your goal is to strengthen the conclusion that comes before, even if that conclusion contains a *not* or is otherwise worded negatively.

Alternative Wording

The *since* _____ or *because* _____ variations are the two most common ways in which FitB questions can be presented. There are a few alternative examples, however, that might pop up. Students aiming for 90th percentile or higher on the Verbal section may want to be prepared for these rare variations; otherwise, it's fine to skip this section.

The rare variants will still typically include the conclusion or claim in the final sentence with the blank, but the "lead-in" wording to the blank will be different, signaling a different question type as shown below:

"Lead-In" Wording	Answer Choice Should	Question Type
If (some claim is true), "it should be expected that" _____	represent something that must be true given the information in the argument	Inference
(In order for some claim to be true), "it must be shown that" _____	represent something that must be true given the information in the argument	Inference
(Something is true) "assuming that" _____	articulate an assumption used to draw the conclusion	Find the Assumption

Common Trap Answers

The common trap answers will mirror the trap answers given on the regular question type. For example, if the question is a Strengthen, then expect to see the same trap answers that you see on regular Strengthen questions: Reverse Logic (weakens rather than strengthens) and No Tie to the Argument.

Weaken the Argument Questions

Weaken the Argument questions ask you to find a *new* piece of information that, if added to the existing argument, will make the argument less likely to be valid. Your goal, then, is to *attack* the argument. The correct answer will generally attack some assumption made by the author.

Most Weaken question stems contain either the word *weaken* or a synonym of it. You will also typically see the phrase *if true* and question stems similar to these examples:

- Which of the following, if true, most seriously weakens the conclusion?
- Which of the following, if true, would cast the most serious doubt on the validity of the argument?
- Which of the following, if true, would raise the most serious doubt regarding the conclusion of the argument?
- Which of the following, if true, most strongly calls into question the author's conclusion?
- Which of the following, if true, most seriously undermines the mayor's claim?

Sometimes, the question stem will contain more unusual language, such as the words in quotes below:

- Find a "disadvantage" or what is "damaging" to the argument
- A plan is "ill-suited" or otherwise unlikely to succeed
- Find a "criticism" of the argument

Now, try the same short argument about QuestCorp from earlier in the chapter, but with a different question stem and answers:

> At QuestCorp, many employees have quit recently and taken jobs with a competitor. Shortly before the employees quit, QuestCorp lost its largest client. Clearly, the employees were no longer confident in QuestCorp's long-term viability.
>
> Which of the following, if true, most seriously undermines the claim that concerns about QuestCorp's viability caused the employees to quit?
>
> (A) A new competitor in the same town provides health insurance for its employees, a benefit that QuestCorp lacks.
>
> (B) QuestCorp is unlikely to be able to replace the lost revenue via either an increase in existing client sales or the attraction of new clients.
>
> (C) Many prospective hires who have interviewed with QuestCorp ultimately accepted jobs with other companies.

The question stem indicates that this is a Weaken question. In your mind or on your paper, the argument core might look like this:

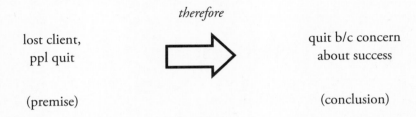

therefore

lost client,	quit b/c concern
ppl quit	about success
(premise)	(conclusion)

As always, make sure that you understand what the argument is trying to say. The author claims that losing this client caused employees to lose confidence in QuestCorp, leading them to quit. The author is assuming that losing this one client was serious enough to result in a major problem for the company. Is that necessarily the case?

Remind yourself of your goal:

This is a Weaken question, so I have to find some evidence that makes it less *likely that people quit for that reason. That could be because it wasn't really a big problem, or it could be that there was some other reason that people quit.*

(A) A new competitor in the same town provides health insurance for its employees, a benefit that QuestCorp lacks.	*The argument claims that people left for one reason, but this answer actually provides an alternative. Maybe people quit because they could get better benefits at the other company. This would weaken the claim that people quit specifically because of concerns over QuestCorp's viability as a company.*	A ~
(B) QuestCorp is unlikely to be able to replace the lost revenue via either an increase in existing client sales or the attraction of new clients.	*So QuestCorp lost its largest client, which means a loss of revenue, and the company probably can't find a way to make up that revenue through other sales. That definitely reinforces the problem described in the argument. This actually strengthens the argument; that's the opposite of what I want.*	~~B~~
(C) Many prospective hires who have interviewed with QuestCorp ultimately accepted jobs with other companies.	*Hmm.* Prospective hires *are not* employees. *I was asked to weaken the part about employees losing confidence in QuestCorp. I could speculate that maybe something is wrong with the company if people take other jobs... but the answer doesn't even tell me* why *these people took other jobs. Maybe QuestCorp rejected them!*	~~C~~

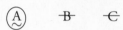

The correct answer is (A).

Answer (B) repeats the common Reverse Logic trap discussed earlier: It strengthens the argument. Answer (C) attempts to distract you by talking about a different part of the argument—perhaps you'll reason that, if interviewees took different jobs, then they didn't believe QuestCorp was a good company. You have no idea why these prospective hires ended up working for another company, though—it's entirely possible that QuestCorp didn't extend a job offer to these people.

Note that the problem used the exact same answer choice (C) for both the Strengthen and Weaken versions of this QuestCorp problem. If a choice is irrelevant to the argument, as choice (C) is, then it doesn't matter whether you're asked to strengthen or weaken the argument. An irrelevant choice doesn't affect the argument at all.

Try this full example:

> The national infrastructure for airport runways and air traffic control requires immediate expansion to accommodate the increase in smaller private planes. To help fund this expansion, the Federal Aviation Authority has proposed a fee for all air travelers. However, this fee would be unfair, as it would impose costs on all travelers to benefit only the few who utilize the new private planes.
>
> Which of the following, if true, would cast the most doubt on the claim that the proposed fee would be unfair?
>
> (A) The existing national airport infrastructure benefits all air travelers.
> (B) The fee, if imposed, will have a negligible impact on the overall volume of air travel.
> (C) The expansion would reduce the number of delayed flights resulting from small private planes congesting runways.
> (D) Travelers who use small private planes are almost uniformly wealthy or traveling on business.
> (E) A substantial fee would need to be imposed in order to pay for the expansion costs.

Step 1: Identify the Question

Which of the following, if true, would cast the most doubt on the claim that the proposed fee would be unfair?	*The language* cast the most doubt on the claim *indicates that this is a Weaken question.* Attack: *The proposed fee would be unfair.*	W A B C D E Ⓒ fee = unfair

12

Step 2: Deconstruct the Argument

The national infrastructure for airport runways and air traffic control requires immediate expansion to accommodate the increase in smaller, private planes.	*This is written as a fact and appears to be stating something that has already been established; I'm guessing it's background info, not the conclusion, but I'm not 100% sure.*	To handle more small priv planes → must expand infra
To help fund this expansion, the Federal Aviation Authority has proposed a fee for all air travelers.	*Okay, here's a plan. It could be the conclusion. The FAA wants to charge a fee to pay for the expansion.*	FAA: fee → fund exp
However, this fee would be unfair, as it would impose costs on all travelers to benefit only the few who utilize the new private planes.	*Change of direction! The author disagrees with the plan, claiming it's unfair. The author's reasoning: Everyone would have to pay the fee, but only a few people would benefit.* *Why wouldn't everyone benefit? If there's more space, then all the planes will be able to take off more quickly. The author is assuming the benefit is only for the people flying in small planes.*	BUT fee = unfair b/c all pay to benef few

Step 3: State the Goal

The airports are congested because there are so many small planes, and the FAA wants to charge a fee to expand the airports. The author claims that this is unfair because the fee would be paid by all but the expansion would only benefit a few.

I want to weaken the author's conclusion, so I need to find some reason why it really isn't unfair. One possibility: Maybe more people will benefit than just the small plane people.

Step 4: Work from Wrong to Right

(A) The existing national airport infrastructure benefits all air travelers.	*This sounds like what I was thinking before—everyone benefits, so why is it unfair for everyone to pay? Great; I'll leave it in.*	A ~
(B) The fee, if imposed, will have a negligible impact on the overall volume of air travel.	*A negligible impact means it won't really change anything. The fee won't change the volume of planes trying to fly…but that was never the plan. The plan was to raise money to expand the infrastructure—then they'll be able to handle more volume. This answer doesn't address the right thing.*	~~B~~
(C) The expansion would reduce the number of delayed flights resulting from small private planes congesting runways.	*Hmm. This is another potential benefit for everyone—a reduction in the number of flight delays. I'll leave this one in, too.*	C ~
(D) Travelers who use small private planes are almost uniformly wealthy or traveling on business.	*That's nice for them, but what does it have to do with this argument? Maybe you could say, "So they can afford to pay more," but that isn't the point of the argument. The point of the argument is that it's unfair to make the regular travelers pay for something that doesn't benefit them (according to the author).*	~~D~~
(E) A substantial fee would need to be imposed in order to pay for the expansion costs.	*So the fee would have to be pretty large. If anything, doesn't that make it even more unfair? Though, actually, I don't think it really addresses the fairness at all. Either it is fair, in which case the size of the fee doesn't matter, or it isn't fair…in which case the size of the fee still doesn't matter.*	~~E~~
Examine (A) and (C) again.	*Compare choices (A) and (C). Both say that this expansion would benefit everyone…wait a second. Choice (C) does explicitly mention the expansion, but (A) says the existing…infrastructure. Existing? Of course, the existing structure benefits everyone who uses it—the argument isn't about that. It's about whether the expansion would benefit everyone. Only choice (C) actually says that; I missed that the first time around.*	~~A~~ ~ Ⓒ

~~A~~   ~~B~~   Ⓒ   ~~D~~   ~~E~~

Right Answers

As discussed with Strengthen questions, for Weaken questions, look for an answer that has a logical connection to the conclusion, in this case one that makes the conclusion less likely to be true. You will often see new language and ideas in correct answers because one way to weaken an argument is to bring up an issue that the author did not discuss. For example, in the previous example, the author had not discussed flight delays in the original argument. Below are some common ways to weaken different argument types:

- **Causation:** Provide an alternate cause for the situation.
- **Plan:** Present an unexpected cost of the plan or reason the plan will not work as expected.
- **Prediction:** Discuss additional circumstances or future changes that might affect the prediction.
- **Profit:** Provide additional information about costs or revenues (often the one not discussed in the argument). Be careful about how the direction of a change relates to the conclusion (e.g., an answer that provides a reason that costs may increase weakens an argument that profits will increase).

An argument of each of type is provided below. For each argument, first identify the argument type. Second, find a way to weaken the argument in the manner described above.

1. This year's spring festival takes place next weekend. A large number of attendees at last year's festival have recently shared positive posts about the festival on social media. Also, the advertising budget for the festival is 50% higher than last year's budget. Therefore, attendance at this year's spring festival will exceed attendance at last year's festival.

2. Jitters Coffee Shop offers free Wi-Fi for use by its customers. The manager is concerned that the free Wi-Fi results in customers sitting at tables for extended periods, driving away new customers who cannot find a table. In order to increase sales, the manager plans to limit WiFi use to 30 minutes per session.

3. A teacher observed that students who consistently sat in the first three rows of the classroom scored an average of 12 points higher on the final exam than students who consistently sat in the last three rows. Thus, sitting in the front of the classroom causes enhanced retention of course material.

4. Workers at Tangerine Corporation receive overtime pay equal to one and a half times their normal hourly pay when they work more than 40 hours in a given week. Recently, Tangerine implemented a policy requiring approval from a manager for any employee to exceed the 40-hour threshold. By limiting overtime pay, this policy will increase profits for Tangerine.

Take a look at the suggested answers below. There are multiple ways to weaken any argument, so you may have thought of a different answer.

1. **Prediction.** This conclusion is a prediction about increased attendance at the festival. The premises in the argument only discuss publicity via both social media and advertising. You can weaken this argument by providing any other issue that might decrease attendance (bad weather, fewer attractions at this year's festival). For example, a major snowstorm is predicted for the weekend of the festival this year.

2. **Plan.** The manager provides a plan to increase sales: limit WiFi to 30 minutes so more customers can sit down. You can weaken this argument by providing reasons this plan might not increase sales or even decrease sales. For example, most customers who use the WiFi for over an hour make multiple purchases during their stay. If this were the case, the plan could actually lead to losing some sales.

12

3. **Causation.** The teacher has made an observation that two things occur together: sitting in the front and higher test scores. The conclusion introduces causation: Sitting in front causes enhanced retention of the course material. You can weaken this argument by providing another cause for the teacher's observation: either reverse causation or an outside cause for both factors. Reverse causation in this case would mean high test grades are causing students to sit in the front of the room. While that idea doesn't make complete sense, it might get you thinking about what types of students might choose to sit in the front. For example, students who report studying more hours per week tend to select seats in the front of the classroom.

4. **Profit** (also a Plan). The argument states that profits will increase, but the information provided only discusses potentially reducing costs through limiting overtime pay. You can weaken this plan by providing a reason that the plan may reduce revenues (or a reason it might not reduce costs). For example, most overtime work results in additional sales to new clients.

Common Trap Answers

Weaken questions contain the same kind of common trap answers that show up on Strengthen questions.

One of the trickiest types is the Reverse Logic trap: The question asks you to weaken, but a trap answer choice strengthens the argument instead. You will also again see the No Tie to the Argument traps—choices that might discuss something in a premise but don't affect the argument.

The most tempting wrong answer in the airport expansion problem, answer choice (A), is actually a No Tie trap. Almost everything in the choice was addressing the right thing, but one word made it wrong: *existing*. The conclusion was about the future infrastructure, after an expansion, so limiting the answer to the existing infrastructure meant that the information didn't affect the conclusion after all.

EXCEPT Questions

Assumption Family questions may also be presented in a "negative" form that is commonly referred to as EXCEPT questions.

A regular Weaken question might read:

> Which of the following, if true, most seriously weakens the conclusion?

A Weaken EXCEPT question might read:

> Each of the following, if true, weakens the conclusion EXCEPT:

What is the difference in wording between those two questions?

The first one indicates that one answer choice, and only one, weakens the argument. You want to pick that choice.

The second one indicates that four answer choices weaken the argument. These four are all wrong answers. What about the fifth answer—what does that one do?

Many people assume that the fifth one must do the opposite: strengthen the argument. *This is not necessarily true.* The fifth one certainly does not weaken the argument, but it may not strengthen the argument either. It might have no impact whatsoever on the argument.

12

For these negatively worded questions, use the "odd one out" strategy. Four of the answer choices will do the same thing; in the case of the example above, four answers will weaken the argument. The fifth choice, the correct one, will do something else. It doesn't matter whether the fifth one strengthens the argument or does nothing—all that matters is that it is the odd one out, the one that does *not* weaken. In order to keep track of the four similar answers versus the odd one out, label the choices as you assess them with an S for Strengthen, a W for Weaken, and an N for Neutral or "does Nothing."

Try this example:

> Supporters of a costly new Defense Advanced Research Projects Agency (DARPA) initiative assert that the project will benefit industrial companies as well as the military itself. In many instances, military research has resulted in technologies that have fueled corporate development and growth, and this pattern can be expected to continue.

Each of the following, if true, serves to weaken the argument above EXCEPT:

(A) The research initiative will occupy many talented scientists, many of whom would otherwise have worked for private corporations.

(B) In the past decade, DARPA has adopted an increasingly restrictive stance regarding the use of intellectual property resulting from its research.

(C) If the DARPA initiative hadn't been approved, much of the funding would instead have been directed toward tax breaks for various businesses.

(D) At any given time, DARPA is conducting a wide variety of costly research projects.

(E) The research initiative is focused on specific defense mechanisms that would be ineffective for private corporations.

Step 1: Identify the Question

Each of the following, if true, serves to weaken the argument above EXCEPT:	*The language* serves to weaken *indicates that this is a Weaken question. The word* EXCEPT *indicates that the four wrong answers will weaken, and I want to pick the "odd one out" answer.*	WEx A B C D E

Step 2: Deconstruct the Argument

Supporters of a costly new Defense Advanced Research Projects Agency (DARPA) initiative assert that the project will benefit industrial companies as well as the military itself.	*The supporters of DARPA think that this costly project will be good for companies and for the military.*	© Supporters: Costly proj will benef co's & mil
In many instances, military research has resulted in technologies that have fueled corporate development and growth, and this pattern can be expected to continue.	*Research has helped companies in the past, and the author claims this will keep happening in the future. That all supports the claim of the supporters: that the specific DARPA project will be beneficial for companies.*	Past: mil research → techs help co's, will cont

Step 3: State the Goal

In the past, military research has helped companies, and the claim is that this DARPA project will also help companies.

I want to find four answers that weaken the argument. The answer that doesn't weaken—the odd one out—is the correct answer.

Step 4: Work from Wrong to Right

(A) The research initiative will occupy many talented scientists, many of whom would otherwise have worked for private corporations.	*This benefits the military and specifically does not benefit the companies. That does weaken the idea that companies will benefit.*	~~A~~ W
(B) In the past decade, DARPA has adopted an increasingly restrictive stance regarding the use of intellectual property resulting from its research.	Hmm. Restrictive *makes it sound like DARPA doesn't let others use its research as much. If that's the case, then that would weaken the idea that companies will benefit. I'm not totally sure that's what this means though—the wording is tricky—so I'm going to give this a question mark and come back to it later.*	B W ?
(C) If the DARPA initiative hadn't been approved, much of the funding would instead have been directed toward tax breaks for various businesses.	*A tax break is a good thing. This choice is saying that the funding for the DARPA project would instead have been spent on tax breaks, which is a definite benefit. So not giving those tax breaks is a bad thing for the companies; this does weaken the argument.*	~~C~~ W
(D) At any given time, DARPA is conducting a wide variety of costly research projects.	*This choice talks about all research projects DARPA is conducting. Hmm. The argument makes a claim only about one specific project. Does this information make that claim more or less likely to be valid? I can't really see how it affects the argument's conclusion at all.*	D N
(E) The research initiative is focused on specific defense mechanisms that would be ineffective for private corporations.	*The key here is the language* ineffective for private corporations. *If the private companies can't make effective use of the results of this particular research, then that weakens the claim that the DARPA research will benefit companies.*	~~E~~ W
Examine (B) and (D) again.	*I need to compare answers (B) and (D). I thought (B) might weaken a little bit, and I thought (D) didn't do anything to the argument. Between those two, I should choose the one that doesn't weaken at all, so I'm going to choose choice (D).*	~~B~~ ⑩ W N

~~A~~   ~~B~~   ~~C~~   Ⓓ   ~~E~~

The biggest trap answer on an EXCEPT question is simply to forget halfway through that you're working on an EXCEPT question. If this happens, you might accidentally pick a Weaken answer or pick the answer that you think *most* weakens the argument. The *W* labels under your Weaken answers will help to remind you that multiple answers weaken, so that is not what you want to pick.

Strengthen the Argument Cheat Sheet

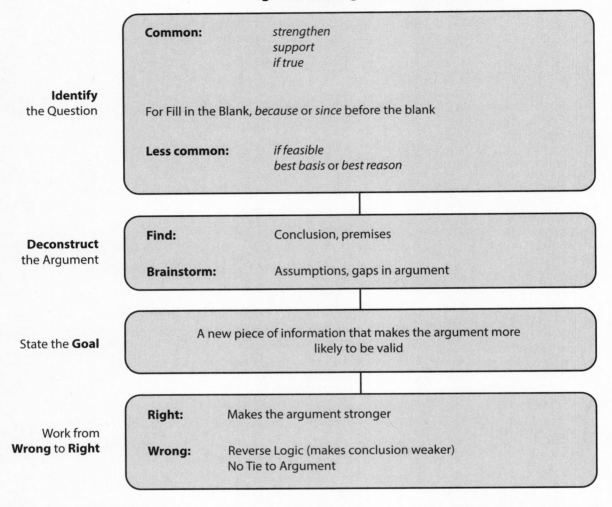

Strengthen the Argument Cheat Sheet

Identify the Question

Common:
strengthen
support
if true

For Fill in the Blank, *because* or *since* before the blank

Less common:
if feasible
best basis or *best reason*

Deconstruct the Argument

Find: Conclusion, premises

Brainstorm: Assumptions, gaps in argument

State the **Goal**

A new piece of information that makes the argument more likely to be valid

Work from **Wrong** to **Right**

Right: Makes the argument stronger

Wrong: Reverse Logic (makes conclusion weaker)
No Tie to Argument

Note: Fill in the Blank is almost always Strengthen, because the blank is usually preceded by *since* or *because*. When in doubt, assume that the question type is Strengthen.

Take a picture of this page and keep it with the review sheets you're creating as you study. Better yet, use this page as a guide to create your own review sheet—you'll remember the material better if you write it down yourself. Where appropriate, put it in your own words and you'll remember it even better.

Weaken the Argument Cheat Sheet

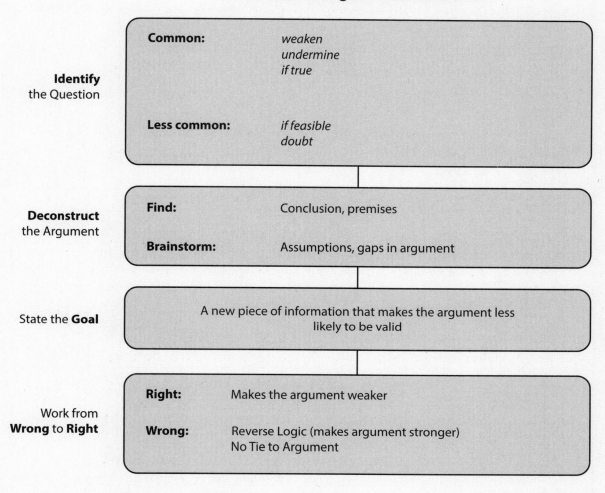

Weaken the Argument Cheat Sheet

Identify the Question	**Common:**	*weaken* *undermine* *if true*
	Less common:	*if feasible* *doubt*
Deconstruct the Argument	**Find:**	Conclusion, premises
	Brainstorm:	Assumptions, gaps in argument
State the **Goal**		A new piece of information that makes the argument less likely to be valid
Work from **Wrong** to **Right**	**Right:**	Makes the argument weaker
	Wrong:	Reverse Logic (makes argument stronger) No Tie to Argument

Take a picture of this page and keep it with the review sheets you're creating as you study. Better yet, use this page as a guide to create your own review sheet—you'll remember the material better if you write it down yourself. Where appropriate, put it in your own words and you'll remember it even better.

Problem Set

Answer each question using the 4-step Critical Reasoning process.

1. **Identify the question:** Is this a Strengthen the Argument question or a Weaken the Argument question?

2. **Deconstruct the argument:** Find the conclusion and map the argument on your paper.

3. **State the goal:** What will the right answer need to do?

4. **Work from wrong to right:** Eliminate four wrong answers. Watch out for common wrong answer types.

Before you check your answers, identify as many Reverse Logic wrong answers as you can in each problem. Every problem has at least one!

5. *Motor City*

   Which of the following best completes the passage below?

   A nonprofit organization in Motor City has proposed that local college students be given the option to buy half-price monthly passes for the city's public transportation system. The nonprofit claims that this plan will reduce air pollution in Motor City while increasing profits for the city's public transportation system. However, this plan is unlikely to meet its goals, since _____ .

   (A) most college students in Motor City view public transportation as unsafe

   (B) most college students in Motor City view public transportation as prohibitively expensive

   (C) college students typically do not have the 9-to-5 schedules of most workers, and can thus be expected to ride public transportation at times when there are plenty of empty seats

   (D) a bus produces more air pollution per mile than does a car

   (E) a large proportion of the college students in Motor City live off campus

6. *Smithtown Theater*

   The Smithtown Theater, which stages old plays, has announced an expansion that will double its capacity along with its operating costs. The theater is only slightly profitable at present. In addition, all of the current customers live in Smithtown, and the population of the town is not expected to increase in the next several years. Thus, the expansion of the Smithtown Theater will prove unprofitable.

   Which of the following, if true, would most seriously weaken the argument?

   (A) A large movie chain plans to open a new multiplex location in Smithtown later this year.

   (B) Concession sales in the Smithtown Theater comprise a substantial proportion of the theater's revenues.

   (C) Many recent arrivals to Smithtown are students who are less likely to attend the Smithtown Theater than are older residents.

   (D) The expansion would allow the Smithtown Theater to stage larger, more popular shows that will attract customers from neighboring towns.

   (E) The Board of the Smithtown Theater often solicits input from residents of the town when choosing which shows to stage.

7. *Books and Coffee*

    The owners of a book store and a nearby coffee shop have decided to combine their businesses. Both owners believe that this merger will increase the number of customers and therefore the gross revenue, because customers who come for one reason may also decide to purchase something else.

    Which of the following, if true, most weakens the owners' conclusion that a merger will increase revenue?

    (A) Books and drinks can both be considered impulse purchases; often, they are purchased by customers without forethought.

    (B) Profit margins at a coffee shop are generally significantly higher than profit margins at a book store.

    (C) People who are able to read the first chapter of a book before buying are more likely to decide to buy the book.

    (D) A large majority of the book store's current customer base already frequents the coffee shop.

    (E) A combination book store and coffee shop that opened in a neighboring city last year has already earned higher than expected profits.

8. *Teacher Compensation*

    Traditionally, public school instructors have been compensated according to seniority. Recently, education experts have criticized the system as one that rewards lackadaisical teaching and reduces motivation to excel. Instead, these experts argue that, to retain exceptional teachers and maintain quality instruction, teachers should receive salaries or bonuses based on performance rather than seniority.

    Which of the following, if true, most weakens the argument of the education experts?

    (A) Some teachers express that financial compensation is not the only factor contributing to job satisfaction and teaching performance.

    (B) School districts will develop their own unique compensation structures that may differ greatly from those of other school districts.

    (C) Upon leaving the teaching profession, many young, effective teachers cite a lack of opportunity for more rapid financial advancement as a primary factor in the decision to change careers.

    (D) In school districts that have implemented pay for performance compensation structures, standardized test scores have dramatically increased.

    (E) A merit-based system that bases compensation on teacher performance reduces collaboration, which is an integral component of quality instruction.

9. *Machu Picchu*

In 2001, the Peruvian government began requiring tourists to buy permits to hike the Inca Trail to the ancient city of Machu Picchu. Only 500 people per day are given permission to hike the Inca Trail, whereas before 2001 daily visitors numbered in the thousands. The Peruvian government claims that this permit program has successfully prevented deterioration of archaeological treasures along the Inca Trail.

Which of the following, if true, most strengthens the argument above?

(A) Since 2001, Incan ruins similar to Machu Picchu but without a visitor limit have disintegrated at a significantly greater rate than those on the Inca Trail.

(B) Villages near Machu Picchu have experienced declines in income, as fewer tourists buy fewer craft goods and refreshments.

(C) Many of the funds from the sale of Inca Trail permits are used to hire guards for archaeological sites without permit programs.

(D) Since 2001, tourist guides along the Inca Trail have received 50% to 100% increases in take-home pay.

(E) Due to limited enforcement, the majority of tourists hiking the Inca Trail currently do so without a permit.

10. *Digital Video Recorders*

Advertising Executive: More than 10 million households now own digital video recorders that can fast-forward over television commercials; approximately 75% of these households fast-forward over at least one commercial per 30-minute program. Because television commercials are not as widely watched as they used to be, they are much less cost-effective today.

Which of the following is required in order for the advertising executive to claim that television commercials are less cost-effective today?

(A) Product placement within television programs is a viable alternative to traditional television commercials.

(B) The television programs preferred by consumers without digital video recorders are similar to those preferred by consumers with the devices.

(C) Prior to the advent of digital video recorders, very few television viewers switched channels or left the room when commercials began.

(D) The cost-effectiveness of television advertising is based less upon how many people watch a particular commercial and more upon the appropriateness of the demographic.

(E) The amount that television channels charge for advertisers to air commercials on their channel has increased steadily over the last decade.

11. *APR*

CEO: Over the past several years, we have more than doubled our revenues, but profits have steadily declined because an increasing number of customers have failed to pay their balances. In order to compensate for these higher default rates, we will increase the interest charged on outstanding balances from an annual percentage rate (APR) of 9.5% to an APR of 12%. This increase will be sufficient to compensate for the current rate of defaults and allow us to increase our profits.

Which of the following statements, if true, would most seriously undermine a plan to increase interest rates in order to spur profitable growth?

(A) Many other companies have experienced a similar trend in their default rates.

(B) The company's operating expenses are above the industry average and can be substantially reduced, thus increasing margins.

(C) The increase in default rates was due to a rise in unemployment, but unemployment rates are expected to drop in the coming months.

(D) The proposed increase in the APR will, alone, more than double the company's profit margins.

(E) An increase in the APR charged on credit card balances often results in higher rates of default.

12. *Jupiter vs. Mars*

Scientists suspect that Europa, a moon orbiting Jupiter, may contain living organisms. However, the government recently scrapped an unmanned science mission to Europa and replaced it with a project aimed at landing an astronaut on Mars. Polls show that the public is far more fascinated by space travel than by discovering life elsewhere in the universe. Critics argue that the government's decision-making process places a greater emphasis on popularity than it does on the importance of scientific research.

Which of the following, if true, would most strengthen a contention by the government that the critics' accusation is incorrect?

(A) In the first year of the project, the government will spend 30% of its total budget on developing a space shuttle that can travel to Mars; that figure is expected to drop to 0% after five years.

(B) The government cannot be absolutely certain of the chances for success of either project.

(C) Some scientists are convinced that a mission to Europa would add immeasurably to our understanding of the universe.

(D) A new telescope that has just become available to scientists promises to yield more information than the planned mission to Europa was designed to provide.

(E) Most people feel that a shuttle to Mars would represent a first step toward an extensive program of space travel.

13. *Deep-Brain Stimulation*

Which of the following most logically completes the argument given below?

Deep-brain stimulation is a new technique for combating severe depression. In a recent experiment, electrodes were implanted into the brains of six patients who had not responded to any currently approved treatment for depression. When an electrical current to the electrodes was switched on, four of the patients reported feeling a dramatic reduction in depressive symptoms. The long-term prospects of the new treatment are not promising, however, because _____ .

(A) other treatments for depression may also be effective

(B) the other two patients reported only a slight reduction of depressive symptoms during the treatment

(C) deep-brain stimulation relies on the expertise of highly skilled physicians

(D) when the electrical current is interrupted, the effects of the treatment are reversed

(E) in a subsequent experiment, a one-hour treatment with the electrodes resulted in a sustained remission from depression in the four patients for six months

12

Solutions

1. Motor City: The correct answer is **(A)**. Remember to identify any Reverse Logic answers before you read the explanation!

Step 1: Identify the Question

Which of the following best completes the passage below?	*The blank at the end signals a Fill in the Blank format. The word* since *just before the blank indicates that this is a Strengthen question.*	S A B C D E

Step 2: Deconstruct the Argument

A nonprofit organization in Motor City has proposed that local college students be given the option to buy half-price monthly passes for the city's public transportation system.	*This is a fact—the organization has proposed this plan.*	Nonprof: give coll stud 1/2 off pub trans
The nonprofit claims that this plan will reduce air pollution in Motor City while increasing profits for the city's public transportation system.	*Okay, the nonprofit claims something. Is this the final conclusion? Keep reading.*	→ ↓ air poll, ↑ prof
However, this plan is unlikely to meet its goals, since _____.	*This is the conclusion. The author thinks the plan won't work. Why?*	Ⓒ BUT unlikely to work

Step 3: State the Goal

The author believes that the nonprofit's plan is not going to work, and I need to find a reason that supports this author's belief. The plan is to let college students buy public transportation passes for half price in order to reduce air pollution and increase profits. Which answer choice supports the idea that this plan will not *work?*

Step 4: Work from Wrong to Right

(A) most college students in Motor City view public transportation as unsafe	*If this is the case, then the students wouldn't want to use public transport at all, even if they were given a discount. That would make the plan unlikely to succeed. This might be it!*	A $\sim$
(B) most college students in Motor City view public transportation as prohibitively expensive	***Reverse logic.*** *Giving the students a discount is likely to make them use public transport more. This makes the plan more likely to succeed, not less likely.*	B̶
(C) college students typically do not have the 9-to-5 schedules of most workers, and can thus be expected to ride public transportation at times when there are plenty of empty seats	***Reverse logic.*** *If this were true, it'd be good news for the public transport's profits—the students would be filling what are currently empty seats.*	C̶
(D) a bus produces more air pollution per mile than does a car	*At first, this sounds good—if a bus produces more air pollution than a car, then using more buses would create more air pollution, which would hurt the plan. But the plan isn't to add more buses; it's to put more people on the already-running buses. Plus, one car won't be replaced with one bus! A bus might replace 10 or more cars.*	D̶
(E) a large proportion of the college students in Motor City live off campus	***Reverse logic.*** *This makes it likely that the students need some method of transportation to get to school—if they're using cars now and switch to buses, then the plan just might work.*	E̶

2. Smithtown Theater: The correct answer is **(D)**. Remember to identify any Reverse Logic answers before you read the explanation!

Step 1: Identify the Question

Which of the following, if true, would most seriously weaken the argument?	*The words* if true *and* weaken *indicate that this is a Weaken question.*	W A B C D E

Step 2: Deconstruct the Argument

The Smithtown Theater, which stages old plays, has announced an expansion that will double its capacity along with its operating costs.	*They have a plan. It's future, so it could be the conclusion, but I'm guessing there'll be more of a claim like "The theater will (or will not) be successful with its plan" or something like that.*	Theater: expand to ↑↑ cap & cost
The theater is only slightly profitable at present.	*This is a fact. I wonder: If the theater expands, will it get enough new business to continue covering costs?*	Now: barely prof
In addition, all of the current customers live in Smithtown, and the population of the town is not expected to increase in the next several years.	*The first half is a fact; the second half is a future prediction. So far, the case for the theater's new plan doesn't sound very good.*	Cust live in S, prob won't be more from S
Thus, the expansion of the Smithtown Theater will prove unprofitable.	*Okay, here's the conclusion. The author thinks the plan will fail and provides some pieces of evidence to support that claim.*	© Theater expansion unprof

Step 3: State the Goal

The theater has a plan to expand, but the author claims that the plan will fail. The author reasons that the theater is only barely profitable right now, and it doesn't seem like there are a lot more opportunities to get new customers.

I want something that will weaken the author's claim. I have to be careful here: I should weaken the idea that the plan will fail, not weaken the plan itself. The right answer will actually strengthen the plan and show that the expansion may work.

Step 4: Work from Wrong to Right

(A) A large movie chain plans to open a new multiplex location in Smithtown later this year.	***Reverse logic.*** *If anything, you'd have to say that the new movie theater would take business from the theater, which would strengthen the author's claim that the theater will fail.*	~~A~~
(B) Concession sales in the Smithtown Theater comprise a substantial proportion of the theater's revenues.	*How would this change if the theater expanded? That still depends upon whether they can get more people to come to the theater, so this doesn't really tell me anything new.*	~~B~~
(C) Many recent arrivals to Smithtown are students who are less likely to attend the Smithtown Theater than are older residents.	***Reverse logic.*** *The new people moving to town are people who aren't likely to start going to the theater. That strengthens the author's claim that ST's expansion is going to fail.*	~~C~~
(D) The expansion would allow the Smithtown Theater to stage larger, more popular shows that will attract patrons from neighboring towns.	*Hmm. This basically means that the expansion would attract a greater audience—that helps! If they have more people, they can fill the larger theater and make more money. This one is looking good as a weakener for the claim that the expansion will fail.*	D ∼
(E) The Board of the Smithtown Theater often solicits input from residents of the town when choosing which shows to stage.	*This is how they do things now. Would it stay the same or change when they expand? I have no idea.*	~~E~~

3. Books and Coffee: The correct answer is (D). Remember to identify any Reverse Logic answers before you read the explanation!

Step 1: Identify the Question

Which of the following, if true, most weakens the owners' conclusion that a merger will increase revenue?	*The words* if true *and* weakens *tell me that this is a Weaken question. Further, I now know the conclusion: Some merger will result in increased revenue.*	W A B C D E Ⓒ Merger → ↑ rev

Step 2: Deconstruct the Argument

The owners of a book store and a nearby coffee shop have decided to combine their businesses.	*This is a fact; they have already made this decision, although it sounds like they haven't actually merged yet.*	Book + coffee combining
Both owners believe that this merger will increase the number of customers and therefore the gross revenue,	*This is the same thing the Q stem said: The merger will increase revenue.*	Will → ↑ cust, rev
because customers who come for one reason may also decide to purchase something else.	*According to the owners, the individual customers of each store will end up buying both books and coffee, so there'll be more customers for both, which means more revenue for both.*	B/c cross-sell

Step 3: State the Goal

The owners think that merging will lead to increased revenue because it'll increase the number of customers and the customers will buy more stuff. This assumes that the same customers weren't already going to both stores and buying stuff.

This is a Weaken question, so I need to find something that will make the conclusion less likely to be valid. The right answer will show that revenue might not increase.

Step 4: Work from Wrong to Right

(A) Books and drinks can both be considered impulse purchases; often, they are purchased by customers without forethought.	***Reverse logic.*** *If people normally just buy coffee but see a book they like, maybe they'll be more likely to buy. That would strengthen the plan to merge, but I want to weaken the plan.*	~~A~~
(B) Profit margins at a coffee shop are generally significantly higher than profit margins at a book store.	*That might make the coffee shop owner not want to merge, but it doesn't address the revenue side of the equation at all—and the conclusion has to do with revenues, not profits.*	~~B~~
(C) People who are able to read the first chapter of a book before buying are more likely to decide to buy the book.	***Reverse logic.*** *This helps the owners' argument again! If I can sit there and read while having my coffee, then I'm more likely to buy the book, which would increase revenues.*	~~C~~
(D) A large majority of the book store's current customer base already frequents the coffee shop.	*Most of the people who shop at the book store also already go to the coffee shop. That's bad for the owners' plan—it means that they're not going to pick up as many new customers as I might have thought before.*	D $\sim$
(E) A combination book store and coffee shop that opened in a neighboring city last year has already earned higher than expected profits.	*Two problems here. One, the author's not talking about the same book store and coffee shop. Two, this choice talks about profits, not revenues.*	~~E~~

~~A~~   ~~B~~   ~~C~~   Ⓓ   ~~E~~

4. Teacher Compensation: The correct answer is (**E**). Remember to identify any Reverse Logic answers before you read the explanation!

Step 1: Identify the Question

Which of the following, if true, most weakens the argument of the educational experts?	*The language* if true *and weakens* tells *me this is a Weaken question. In addition, the question tells me that I need to look for a reference to* education experts *because whatever they claim is the conclusion.*	W A B C D E

Step 2: Deconstruct the Argument

Traditionally, public school instructors have been compensated according to seniority.	*Fact: Teachers have been getting paid based upon how long they've worked.*	Trad: Pub school teachers = $ by seniority
Recently, education experts have criticized the system as one that rewards lackadaisical teaching and reduces motivation to excel.	*Supposedly, paying teachers by seniority makes them less likely to work hard.*	Experts: ↓ motiv
Instead, these experts argue that, to retain exceptional teachers and maintain quality instruction, teachers should receive salaries or bonuses based on performance rather than seniority.	*The experts want to base compensation on performance, and they claim this will lead to better teachers and instruction. This is the conclusion.*	ⓒ Base comp on perform → keep great teachers

Step 3: State the Goal

Teachers normally get paid based on seniority, but these experts think that paying them based on performance will help teacher quality.

I need to find something that weakens this plan. The right answer should show that paying teachers based on performance won't get us better teachers.

12

Step 4: Work from Wrong to Right

(A) Some teachers express that financial compensation is not the only factor contributing to job satisfaction and teaching performance.	*This answer is going in the right direction. If financial compensation isn't the only factor, then maybe paying teachers based on performance won't make them perform better. But there are a few problems: First, this answer says it isn't the only factor. But if it isn't the only factor, that means compensation is still a factor! Plus, this is just about what some teachers say. Even if some teachers claim to disagree, they might not be right, and they might not represent the majority.*	~~A~~
(B) School districts will develop their own unique compensation structures that may differ greatly from those of other school districts.	*The argument isn't claiming that every school district has to be identical. It just makes a recommendation that compensation be tied to performance in general.*	~~B~~
(C) Upon leaving the teaching profession, many young, effective teachers cite a lack of opportunity for more rapid financial advancement as a primary factor in the decision to change careers.	***Reverse logic.*** *This shows that teachers do care about the financial side of things. So, paying effective teachers more will probably help schools hang on to them.*	~~C~~
(D) In school districts that have implemented pay for performance compensation structures, standardized test scores have dramatically increased.	***Reverse logic.*** *If paying for teacher performance helps the students, then the experts' plan is probably a good one.*	~~D~~
(E) A merit-based system that bases compensation on teacher performance reduces collaboration, which is an integral component of quality instruction.	*The experts' plan has a drawback: It reduces something that is considered an integral component of good teaching. If that's true, it could hurt the idea that basing compensation on performance will result in maintaining good instruction.*	E ~

5. Machu Picchu: The correct answer is **(A)**. Remember to identify any Reverse Logic answers before you read the explanation!

    Step 1: Identify the Question

Which of the following, if true, most strengthens the argument above?	*The words* if true *and* strengthens the argument *indicate that this is a Strengthen question.*	S A B C D E

    Step 2: Deconstruct the Argument

In 2001, the Peruvian government began requiring tourists to buy permits to hike the Inca Trail to the ancient city of Machu Picchu.	*This is a fact. People now have to pay to hike the Inca Trail.*	2001 Peru gov: req permits to hike Inca Trail
Only 500 people per day are given permission to hike the Inca Trail, whereas before 2001 daily visitors numbered in the thousands.	*More facts. Now, only 500 people a day are allowed; before, there were thousands a day.*	Now: 500/day (old = 1000's)
The Peruvian government claims that this permit program has successfully prevented deterioration of archaeological treasures along the Inca Trail.	*Here's the claim: The PG specifically says that the permit program is responsible for preventing deterioration along the trail.*	© Gov: permits → ↓ damage

    Step 3: State the Goal

    The Peruvian government claims that its permit program has been responsible for preventing deterioration along the Inca Trail. This is a cause-and-effect relationship. Since I need to strengthen the argument, the right answer should show that the permit program probably has reduced the damage.

Step 4: Work from Wrong to Right

(A) Since 2001, Incan ruins similar to Machu Picchu but without a visitor limit have disintegrated at a significantly greater rate than those on the Inca Trail.	*This sounds promising. The government's assumption was that the visitor limit helped prevent deterioration, so showing that other sites without limits did experience deterioration would make it more likely that the government's reasoning is valid. I'll definitely keep this one in.*	A ~
(B) Villages near Machu Picchu have experienced declines in income, as fewer tourists buy fewer craft goods and refreshments.	*This sounds bad for the villages, but it doesn't impact the specific claim about preventing deterioration along the trail.*	~~B~~
(C) Many of the funds from the sale of Inca Trail permits are used to hire guards for archaeological sites without permit programs.	*All this tells me is that* other *sites are better protected due to the guards. It doesn't tell me whether the program is protecting the Inca Trail itself.*	~~C~~
(D) Since 2001, tourist guides along the Inca Trail have received 50% to 100% increases in take-home pay.	*This doesn't tell me anything about the damage to the trail.*	~~D~~
(E) Due to limited enforcement, the majority of tourists hiking the Inca Trail currently do so without a permit.	***Reverse logic.*** *This one makes me think that even though only 500 people per day are allowed on the trail, the actual number is much higher. So, the permit program probably isn't working very well.*	~~E~~

6. Digital Video Recorders: The correct answer is (**C**).

Did this one seem a little different from all of the others? We set a trap for you! This is a Find the Assumption question, not a Strengthen or a Weaken. We discussed Find the Assumption questions in the previous chapter (though we used a less common variant for the question wording, just to see whether you were paying attention). We did warn you at the beginning of this chapter to read the previous chapter first!

On the real test, you'll never have the luxury of knowing that the next question will be a certain type. Be prepared for *anything*.

Step 1: Identify the Question

Which of the following is required in order for the advertising executive to claim that television commercials are less cost-effective today?	*The words* required in order to claim *indicate that this is a Find the Assumption question.*	FA A B C D E

Step 2: Deconstruct the Argument

Advertising Executive: More than 10 million households now own digital video recorders that can fast-forward over television commercials;	*This is just a fact.*	Exec: 10 mill + HH's = DVR
approximately 75% of these house-holds fast-forward over at least one commercial per 30-minute program.	*Another fact. I don't think I need to write down the exact numerical details right now, but I'll note that there are numerical details with a # just to remind myself.*	75% skip ads (#)
Because television commercials are not as widely watched as they used to be, they are much less cost-effective today.	*This contains another premise and the conclusion. The premise: TV ads aren't as widely watched today. The conclusion: TV ads are much less cost-effective than they used to be.*	B/c ads now watched less, ads = less cost eff

Step 3: State the Goal

Okay, the advertising executive claims that TV ads are not as cost-effective specifically because people aren't watching them as much, and that is specifically because a lot of people fast-forward over at least some commercials. I want an answer that the author must believe to be true in order to draw that conclusion. What assumptions are being made?

Let's see. They're assuming that people really did watch TV commercials more before, instead of changing channels or something. They're also assuming that if fewer people are watching, that's actually hurting the cost-effectiveness. Maybe commercials are worth more per viewer these days?

Step 4: Work from Wrong to Right

(A) Product placement within television programs is a viable alternative to traditional television commercials.	*That's nice for the advertisers who want to make money, but this doesn't have to be true in order to claim that TV commercials are less cost-effective now.*	~~A~~
(B) The television programs preferred by consumers without digital video recorders are similar to those preferred by consumers with the devices.	*The DVR thing was used as evidence to show how some people are skipping commercials. I don't think making a distinction about people with or without the DVRs really tells us anything. The conclusion is about commercials, not what programs people watch.*	~~B~~
(C) Prior to the advent of digital video recorders, very few television viewers switched channels or left the room when commercials began.	*That's interesting. People didn't used to change channels or leave the room, so maybe they really were watching more TV commercials. If I negate this answer, then it would say that people did switch channels or leave the room. If that were the case, then it'd be tough to claim that people watch fewer commercials nowadays. This choice looks good.*	C ~
(D) The cost-effectiveness of television advertising is based less upon how many people watch a particular commercial and more upon the appropriateness of the demographic.	*Hmm. They're saying that cost-effectiveness isn't measured based on how many people watch the commercials. That actually hurts the argument! If viewing doesn't matter for cost-effectiveness, then cost-effectiveness probably isn't going down. An assumption will never hurt the argument, so I can eliminate this.*	~~D~~
(E) The amount that television channels charge for advertisers to air commercials on their channel has increased steadily over the last decade.	*This definitely helps the argument, since it makes it seem like the commercials are less cost-effective now. But it isn't an assumption, because it doesn't have to be true for the argument to make sense. It would be helpful if it was true, but it's not a big deal if it isn't.*	~~E~~

~~A~~   ~~B~~   Ⓒ   ~~D~~   ~~E~~

7. APR: The correct answer is (**E**). Remember to identify any Reverse Logic answers before you read the explanation!

Step 1: Identify the Question

Which of the following statements, if true, would most seriously undermine a plan to increase interest rates in order to spur profitable growth?	*The* undermine *and if true* language *indicates that this is a Weaken question. Further, the question stem tells me the conclusion: There's a plan to increase interest rates that will supposedly cause profits to grow.*	W A B C D E Ⓒ Plan: ↑ int rats → ↑ prof growth

Step 2: Deconstruct the Argument

CEO: Over the past several years, we have more than doubled our revenues, but profits have steadily declined because an increasing number of customers have failed to pay their balances.	*Several facts here. Revenues have gone up but profits have gone down because the customers aren't paying what they owe.*	CEO: 2x rev but ↓ prof b/c cust not pay bills
In order to compensate for these higher default rates, we will increase the interest charged on outstanding balances from an annual percentage rate (APR) of 9.5% to an APR of 12%.	*Okay, here's the plan. They'll charge more interest to everyone to compensate for the people who aren't paying their bills.*	↑ % int rate to comp
This increase will be sufficient to compensate for the current rate of defaults and allow us to increase our profits.	*Hmm. They're claiming that 12% will be enough to compensate for the* current *rate of people who don't pay so that they can increase profits (which is the conclusion I already wrote down). They're assuming that the current rate isn't going to get worse in the future.*	12% will be enough

Step 3: State the Goal

The company plans to charge higher interest rates in order to become profitable again. This is a Weaken question, so the right answer should show that this might not actually help profits.

Step 4: Work from Wrong to Right

(A) Many other companies have experienced a similar trend in their default rates.	*This doesn't address the company's plan to fix the problem: increasing the interest rate. This doesn't impact the conclusion at all.*	~~A~~
(B) The company's operating expenses are above the industry average and can be substantially reduced, thus increasing margins.	*If the company does this, it could increase profits, which is the company's goal... but the conclusion is that the plan to increase interest rates will improve profits. The right answer needs to weaken that specific plan, not the company's goal in general.*	~~B~~
(C) The increase in default rates was due to a rise in unemployment, but unemployment rates are expected to drop in the coming months.	**Reverse logic.** *If unemployment caused people not to pay their bills, and fewer people are going to be unemployed, then maybe more will pay their bills? That would help the company, but I want something that will weaken the conclusion. This isn't even a great strengthener, since it doesn't talk about the actual plan in the argument.*	~~C~~
(D) The proposed increase in the APR will, alone, more than double the company's profit margins.	**Reverse logic.** *This supports the company's claim that increasing the interest rate will help raise profits. I want something that weakens that claim.*	~~D~~
(E) An increase in the APR charged on credit card balances often results in higher rates of default.	*Okay, if they do increase the APR, then more people may stop paying their bills as a result! The conclusion specifically said that raising the APR would compensate for the current rate of defaults, so if the rate goes up, then the company is less likely to increase its profits. This does weaken the conclusion.*	E ~

12

8. Jupiter vs. Mars: The correct answer is (**D**). Remember to identify any Reverse Logic answers before you read the explanation!

Step 1: Identify the Question

Which of the following, if true, would most strengthen a contention by the government that the critics' accusation is incorrect?	*The words* if true *and* strengthen a contention *indicate that this is a Strengthen question. The conclusion is also in the question stem: that the critics are wrong.*	S A B C D E ⓒ Gov: critics wrong

Step 2: Deconstruct the Argument

Scientists suspect that Europa, a moon orbiting Jupiter, may contain living organisms.	*There is a fact: Scientists suspect something is true. I don't actually know whether it's true, though.*	Sci: Europa may have life
However, the government recently scrapped an unmanned science mission to Europa and replaced it with a project aimed at landing an astronaut on Mars.	*There was a project to send an unmanned mission to Europa, but that was replaced by another project to send a person to Mars. More facts.*	BUT gov replaced w/Mars proj
Polls show that the public is far more fascinated by space travel than by discovering life elsewhere in the universe.	*More facts—a survey showed that people like space travel more.*	Ppl like space travel more
Critics argue that the government's decision-making process places a greater emphasis on popularity than it does on the importance of scientific research.	*This is a counterconclusion. The critics say that the government is just paying attention to popularity of projects, but the question stem told me that the government claims that the new project is a better use of funds.*	Critics: gov cares more ab popularity

Step 3: State the goal.

There are two opposing points of view, the government and the critics. The government claims that the critics are wrong. So, the government is claiming that it doesn't actually care more about popularity than about science. I need to strengthen that claim by showing that the government actually does care about science. I should be really careful not to strengthen the critics' claim, which is that the government cares more about popularity!

Step 4: Work from wrong to right.

(A) In the first year of the project, the government will spend 30% of its total budget on developing a space shuttle that can travel to Mars; that figure is expected to drop to 0% after five years.	*This doesn't give me any additional information as to why the Mars project is better than the Europa project. I don't know whether they'd be spending more or less on the Europa project, nor do I know what kind of good research they'll expect to get in return.*	A̶
(B) The government cannot be absolutely certain of the chances for success of either project.	*Was there anything in the argument that hinged on being absolutely certain of success? No. If they told me that the Mars project has a greater chance for success, that would be good—but knowing that, I don't know the chances for either project... that doesn't add anything.*	B̶
(C) Some scientists are convinced that a mission to Europa would add immeasurably to our understanding of the universe.	**Reverse logic.** *This one tells me that the Europa mission is important for science. But, the government didn't fund it! That makes it more likely that the government only cares about popularity. So, this strengthens the critics' argument, not the government's.*	C̶
(D) A new telescope that has just become available to scientists promises to yield more information than the planned mission to Europa was designed to provide.	*Now they have a new telescope that they can use to get even more research than they would have if they sent an unmanned mission? It looks like the government canceled the Europa mission because it wasn't the best choice for science, not because it was less popular! Maybe the government really does care about science.*	D ~
(E) Most people feel that a shuttle to Mars would represent a first step towards an extensive program of space travel.	*This explains why people find the shuttle to Mars interesting, but it doesn't actually tell me anything new about the government's decision. It still looks like the government picked this program because it was popular with many people, regardless of the reason that it was popular.*	E̶

9. Deep-Brain Stimulation: The correct answer is **(D)**. Remember to identify any Reverse Logic answers before you read the explanation!

Step 1: Identify the Question

Which of the following most logically completes the argument given below?	*The blank at the end signals a Fill in the Blank format. The word* because *just before the blank indicates that this is a Strengthen question.*	S A B C D E

Step 2: Deconstruct the Argument

Deep-brain stimulation is a new technique for combating severe depression.	*Straight fact.*	Deep-brain stim combats depression
In a recent experiment, electrodes were implanted into the brains of six patients who had not responded to any currently approved treatment for depression.	*This tells me how it works and that they tested it on six people.*	Tested on 6 ppl
When an electrical current to the electrodes was switched on, four of the patients reported feeling a dramatic reduction in depressive symptoms.	*And four of the people got a lot better.*	4 better
The long-term prospects of the new treatment are not promising, however, because _____.	*Oh, but the author thinks the treatment's not really going to work long-term. Why?*	© BUT probably won't work, b/c...

Step 3: State the Goal

The author describes a new medical treatment but says it's probably not going to be good long-term; I need to find a reason why. The right answer should say something negative about the treatment's long-term prospects.

Step 4: Work from Wrong to Right

(A) other treatments for depression may also be effective	*Talking about other treatments doesn't explain why deep-brain stimulation won't be a good treatment long-term. The conclusion is only about deep-brain stimulation, not about depression treatment in general.*	A̶
(B) the other two patients reported only a slight reduction of depressive symptoms during the treatment	*This looks like a negative at first glance, but then I remembered that the first four patients were helped dramatically. Technically, the treatment helped every patient! That doesn't hurt the treatment's prospects.*	B̶
(C) deep-brain stimulation relies on the expertise of highly skilled physicians	*This is probably true, but the right answer needs to be a downside of the treatment. Is relying on the expertise of physicians a downside? Possibly, but it's a real stretch. I'd have to assume that requiring skilled physicians has other consequences, like increasing the cost—and I don't know that.*	C̶
(D) when the electrical current is interrupted, the effects of the treatment are reversed	*When the current is on, the symptoms go away, but when the current is off, the depression comes back. That means they'd have to be connected to some machine all the time—they couldn't just get a treatment once a week or once a month. That definitely makes the treatment less practical and promising. Unless choice (E) is better, this looks like the answer.*	D∼
(E) in a subsequent experiment, a one-hour treatment with the electrodes resulted in a sustained remission from depression in the four patients for six months	***Reverse logic.*** *This is almost the opposite of choice (D). If you get a one-hour treatment, then the symptoms go away for 6 months— that's great for deep-brain stimulation! This can't be the right answer.*	E̶

The Assumption Family: Evaluate the Argument and Find the Flaw

In This Chapter...

In this chapter, you will learn how to apply your knowledge of Strengthen and Weaken questions to the fourth type of Assumption question: Evaluate.

You will also learn how to address the final (and not very common) Assumption question type: Flaw.

CHAPTER 13 The Assumption Family: Evaluate the Argument and Find the Flaw

In the previous two chapters, you learned about the three major question types in the Assumption Family: Find the Assumption, Strengthen, and Weaken. If you haven't read those chapters yet, please do so before reading this chapter.

In addition, think about how much time you want to put into this chapter. **Evaluate the Argument** questions are somewhat uncommon—you'll most likely see just one or two. **Find the Flaw** questions are even rarer. If you have a very high Verbal goal (90th percentile or higher), then study these two question types. If your Verbal score goal is lower, consider guessing on Flaw questions. If you struggle with Evaluate questions, you might want to guess on those as well.

The Assumption lessons you learned earlier still apply to Evaluate and Flaw questions:

- Assumptions are something an author must believe to be true in order to draw his or her conclusion. These assumptions are not stated explicitly in the argument.

- All assumption arguments will contain a core: a conclusion and the major premise or premises that lead to it.

- All assumption arguments will include at least one (and probably more than one) unstated assumption.

Evaluate the Argument Questions

For Evaluate questions, your first step is still to find an assumption, but you have to do a little more work to get to the answer. At heart, you are asked what additional information would help to determine whether the assumption is valid or invalid.

Most Evaluate question stems will contain one or more of the following:

- The word *evaluate* or a synonym
- The word *determine* or a synonym
- Language asking what would be *useful to know* (or *establish*) or *important to know*

For example, an Evaluate question stem might ask:

> Which of the following must be studied in order to evaluate the argument?

> Which of the following would it be most useful to know in determining whether the mayor's plan is likely to be successful?

Occasionally, an Evaluate question will use other wording, but the question will still get at the same overall idea—what information would help to evaluate the given argument? That information, if made available, would either strengthen or weaken that argument.

The Strengthen/Weaken Strategy

13

Evaluate answer choices will often be in the form of a question or in the form of a "one way or the other" statement. Imagine you have to take a stand on whether you agree with the conclusion of the argument: What question would you ask the author to help your decision? For example, say you're asked to evaluate this argument:

> In order to increase its profits, MillCo plans to reduce costs by laying off any nonessential employees.

Hmm. According to the argument:

> MillCo will lay off nonessential employees → reduce costs → increase profits

Does that sound like a good plan? What additional information would help you evaluate this plan?

Profits are equal to revenues minus costs. The argument says costs will go down, but no information is given about revenues. It seems pretty important to have some information about revenues to draw a conclusion about profits. One question might be: How will revenues be affected by this plan?

The question associated with the argument and the correct answer might read:

> Which of the following would be most important to determine to evaluate the argument?

> Whether revenues will be affected adversely enough to threaten MillCo's profit structure

This *whether* does something very interesting to the argument. Imagine that you could find out whether revenues will be affected adversely. The argument would be strengthened one way and weakened the other. Take a look:

> Yes, the plan *will* affect MillCo's revenues adversely enough to threaten profits. In this case, the plan to increase profits is less likely to work, so the argument is weakened.

> No, the plan *won't* affect MillCo's revenues adversely enough to threaten profits. In this case, the plan to increase profits is a little more likely to work, so the argument is strengthened.

If the answer goes one way, the argument is strengthened, and if it goes the other way, the argument is weakened.

The correct answer will be structured in such a way that these two possible "paths" exist, one strengthening and one weakening the argument.

The incorrect answers will be presented in a similar format, but won't actually test the strength of the argument. What if you had the following answer choice?

> Whether MillCo might reduce its costs more by eliminating some health insurance benefits for the remaining employees

Evaluate the two paths:

> Yes, MillCo can reduce costs more by eliminating some health benefits. How will this affect the given plan to lay off employees? Technically, this doesn't impact whether laying off certain employees will improve profits. It is true that reducing costs could help to increase profits, but the argument specifies that MillCo will reduce costs specifically by laying off nonessential employees. Whether the company could also reduce costs in some other way has no bearing on this specific argument.

> No, MillCo cannot reduce costs more by eliminating some health benefits. This certainly doesn't strengthen the argument. It doesn't weaken the argument either, though, since the argument hinges on laying off employees. This path does nothing to the argument.

This incorrect answer choice is trying to distract you by offering a different way to increase profits, but you aren't asked to find alternative ways to increase profits. You're asked to evaluate whether the *existing argument* involving this particular path to profits is valid. The answer doesn't provide a strengthen/weaken pair here, so the choice cannot be the right answer.

On Evaluate questions, after reading the question, you're going to focus on the argument:

First, find the core (conclusion plus major premises).

Second, briefly think about the questions you have or additional information you would want in order to evaluate the conclusion.

As you move to the answer choices, look for an answer similar to the questions you identified. Make sure to be flexible because the correct answer may not be something you identified. The correct answer should offer two different paths: one that would make the argument stronger and one that would make the argument weaker.

Try a full example; set your timer for 2 minutes. If you get stuck, pick an answer before you read the explanation. During the real test, you'll have to pick an answer in order to move on, so practice letting go and guessing.

> Food allergies account for more than 30,000 emergency room visits each year. Often, victims of these episodes are completely unaware of their allergies until they experience a major reaction. Studies show that 90% of food allergy reactions are caused by only eight distinct foods. For this reason, parents should feed a minuscule portion of each of these foods to their children to determine whether the children have these particular food allergies.

> Which of the following must be studied in order to evaluate the recommendation made in the argument?

> (A) The percentage of allergy victims who were not aware of the allergy before a major episode

> (B) The percentage of the population that is at risk for allergic reactions

> (C) Whether some of the eight foods are common ingredients used in cooking

> (D) Whether an allergy to one type of food makes someone more likely to be allergic to other types of food

> (E) Whether ingesting a very small amount of an allergen is sufficient to provoke an allergic reaction in a susceptible individual

13

Step 1: Identify the Question

Which of the following must be studied in order to evaluate the recommendation made in the argument?	*The words* must be studied *and* evaluate *indicate that this is an Evaluate question.*	Ev A B C D E

Step 2: Deconstruct the Argument

Food allergies account for more than 30,000 emergency room visits each year.	*This is a fact.*	Food allerg → 30k ER/yr
Often, victims of these episodes are completely unaware of their allergies until they experience a major reaction.	*Fact, but more fuzzy. A lot of people don't know they're allergic till they have a major reaction.*	Ppl unaware till have rxn
Studies show that 90% of food allergy reactions are caused by only eight distinct foods.	*More facts! That's interesting. Only eight foods cause most allergic reactions.*	Only 8 foods → 90% rxn
For this reason, parents should feed a minuscule portion of each of these foods to their children to determine whether the children have these particular food allergies.	*This is the conclusion. The author's saying parents should give a tiny bit of these eight foods to see what happens.*	© Give child tiny bit of 8 foods to test

Step 3: State the Goal

This is an Evaluate question, so I need to find an answer that will help to determine whether or not the conclusion is likely to be valid. The correct answer will have two paths: one path will make the conclusion a little more likely to be valid and the other will make the conclusion a little less likely to be valid.

In this case, the author recommends that we all try tiny bits of these eight foods to see whether we're allergic. What will help determine if this is a good idea? Could these tests actually cause harm if children have severe reactions to the sample amounts? Will these tests actually work? How much do you need to eat to cause an allergic reaction (are the minuscule bits enough)?

Step 4: Work from Wrong to Right

(A) The percentage of allergy victims who were not aware of the allergy before a major episode	*The argument said that victims* often *aren't aware of the allergy beforehand. If I knew that 90% weren't aware, that would go along with what the argument already says. If I knew that 50% weren't aware...hmm, that wouldn't change the argument. In general, knowing the exact percentage doesn't change anything.*	~~A~~

13

(B) The percentage of the population that is at risk for allergic reactions	*If a really high percentage is at risk for allergies, then it's probably important to figure out whether people are allergic…but that doesn't mean that the specific recommendation in the conclusion here is a good one or bad one. Also, this answer choice doesn't specifically limit itself to food allergies; it mentions all allergies in general.*	~~B~~
(C) Whether some of the eight foods are common ingredients used in cooking	*If yes, then many people may have already tried small amounts of these foods. That doesn't actually tell me, though, whether the recommendation is a good one. If no, then it doesn't affect the conclusion at all—I still don't know whether it's a good recommendation.*	~~C~~
(D) Whether an allergy to one type of food makes someone more likely to be allergic to other types of food	*If yes or if no, I'd still want to test people to see whether they're allergic to anything. This choice doesn't have two paths that lead to alternate outcomes.*	~~D~~
(E) Whether ingesting a very small amount of an allergen is sufficient to provoke an allergic reaction in a susceptible individual	*If yes, then the author's plan will work: Children will be able to try small amounts and determine whether they're allergic. If no, then the author's plan is not a good one: Trying small amounts won't actually help you tell whether a child is allergic.*	E ~

~~A~~   ~~B~~   ~~C~~   ~~D~~   Ⓔ

In the prior example, the student brainstormed multiple relevant questions in step 3, and one was available as an answer choice. Make sure not to get hung up on the specific questions you thought of when working through the answers; most arguments have multiple relevant questions and only one will be in the answer choices. (Also: You won't always be so lucky as to brainstorm the question that actually does appear in the answers!)

Correct Answers

The correct answer will be information important to determining if the conclusion is valid. You don't get follow-up questions on the GMAT. The answer to the question in the correct answer choice must help you evaluate the conclusion on its own without any additional information or clarification. One answer to the question posed in the correct answer will clearly strengthen the argument and the other will clearly weaken it.

Common Trap Answers

The incorrect answers are very tricky. How do the test writers get you to pick trap answers on Evaluate questions?

No Effect on the Conclusion

Answer (C) presented something that seemed like it would matter: Maybe lots of people have already tried the eight foods. What does that mean for the recommendation? Maybe some people have already had reactions to some foods. But some people might have tried only six of the eight, so maybe they should still try the other two. Or, maybe…You could speculate endlessly, but all paths lead to the same place: This choice doesn't impact whether the specific recommendation made is good or bad.

The correct answer should *clearly strengthen* the conclusion if it goes one way and *clearly weaken* if it goes the other. Be careful of answers that only *might strengthen* or *might weaken* or *might do nothing*, especially if you need additional information to make the determination.

Irrelevant Distinction or Comparison

You saw this trap for the first time in the Find the Assumption chapter. In the problem above, answer (D) does discuss something mentioned by the argument—allergies—but tries to talk about whether someone might have more than one allergy; this is not at issue in the argument. The argument only distinguishes those with allergies and those without.

Find the Flaw Questions

Find the Flaw questions are the least common of the five Assumption Family question types. The question stems will almost always contain some form of the word *flaw*, but be careful: Weaken the Argument questions also might contain the word *flaw* in the question stem.

Here's how to tell the difference. Weaken questions will also contain *if true* language. Flaw questions will *not* contain this language. Take a look at the chart below:

Flaw	Weaken
Look for this first:	
Contains the word *flaw* but NOT *if true* language.	Contains the word *flaw* AND the words *if true* (or an equivalent synonym).
If you're still not sure, try this:	
Answer choices are a bit more abstract, similar to but not as abstract as Structure Family questions.	Answer choices represent a new piece of information (as described in the discussion of the Weaken question type).
Example:	
Which of the following indicates a *flaw* in the reasoning above?	Which of the following, *if true*, would indicate a *flaw* in the teacher's plan?

On occasion, a Flaw question may contain a synonym of the word *flaw*, such as *vulnerable to criticism*.

As with the other Assumption Family questions, Find the Flaw questions will contain an argument core, and it's great if you notice assumptions that the author makes. The correct answer, though, will be essentially the opposite of the correct answer on a Find the Assumption question. On Find the Assumption, you pick an answer that articulates an assumption that is necessary to the argument. On Flaw questions, by contrast, you are looking for wording that indicates why it is *flawed* thinking to believe that this assumption is true.

For example:

> Pierre was recovering from the flu when he visited Shelley last week, and now Shelley is showing signs of the flu. If Pierre had waited until he was no longer contagious, Shelley would not have become ill.

The author is assuming that Pierre was definitely the one to infect Shelley. The author is also assuming that there is no other way Shelley could have gotten sick. Perhaps it is flu season, and many people with whom Shelley came in contact had the flu!

The correct answer might be something like:

> The author fails to consider that there are alternate paths by which Shelley could have become infected.

Contrast that language with the assumption itself: The author assumes that only Pierre could have infected Shelley. If that's true, then that piece of information at least partially fixes the author's argument. When you take the same information, though, and flip it around into a flaw, you harm the author's argument:

Pierre was recovering from the flu when he visited Shelley last week, and now Shelley is showing signs of the flu. If Pierre had waited until he was no longer contagious, Shelley would not have become ill.	
Assumption	*Flaw*
Only Pierre could have infected Shelley.	The author fails to consider that there are alternate paths by which Shelley could have become infected.
The argument is made stronger.	*The argument is made weaker.*

In sum, think of Flaw questions as the "reverse" of Assumption questions. The answer still hinges on an assumption, but the correct answer will word that assumption in a way that hurts the argument.

In addition, the answer choice language may be a bit more abstract than the answer choices on other Assumption Family questions. Often, the answer choices will talk about what the author "fails to consider (or establish)," "does not specify (or identify)," or something along those lines.

Try this full example:

> Environmentalist: Bando Inc.'s manufacturing process releases pollution into the atmosphere. In order to convince the company to change processes, we will organize a boycott of the product that represents its highest sales volume, light bulbs. Because Bando sells more light bulbs than any other product, a boycott of light bulbs will cause the most damage to the company's profits.
>
> The environmentalist's reasoning is flawed because it fails to
>
> (A) allow for the possibility that Bando may not want to change its manufacturing process
> (B) supply information about other possible ways for Bando to reduce pollution
> (C) consider that the relative sales volumes of a company's products are not necessarily proportional to profits
> (D) identify any alternate methods by which to convince Bando to change its manufacturing process
> (E) consider that a boycott may take too long to achieve its purpose

Step 1: Identify the Question

The environmentalist's reasoning is flawed because it fails to	*The word* flawed *indicates that this is either a Flaw or a Weaken question. If* true *does not appear, so this is a Flaw question. I'll write down "Fl" on my scrap paper.*	Fl A B C D E

13

Step 2: Deconstruct the Argument

Environmentalist: Bando Inc.'s manufacturing process releases pollution into the atmosphere.	*This is a fact (assume the environmentalist is telling the truth).*	Environ-ist: manuf → atmo pollutn
In order to convince the company to change processes, we will organize a boycott of the product that represents its highest sales volume, light bulbs.	*Okay, here's a plan, so it's likely a conclusion. They think if they boycott something, this company might change its manufacturing process. So they're going to boycott light bulbs because Bando sells more light bulbs than anything else.*	boyc bulbs (↑ sales) → so company Δ manuf
Because Bando sells more light bulbs than any other product, a boycott of light bulbs will cause the most damage to the company's profits.	*Another claim. Because they sell more light bulbs than anything else, the environmentalist figures that a boycott of light bulbs will do the most damage to profits. Profits? How profitable are the light bulbs?* *Okay, the conclusion was the previous sentence, because all of this is designed to convince Bando to change its manufacturing process.*	Bando sells ↑ bulbs → boyc → ↑ damage to prof

Step 3: State the Goal

The environmentalist doesn't like that Bando pollutes. Bando sells more light bulbs than any other product, so the environmentalist wants to boycott those bulbs to do the most damage to Bando's profits (according to this environmentalist, anyway), and then the hope is that this will all cause the company to change its manufacturing process.

I need to find an answer that will articulate a flaw in that reasoning. I've already thought of one. The environmentalist is assuming that just because Bando sells more light bulbs than anything else, the company is also earning the most profits from those products. But there's no evidence to support that. Also, consumers might not actually agree to boycott Bando.

Step 4: Work from Wrong to Right

(A) allow for the possibility that Bando may not want to change its manufacturing process	*If anything, it could be argued that the environmentalist is already assuming the company will not want to change. That's why the environmentalist is trying to organize a boycott—to get the company to change!*	~~A~~
(B) does not supply information about other possible ways for Bando to reduce pollution	*In the real world, I agree that environmentalists should explore all possible ways . . . but the question asks me to find a flaw in this particular plan about the boycott. This doesn't apply to that plan.*	~~B~~

(C) consider that the relative sales volumes of a company's products are not necessarily proportional to profits	*This sounds kind of like what I said before. It's a little abstract, so I'm not sure I fully understand all of it, but it does say that sales aren't necessarily proportional to profits. I'll keep this one in.*	C ~
(D) identify any alternative methods by which to convince Bando to change its manufacturing process	*This is like choice (B). It'd be good in general for the environmentalist to do this…but this doesn't help me figure out a flaw in the boycott plan specifically.*	~~D~~
(E) consider that a boycott may take too long to achieve its purpose	*I think what really matters is whether the plan is going to work at all, not how long it takes. The argument doesn't have any requirements about how long it will take to get Bando to change its process.*	~~E~~

~~A~~   ~~B~~   Ⓒ   ~~D~~   ~~E~~

Common Trap Answers

Irrelevant Distinction or Comparison

This type of trap discusses alternative plans or paths when you were asked to comment on the given plan, similar to answers (B) and (D) in the example above. A choice can also bring up a detail or distinction that does not actually affect the argument, similar to choice (E) in the problem above.

Flaw questions may also occasionally use Reverse Logic, similar to answer choice (A) in the example above.

Evaluate the Argument Cheat Sheet

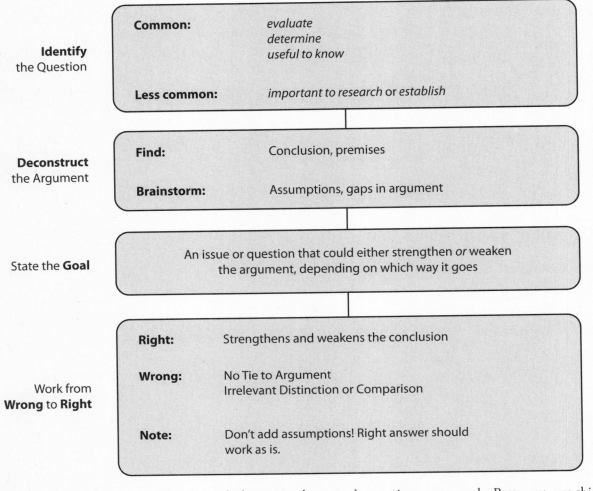

Evaluate the Argument Cheat Sheet

Identify the Question	**Common:**	*evaluate* *determine* *useful to know*
	Less common:	*important to research* or *establish*

Deconstruct the Argument	**Find:**	Conclusion, premises
	Brainstorm:	Assumptions, gaps in argument

State the **Goal**	An issue or question that could either strengthen *or* weaken the argument, depending on which way it goes

Work from **Wrong** to **Right**	**Right:**	Strengthens and weakens the conclusion
	Wrong:	No Tie to Argument Irrelevant Distinction or Comparison
	Note:	Don't add assumptions! Right answer should work as is.

Take a picture of this page and keep it with the review sheets you're creating as you study. Better yet, use this page as a guide to create your own review sheet—you'll remember the material better if you write it down yourself. Where appropriate, put it in your own words and you'll remember it even better.

13

Find the Flaw Cheat Sheet

Find the Flaw Cheat Sheet

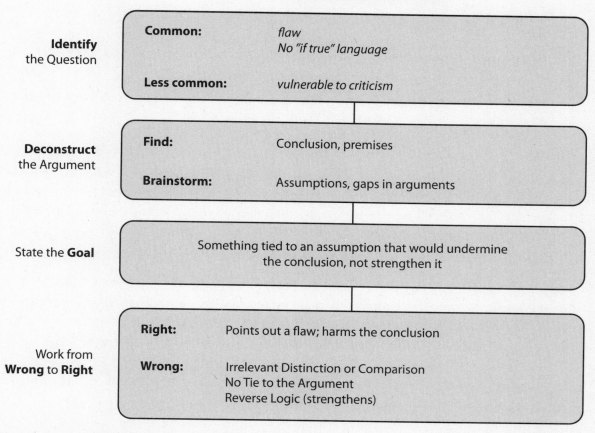

Identify the Question	**Common:**	*flaw* *No "if true" language*
	Less common:	*vulnerable to criticism*
Deconstruct the Argument	**Find:**	Conclusion, premises
	Brainstorm:	Assumptions, gaps in arguments
State the **Goal**		Something tied to an assumption that would undermine the conclusion, not strengthen it
Work from **Wrong** to **Right**	**Right:**	Points out a flaw; harms the conclusion
	Wrong:	Irrelevant Distinction or Comparison No Tie to the Argument Reverse Logic (strengthens)

Take a picture of this page and keep it with the review sheets you're creating as you study. Better yet, use this page as a guide to create your own review sheet—you'll remember the material better if you write it down yourself. Where appropriate, put it in your own words and you'll remember it even better.

Problem Set

Answer each question using the 4-step Critical Reasoning process.

1. **Identify the question:** Is this an Evaluate the Argument question or a Find the Flaw question?

2. **Deconstruct the argument:** Find the conclusion and map the argument on your paper.

3. **State the goal:** What will the right answer need to do?

4. **Work from wrong to right:** Eliminate four wrong answers. Watch out for common wrong answer types.

1. *Tuition*

Recently, the tuition at most elite private high schools has been rising more quickly than inflation. Even before these increases, many low- and middle-income families were unable to afford the full tuition costs for their children at these schools. With the new tuition increases, these schools will soon be attended solely by students from affluent families.

Which of the following would it be most useful to determine in order to evaluate the argument?

(A) Whether students from affluent families are more likely to prefer public or private high schools

(B) Whether most students from low- and middle-income families are academically qualified to attend elite private high schools

(C) Whether low-income families are less likely to be able to afford tuition costs than middle-income families

(D) Whether graduates of elite private high schools typically earn higher salaries as adults than do people who did not graduate from these schools

(E) Whether grants or scholarships are available for students from economically disadvantaged families

2. *Charity*

Studies show that impoverished families give away a larger percentage of their income in charitable donations than do wealthy families. As a result, fundraising consultants recommend that charities direct their marketing efforts toward individuals and families from lower socioeconomic classes in order to maximize the dollar value of incoming donations.

Which of the following best explains why the consultants' reasoning is flawed?

(A) Marketing efforts are only one way to solicit charitable donations.

(B) Not all impoverished families donate to charity.

(C) Some charitable marketing efforts are so expensive that the resulting donations fail to cover the costs of the marketing campaign.

(D) Percentage of income is not necessarily indicative of absolute dollar value.

(E) People are more likely to donate to the same causes to which their friends donate.

3. *CostMart*

Editorial: To avoid increasing the unemployment rate in the city of Dorwall, a CostMart warehouse department store should not be permitted to open within city limits. In the past, when CostMart has opened a new warehouse department store in a city, up to 20% of local retailers—which, in Dorwall, primarily employ local residents—have closed within the next three years.

Which of the following questions would be most useful for evaluating the conclusion of the editorial?

(A) Does the bankruptcy rate of local retailers in a city generally stabilize several years after a CostMart warehouse department store opens?

(B) Are the majority of residents of Dorwall currently employed within the city limits?

(C) Will the number of jobs created by the opening of the CostMart warehouse store be greater than the number of jobs that will be lost when local retailers close?

(D) Have other cities that have permitted CostMart warehouse stores to open within city limits experienced an increase in unemployment within the city?

(E) Does CostMart plan to hire employees exclusively from within Dorwall for the proposed warehouse department store?

4. *Bicycle Manufacturing*

Bicycle Manufacturer: Switching our focus from building aluminum bicycles to primarily building carbon-fiber bicycles will reduce the time taken by our manufacturing process. Although the initial construction of aluminum bicycle frames was significantly faster and simpler than the construction of carbon-fiber frames, each weld in an aluminum frame then needed to be individually checked for integrity. This required that substantial time be spent on quality control to avoid shipping out any defective frames.

Which of the following would be most useful in evaluating the claim made in the argument?

(A) Whether factory workers will require additional training in order to manufacture carbon bicycle frames

(B) Whether the carbon manufacturing process is likely to require time-consuming quality checks

(C) Whether aluminum bicycle frames with defective welds can be fixed or must be thrown away

(D) Whether there are improvements that could be introduced that would significantly reduce the rate of defects in aluminum bicycle frames

(E) Whether the demand for carbon-fiber bicycles is as high as the demand for aluminum bicycles

5.   *Ethanol*

Ethanol, a fuel derived from corn, can be used alone to power vehicles or along with gasoline to reduce the amount of gasoline consumed. Compared with conventional gasoline, pure ethanol produces significantly less pollution per gallon used. In order to combat pollution, many individuals advocate the increased usage of ethanol as a fuel source for vehicles in conjunction with or in place of gasoline.

In evaluating the recommendation to increase the use of ethanol, it would be most important to research which of the following?

(A)   Whether the majority of existing vehicles are capable of using ethanol for fuel, either alone or in conjunction with gasoline

(B)   Whether the process of growing corn to produce ethanol results in significant amounts of pollution

(C)   Whether completely replacing gasoline with ethanol results in less pollution than using ethanol in conjunction with gasoline

(D)   Whether ethanol is more expensive to produce than conventional gasoline

(E)   Whether there are some vehicles in which using ethanol fuel would not result in a significant reduction in pollution compared to conventional gasoline

Solutions

1. Tuition: The correct answer is **(E)**.

    Step 1: Identify the Question

Which of the following would it be most useful to determine in order to evaluate the argument?	*Contains the words* evaluate *and* useful to determine—*this is an Evaluate question.*	Ev A B C D E

    Step 2: Deconstruct the Argument

Recently, the tuition at most elite private high schools has been rising more quickly than inflation.	*Fact: Tuition at this specific type of school has been going up even faster than inflation.*	↑ priv HS tuit > infl
Even before these increases, many low- and middle-income families were unable to afford the full tuition costs for their children at these schools.	*And many people without much money already couldn't afford these schools, even before the tuition went up. Another fact.*	B4: mid inc fams can't afford
With the new tuition increases, these schools will soon be attended solely by students from affluent families.	*This must be the conclusion because the other two were facts, and this is a prediction about the future. Basically, they're saying that only wealthy students are going to be able to afford these schools now.*	© Priv HS will have only rich students

    Step 3: State the Goal

    This is an Evaluate question, so I need to find an answer that will help to determine whether or not the conclusion is likely to be valid. The correct answer will have two paths: One path will make the conclusion a little more likely to be valid and the other will make the conclusion a little less likely to be valid.

    The conclusion is that only wealthy students are going to be able to go to these elite private high schools. What is the author assuming? That there's no way that students from lower-income families can attend these schools: Their families can't take out loans, they can't receive scholarships, etc.

Step 4: Work from Wrong to Right

(A) Whether students from affluent families are more likely to prefer public or private high schools	*The conclusion is that private high schools will only have wealthy students, not that all wealthy students will go to private schools. Even if most wealthy students go to public schools, private schools won't suddenly become affordable for other students. So, this doesn't affect the conclusion.*	~~A~~
(B) Whether most students from low- and middle-income families are academically qualified to attend elite private high schools	*This is interesting. Maybe the lower-income students aren't actually qualified to go to these schools. But on the other hand, regardless of whether they're qualified, they won't be able to afford them! So the conclusion is equally strong either way: If the low-income students are qualified, they can't afford the schools, so they won't attend. And if they aren't qualified, they also won't attend. Either way, these high schools will only be attended by students from wealthy families.*	~~B~~
(C) Whether low-income families are less likely to be able to afford tuition costs than middle-income families	*This answer makes a distinction between low- and middle-income families, but the argument doesn't distinguish between these two groups—it combines them. Logically, it would make sense that the less money a family has, the less likely it could afford the tuition… but this doesn't change anything about the basic argument that low- and middle-income families can't afford the tuition.*	~~C~~
(D) Whether graduates of elite private high schools typically earn higher salaries as adults than do people who did not graduate from these schools	*This answer choice discusses the consequences of attending one of these private high schools. However, the conclusion deals with whether certain students can attend these schools in the first place. The outcome of attending a private school doesn't influence whether a student will be able to afford to attend.*	~~D~~
(E) Whether grants or scholarships are available for students from economically disadvantaged families	*If there are grants and scholarships for lower-income students, then perhaps they can afford to attend these schools—this hurts the argument's conclusion. If there are no grants and scholarships for these students, then the argument's conclusion is more likely to be true: These students won't be able to afford these schools. This answer can either strengthen or weaken the argument, so it's correct.*	E $\sim$

 ~~A~~   ~~B~~   ~~C~~   ~~D~~   Ⓔ

2. Charity: The correct answer is (**D**).

Step 1: Identify the Question

Which of the following best explains why the consultants' reasoning is flawed?	*The word* flawed *indicates that this is either a Flaw or Weaken question. The lack of the words* if true *(or an equivalent) means that this is a Flaw question.*	F A B C D E

Step 2: Deconstruct the Argument

Studies show that impoverished families give away a larger percentage of their income in charitable donations than do wealthy families.	*This is a fact. It's impressive that the poor donate anything, but if they do donate anything, then this fact makes sense because donating $100 is a much greater percentage of your income if you don't have much income.*	Poor donate > % inc than rich
As a result, fundraising consultants recommend that charities direct their marketing efforts toward individuals and families from lower socioeconomic classes in order to maximize the dollar value of incoming donations.	*This is the conclusion. Based on the percentage info, the consultants are saying that the charities should focus on lower-income people... but the consultants are assuming that* greater percentage *equals more money. A very rich person might donate $10 million, a small percentage of income but a very large sum.*	© Consultants: to get most $, char shld focus on ↓ inc ppl

Step 3: State the Goal

For Flaw questions, it's important to find the conclusion and brainstorm any assumptions, if I can. I need to find an answer that hurts the argument or shows why the argument is not a good argument.

In this case, the fundraising consultants are recommending that the charities target lower-income families in order to maximize the number of dollars they get in donations. I've identified one potential assumption: The consultants assume that donating a greater percentage of income also means donating a greater dollar amount collectively. If that's not actually the case, then that's a flaw.

Step 4: Work from Wrong to Right

(A) Marketing efforts are only one way to solicit charitable donations.	*This might be true, but it just indicates that there might be other ways, in addition to marketing efforts, to raise money. That doesn't affect the consultants' recommendation to target lower-income families in particular.*	A̶
(B) Not all impoverished families donate to charity.	*I'm sure this is true, but how does it affect the conclusion? It doesn't. The argument never claims that all impoverished families donate to charity—only that, in general, they donate a larger percentage of income to charity.*	B̶
(C) Some charitable marketing efforts are so expensive that the resulting donations fail to cover the costs of the marketing campaign.	*Oh, maybe this is it. If you spend more on the marketing than you make from donations, that can't be a very successful marketing campaign. What was the conclusion again? Oh, wait, to maximize the dollar value of donations. Whether the marketing covered costs isn't part of the conclusion—it just depends on how much money they get in donations. Tricky, but not correct.*	C̶
(D) Percentage of income is not necessarily indicative of absolute dollar value.	*This is what I was saying before about the really rich person donating $10 million! You can have a bunch of low-income people give 10% of their income and one billionaire give 9% of her income . . . and the billionaire could be giving more in terms of absolute dollars. This indicates the flawed assumption made by the fundraising consultants.*	D̰
(E) People are more likely to donate to the same causes to which their friends donate.	*I can believe that this is true, but the argument doesn't address which causes people choose for charity. Rather, the argument talks about amount of money donated.*	E̶

13

3.   CostMart: The correct answer is (**C**).

Step 1: Identify the Question

Which of the following questions would be most useful for evaluating the conclusion of the editorial?	*The language* most useful *and* evaluating *indicates that this is an Evaluate question.*	Ev A B C D E

Step 2: Deconstruct the Argument

Editorial: To avoid increasing the unemployment rate in the city of Dorwall, a CostMart warehouse department store should not be permitted to open within city limits.	*This seems like the conclusion: It's telling me what Dorwall should do. Also, it doesn't just say that Dorwall should ban CostMart. The conclusion is specifically about unemployment.*	© Dorwall shld ban CostMart in city → unempl. not ↑
In the past, when CostMart has opened a new warehouse department store in a city, up to 20% of local retailers—which, in Dorwall, primarily employ local residents—have closed within the next three years.	*The author is explaining why CostMart will increase unemployment. A lot of local stores will close, so locals will lose their jobs.*	new store → 20% of local stores close

Step 3: State the Goal

I need to find an answer that will have two possible paths—one way will strengthen the author's claim and the other way will weaken it. The author's claim is that banning CostMart will prevent an increase in unemployment. One path will show that CostMart might cause unemployment and the other path will show that it might not.

Step 4: Work from Wrong to Right

(A) Does the bankruptcy rate of local retailers in a city generally stabilize several years after a CostMart warehouse department store opens?	*If yes, then unemployment wouldn't continue to worsen over time… but it would still happen in the first place! Even if the bankruptcy rate stabilizes, the editorial still has a good point.*	A̶
(B) Are the majority of residents of Dorwall currently employed within the city limits?	*If yes, then… I'm not sure what this has to do with the conclusion. The argument says that local retailers primarily employ Dorwall residents. Even if most of the other residents are employed outside of the city, the ones who work at local retailers are at risk of losing their jobs.*	B̶
(C) Will the number of jobs created by the opening of the CostMart warehouse store be greater than the number of jobs that will be lost when local retailers close?	*If yes, then the opening of CostMart will result in a net gain in jobs within the Dorwall city limits. That weakens the author's point about unemployment. If no, then some of the residents who lose their jobs might not be able to find new ones, which makes the author's point stronger.*	C̰
(D) Have other cities that have permitted CostMart warehouse stores to open within city limits experienced an increase in unemployment within the city?	*This could be right. If CostMart has increased unemployment in other cities, isn't it more likely to increase unemployment in Dorwall? Well, not necessarily—there's no way to know whether the other cities had the same economic situation as Dorwall. We just knew that their local retailers closed; if that happened in Dorwall, jobs would be lost.*	D̶
(E) Does CostMart plan to hire employees exclusively from within Dorwall for the proposed warehouse department store?	*This one could be good, too. If yes, then that would reduce unemployment! If no, then… hmm… it's not bad necessarily but it's not good either, so I'll have to be sure.*	Ḛ
Compare (C) and (E).	*Wait. (C) specifically says that the number of jobs created will be greater than the ones that are lost. (E) doesn't demonstrate this. Maybe CostMart will only hire Dorwall employees, but there still won't be enough jobs for all of them. Or, maybe CostMart will hire a few people from outside of Dorwall, but there will be enough jobs for the Dorwall residents, too.*	C̰ Ḛ

A̶   B̶   Ⓒ   D̶   Ḛ

4. Bicycle Manufacturing: The correct answer is (**B**).

Step 1: Identify the Question

Which of the following would be most useful in evaluating the claim made in the argument?	*The language* most useful in evaluating *indicates that this is an Evaluate question.*	Ev A B C D E

Step 2: Deconstruct the Argument

Bicycle Manufacturer: Switching our focus from building aluminum bicycles to primarily building carbon-fiber bicycles will reduce the time taken by our manufacturing process.	*This looks like a prediction. It's probably the manufacturer's conclusion.*	© Alum → CF = time ↓
Although the initial construction of aluminum bicycle frames was significantly faster and simpler than the construction of carbon-fiber frames, each weld in an aluminum frame then needed to be individually checked for integrity.	*Now I know why it took longer to make the aluminum bikes. They were faster to make, but the quality control took a long time.*	Alum: faster originally, but QC = time ↑
This required that substantial time be spent on quality control to avoid shipping out any defective frames.	*This really just confirms what we found out in the last sentence! Since we had to check all of those welds, QC took forever.*	

Step 3: State the Goal

The right answer will have two possible paths. One should show that switching to carbon manufacturing might save time. The other should show that it won't actually save time. There might be a drawback to the carbon manufacturing process: Maybe some other part of it actually takes extra time?

Step 4: Work from Wrong to Right

(A) Whether factory workers will require additional training in order to manufacture carbon bicycle frames	*This seems reasonable. If it takes extra training to make the new frames, it'll probably take more time.*	A⁓
(B) Whether the carbon manufacturing process is likely to require time-consuming quality checks	*Okay, this directly addresses the time issue! If it goes one way, then carbon manufacturing might actually take longer. If it goes the other way, carbon should save time. This is stronger than (A), because it definitely affects the time spent. I don't have to just guess that it'll take more time.*	B⁓
(C) Whether aluminum bicycle frames with defective welds can be fixed or must be thrown away	*This might explain why aluminum manufacturing took a long time, but it doesn't say anything about whether switching to carbon would help.*	C̶
(D) Whether there are improvements that could be introduced that would significantly reduce the rate of defects in aluminum bicycle frames	*Interesting. If this is true, then maybe the aluminum process could be made faster. But the problem is, the conclusion is about whether switching to carbon would help or not. It's not about whether something else could help.*	D̶
(E) Whether the demand for carbon-fiber bicycles is as high as the demand for aluminum bicycles	*This doesn't mention manufacturing time at all. If I wanted to relate it to time, I'd need to make some serious assumptions.*	E̶

5. Ethanol: The correct answer is (**B**).

Step 1: Identify the Question

In evaluating the recommenda-tion to increase the use of ethanol, it would be most important to research which of the following?	*This question asks me to evaluate a recommendation, so it's an Evaluate question.*	Ev A B C D E

Step 2: Deconstruct the Argument

Ethanol, a fuel derived from corn, can be used alone to power vehicles or along with gasoline to reduce the amount of gasoline consumed.	*This is a fact. Ethanol, alone or with gas, can power vehicles.*	Eth OR eth + gas can power veh.
Compared with conventional gasoline, pure ethanol pro-duces significantly less pollu-tion per gallon used.	*Another fact. This is just about pure ethanol, though. Weren't we just talking about combining it with gasoline?*	PURE eth = pollution < than gas
In order to combat pollution, many individuals advocate the increased usage of ethanol as a fuel source for vehicles in conjunction with or in place of gasoline.	*Here's the conclusion. It's very specific: In order to combat pollution, we should use more ethanol, alone or with gas.*	© Eth or eth + gas → pollution ↓

Step 3: State the Goal

This is an Evaluate question, so the right answer will be able to both strengthen and weaken the argument. It has to show that the ethanol plan might decrease pollution, but on the other hand, it might not. I'll have to avoid trap answer choices that don't mention pollution, though.

Step 4: Work from Wrong to Right

(A) Whether the majority of existing vehicles are capable of using ethanol for fuel, either alone or in conjunction with gasoline	*If most vehicles can use ethanol, the plan is good to go. What if most vehicles can't use ethanol? Well, switching as many as possible over to ethanol would still reduce pollution. This doesn't say that switching wouldn't reduce pollution! It just says that switching might be difficult.*	~~A~~
(B) Whether the process of growing corn to produce ethanol results in significant amounts of pollution	*This is a drawback to using ethanol! If making ethanol fuel produces a lot of pollution, then switching won't actually cut down on pollution. But if it can be produced cleanly, the switch will cut pollution a lot. It can go either way, so it might be right.*	B ~
(C) Whether completely replacing gasoline with ethanol results in less pollution than using ethanol in conjunction with gasoline	*The conclusion combines these two things together, but the answer choice splits them up. Even if one produces less pollution than the other, they might or might not make less pollution than pure gasoline. There's no way to know, so it's wrong!*	~~C~~
(D) Whether ethanol is more expensive to produce than conventional gasoline	*Cost might be a drawback to ethanol in general, but the conclusion is about pollution, not cost.*	~~D~~
(E) Whether there are some vehicles in which using ethanol fuel would not result in a significant reduction in pollution compared to conventional gasoline	*This talks about* some *vehicles. Okay, if switching won't cut pollution from some vehicles, will the overall switch still cut pollution? I don't know, since I don't know how many vehicles we're talking about. This doesn't tell me that the switch would or wouldn't work.*	~~E~~

The Evidence Family

In This Chapter...

- What Are Inferences?
- Inference Questions
- Explain a Discrepancy
- EXCEPT Questions
- Inference Cheat Sheet
- Explain a Discrepancy Cheat Sheet
- Problem Set
- Solutions

In this chapter, you will learn how to recognize and answer two question types that differ from the rest in one crucial way: Evidence Family arguments typically do *not* contain conclusions. You will also learn how to distinguish Inference questions from Strengthen questions, allowing you to avoid traps.

CHAPTER 14 The Evidence Family

The **Evidence Family** of questions is the second main family. Here's a short recap of what you learned about this family earlier in the book:

- There are no conclusions. Evidence Family questions are made up entirely of premises.
- There are no assumptions either. Just premises.
- There are two main question types: **Inference** and **Explain a Discrepancy**.

Inference questions require you to find a piece of information that *must be true* according to the premises given in the argument.

Explain a Discrepancy questions require you to identify some kind of paradox or puzzling result in an argument and find an answer that explains, or resolves, the puzzling part of the argument. Before delving further into each type, let's talk about what inferences are on the GMAT.

What Are Inferences?

In GMAT world, an inference is something that absolutely *must* be true according to the evidence given in the argument. You don't usually think of inferences this way; rather, in the real world, inferences are *likely* to be true based on the available evidence, but they don't absolutely have to be true. In the real world, an inference is a good guess or conjecture. In GMAT world, an inference is a bulletproof logical consequence.

For example, if a friend tells you that chocolate is her favorite flavor of ice cream, what kind of real-world inferences might you make? You might infer that she likes chocolate in general and that she likes ice cream in general. Maybe she likes all desserts in general—perhaps she has a sweet tooth. All of these things are perfectly reasonable to infer in the real world, but not a single one *has* to be true. It's possible that she likes chocolate only when it's in the form of ice cream or that she likes ice cream only when it's chocolate. The kinds of answers discussed in this paragraph would be tempting *incorrect* answers on the GMAT.

What would be good GMAT inferences? Well, what *must* be true? She can't like vanilla ice cream better than she likes chocolate ice cream—if chocolate is her *favorite* flavor of ice cream, then by definition she doesn't like any other flavor better. She has to have tried at least one other flavor of ice cream at some point in her life—she has to have had the ability to compare with at least one other flavor in order to decide that chocolate is her *favorite* flavor. These kinds of inferences would be correct answers on the GMAT.

All inference lessons refer to the GMAT's definition: something that *must* be true based on the available evidence.

Inference Questions

Inference questions require you to find an answer that must be true according to the information in the argument.

Most Inference question stems contain some form of the words *conclude* or *infer*, although some variations don't include those specific words. Here are examples of phrasing in Inference questions:

Which answer can be "logically concluded"?

The "statements above most strongly support which of the following conclusions"?

Which answer can be "properly inferred"?

The statements above "best support" which of the following "assertions"?

Which answer "must be true" based upon the statements above?

Note: Inference question stems can contain the language "most strongly support," which you also saw on Strengthen questions.

The diagram below shows how to tell whether the word *support* indicates Strengthen or Inference. On Inference questions, the argument (above) is used to support the correct answer (below). On Strengthen questions, the correct answer (below) is used to support the conclusion of the argument (above):

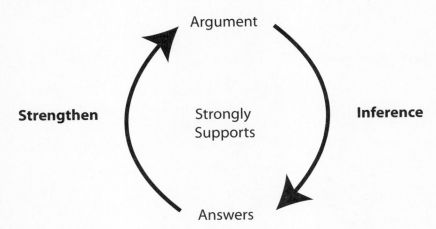

Inference questions will ask you to **use the argument to support an answer choice**. Also, Inference arguments will *not* contain a conclusion in the argument or question stem; they will consist only of premises.

By contrast, Strengthen questions will ask you to **use an answer to support the argument**. The correct answer would serve as an additional premise to support the argument's conclusion. Also, Strengthen questions will contain a conclusion in the argument or question stem.

Try this short example:

> Both enrollment and total tuition revenue at Brownsville University have increased during each of the last four years. During the same period, enrollment at Canterbury University has steadily decreased, while total tuition revenue has remained constant.
>
> Which of the following hypotheses is best supported by the statement given?
>
> (F)   Brownsville University now collects more total revenue from tuition than does Canterbury University.
>
> (G)   The per-student tuition at Canterbury University has risen over the last four years.
>
> (H)   Brownsville University will continue to increase its revenues as long as it continues to increase enrollment.

The question stem uses the word *hypotheses* instead of the more common *conclusions*, but it signals the same thing: an Inference question. Your notes might look like this:

4 yrs:

BU: enrol, tuit ↑

CU: enrol ↓, tuit =

(premise)

There are two schools but different trends are happening. BU's enrollment and tuition revenues are both going up. CU's enrollment is going down, but tuition revenues are the same.

State your goal: *This is an Inference question, so I have to find an answer that must be true according to the premises.*

(A) Brownsville University now collects more total revenue from tuition than does Canterbury University.	*Things have certainly been looking up for BU lately, but the argument says nothing about the actual dollar values that the schools are collecting. It's entirely possible that CU still collects more money than BU.*	~~A~~
(B) The per-student tuition at Canterbury University has risen over the last four years.	*Let's see.* Per-student tuition = *revenues/# of students. CU has the same revenues today, so the numerator stays the same, but fewer students, so the denominator gets smaller. Dividing by a smaller number = a larger number. This must be true! I'll check (C), just in case.*	B̰
(C) Brownsville University will continue to increase its revenues as long as it continues to increase enrollment.	*This might be reasonable to believe in the real world, but it doesn't have to be true. A trend never absolutely has to continue in the future.*	~~C~~

~~A~~   (B)   ~~C~~

The argument provides several fact-based premises. (It is also possible to have premises that are somewhat more claim-based.) The correct answer must be true based on those premises, though in this case, you only needed to use the information about Canterbury in order to draw the correct conclusion. Answer (B) didn't use the Brownsville data at all. That's perfectly acceptable; you may need to use only some of the information in the argument, not all of it.

Answer (A) tried to trap you into concluding something based on information you don't have (actual dollar values). Answer (C) is a classic Real-World Distraction trap—it might be reasonable to believe that the trend will continue, but nothing says that a trend must continue in the future.

Quick quiz! What can you infer in the situation described below?

Imagine two ice cream companies, X and Y. Chocolate ice cream represents 60% of Company X's sales and 50% of Company Y's sales. Clearly, Company X sells more chocolate ice cream than Company Y.

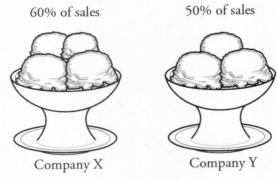

The conclusion above is not necessarily true. You know nothing about the actual sales' numbers, nor about how those percentages relate to each other. What if company Y has $1 million in annual revenues and company X has only $10,000 in annual revenues? In that case, company Y sells a lot more chocolate ice cream than company X. You can't conclude anything about actual dollar amounts from this limited information about percentages.

Try this problem:

A particular company sells only vanilla and chocolate ice cream. Last year, 55% of the company's profits were derived from chocolate ice cream sales and 40% of the revenues were derived from vanilla ice cream sales. What can you infer?

(A) Chocolate ice cream is more popular than vanilla ice cream.

(B) The company's vanilla ice cream produces more profit per dollar of sales than does the company's chocolate ice cream.

Yes, they might actually test your math skills on critical reasoning! Because you know that the company sells only these two products, you can figure out two additional percentages. If 55% of profits came from chocolate, then 45% of profits came from vanilla. If 40% of revenues came from vanilla, then 60% of revenues came from chocolate. These things must be true, but these inferences are probably too easy for any GMAT question. What else can you infer?

The company earned 60% of its revenues, but only 55% of its profits, from chocolate. By contrast, the company earned 40% of its revenues and a *higher* percentage of its profits, 45%, from vanilla. That's interesting. The company made more profit on vanilla and less profit on chocolate than you might have expected based on the percentage of revenues that each product generates. *Profitability* is a measure of profit per dollar of revenues. The vanilla ice cream product is more *profitable* than the chocolate ice cream product. That must be true, so answer (B) is correct.

What doesn't have to be true? It doesn't have to be true that vanilla will continue to be more profitable in the future. The trend might not continue. It also doesn't have to be true that chocolate ice cream is more popular or even that more is sold by the industry in general—maybe this company makes a fantastic chocolate ice cream, but some other company makes a much better vanilla. Notice that answer (A) focuses on how popular chocolate ice cream is in general, not just this company's chocolate ice cream. You don't have any information about how popular chocolate ice cream is overall.

When you are given numbers, proportions, or any other mathematical information, do two things:

1. Confirm whether you have real numbers or percentages.

2. Figure out any other values or relationships that must be mathematically true.

Try a full example. Set your timer for two minutes:

> Reducing government spending has been demonstrated to raise the value of a country's currency over time. However, many economists no longer recommend this policy. A currency of lesser value causes a country's exports to be more competitive in the international market, encouraging domestic industries and making the economy more attractive to foreign investment.
>
> The statements above most strongly support which of the following inferences?
>
> (A) Limited government spending can also lead to a reduction in the national deficit.
> (B) Reducing government spending can make a country's exports less competitive.
> (C) Many economists now recommend higher levels of government spending.
> (D) An increase in the value of a currency will result in reduced government spending.
> (E) Competitive exports indicate a weak currency.

Step 1: Identify the Question

The statements above most strongly support which of the following inferences?	*They're asking to support something below (in the answers), and they use the word inference.* This is an Inference question.	In A B C D E

Step 2: Deconstruct the Argument

Reducing government spending has been demonstrated to raise the value of a country's currency over time.	*This is a fact (that is, I should take it as one in the world of this argument). One thing demonstrably leads to another.*	↓ gov spend → ↑ val curr
However, many economists no longer recommend this policy.	*Hmm. According to the first sentence, raising the value of currency sounds like a good thing, so why wouldn't the economists want to do that?*	BUT econs no longer rec
A currency of lesser value causes a country's exports to be more competitive in the international market, encouraging domestic industries and making the economy more attractive to foreign investment.	*Oh, okay, so there are some good reasons to have a lower currency value. I guess the economists think these benefits outweigh the lower value.*	↓ val curr → exports more > compet → various benefits

Step 3: State the Goal

Reducing government spending will increase currency value. It seems like it would be good to have a high currency value, but some economists disagree, because there are other benefits involved in having a lower currency value.

I need to find an answer that must be true given the information in the argument. I don't need to use all of the info in the argument, though I may.

Step 4: Work from Wrong to Right

(A) Limited government spending can also lead to a reduction in the national deficit.	*Deficit? This might be reasonable to believe in the real world, but there was nothing about the deficit in the argument—there's no evidence to support this statement.*	~~A~~
(B) Reducing government spending can make a country's exports less competitive.	*Let's see. The author said that reducing spending leads to a higher currency value. And then the economists said that a lower currency value makes exports more competitive. If that's true, then a higher currency value could make exports less competitive... so it is actually the case that reducing spending might lead to less competitive exports! Keep this one in.*	B ~
(C) Many economists now recommend higher levels of government spending.	*The argument says* many economists *and the answer says* many economists, *so that part is okay. If you tell someone not to lower their spending, is that the same thing as telling them to increase their spending? No. You could also recommend spending the same amount. Tricky! This one isn't a "must be true" statement.*	~~C~~
(D) An increase in the value of a currency will result in reduced government spending.	*This one feels similar to (B)—language pretty similar to the argument, and I have to figure out what leads to what. The author said that X (reducing spending) will lead to Y (a higher currency value). This answer reverses the direction: Y will lead to X. That's not what the author said!*	~~D~~

14

| (E) Competitive exports indicate a weak currency. | *The economists said that a lower currency value leads to more competitive exports. Hmm. These things do seem to go together, according to the argument. I'll leave this one in and compare it to answer (B).* | E̲ |
| Compare (B) and (E). | *Now I need to compare (B) and (E). I'll check the wording of the answers to make sure I'm reading them correctly. Oh, I see. Answer (B) says that reducing spending can make exports less competitive, which is true, while (E) says that competitive exports indicate a weak currency. The argument says that a weaker currency leads to more competitive exports, but it doesn't say that the ONLY way to competitive exports is to have a weak currency. Maybe you can have competitive exports by investing in great research and development nationally or in some other fashion, so (E) isn't necessarily true and I can eliminate it.* | B̲ E̲ |

Right Answers

Right answers on Inference questions must be entirely supported by the information provided in the argument. Often, the right answer will bring together two or more of the premises in the argument, but not necessarily all the premises. This was the case in the prior example where the right answer linked reduced government spending (first sentence) to exports (last sentence). Occasionally, you may see a right answer that only draws from one premise in the argument.

Common Trap Answers

Real-World Distraction

The most tempting wrong answers on Inference questions tend to revolve around Real-World Distractions—things that you would reasonably assume to be true in the real world, but that don't absolutely have to be true. Some of these trap answers may quite obviously go way too far, but the trickiest ones will seem very reasonable...until you ask yourself whether that answer must be true.

Choices (C) and (E) from the last problem both seem reasonable in the real world, but neither one has to be true. The argument said merely that economists no longer recommend a policy to *reduce* spending. That doesn't necessarily mean that the economists recommend *higher* spending, as choice (C) says. There's also a third option: maintaining the same level of spending. Choice (E) didn't qualify the claim with a *could* or *can*. It isn't the case that competitive exports must always indicate a weak currency; they might have been caused by something else.

Reverse Logic

Other trap answers will use language very similar to the language in the argument but will reverse the proper direction of the information. If you're told that eating honey causes people to hiccup, then a wrong answer might say that hiccuping causes people to eat honey. In the last problem, choice (D) used Reverse Logic, as did answer choice (E).

Too Broad

If you're told that the flu often results in weight loss, then a trap answer might say that illness causes people not to be hungry. All illnesses? The flu is just one example; it isn't reasonable to conclude something about illnesses in general. (In addition, perhaps people are hungry when they have the flu, but they feel so nauseous that they can't eat!). Often, wrong answers on the GMAT will include a claim that is broader than the information in the argument; these broader claims, although common when making inferences in the real world, are not valid GMAT inferences.

Explain a Discrepancy

As with Inference questions, **Discrepancy questions** consist only of premises, mostly on the fact-based side (though it is possible to have more claim-like premises). Most of the time, two sets of premises will be presented, and those premises will seem to be contradictory in some way. They won't "make sense" together. Sometimes, the argument will include indicator words such as *surprisingly* or *yet*.

Most Discrepancy question stems will include some form of the words *explain* or *resolve*, and the vast majority will also contain the words *if true*. Here are two typical examples:

> Which of the following, if true, most helps to resolve the paradox described above?

> Which of the following, if true, best explains the fact that many economists no longer recommend reducing spending in order to increase currency values?

Your task on Discrepancy questions is to find an answer that *resolves* or *fixes* the discrepancy—that is, all of the information now makes sense together. If you leave the argument as is, people should say, "Wait. That doesn't make sense." If you add the correct answer into the argument, people should say, "Oh, I see. That makes sense now."

Take a look at this short example:

> According to researchers, low dosages of aspirin taken daily can significantly reduce the risk of heart attack or stroke. Yet doctors have stopped recommending daily aspirin for most patients.

> Which of the following, if true, most helps to explain why doctors no longer recommend daily low dosages of aspirin?

> (A) Only a small percentage of patients have already experienced a heart attack or stroke.

> (B) Patients who are at low risk for heart attack or stroke are less likely to comply with a doctor's recommendation to take aspirin daily.

> (C) Aspirin acts as a blood thinner, which can lead to internal bleeding, particularly in the stomach or brain.

The question stem asks you to *explain* something that doesn't make sense: Aspirin is apparently beneficial, but "doctors have *stopped* recommending" its use for most people (implying that they used to recommend it more). Why would they do that? You might sketch or think of the info visually in this way:

daily aspirin ↓   *BUT*   Drs stop recomm

heart attack, stroke   for most

WHY?

You're trying to highlight the apparent discrepancy between the two facts: On the one hand, daily aspirin is beneficial, and, on the other, doctors have stopped recommending it.

Go back to step 3, and state the goal:

So far, they've told me something really good about taking aspirin daily: It significantly reduces the risk of some pretty bad things. The fact that the doctors have stopped recommending it means that they used to recommend it, so why would they stop doing so? Maybe there's something else that's bad about taking aspirin daily.

(A) Only a small percentage of patients have already experienced a heart attack or stroke.	*So maybe this means the doctors think it won't help that many people? Wait. The purpose of taking the aspirin is to try to prevent a heart attack or stroke. If most people haven't had a heart attack or stroke, you'd want them to do something that would help lower the risk.*	A̶
(B) Patients who are at low risk for heart attack or stroke are less likely to comply with a doctor's recommendation to take aspirin daily.	*I can believe this is true in the real world, but is a doctor really going to say, "Oh, I know a lot of people won't take the life-saving medication properly, so I just won't bother to prescribe it." I hope not! Plus, why would they recommend aspirin to people who are at low risk?*	B̶
(C) Aspirin acts as a blood thinner, which can lead to internal bleeding, particularly in the stomach or brain.	*Oh, this is a bad thing about aspirin—it can cause you to bleed! Yeah, if it could make your brain start bleeding, I can imagine that doctors would want to avoid prescribing it unless there was a really good reason to do so.*	C̰

A̶   B̶   Ⓒ

Answer (C) indicates a bad consequence that can result from taking aspirin. If you add it to the argument, now it's understandable why doctors might be reluctant to have people take aspirin regularly.

Answer (A) talks about the wrong group. The argument talks about preventing heart attacks or strokes in the general population, not only among those who have already experienced these maladies.

Answer (B) might be true, but this doesn't explain why doctors would stop recommending aspirin in general. In addition, this choice limits itself to those who are at low risk for heart attack or stroke—why would doctors need to recommend daily aspirin for a group that doesn't have the risk factors?

As you read that argument, the surprising finding (aspirin no longer recommended) may have seemed a lot like what has previously been classified as a conclusion. It is not actually a conclusion because there was nothing in the existing argument to support that claim; a claim is only a conclusion if it is supported by at least one premise. In fact, the only information in the argument went against that claim. Once you add the answer choice, you actually do have an argument with a counterpoint, premise (the answer), and conclusion. This approach provides another way to think about answering Discrepancy questions: Find a premise to support the surprising claim in the argument.

Try another example:

> In a recent poll, 71% of respondents reported that they cast votes in the most recent national election. Voting records show, however, that only 60% of eligible voters actually voted in that election.
>
> Which of the following pieces of evidence, if true, would provide the best explanation for the discrepancy?
>
> (A) The margin of error for the survey was plus or minus five percentage points.
>
> (B) Fifteen percent of the survey's respondents were living overseas at the time of the election.
>
> (C) Prior research has shown that people who actually do vote are also more likely to respond to polls than those who do not vote.
>
> (D) Some people who intend to vote are prevented from doing so by last-minute conflicts or other complications.
>
> (E) People are less likely to respond to a voting poll on the same day that they voted.

14

Step 1: Identify the Question

Which of the following pieces of evidence, if true, would provide the best explanation for the discrepancy?	*The question stem uses the word* explanation *and explicitly mentions a* discrepancy, *so this is an Explain the Discrepancy question.*	ED A B C D E

Step 2: Deconstruct the Argument

In a recent poll, 71% of respondents reported that they cast votes in the most recent national election.	*Pure fact. There was a poll, and 71% of the people who responded said they voted in the last election.*	Poll: 71% voted
Voting records show, however, that only 60% of eligible voters actually voted in that election.	*Okay, that's strange. Records show that only 60% of people who were allowed to vote actually voted.*	BUT records: only 60% of elig voters voted

Step 3: State the Goal

How can it be the case that, when asked, 71% of the people said they voted, but records show only 60% of those who were allowed to vote actually voted? I don't think it would be because some people voted who weren't allowed to—that would technically resolve the discrepancy, but I doubt the GMAT is going to say that. So what could it have been? Maybe some people are remembering incorrectly or mixing up the election in question. Oh, I know! Polls always have a margin of error, so maybe the margin of error accounts for the discrepancy.

Okay, I need to find something that will make the whole thing make sense—it'll explain why 71% said they voted but records showed that only 60% actually voted.

Step 4: Work from Wrong to Right

(A) The margin of error for the survey was plus or minus five percentage points.	*Margin of error, bingo! Excellent. So the real percentage could've been anywhere from... 71% + 5% to 71% − 5%, which is still 66%. This doesn't go far enough. Still, it's about margin of error. I'm going to keep this one and come back to it later.*	A̰
(B) Fifteen percent of the survey's respondents were living overseas at the time of the election.	*This percentage is larger than the 11% discrepancy mentioned in the argument. But what group are they talking about? Are these the people who did vote, or didn't vote, or some mix of the two? And what does living overseas imply? This country might allow people to vote by absentee ballot. This doesn't resolve anything.*	B̶
(C) Prior research has shown that people who actually do vote are also more likely to respond to polls than those who do not vote.	*People who vote are also more likely to respond to a survey. What does that mean? Of the people who responded, more were likely to have been voters than is represented in the overall population. Oh, I see—the survey group was skewed toward those who voted. That's why 71% of that subgroup could have voted while only 60% of the overall population of eligible voters voted. That's better than (A)—I'll get rid of (A).*	C̰
(D) Some people who intend to vote are prevented from doing so by last-minute conflicts or other complications.	*I'm sure this is true in the real world. How does it affect this argument? The survey took place after the election; it asked people whether they had voted in the past. It doesn't address what people intended to do before the election.*	D̶
(E) People are less likely to respond to a voting poll on the same day that they voted.	*I have no idea when the poll was taken, so I can't do much with this. Even if the poll was done the same day as the election, this just highlights the discrepancy—it's even more puzzling now. I would expect the percentage of people who said they voted to be lower than the real percentage because those who didn't vote that day would be more likely to agree to participate in the poll.*	E̶

A̰   B̶   Ⓒ   D̶   E̶

Right Answers

The right answer on a Discrepancy question should provide an explanation for the surprising finding presented in the argument. New language, information, and ideas are common in right answers because the finding was not explained by the original information in the argument.

Common Trap Answers

Half Way

One common wrong answer trap will seem to be on topic because it will address one of the premises, but it won't actually resolve the discrepancy between the two premises. Thus, this trap answer only goes Half Way. Some of these will more obviously fall short, such as answer (D) in the previous problem, while others will be trickier because they just don't go quite far enough, such as answer (A). If answer (A) had said that the margin of error was plus or minus 15 percentage points, it could have been the correct answer.

Reverse Logic

You may also see Reverse Logic traps, where the answer choice actually highlights or even heightens the discrepancy—that is, the choice makes the surprise even more surprising. Answer (E) could fall into this category: If the poll was taken the same day as the election, then the fact that the numbers don't match would be even more puzzling. People probably wouldn't have forgotten whether they just voted, so did some of them lie?

EXCEPT Questions

As with Assumption Family questions, Evidence Family questions can also be presented in the negative EXCEPT format. These are more likely to occur on Discrepancy questions than on Inference questions.

A regular Discrepancy question might read:

> Which of the following, if true, would best help to explain the surprising finding?

An EXCEPT Discrepancy question might read:

> Each of the following, if true, could help to explain the surprising finding EXCEPT

What is the difference in wording between those two questions?

The first one indicates that one answer choice, and only one, explains the discrepancy. That is the answer choice that you want to pick.

The second one indicates that four answer choices explain the discrepancy. These four are all wrong answers. The fifth answer will *not* explain or resolve the discrepancy. This is the odd one out and the correct answer.

Similarly, on an Inference EXCEPT question, four answer choices will represent things that must be true according to the argument; eliminate these four. One answer will represent something that does not have to be true. This is the odd one out; pick it.

Inference Cheat Sheet

Inference Cheat Sheet

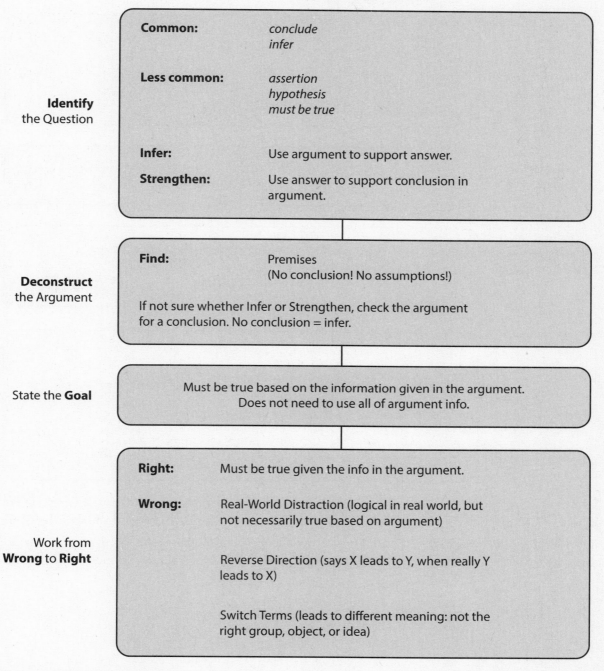

Identify the Question	**Common:**	*conclude* *infer*
	Less common:	*assertion* *hypothesis* *must be true*
	Infer:	Use argument to support answer.
	Strengthen:	Use answer to support conclusion in argument.

Deconstruct the Argument

Find: Premises (No conclusion! No assumptions!)

If not sure whether Infer or Strengthen, check the argument for a conclusion. No conclusion = infer.

State the **Goal**

Must be true based on the information given in the argument. Does not need to use all of argument info.

Work from **Wrong** to **Right**

Right: Must be true given the info in the argument.

Wrong: Real-World Distraction (logical in real world, but not necessarily true based on argument)

Reverse Direction (says X leads to Y, when really Y leads to X)

Switch Terms (leads to different meaning: not the right group, object, or idea)

Take a picture of this page and keep it with the review sheets you're creating as you study. Better yet, use this page as a guide to create your own review sheet—you'll remember the material better if you write it down yourself. Where appropriate, put it in your own words and you'll remember it even better.

Explain a Discrepancy Cheat Sheet

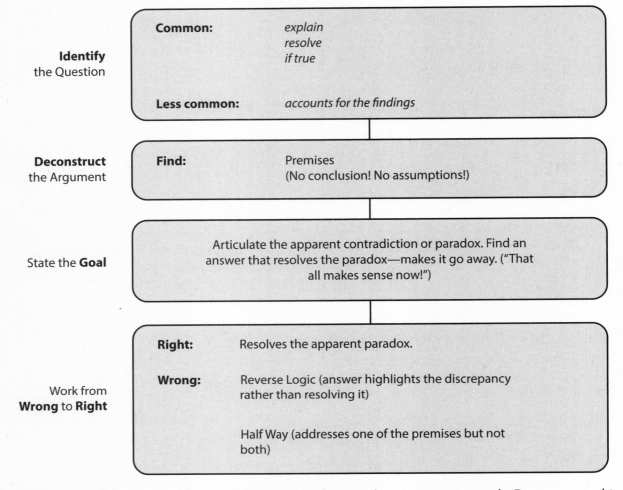

Explain a Discrepancy Cheat Sheet

Identify
the Question

Common: *explain*
resolve
if true

Less common: *accounts for the findings*

Deconstruct
the Argument

Find: Premises
(No conclusion! No assumptions!)

State the **Goal**

Articulate the apparent contradiction or paradox. Find an answer that resolves the paradox—makes it go away. ("That all makes sense now!")

Work from
Wrong to **Right**

Right: Resolves the apparent paradox.

Wrong: Reverse Logic (answer highlights the discrepancy rather than resolving it)

Half Way (addresses one of the premises but not both)

Take a picture of this page and keep it with the review sheets you're creating as you study. Better yet, use this page as a guide to create your own review sheet—you'll remember the material better if you write it down yourself. Where appropriate, put it in your own words and you'll remember it even better.

Problem Set

Answer each question using the 4-step Critical Reasoning process.

1. **Identify the question:** Is this an Inference question or an Explain the Discrepancy question?

2. **Deconstruct the argument:** Map the argument on your paper. Remember that there won't be a conclusion.

3. **State the goal:** What will the right answer need to do?

4. **Work from wrong to right:** Eliminate four wrong answers. Watch out for common wrong answer types.

1. *Mycenaean Vase*

Museum A will display only objects that are undamaged and that have been definitively proven to be authentic. Doubts have been raised about the origins of a supposedly Mycenaean vase currently on display in the museum's antiquities wing. The only way to establish this vase's authenticity would be to pulverize it, then subject the dust to spectroscopic analysis.

The claims above, if true, most strongly support which of the following conclusions?

(A) Authentic Mycenaean vases are valuable and rare.

(B) Museum A was not sufficiently diligent in establishing the authenticity of the vase before displaying it.

(C) The vase in question will no longer be displayed in Museum A.

(D) Spectroscopic analysis is the only method used by Museum A to establish the authenticity of objects.

(E) Many of the world's museums unknowingly display forgeries.

2. *Gas Mileage*

The average fuel efficiency of vehicles sold nationwide during the period 2000–2004 was 25 miles per gallon; the corresponding figure during the period 1995–1999 was 20 miles per gallon. The national average price of gasoline during the period 2000–2004 was $2 per gallon; the corresponding figure during the period 1995–1999 was $1.60 per gallon.

The statements above, if true, best support which of the following conclusions?

(A) The average fuel efficiency of vehicles sold nationwide should reach 30 miles per gallon for the period 2005–2009.

(B) The cost of gasoline for an average trip in a vehicle was higher during the period 1995–1999 than during the period 2000–2004.

(C) Rising gasoline prices lead consumers to purchase more fuel-efficient cars.

(D) The ratio of average fuel efficiency to average price of gasoline from the 1995–1999 period was roughly equal to the ratio from the 2000–2004 period.

(E) Consumers spent more money on gasoline during the period 2000–2004 than during the period 1995–1999.

3. *CarStore*

   CarStore's sales personnel have an average of 15 years' experience selling automobiles, and for the last 5 years, they have sold more cars each year than other local dealers. Despite this, CarStore management has decided to implement a mandatory training program for all sales personnel.

   Which of the following, if true, best explains the facts given above?

   (A) Sales personnel at CarStore earn significantly more money than those who work for other local dealers.

   (B) Within the last 5 years, a number of other local dealers have implemented mandatory training programs.

   (C) It is common for new or less experienced employees to participate in training programs.

   (D) A website has recently released confidential pricing information for the cars sold by CarStore, and customers have begun trying to negotiate lower prices using this data.

   (E) Several retailers that compete directly with CarStore use "customer-centered" sales approaches.

4. *Stem Cell Research*

   Government restrictions have severely limited the amount of stem cell research U.S. companies can conduct. Because of these restrictions, many U.S. scientists who specialize in the field of stem cell research have signed long-term contracts to work for foreign companies. Recently, Congress has proposed lifting all restrictions on stem cell research.

   Which of the following statements can most properly be inferred from the information above?

   (A) Some foreign companies that conduct stem cell research work under fewer restrictions than some U.S. companies do.

   (B) Because U.S. scientists are under long-term contracts to foreign companies, there will be a significant influx of foreign professionals into the U.S.

   (C) In all parts of the world, stem cell research is dependent on the financial backing of local government.

   (D) In the near future, U.S. companies will no longer be at the forefront of stem cell research.

   (E) If restrictions on stem cell research are lifted, many of the U.S. scientists will break their contracts to return to U.S. companies.

5. *Hunting Season*

In an effort to reduce the number of deer, and therefore decrease the number of automobile accidents caused by deer, the government lengthened the deer hunting season earlier this year. Surprisingly, the number of accidents caused by deer has increased substantially since the introduction of the longer hunting season.

All of the following, if true, help to explain the increase in traffic accidents caused by deer EXCEPT

(A) The presence of humans in the woods causes the deer to move to new areas, which causes the deer to cross roads more frequently than normal.

(B) In the area where the deer live, the lengthened hunting season attracted a significantly greater amount of traffic than usual this year.

(C) Most automobile accidents involving deer result from cars swerving to avoid deer, and they leave the deer in question unharmed.

(D) Deer tend to bolt when hearing gunshots or other loud sounds and are more likely to run across a road without warning.

(E) A new highway was recently built directly through the state's largest forest, which is the primary habitat of the state's deer population.

6. *World Bank*

In 2010, China comprised about 10 percent of the world's gross domestic product (GDP), and its voting share in the World Bank was increased from less than 3% to 4.4%. During the same time frame, France comprised about 4% of the world's GDP and saw its voting share in the World Bank drop from 4.3% to 3.8%.

Which of the following can be logically concluded from the passage above?

(A) Prior to 2010, China comprised less than 10 percent of the world's gross domestic product.

(B) Voting share in the World Bank is not directly proportional to each country's share of the world's GDP.

(C) China's share in the world's gross domestic product is increasing more rapidly than France's share.

(D) The Chinese government is likely to be dissatisfied with the degree of the increase in its voting share.

(E) World Bank voting shares are allocated based upon each country's share of the world's GDP during previous years, not during the present year.

14

7. *Barcodes*

Two-dimensional barcodes are omni-directional; that is, unlike one-dimensional barcodes, they can be scanned from any direction. Additionally, two-dimensional barcodes are smaller and can store more data than their one-dimensional counterparts. Despite such advantages, two-dimensional barcodes account for a much smaller portion of total barcode usage than one-dimensional barcodes.

Which of the following, if true, most helps to resolve the apparent paradox?

(A) Many smaller stores do not use barcodes at all because of the expense.

(B) For some products, the amount of data necessary to be coded is small enough to fit fully on a one-dimensional barcode.

(C) Two-dimensional barcodes are, on average, less expensive than one-dimensional barcodes.

(D) Two-dimensional barcodes can also be scanned by consumer devices, such as cell phones.

(E) One-dimensional barcodes last longer and are less prone to error than two-dimensional barcodes.

14

Solutions

1. Mycenaean Vase: The correct answer is **(C)**.

Step 1: Identify the Question

The claims above, if true, most strongly support which of the following conclusions?	*The language* strongly support *could indicate an Inference or a Strengthen question. Since the question stem says* which of the following conclusions, *the conclusion will be in the answer choices, not in the argument. This is an Inference problem.*	In A B C D E

Step 2: Deconstruct the Argument

Museum A will display only objects that are undamaged and that have been definitively proven to be authentic.	*This is a fact—all objects have to be perfect and authenticated for this museum to display them.*	Mus: only perfect, auth objects
Doubts have been raised about the origins of a supposedly Mycenaean vase currently on display in the museum's antiquities wing.	*Another fact: They're not sure whether this vase is authentic.*	Doubts about Myc vase
The only way to establish this vase's authenticity would be to pulverize it, then subject the dust to spectroscopic analysis.	*That's interesting and kind of sad. In order to prove whether the vase is authentic, they've got to destroy it!*	To auth, must destroy!

Step 3: State the Goal

This is an Inference question; I need to find something that must be true according to the info given in the argument. In this case, they're not sure whether this vase is authentic and the only way to establish its authenticity is to destroy it. What follows logically from that? They can't display a fake vase, and they can't display a pulverized vase, so they won't be able to display it at all.

Step 4: Work from Wrong to Right

(A) Authentic Mycenaean vases are valuable and rare.	*This might be true, but I can't prove it using only what's in the argument.*	A̶
(B) Museum A was not sufficiently diligent in establishing the authenticity of the vase before displaying it.	*That seems a little judgmental, but reasonable. The museum only wants to display authentic objects, so why were they displaying this vase?*	B̰
(C) The vase in question will no longer be displayed in Museum A.	*I can prove that this answer choice is true! Since they only display objects they know are authentic, if they want to display the vase, they have to authenticate it. But to authenticate it, they have to destroy it! No matter what, they won't be able to display the vase. This is better than (B), since it's something I can prove using logic, not a value judgment.*	C̰
(D) Spectroscopic analysis is the only method used by Museum A to establish the authenticity of objects.	*That's not necessarily true. They have to use it for this vase, but they might have other methods for other objects.*	D̶
(D) Many of the world's museums unknowingly display forgeries.	*This makes sense in the real world, but I can't prove it using only the information here. I only know about one museum and one object, not many of the world's museums.*	E̶

2. Gas Mileage: The correct answer is **(D)**.

Step 1: Identify the Question

The statements above, if true, best support which of the following conclusions?	*The language best support could indicate an Inference or a Strengthen question. The rest of the question says that the conclusion will be one of the answer choices, so this is an Inference question.*	In A B C D E

Step 2: Deconstruct the Argument

The average fuel efficiency of vehicles sold nationwide during the period 2000–2004 was 25 miles per gallon; the corresponding figure during the period 1995–1999 was 20 miles per gallon.	*These are both facts, which I'm expecting because this is an Inference question. They're talking about time periods and figures, so maybe a table is the best way to keep track.*	**95–99**	**00–04**
		Fuel eff 20 mpg	25
The national average price of gasoline during the period 2000–2004 was $2 per gallon; the corresponding figure during the period 1995–1999 was $1.60 per gallon.	*Yep, a table was a good idea! More facts and figures for the same time frame.*	$1.60 per gal	$2

Step 3: State the Goal

This is an Inference question, so I'm looking for something that must be true based on all this data. I was given specific figures for average fuel efficiency and average gas price for two time periods. Both went up over time. I imagine that I'll need to make a mathematical inference.

Step 4: Work from Wrong to Right

(A) The average fuel efficiency of vehicles sold nationwide should reach 30 miles per gallon for the period 2005–2009.	*Should reach? That doesn't have to be true. Who knows what's going to happen in the future?*	A̶
(B) The cost of gasoline for an average trip in a vehicle was higher during the period 1995–1999 than during the period 2000–2004.	*Interesting. Gas efficiency was lower in the first time period, but gas also cost less. On top of that, I don't know whether the number or length of trips changed. I don't have enough information to prove this.*	B̶
(C) Rising gasoline prices lead consumers to purchase more fuel-efficient cars.	*This statement is logical, but I can't prove it using only what's in the argument, and I'm not allowed to use outside knowledge. The argument doesn't say anything about why consumers decide to purchase certain cars.*	C̶
(D) The ratio of average fuel efficiency to average price of gasoline from the 1995–1999 period was roughly equal to the ratio from the 2000–2004 period.	*The ratio? Hmm. I don't know, but I can calculate based on the figures I was already given. In the first period, the fuel efficiency number was 20 miles per gallon, and the cost of gas was \$1.60. 20/\$1.60 = 20/(8/5) = 100/8 = 12.5. In the second period, the numbers were 25 and \$2. That's also a ratio of 12.5. They're equal!*	D̰
(E) Consumers spent more money on gasoline during the period 2000–2004 than during the period 1995–1999.	*Tricky! This one seems pretty good at first glance, but average price per gallon is not the same thing as total amount of money spent. It's true that the average price was higher, but maybe people bought fewer gallons of gasoline (especially because fuel efficiency was better!). This one might be true, but it doesn't have to be.*	E̶

14

3. CarStore: The correct answer is (**D**).

Step 1: Identify the Question

Which of the following, if true, best explains the facts given above?	*The language* best explains the facts *is slightly unusual. But since I need to explain something, it's a Discrepancy problem.*	ED A B C D E

Step 2: Deconstruct the Argument

CarStore's sales personnel have an average of 15 years' experience selling automobiles, and for the last 5 years, they have sold more cars each year than other local dealers.	*CarStore's people have 15 years' experience on average, and they sell more cars than the competition. These are facts.*	Sales ppl: avg 15y exper, sell more than comp
Despite this, CarStore has decided to implement a mandatory training program for all sales personnel.	*Here's the contrast. Why are they going to make them all go through training? Maybe something has changed in the marketplace?*	BUT store now req training for all

Step 3: State the Goal

This is a Discrepancy question, so I need to find an answer that explains the surprise. What is the reason for the new training?

Step 4: Work from Wrong to Right

(A) Sales personnel at CarStore earn significantly more money than those who work for other local dealers.	*Maybe they want to train their employees because they're investing a lot of money into them? No, that's too much of a stretch. It doesn't clearly explain why management suddenly made this decision.*	~~A~~
(B) Within the last 5 years, a number of other local dealers have implemented mandatory training programs.	*This would be a good explanation if I didn't know that CarStore employees were selling more cars than employees at other dealers. But, the argument makes it sound like if this is true, then the training programs at the other dealerships don't work. Why would CarStore copy them?*	~~B~~
(C) It is common for new or less experienced employees to participate in training programs.	*This makes sense, but doesn't explain why the employees who average 15 years' experience need training. The argument said that all sales personnel have to undergo the training, not just the new ones.*	~~C~~
(D) A website has recently released confidential pricing information for the cars sold by CarStore, and customers have begun trying to negotiate lower prices using this data.	*This describes a change, which is promising. A change in the situation might explain why management wants to train the sales personnel now. And this change makes sense, too: Customers are using a new negotiating tactic, so CarStore employees should be trained to respond to it.*	D̰
(E) Several retailers that compete directly with CarStore use "customer-centered" sales approaches.	*The other retailers aren't doing as well as CarStore is, so this doesn't explain why the CarStore employees need training. We also don't know whether CarStore already uses this approach or whether it has something better.*	~~E~~

~~A~~   ~~B~~   ~~C~~   Ⓓ   ~~E~~

4. Stem Cell Research: The correct answer is **(A)**.

Step 1: Identify the Question

Which of the following statements can most properly be inferred from the information above?	*The word* inferred *indicates that this is an Inference question.*	In A B C D E

Step 2: Deconstruct the Argument

Government restrictions have severely limited the amount of stem cell research U.S. companies can conduct.	*This is a fact. The U.S. government restricts this stem cell research.*	In A B C D E Stem cell res restrict by U.S. gov
Because of these restrictions, many U.S. scientists who specialize in the field of stem cell research have signed long-term contracts to work for foreign companies.	*Because of that—so the first sentence leads to the second sentence.*	→ U.S. sci work foreign coms instead
Recently, Congress has proposed lifting all restrictions on stem cell research.	*Still a fact: The government is considering lifting the restrictions. Maybe that'll bring the scientists back to work for U.S. companies?*	U.S. gov: maybe lift restrict?

Step 3: State the Goal

This is an Inference question, so I need to find something that's definitely true based on the information so far. The U.S. government restricts a certain kind of research, so many U.S. scientists who do this type of research are working for foreign companies instead. Congress might lift the restrictions.

14

Step 4: Work from Wrong to Right

(A) Some foreign companies that conduct stem cell research work under fewer restrictions than some U.S. companies do.	*If the researchers decided to work for foreign companies specifically because the U.S. companies had restrictions, then that would mean that at least some foreign companies did have fewer restrictions. Yes, this one must be true! I'll check the other answers just in case, though.*	A̰
(B) Because U.S. scientists are under long-term contracts to foreign companies, there will be a significant influx of foreign professionals into the U.S.	*This might be true, but it certainly doesn't have to be true. The argument doesn't say anything about foreign professionals coming into the United States.*	B̶
(C) In all parts of the world, stem cell research is dependent on the financial backing of local government.	*The argument doesn't say anything about how this type of research gets its financial backing. This doesn't have to be true.*	C̶
(D) In the near future, U.S. companies will no longer be at the forefront of stem cell research.	*Irrelevant. The argument doesn't discuss who is or will be at the forefront of this kind of research.*	D̶
(E) If restrictions on stem cell research are lifted, many of the U.S. scientists will break their contracts to return to U.S. companies.	*This might happen, but we can't necessarily predict what will happen in the future.*	E̶

14

5. Hunting Season: The correct answer is **(C)**.

Step 1: Identify the Question

All of the following, if true, help to explain the increase in traffic accidents caused by deer EXCEPT	*The language* help to explain *indicates that this is a Discrepancy question. This is also an EXCEPT question.*	ED Ex A B C D E

Step 2: Deconstruct the Argument

In an effort to reduce the number of deer, and therefore decrease the number of automobile accidents caused by deer, the government lengthened the deer hunting season earlier this year.	*Multiple levels here. First, the government lengthened the hunting season, which is supposed to reduce the number of deer, which is then supposed to reduce the number of car accidents caused by deer.*	Gov: ↑ hunt seas → ↓ deer → ↓ car acc
Surprisingly, the number of accidents caused by deer has increased substantially since the introduction of the longer hunting season.	*That's weird. The exact opposite has happened: There have been more car accidents caused by deer!*	BUT # car acc ↑

Step 3: State the Goal

This is a Discrepancy EXCEPT question. Normally on Discrepancy questions, I'm looking for the answer that makes the contradictory evidence make sense. On this one, though, all four wrong answers will fix the discrepancy. The odd one out—the one that doesn't fix the discrepancy—will be the right answer.

So I need to find (and cross off) four things that explain why there have been even more car accidents caused by deer.

Step 4: Work from Wrong to Right

(A) The presence of humans in the woods causes the deer to move to new areas, which causes the deer to cross roads more frequently than normal.	*If hunting season is lengthened, then there will be people in the woods for a longer period of time. According to this choice, that means the deer are going to cross the roads more frequently than they otherwise would have. That could increase the likelihood of accidents due to deer, which explains the discrepancy. Cross this one off.*	~~A~~
(B) In the area where the deer live, the lengthened hunting season attracted a significantly greater amount of traffic than usual to the area this year.	*Oh, this makes sense. The lengthened hunting season actually caused more traffic, so there are more chances for accidents between cars and deer where the deer live. This explains the discrepancy, too.*	~~B~~
(C) Most automobile accidents involving deer result from cars swerving to avoid deer, and they leave the deer in question unharmed.	*This one is tricky! It explains how the accidents happen, which makes sense. But the right answer has to explain why there are* more *accidents. This doesn't show anything about the number of accidents.*	C
(D) Deer tend to bolt when hearing gunshots or other loud sounds and are more likely to run across a road without warning.	*If there are gunshots for a longer length of time, then there are more chances for the deer to bolt and cross the road suddenly…increasing the chances of an accident.*	~~D~~
(E) A new highway was recently built directly through the state's largest forest, which is the primary habitat of the state's deer population.	*The situation has changed from the year before: A new highway was built right through the area where the deer live. So it would make sense that there are now more accidents caused by deer.*	~~E~~

14

6. World Bank: The correct answer is (**B**).

Step 1: Identify the Question

Which of the following can be logically concluded from the passage above?	*The language* logically concluded *indicates that this is an Inference question.*	In A B C D E

Step 2: Deconstruct the Argument

In 2010, China comprised about 10% of the world's gross domestic product (GDP), and its voting share in the World Bank was increased from less than 3% to 4.4%.	*A bunch of stats about China in 2010. I just need to keep this straight because, glancing down, I can see the next sentence has more numbers.*	<table><tr><td>2010</td><td>GDP</td><td>Vote Share</td></tr><tr><td>China</td><td>10</td><td><3 → 4.4</td></tr></table>
During the same time frame, France comprised about 4% of the world's GDP and saw its voting share in the World Bank drop from 4.3% to 3.8%.	*Same type of stats, but about France this time. Same time frame.*	<table><tr><td>Fra</td><td>4</td><td>4.3 → 3.8</td></tr></table>

Step 3: State the Goal

This is an Inference question, so I need to find something that must be true based upon the info given so far. There are a lot of numbers to keep straight, but generally, China has a larger share of the world GDP than France. China used to have a lower voting share than France, but now it has a higher share.

Step 4: Work from Wrong to Right

(A) Prior to 2010, China comprised less than 10 percent of the world's GDP.	*China's voting share increased in 2010. Maybe that happened because its GDP was lower than 10 percent, and then it increased? On the other hand, I don't actually know that the voting share is based on the GDP. They could have nothing to do with each other. This doesn't have to be true.*	A̶
(B) Voting share in the World Bank is not directly proportional to each country's share of the world's GDP.	*If they were directly proportional, a country with twice the GDP would also have twice the voting share. But China's GDP is more than twice France's and their voting shares are almost the same. The voting share must not be directly proportional! This is probably right.*	B̰
(C) China's share in the world's GDP is increasing more rapidly than France's share.	*China's share is higher now, but I don't actually know whether France's share is increasing or how quickly.*	C̶
(D) The Chinese government is likely to be dissatisfied with the degree of the increase in its voting share.	*There's no way to know this using only the information in the argument. I don't even know whether an increase from 3% to 4.4% is considered small or large.*	D̶
(E) World Bank voting shares are allocated based upon each country's share of the world's GDP during previous years, not during the present year.	*I could speculate that this was true, but I can't prove it. I don't have enough information to tell where these numbers came from.*	E̶

14

7. Barcodes: The correct answer is (**E**).

Step 1: Identify the Question

Which of the following, if true, most helps to resolve the apparent paradox?	*The word* paradox *indicates that this is a Discrepancy question.*	ED A B C D E

Step 2: Deconstruct the Argument

Two-dimensional barcodes are omni-directional; that is, unlike one-dimensional barcodes, they can be scanned from any direction.	*Okay, so 2D barcodes have a better feature than 1D barcodes.*	2D barcodes scan any dir, unlike 1D
Additionally, two-dimensional barcodes are smaller and can store more data than their one-dimensional counterparts.	*Even more advantages for the 2D barcodes.*	Also 2D smaller, more data
Despite such advantages, two-dimensional barcodes account for a much smaller portion of total barcode usage than one-dimensional barcodes.	*But the 1D barcodes are used a lot more—why? There must be some advantages to the 1Ds or disadvantages to the 2Ds that I don't yet know about.*	BUT 1D is used >>

Step 3: State the Goal

I need to find something that fixes the discrepancy described in the argument: The 2D barcodes have a bunch of advantages, but people mostly still use the 1D barcodes. Why? Maybe the 2D ones are super-expensive or something like that.

Step 4: Work from Wrong to Right

(A) Many smaller stores do not use barcodes at all because of the expense.	*Expense—does this explain why 1D barcodes are still being used? No, wait—this says the stores aren't using any type of barcode at all. So that doesn't explain why the ones that do use barcodes seem to prefer the 1D models.*	A̶
(B) For some products, the amount of data necessary to be coded is small enough to fit fully on a one-dimensional barcode.	*Okay, so some products might not need the 2D barcodes. Except, this only mentions some products, while the argument says that the 2D barcodes are a much smaller portion of total usage. This doesn't fully explain the discrepancy.*	B̶
(C) Two-dimensional barcodes are, on average, less expensive than one-dimensional barcodes.	*Less expensive, this is it! Wait a second. No, this says the 2D barcodes are less expensive—that gives them yet another advantage! If they're less expensive, I'd expect people to use them more. This isn't it.*	C̶
(D) Two-dimensional barcodes can also be scanned by consumer devices, such as cell phones.	*This sounds like yet another advantage of the 2D barcodes. This isn't it either!*	D̶
(E) One-dimensional barcodes last longer and are less prone to error than two-dimensional barcodes.	*Here are two advantages of the 1D barcodes. If it's true that they last longer and are less prone to error, then that would explain why people would want to use them rather than the 2D barcodes.*	Ḛ

14

A̶   B̶   C̶   D̶   Ⓔ̰

The Structure Family

In This Chapter...

In this chapter, you will learn how to answer Critical Reasoning question types that test your ability to deconstruct arguments and to identify the role played by specific information or the logic underlying the argument.

CHAPTER 15 The Structure Family

As the name implies, these questions require you to understand the structure of the argument. What kinds of building blocks are present in the argument? What role does each building block play?

There are two main Structure question types: **Describe the Role** and **Describe the Argument**.

Describe the Role

Of the two types, Describe the Role is more common. These problems present a standard argument, with one or two portions in **boldface** font. You are asked to describe the *role* that each portion of boldface font plays.

Role is just another term for concepts you already know. A bolded portion could be a premise, a conclusion, a counterpoint, an intermediate conclusion, or background information. It could also be an opposing conclusion, which goes against the author's main conclusion. You might think of this as the final claim of the *other* side of the argument.

These question types are easy to identify, because one or (usually) two statements will be presented in boldface font and the question stem will include the word *boldface*.

You're going to learn two methods to determine the role of each boldface statement. The Primary Method will always work, but it may be a little more complicated and time-consuming to use. The Secondary Method will allow you to narrow down the answer choices more easily but may not get you all the way to one answer—that is, you may have to guess from a narrowed set of answers. Regardless of the method you use, do still read and deconstruct the argument before moving on to classifying the boldface statements.

Primary Method
Classify each statement in boldface as one of the following three things:
1. (C) The author's **conclusion**
2. (P) A **premise** (it supports the author's conclusion)
3. (X) **Something else** (maybe a counterpoint, background information, acknowledgment of a weakness in the argument . . .)

In your notes, you'll classify each statement using the labels C, P, or X, as described above. When you evaluate the answer choices, you'll look for language that matches your labels.

Try this example:

> CEO: Now that Apex Corporation has begun to compete in our market, investors are expecting us to cut our prices to maintain market share. I don't believe this is necessary, however, because the market is growing rapidly and **a certain percentage of customers will always pay more for high-quality products**.
>
> In the argument above, the portion in boldface plays which of the following roles?

How does this argument work? First, the CEO states that investors are expecting a certain action, but she disagrees. She then provides two pieces of evidence intended to support her opinion: The market is growing and some number of customers are willing to pay higher prices. The boldface portion, then, is a premise: It supports the CEO's conclusion that the company does not need to cut prices in order to maintain market share.

Next, look for a P among the answer choices. The answer choices tend to be written in a difficult, abstract style. For example, some answers might read:

(A) The statement is evidence that has been used to weaken a claim made by the argument.

(B) The statement has been used to support a claim made by the argument.

(C) The statement is the primary claim made in the argument.

Start with the most basic piece: a building block. The word *claim* is typically a synonym for the conclusion. The first answer says that the statement weakens the conclusion. Something used to weaken the conclusion is a counterpoint; such a statement would be labeled X, not P. Choice (A) is not the correct answer.

The second answer talks about something that *supports a claim*. Since the claim is the conclusion, this answer choice does indeed describe a P, or premise, supporting the conclusion. This is probably the correct answer, but check choice (C) just to make sure.

The third answer describes the conclusion itself, not a premise supporting the conclusion. This choice is incorrect, so choice (B) is the correct answer.

You may have noticed that all the answer choices refer to how the statement relates to *the argument*. On the GMAT, when an answer choice refers to *the argument*, it refers to the perspective of the person making the argument. For instance, this argument is made by the CEO, even though it also describes the perspective of investors. If an answer choice says that a sentence *supports the argument*, it must support the perspective of the CEO, not the investors. Describe the Role questions often feature multiple perspectives; be careful to keep the different perspectives straight.

15

If you can use this method accurately, you will be able to eliminate the four wrong answers and get to the right answer. You might take too much time to do so, though, because of the strange format of the answers (and don't forget that the official questions typically have two boldface statements, not just one). The Secondary Method may allow you to get rid of some answers more quickly. Find the conclusion first, then ask yourself these three questions:

Secondary Method
1. Is the statement a *fact* (F) or an *opinion* (O)?
2. Is the statement *for* (+) or *against* (−) the conclusion?
3. If there are two statements, are they on the *same* side of the fence or *opposite* sides?

Strategy Tip: You can use the same side/opposite side trick with the Primary Method, too: C's and P's are on one side, while X's are on the other.

As with the Primary Method, you then look in the answer choices for matching language. How would this method work on the market share problem? The boldface statement is an *opinion* (she hasn't cited actual evidence from customers to support the claim). In addition, the statement is *for* the conclusion. The problem had only one statement, so the third question doesn't apply.

Next, check the answer choices. The word *evidence* typically indicates a fact, not an opinion, so answer (A) is likely incorrect. Answers (B) and (C) both describe claims, or opinions, and both are for the conclusion, so the Secondary Method wouldn't necessarily allow you to choose between the two. (In this case, you might notice the distinction between a conclusion and a premise and be able to choose the correct answer. This problem, though, is on the easier side.)

Common Trap Answers

The most tempting trap answers on Role questions tend to be "off" by just one word, often at the end of the sentence. For example, imagine that you've decided the first boldface is a premise in support of the author's conclusion. A tempting wrong answer might read:

> (A) The first **[boldface statement]** provides evidence in support of the position that the argument seeks to reject.

Every word of that answer matches what you want to find with the exception of the very last word, *reject*. In fact, if you changed that one word, the answer would be correct:

> (A) The first **[boldface statement]** provides evidence in support of the position that the argument seeks to establish.

The first version of the answer choice says that the first boldface statement is a premise in support of some *counter* conclusion. That's not the kind of premise you want! Read every word carefully, all the way to the end of each answer choice.

Putting It All Together

Try a full example:

> Mathematician: Recently, Zubin Ghosh made headlines when he was recognized to have solved the Hilbert Conjecture. Ghosh posted his work on the internet, rather than submitting it to established journals. In fact, **he has no job, let alone a university position**; he lives alone and has refused all acclaim. In reporting on Ghosh, the press unfortunately has reinforced the popular view that mathematicians are antisocial loners. But **mathematicians clearly form a tightly knit community**, frequently collaborating on important efforts; indeed, teams of researchers are working together to extend Ghosh's findings.

In the argument above, the two portions in boldface play which of the following roles?

(A) The first is an observation the author makes to illustrate a social pattern; the second is a generalization of that pattern.

(B) The first is evidence in favor of the popular view expressed in the argument; the second is a brief restatement of that view.

(C) The first is a specific example of a generalization that the author contradicts; the second is a reiteration of that generalization.

(D) The first is a specific counterexample to a generalization that the author asserts; the second is that generalization.

(E) The first is a judgment that counters the primary assertion expressed in the argument; the second is a circumstance on which that judgment is based.

Step 1: Identify the Question

In the argument above, the two portions in boldface play which of the following roles?	*This is a Role question. The argument contains bold font, and the question stem contains the words* boldface *and* role.	R A B C D E

Step 2: Deconstruct the Argument

Mathematician: Recently, Zubin Ghosh made headlines when he was recognized to have solved the Hilbert Conjecture.	*A past fact—this is likely background. Still, jot down a note.*	M: Ghosh solved conjecture
Ghosh simply posted his work on the internet, rather than submitting it to established journals.	*Sounds like more background.*	posted on int
In fact, **he has no job, let alone a university position**; he lives alone and has refused all acclaim.	*Here's the first boldface. He's not a mathematician; that's surprising. Still, I don't know what the conclusion is, so I don't know what role this sentence is playing.*	No job

In reporting on Ghosh, the press unfortunately has reinforced the popular view that mathematicians are antisocial loners.	*So the first boldface is* evidence of *the popular view* that mathematicians are loners ... but the sentence also uses the word unfortunately, *so it sounds like the author doesn't agree ...*	Press: math = loners
But **mathematicians clearly form a tightly knit community**, frequently collaborating on important efforts; indeed, teams of researchers are working together to extend Ghosh's findings.	*I was right; the author disagrees. The author's conclusion is this second boldface statement, so I can label it with a ©.*	© BUT math = commun, collab
	Now, what about that first boldface statement? It's not the conclusion, and it doesn't support the conclusion, so it must be an X: something else.	R A B C D E Ghosh solved conjecture posted on int ⊗ No job Press: math = loners © BUT math = commun, collab

Step 3: State the Goal

The first boldface statement is an X; that is, it is neither the conclusion nor a premise. In this case, it supports the alternate point of view, so call it a counterpoint. It goes against the conclusion. The second boldface statement is a C; it is the author's conclusion.

Remind yourself:

In the right answer, the first statement will be consistent with an X label and the second statement will be consistent with a C label. I'm looking for an XC combo, and those two labels are on opposite sides.

Step 4: Work from Wrong to Right

(A) The first is an observation the author makes to illustrate a social pattern; the second is a generalization of that pattern.	*Hmm. I'm not 100% sure what they mean by* illustrate a social pattern, *but the description of the two statements here makes them sound like they're on the same "side"—the first illustrates something, and the second generalizes that same thing. I want an "opposite sides" answer.*	~~A~~
(B) The first is evidence in favor of the popular view expressed in the argument; the second is a brief restatement of that view.	*The first supports a popular view … okay, maybe. You could call the press view the popular view. Oh, but then it says that the second restates that same view. These two are on the same side again, and I want an opposite sides answer.*	~~B~~
(C) The first is a specific example of a generalization that the author contradicts; the second is a reiteration of that generalization.	*"The first is a [something] that the author contradicts." The [something] part confuses me, but I agree that the author contradicts the first one; this is a good description of a "label X" statement. Hmm. The second repeats that generalization—the same one mentioned in the first statement? No, I'm looking for opposite sides, not a repetition.*	~~C~~
(D) The first is a specific counter example to a generalization that the author asserts; the second is that generalization.	*The first is a counterexample to something the author says? Yes, that accurately describes a "label X." The second is that generalization. I crossed off the last one for this same language. But wait … which generalization is this referring to this time? Oh, a generalization that the author asserts; that's the conclusion, which is a "label C." Leave this answer in.*	D
(E) The first is a judgment that counters the primary assertion expressed in the argument; the second is a circumstance on which that judgment is based.	*Counters language—yes, the first statement does counter the conclusion, which is consistent with the label X. That judgment = the first boldface. The second is not something on which the first one is based—that would be same side, and I want opposite sides.*	~~E~~

~~A~~   ~~B~~   ~~C~~   (D)   ~~E~~

The correct answer is (D).

Common Trap Answers

Half Right

The test writers try to set some traps for you on incorrect Describe the Role answers. For example, one of the descriptions might match one of the boldface statements, but the other one won't match. Several of the wrong answers in the last problem were **Half Right** in this way.

One Word Off

In addition, a very tricky trap answer might be wrong by just one word; we call this the **One Word Off** trap. For example, you might be looking for a premise that supports the conclusion. The answer choice might say, "The first boldface supports a claim that the argument as a whole argues against."

What does that really mean? This choice says that the boldface statement supports a counterconclusion, not the author's conclusion—but you wouldn't know until you read the very last word of the sentence. In fact, if you changed the word *against* to the word *for*, then the choice would be describing a premise in support of the conclusion!

Describe the Argument

Describe the Argument questions can be similar to Role questions: Both often offer "abstract" answer choices based on the *structure* of the argument, perhaps referring to the various building blocks (conclusions, premises, and so on). The majority of these Argument questions will offer two competing points of view in a dialogue format. Then, you might be asked how the second person responds to the first person's argument.

Important note: Other question types can also be presented in this "two people speaking" format—the mere existence of two speakers does not make the problem a Describe the Argument problem. *Always identify the question type using the question stem.*

A minority of these questions will offer just one point of view and ask you how the author of that argument develops their point of view.

Common question formulations include:

> Baram responds to Sadie's argument by . . .
>
> Baram challenges Sadie's argument by . . .
>
> The author develops the argument by doing which of the following?

These all indicate that you have a Describe the Argument question.

Your task is to determine how a particular part of the text was constructed. When the text is a dialogue between two people, read and deconstruct the first person's complete argument just as you would do for any other GMAT argument. Next, examine the response and figure out which piece of the argument the response attacks.

Try an example:

> Baram: I need to learn the names of 100 muscles for the anatomy exam in two hours. I've just memorized 5 of them in 5 minutes, so I only need 95 more minutes to study. Therefore, I'll have plenty of time to memorize everything and get a perfect score on the test.
>
> Sadie: Are you sure? Perhaps the more you memorize, the harder it gets.
>
> Sadie responds to Baram by

What is Baram's argument? What is his conclusion and how does he support it?

> must learn 100 names in 2h
>
> mem 5 in 5m, so need 95m
>
> ⓒ will get 100%

Which part does Sadie attack? Does she attack the conclusion directly? No, but her words certainly cast doubt on Baram's eventual conclusion. She attacks Baram's assumption that he can maintain the same rate of learning, 1 name every minute, for all 100 names. He doesn't explicitly state that he can maintain that rate, but he clearly believes it to be true. The correct answer might be something like:

> Sadie calls into question an assumption Baram makes about the efficacy of his plan.

This answer addresses the appropriate part of the argument—an assumption that Baram makes about his plan. An incorrect answer might look something like:

> Sadie introduces new evidence that contradicts one of Baram's premises.

Sadie does say something new, but does it rise to the level of evidence? She only suggests that his memorization rate might not be constant; she doesn't prove that it is not. While you might be able to argue that the word *evidence* is okay, the word *contradicts* clearly takes things too far. Sadie does not definitively contradict Baram's premise that he will need only 95 more minutes; rather, she raises a question as to *whether* he can memorize the words in only 95 minutes.

Ultimately, the attack is designed to find fault with the conclusion, but don't assume that the second person is attacking the conclusion directly. Tearing down any piece of the argument would ultimately undermine the conclusion, so find the piece that the second person most directly attacks.

You probably won't be able to anticipate the exact wording of the correct answer, but if you can identify the part of the argument addressed, then you are in a much better position to identify the appropriate "matching" language in the correct answer.

Try a full example:

> Mayor: The recycling program costs us nearly $1 million to operate every year, and our budget shortfall this year is projected to be $5 million. Cutting the recycling program will help balance the budget.
>
> Consumer Advocate: It costs the city more to throw something out than to recycle it.
>
> The consumer advocate responds to the mayor by
>
> (A) establishing that the mayor's figures were incorrectly calculated
> (B) accepting the mayor's conclusion but questioning the legality of the plan
> (C) interpreting the mayor's evidence in a way that reduces the validity of the mayor's claim
> (D) introducing a new piece of information that calls into question the validity of the mayor's conclusion
> (E) pointing out that the mayor has not adequately considered the potential causes and effects of the budget shortfall

Step 1: Identify the Question

The consumer advocate responds to the mayor by	*This is a Describe the Argument question. Two people are talking, and I have to explain how one responds to the other.*	DA A B C D E

Step 2: Deconstruct the Argument

Mayor: The recycling program costs us nearly $1 million to operate every year, and our budget shortfall this year is projected to be $5 million.	*The mayor is stating a couple of facts—recycling costs $1m and they're going to miss their budget by $5m.*	M: Recyc cost $1m; this yr $5m short

15

| Cutting the recycling program will help balance the budget. | *So the mayor suggests that they cut the R program in order to help balance the budget.* | → Cut R → bal budg © |
| Consumer Advocate: It costs the city more to throw something out than to recycle it. | *That's interesting. The advocate says that it costs even more to throw something out. Why does this matter? If you can't recycle something, what are you going to do with it instead? Probably throw it out.* | Advoc: Throw away costs > R |

Step 3: State the Goal

For Describe the Argument questions, you have to address how some part of the argument is made: in this case, how the consumer advocate responds to the mayor. First, it sounds as if the advocate thinks that the mayor's plan isn't going to work since the advocate says that throwing stuff out is more costly than recycling it. If that's true, then the plan to cut the recycling program just got a bit worse—it might not actually achieve the ultimate goal, which is to save money and balance the budget.

State your goal briefly to yourself before going to the answers:

The answer I find should indicate that the consumer advocate disagrees with the mayor, specifically questioning whether the suggested action (cutting the recycling program) will result in the desired outcome (saving money, helping to balance the budget).

Step 4: Work from Wrong to Right

(A) establishing that the mayor's figures were incorrectly calculated	*The consumer advocate doesn't say anything about the mayor's figures—in fact, the advocate doesn't dispute the mayor's evidence at all. Rather, the advocate attacks the mayor's assumption that cutting the program will lead to balancing the budget.*	A̶
(B) accepting the mayor's conclusion but questioning the legality of the plan	*The advocate doesn't accept the conclusion, nor does the advocate say anything about legality. Rather, the advocate questions whether the plan will really lead to saving money.*	B̶
(C) interpreting the mayor's evidence in a way that reduces the validity of the mayor's claim	*Hmm. Maybe. The advocate does reduce the validity of the mayor's claim. I'm not 100% sure what interpreting the evidence means. I'll leave this in for now.*	C ~
(D) introducing a new piece of information that calls into question the validity of the mayor's conclusion	*The advocate does call the mayor's conclusion into question, yes. Oh, I see—this one is better than answer (C) because the advocate does introduce a new piece of info (that it costs more to throw something away).*	D ~
(E) pointing out that the mayor has not adequately considered the potential causes and effects of the budget shortfall	*This one is tricky. It's true that the mayor hasn't fully considered the potential effects of the plan to cut the recycling program—but that's not what this choice says. It talks about the causes and effects of the budget shortfall.*	E̶

A̶   B̶   C̶   Ⓓ   E̶

Common Trap Answers

One Word Off

The most tempting trap answers on Describe the Argument questions are similar to those on Role questions: Most of the answer is fine, but one or two words will throw the answer off.

In addition, because most of these arguments will consist of a second person objecting to something the first person says, it will always be tempting to choose an answer that indicates that, for example, the consumer advocate rejects the mayor's conclusion. The advocate's comment does weaken the mayor's conclusion, but it may not directly attack the conclusion—and the question asks you to articulate what the advocate directly attacks.

Drill 15.1—Understanding Answer Choices

One of the toughest things about Describe the Role problems is understanding the language in the answer choices. Before you do a full problem set, warm up by translating some answer choices for practice.

Each question gives you sample answer choice text from a Describe the Role problem. Your job is to determine what part of an argument that answer choice is actually referring to.

1. A claim upon which the author's argument depends

    (A)   Author's premise

    (B)   Author's conclusion

    (C)   Premise of a counterargument

    (D)   Conclusion of a counterargument

2. A conclusion that the author believes has been incorrectly drawn

    (A)   Author's premise

    (B)   Author's conclusion

    (C)   Premise of a counterargument

    (D)   Conclusion of a counterargument

3. Reasoning that has been used to support the claim made by the opposing scientists

    (A)   Author's premise

    (B)   Author's conclusion

    (C)   Premise of a counterargument

    (D)   Conclusion of a counterargument

4. A prediction supported by the author's interpretation of existing evidence

    (A)   Author's premise

    (B)   Author's conclusion

    (C)   Premise of a counterargument

    (D)   Conclusion of a counterargument

5. The desired outcome of a plan, which the author believes will be more successful than the previous approach

    (A)   Author's premise

    (B)   Author's conclusion

    (C)   Premise of a counterargument

    (D)   Conclusion of a counterargument

15

Answers to Drill Set

Drill 15.1—Understanding Answer Choices

1. **(A) Author's premise:** *Claim* usually refers to the conclusion of an argument. However, the author's argument *depends* on this claim. Something that an argument depends on is a premise: Conclusions always depend on premises.

2. **(D) Conclusion of a counterargument:** Since the author believes that this conclusion has been *incorrectly drawn*, it must be part of a counterargument that the author disagrees with.

3. **(C) Premise of a counterargument:** Something that *supports a claim* is a premise. Since this claim belongs to the *opposing scientists*, it's one that the author disagrees with, so it's part of a counterargument.

4. **(B) Author's conclusion:** A prediction is often a conclusion, and this one is *supported*: The rest of an argument always supports its conclusion. Since it's supported by the author's interpretation, it's part of the author's argument.

5. **(B) Author's conclusion:** When an argument discusses a plan, the desired outcome of that plan—even if it's just that the plan will succeed—is the conclusion of the argument.

Describe the Role Cheat Sheet

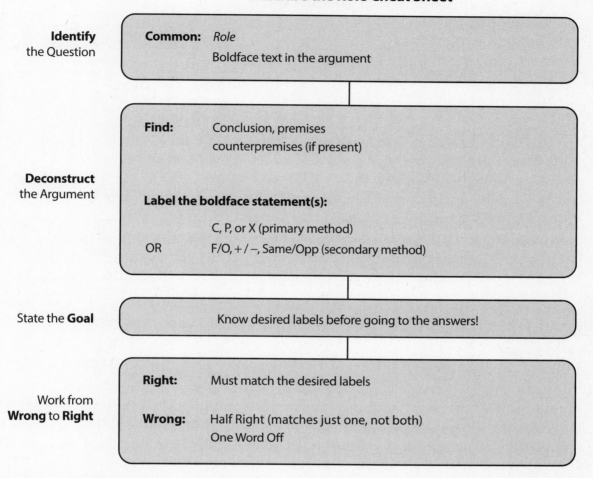

Describe the Role Cheat Sheet

Identify the Question	**Common:** *Role* Boldface text in the argument
Deconstruct the Argument	**Find:** Conclusion, premises counterpremises (if present) **Label the boldface statement(s):** C, P, or X (primary method) OR F/O, + / −, Same/Opp (secondary method)
State the **Goal**	Know desired labels before going to the answers!
Work from **Wrong** to **Right**	**Right:** Must match the desired labels **Wrong:** Half Right (matches just one, not both) One Word Off

Take a picture of this page and keep it with the review sheets you're creating as you study. Better yet, use this page as a guide to create your own review sheet—you'll remember the material better if you write it down yourself. Where appropriate, put it in your own words and you'll remember it even better.

Describe the Argument Cheat Sheet

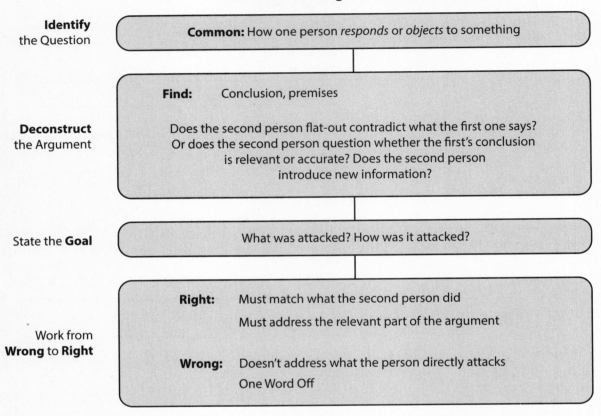

Describe the Argument Cheat Sheet

Identify the Question	**Common:** How one person *responds* or *objects* to something
Deconstruct the Argument	**Find:** Conclusion, premises Does the second person flat-out contradict what the first one says? Or does the second person question whether the first's conclusion is relevant or accurate? Does the second person introduce new information?
State the **Goal**	What was attacked? How was it attacked?
Work from **Wrong** to **Right**	**Right:** Must match what the second person did Must address the relevant part of the argument **Wrong:** Doesn't address what the person directly attacks One Word Off

Take a picture of this page and keep it with the review sheets you're creating as you study. Better yet, use this page as a guide to create your own review sheet—you'll remember the material better if you write it down yourself. Where appropriate, put it in your own words and you'll remember it even better.

15

Problem Set

Answer each question using the 4-step Critical Reasoning process.

1. **Identify the question:** Is this a Describe the Role question or a Describe the Argument question?

2. **Deconstruct the argument:** Find the conclusion and map the argument on your paper.

3. **State the goal:** What will the right answer need to do?

4. **Work from wrong to right:** Eliminate four wrong answers. Watch out for common wrong answer types.

1. *Ad Revenues*

Media Critic: Network executives allege that television viewership is decreasing due to the availability of television programs on other platforms, such as the internet and mobile devices. These executives claim that **declining viewership will cause advertising revenue to fall and networks will thus be unable to spend the large sums necessary to produce high-quality programming**. That development, in turn, will lead to a dearth of programming for the very devices that cannibalized television's audience. However, research shows that users of alternative platforms are exposed to new programs and, **as a result, actually increase the number of hours per week that they watch television**. This demonstrates that alternative platforms will not prevent networks from increasing advertising revenue.

The portions in boldface play which of the following roles in the media critic's argument?

(A) The first is a trend that weighs against the critic's claim; the second is that claim.

(B) The first is a prediction that is challenged by the argument; the second is a finding upon which the argument depends.

(C) The first clarifies the reasoning behind the critic's claim; the second demonstrates why that claim is flawed.

(D) The first acknowledges a position that the network executives accept as true; the second is a consequence of that position.

(E) The first opposes the critic's claim through an analogy; the second outlines a scenario in which that claim will not hold.

2.   *Renaissance Masters*

Many people praise High Renaissance painting for creating very realistic images from observation, but **scholars have documented that some High Renaissance painters used pinhole cameras to project the likeness of their subjects onto the canvas and painted from there**. Thus, people who credit High Renaissance painters with superior artistic skills are misguided. **Painting from a projected image requires only an insignificant amount of additional skill beyond that needed to copy a picture outright.**

In the argument given, the two boldfaced portions play which of the following roles?

(A)   The first is a finding that has been used to support a conclusion that the argument rejects; the second is a claim that supports that conclusion.

(B)   The first is a finding that has been used to support a conclusion that the argument rejects; the second is that conclusion.

(C)   The first is a claim put forth to support a conclusion that the argument rejects; the second is a consideration that is introduced to counter the force of that evidence.

(D)   The first is evidence that forms the basis for the position that the argument seeks to establish; the second is a claim presented to solidify that position.

(E)   The first is evidence that forms the basis for the position that the argument seeks to establish; the second is that position.

3.   *Democracy*

As the United States demonstrated during its early development, it is not enough for citizens simply to have rights; the successful functioning of a democracy requires that they also know how to exercise those rights. Access to formal education was one necessary component that helped the U.S. citizenry learn how to exercise its rights. Therefore, in order for a democracy to function successfully, its citizens must have access to a formal education.

The author develops the argument by

(A)   using an analogy to establish a precedent for a planned future event

(B)   illustrating differences in the requirements for the functioning of a democracy depending upon the democracy in question

(C)   introducing an example that illustrates a common principle

(D)   forming a hypothesis that explains apparently contradictory pieces of evidence

(E)   supplying an alternate explanation for a known phenomenon

15

4. *Malaria*

In an attempt to explain the cause of malaria, a deadly infectious disease, early European settlers in Hong Kong attributed the malady to poisonous gases supposedly emanating from low-lying swampland. In the 1880s, however, doctors determined that Anopheles mosquitoes were responsible for transmitting the disease to humans after observing that **the female of the species can carry a parasitic protozoan that is passed on to unsuspecting humans when a mosquito feasts on a person's blood**.

What function does the statement in boldface fulfill with respect to the argument presented above?

(A) It provides support for the explanation of a particular phenomenon.

(B) It presents evidence that contradicts an established fact.

(C) It offers confirmation of a contested assumption.

(D) It identifies the cause of an erroneous conclusion.

(E) It proposes a new conclusion in place of an earlier conjecture.

5. *Digital Marketing*

Sania: The newest workers in the workforce are the most effective digital marketing employees because they are more likely to use social networking websites and tools themselves.

Carlos: But effective digital marketing also requires very technical expertise, such as search engine optimization, that is best learned on the job via prolonged exposure and instruction.

Carlos responds to Sania by

(A) demonstrating that Sania's conclusion is based upon evidence that is not relevant to the given situation

(B) questioning the accuracy of the evidence presented by Sania in support of her conclusion

(C) reinforcing Sania's argument by contributing an additional piece of evidence in support of her conclusion

(D) pointing out differences in the qualifications desired by different employers seeking digital marketing employees

(E) providing an additional piece of evidence that undermines a portion of Sania's claim

6. *Innovative Design*

Products with innovative and appealing designs relative to competing products can often command substantially higher prices in the marketplace. **Because design innovations are quickly copied by other manufacturers**, many consumer technology companies charge as much as possible for their new designs to extract as much value as possible from them. But large profits generated by the innovative designs give competitors stronger incentives to copy the designs. Therefore, **the best strategy to maximize overall profit from an innovative new design is to charge less than the greatest possible price**.

In the argument above, the two portions in boldface play which of the following roles?

(A) The first is an assumption that supports a described course of action; the second provides a consideration to support a preferred course of action.

(B) The first is a consideration that helps explain the appeal of a certain strategy; the second presents an alternative strategy endorsed by the argument.

(C) The first is a phenomenon that makes a specific strategy unlikely to be successful; the second is that strategy.

(D) The first is a consideration that demonstrates why a particular approach is flawed; the second describes a way to amend that approach.

(E) The first is a factor used to rationalize a particular strategy; the second is a factor against that strategy.

7. *Gray Wolf Population*

Government representative: Between 1996 and 2005, the gray wolf population in Minnesota grew nearly 50%; the gray wolf population in Montana increased by only 13% during the same period. Clearly, the Minnesota gray wolf population is more likely to survive and thrive long term.

Environmentalist: But the gray wolf population in Montana is nearly eight times the population in Minnesota; above a certain critical breeding number, the population is stable and does not require growth in order to survive.

The environmentalist challenges the government representative's argument by doing which of the following?

(A) Introducing additional evidence that undermines an assumption made by the representative

(B) Challenging the representative's definition of a critical breeding number

(C) Demonstrating that the critical breeding number of the two wolf populations differs significantly

(D) Implying that the two populations of wolves could be combined in order to preserve the species

(E) Suggesting that the Montana wolf population grew at a faster rate than stated in the representative's argument

15

Solutions

1. Ad Revenues: The correct answer is **(B)**.

   Step 1: Identify the Question

The portions in boldface play which of the following roles in the media critic's argument?	*This is a Role question. The question contains the word* boldface, *and I'm asked to find the* role *of each bold statement.*	R A B C D E

   Step 2: Deconstruct the Argument

Media Critic: Network executives allege that television viewership is decreasing due to the availability of television programs on other platforms, such as the internet and mobile devices.	*The word* allege *tells me this is a claim. Also, the critic is talking about what other people claim, so I'm guessing the critic is going to contradict what they claim—so this is probably a counter-premise.*	Critic: Execs say TV ↓ b/c use other plats
These executives claim that **declining viewership will cause advertising revenue to fall and networks will thus be unable to spend the large sums necessary to produce high-quality programming**.	*More from the execs. More claims about bad things happening. Is the last thing the execs' conclusion? This is the 1st boldface. If the critic contradicts the execs later, then this first boldface will be labeled an X.*	Execs: TV ↓ → ad ↓ → no $ for qual prog
That development, in turn, will lead to a dearth of programming for the very devices that cannibalized television's audience.	*Ah, I see. Ironic. The fact that people are watching on other platforms will eventually lead to not having enough programming for those other platforms. Conclusion of the execs.*	→ No prog for other plats
However, research shows that users of alternative platforms are exposed to new programs and, **as a result, actually increase the number of hours per week that they watch television**.	*Here's the contradiction! I'll wait till I find the conclusion for sure, but the first boldface is probably an X, which would make this one a premise (P).*	BUT users of alt plats watch MORE TV
This demonstrates that alternative platforms will not prevent networks from increasing advertising revenue.	*Okay, the critic is concluding the opposite: that ad rates will go up. And if that's my conclusion, then the first boldface is indeed an X and the second one supports the critic's conclusion, so it's a P.*	© Ad rates Want: X P

15

Step 3: State the Goal

The question asks me to find the role of two boldface statements. The critic's conclusion is in the last line, and the second boldface, right before it, supports that conclusion. The second boldface is a premise (P). The first boldface is part of the executives' argument, which is the opposite of the critic's argument, so the first boldface is an X. I want to find the combo X P (in that order) in an answer choice.

Step 4: Work from Wrong to Right

(A) The first is a trend that weighs against the critic's claim; the second is that claim.	*Weighs against the critic's claim—yes, that's consistent with an X label. The second is that claim, meaning the critic's claim? No. The second boldface is a P supporting the author's conclusion; it's not the author's actual conclusion.*	A̶
(B) The first is a prediction that is challenged by the argument; the second is a finding upon which the argument depends.	*That's true, the critic does challenge the first one. That's an X. And the second one is a P, so this could be something upon which the critic's argument depends. I'll keep it in.*	B ~
(C) The first clarifies the reasoning behind the critic's claim; the second demonstrates why that claim is flawed.	*Clarifies the critic's claim? No. The first one is something the execs claim. I don't even need to read the second half of the answer.*	C̶
(D) The first acknowledges a position that the network executives accept as true; the second is a consequence of that position.	*Yes, the execs do accept the first boldface as true—it's their premise. And they're on the opposite side of the critic, so something they think is an X. Okay, that's fine. The second is a consequence of that position. What position? Oh, they use position in the first half of the sentence . . . the execs' position. The second isn't something about the execs' position. It goes against the execs' position. No.*	D̶
(E) The first opposes the critic's claim through an analogy; the second outlines a scenario in which that claim will not hold.	*The first one does oppose what the critic concludes. I'm not quite sure whether it does so through an analogy. What about the second half? A scenario in which the critic's claim won't hold—meaning something that's on the opposite side of what the critic says. No! The second one outlines a scenario in which the execs' claim, not the critic's claim, won't hold.*	E̶

2. Renaissance Masters: The correct answer is **(D)**.

Step 1: Identify the Question

In the argument given, the two boldfaced portions play which of the following roles?	*The word* boldfaced, *along with the boldface font in the argument, indicates that this is a Role question.*	R A B C D E

Step 2: Deconstruct the Argument

Many people praise High Renaissance painting for creating very realistic images from observation,	*The* many people *intro feels like there's a contrast coming … and there is! Okay, just get this piece down first.*	Many like Hi Ren pics b/c realistic
but **scholars have documented that some High Renaissance painters used pinhole cameras to project the likeness of their subjects onto the canvas and painted from there**.	*People think the High Renaissance painters could paint realistically just by observing, but actually some were just projecting the images onto a canvas and sort of tracing the image.*	BUT some painters just projected + traced
Thus, people who credit High Renaissance painters with superior artistic skills are misguided.	*The word* thus *might mean this is the conclusion. The previous sentence only said that* some *painters did the tracing thing, not all of them. But this sentence seems to be condemning all of them.*	People who like Hi Ren = misguided
Painting from a projected image requires only an insignificant amount of additional skill beyond that needed to copy a picture outright.	*Okay, the last sentence was definitely the conclusion. This sentence is supporting the conclusion. If this is true, then yes, painters who use this technique aren't that great.*	project = low skill
	I'm not 100% sure how to label the first boldface, but I did notice that the first one was a fact and the second one was an opinion. I could use the Secondary Method to solve.	

Step 3: State the Goal

I need to identify the role of the two boldfaced statements as they relate to the conclusion—which was that people who think High Renaissance painters are really skilled are misguided. The first one is a fact, and the second one is an opinion. The first one is FOR the conclusion. So is the second one.

Step 4: Work from Wrong to Right

(A) The first is a finding that has been used to support a conclusion that the argument rejects; the second is a claim that supports that conclusion.	*A finding could be a fact, and a claim is an opinion, so this one is okay so far.*	A ~
(B) The first is a finding that has been used to support a conclusion that the argument rejects; the second is that conclusion.	*A finding could be a fact, and the conclusion is technically an opinion. But the boldface opinion is FOR the conclusion; it's not actually the conclusion itself.*	~~B~~
(C) The first is a claim put forth to support a conclusion that the argument rejects; the second is a consideration that is introduced to counter the force of that evidence.	*A claim is not a fact. I can eliminate this one.*	~~C~~
(D) The first is evidence that forms the basis for the position that the argument seeks to establish; the second is a claim presented to solidify that position.	*Evidence can be a fact, and a claim is an opinion. This one has to stay in, too.*	D ~
(E) The first is evidence that forms the basis for the position that the argument seeks to establish; the second is that position.	*Evidence can be a fact, but the second boldface is an opinion supporting the conclusion, while this choice says that the second boldface is the* position, *or conclusion. I can eliminate this one.*	~~E~~
Compare (A) and (D).	*Based on the fact/opinion technique, I can't get any further; I just have to guess between (A) and (D).* *The main technique can distinguish between (A) and (D): Both boldfaces are premises used to support the author's conclusion. Answer (A) says that the first boldface is used "to support a conclusion that the argument rejects." Eliminate answer (A).*	~~A~~ ~ and D ~

372 Ⓜ **Critical Reasoning**

3. Democracy: The correct answer is (**C**).

Step 1: Identify the Question

The author develops the argument by	*The wording is similar to a Describe the Argument question, though it doesn't have the "two people talking" feature. This might be one of the rare variants that doesn't have two people talking. A quick glance at the abstract wording of the answer choices confirms: This is a Describe Arg question.*	DA A B C D E

Step 2: Deconstruct the Argument

As the United States demonstrated during its early development, it is not enough for citizens simply to have rights; the successful functioning of a democracy requires that they also know how to exercise those rights.	*Okay, specific example of a principle: the U.S. showed that citizens need to have rights AND need to know how to exercise those rights.*	US: not just have rights but know how to exercise → success democ
Access to formal education was one necessary component that helped the U.S. citizenry learn how to exercise its rights.	*More detail on the U.S. example. Access to formal education was needed to know how to exercise those rights.*	Need access to formal educ →
Therefore, in order for a democracy to function successfully, its citizens must have access to a formal education.	*Conclusion. The author's just sort of putting together the two "end" pieces of the argument here.*	© Need formal edu for success democ

Step 3: State the Goal

The author concludes that formal education is necessary in general for a democracy to be successful. The evidence: It happened this way in one country (the U.S.).

15

Step 4: Work from Wrong to Right

(A) using an analogy to establish a precedent for a planned future event	*The argument used an example. Is that the same thing as an analogy? Maybe. Oh, but what's the planned future event? There isn't anything; rather, the author concluded with a general statement, not a discussion of an event.*	~~A~~
(B) illustrating differences in the requirements for the functioning of a democracy depending upon the democracy in question	*I can imagine that it would be true that there are different requirements for different governments . . . but that's not what this argument says. The author only mentions the U.S. and then concludes something in general about that.*	~~B~~
(C) introducing an example that illustrates a common principle	*This looks decent. The argument did introduce an example and then used that to conclude a general principle.*	C̰
(D) forming a hypothesis that explains apparently contradictory pieces of evidence	*It would be reasonable to describe the conclusion as a hypothesis . . . but there aren't any contradictory things in the argument. Rather, the example given does illustrate the conclusion.*	~~D~~
(E) supplying an alternate explanation for a known phenomenon	*The author doesn't supply an alternate explanation; he isn't arguing against anyone. He just concludes something from the U.S. example.*	~~E~~

4. Malaria: The correct answer is **(A)**.

Step 1: Identify the Question

What function does the statement in boldface fulfill with respect to the argument presented above?	*This is a Role question. The question contains the word* boldface, *and I'm asked to find the function of each bold statement.*	R A B C D E

Step 2: Deconstruct the Argument

In an attempt to explain the cause of malaria, a deadly infectious disease, early European settlers in Hong Kong attributed the malady to poisonous gases supposedly emanating from low-lying swampland.	*This is a fact. Likely either background or premise.*	Euros in HK: Poison gas → malaria
In the 1880s, however, doctors determined that Anopheles mosquitoes were responsible for transmitting the disease to humans after observing that **the female of the species can carry a parasitic protozoan that is passed on to unsuspecting humans when a mosquito feasts on a person's blood**.	*Okay, this is still a fact, but it's the conclusion of the story. They used to think it was one thing, and then they figured out it was really the mosquitoes. The boldface language, in particular, is the evidence used to show that it was mosquitoes. That's a premise.*	But 1880s MDs: mosq bite, pass parasite blood Want: P

Step 3: State the Goal

The question specifically asks me what role this information plays: the female carries a parasite that is passed to humans when a mosquito bites someone. Because of that, the scientists decided that the mosquitoes were transmitting the disease. That's the most like a P—a premise that supports some further conclusion.

I need to find the abstract language that indicates some kind of premise or support.

Step 4: Work from Wrong to Right

(A) It provides support for the explanation of a particular phenomenon.	Support—*that's good*—for a phenomenon. *Okay, that's just fancy-speak for: Provides support for something that happened. That sounds okay. Leave it in.*	A̰
(B) It presents evidence that contradicts an established fact.	Evidence—*that's also good. And that evidence does contradict what the earlier settlers thought! Oh, wait—was that an established fact? Let me look at the first sentence again. No, they thought that, but the argument doesn't say it was an* established fact. *Cross this one off.*	~~B~~
(C) It offers confirmation of a contested assumption.	Confirmation *is also good . . . of a contested assumption. I'm not quite sure what they're referring to when they say* assumption, *but nothing was contested here. First, some people thought one thing, and later, new evidence led some doctors to conclude something else. No.*	~~C~~
(D) It identifies the cause of an erroneous conclusion.	*No—the only thing we might be able to describe as an erroneous conclusion is what the early settlers thought. But the bold stuff supports the doctors' conclusion.*	~~D~~
(E) It proposes a new conclusion in place of an earlier conjecture.	*Oh, yes, a new conclusion. Yes, that's exactly what the argument says! Oh, wait—I labeled the boldface stuff a P, not a C. Why was that? Oh, I see—tricky. The first half of the sentence, the non-bold part, is the new conclusion. The bold part is the evidence supporting that. This isn't it after all!*	~~E~~

 Ⓐ ~~B~~ ~~C~~ ~~D~~ ~~E~~

5. Digital Marketing: The correct answer is **(E)**.

Step 1: Identify the Question

Carlos responds to Sania by	The "two person" structure and the focus on how Carlos responds indicate that this is a Describe the Argument question.	DA A B C D E

Step 2: Deconstruct the Argument

Sania: The newest workers in the workforce are the most effective digital marketing employees because they are more likely to use social networking websites and tools themselves.	Sania claims that the workers who use certain online tools are also the most effective at digital marketing and that those people are the newest workers.	Sania: New empl use soc nw → most eff dig mktg ©
Carlos: But effective digital marketing also requires very technical expertise, such as search engine optimization, that is best learned on the job via prolonged exposure and instruction.	Carlos doesn't dispute Sania's evidence, but he brings up a new point: You also need these other skills to be a good digital marketer . . . and those skills are learned on the job over a long (prolonged) time . . . which hurts Sania's claim that the newest workers are the most effective.	Carlos: But eff dig mktg needs tech expertise, best learned on job

Step 3: State the Goal

I need to articulate how Carlos responds to Sania. He doesn't say that she's wrong about the newest workers using social networking tools. Rather, he says that digital marketers also need this other skill that takes a long time to learn on the job. If that's the case, this weakens Sania's claim that the newest workers are the most effective.

Step 4: Work from Wrong to Right

(A) demonstrating that Sania's conclusion is based upon evidence that is not relevant to the given situation	*Carlos doesn't say anything negative about Sania's evidence; rather, he introduces new evidence that attacks Sania's assumption that her piece of evidence is the most important thing to consider.*	~~A~~
(B) questioning the accuracy of the evidence presented by Sania in support of her conclusion	*This is similar to choice (A); Carlos doesn't question Sania's evidence.*	~~B~~
(C) reinforcing Sania's argument by contributing an additional piece of evidence in support of her conclusion	*Carlos does contribute an additional piece of evidence, but his new evidence hurts Sania's argument. Carlos doesn't support Sania's conclusion.*	~~C~~
(D) pointing out differences in the qualifications desired by different employers seeking digital marketing employees	*Carlos does point out a different way to assess the effectiveness of digital marketing employees, but he doesn't mention employers at all or differences among different employers.*	~~D~~
(E) providing an additional piece of evidence that undermines a portion of Sania's claim	*Bingo. This is exactly what Carlos does—a new piece of information that hurts the* newest workers *portion of Sania's claim.*	E

6. Innovative Design: The correct answer is (**B**).

   Step 1: Identify the Question

In the argument above, the two portions in boldface play which of the following roles?	*This is a Role question. The question contains the word* boldface, *and I'm asked to find the* role *of each bold statement.*	R A B C D E

   Step 2: Deconstruct the Argument

Products with innovative and appealing designs relative to competing products can often command substantially higher prices in the marketplace.	*Sort of between a fact and a claim. Probably a premise.*	Innov designs → ↑↑ $
Because design innovations are quickly copied by other manufacturers, many consumer technology companies charge as much as possible for their new designs to extract as much value as possible from them.	*Getting more toward claim-based material, with the first half of the sentence providing support for the second half. I'm not sure yet whether this is the conclusion though.*	Because others copy many co's charge ↑↑ $
But large profits generated by the innovative designs give competitors stronger incentives to copy the designs.	*The word* but *signals a contrast. Oh, so there's actually a drawback to making a lot of money: Competitors will copy even faster so I guess that could hurt market share. That's interesting.*	BUT ↑↑ prof → incent to copy
Therefore, **the best strategy to maximize overall profit from an innovative new design is to charge less than the greatest possible price**.	*Here we go, the conclusion. The person's claiming that companies actually shouldn't charge the largest possible price and this will actually help maximize profits in the end. The second boldface is the conclusion; that gets a C. The first boldface is a premise that supports a strategy the argument disagrees with (that companies should charge the greatest possible price for an ID).*	Ⓒ to max prof charge < than max price Want: X C

15

Step 3: State the Goal

The question asks me to determine the role played by each of two boldface statements. I've decided the second one is the conclusion and the first is a premise supporting an alternate strategy, so I want to find an answer that gives this combo: X C (in that order).

Step 4: Work from Wrong to Right

(A) The first is an assumption that supports a described course of action; the second provides a consideration to support a preferred course of action.	*Hmm, they call the first an assumption, not a premise, but I suppose that's okay; they do say it* supports *something. The second, though, is the actual conclusion—but this answer choice makes the second sound like another premise. I don't think so.*	~~A~~
(B) The first is a consideration that helps explain the appeal of a certain strategy; the second presents an alternative strategy endorsed by the argument.	*The wording for the first statement is a little strange, but I suppose that could be considered a premise. And it does support the greatest-possible-price strategy. The second boldface is the strategy the argument supports. Keep this one.*	B ~
(C) The first is a phenomenon that makes a specific strategy unlikely to be successful; the second is that strategy.	*The first boldface provides support for the first strategy. It definitely doesn't weaken the author's strategy. Eliminate this answer choice.*	~~C~~
(D) The first is a consideration that demonstrates why a particular approach is flawed; the second describes a way to amend that approach.	*No, the first supports the alternate strategy—it doesn't illustrate a flaw. I don't even need to read the second half of this choice.*	~~D~~
(E) The first is a factor used to rationalize a particular strategy; the second is a factor against that strategy.	*Something used to* rationalize *a strategy? Yes, that could be describing a premise that supports the alternate strategy. Oh, but the second goes against the strategy? No! The second is actually the author's strategy.*	~~E~~

7. Gray Wolf Population: The correct answer is (A).

Step 1: Identify the Question

The environmentalist challenges the government representative's argument by doing which of the following?	*There's a 2-person-talking structure, and I'm asked how the second person responds; this is a Describe the Argument question.*	DA A B C D E

Step 2: Deconstruct the Argument

Government representative: Between 1996 and 2005, the gray wolf population in Minnesota grew nearly 50%; the gray wolf population in Montana increased by only 13% during the same period.	*This is just a straight fact. The Minnesota wolf population grew a lot faster in that time period than the Montana wolf population.*	Gov rep: 96–05, wolf in Minn ↑ 50%, in Mont only ↑ 13%
Clearly, the Minnesota gray wolf population is more likely to survive and thrive long term.	*Conclusion! Claiming that Minnesota wolves are more likely to survive and thrive. Certainly, the Minnesota wolf population grew more . . . but does that automatically mean they're more likely to survive and thrive?*	Ⓒ Minn > likely to survive/ thrive
Environmentalist: But the gray wolf population in Montana is nearly eight times the population in Minnesota; above a certain critical breeding number, the population is stable and does not require growth in order to survive.	*Ah, okay. The environmentalist is pointing out that they're not necessarily the same thing. Once the population is large enough, it's already stable, so growth isn't necessarily critical to survival.*	Enviro: BUT Mont 8x Minn; when ↑ enough, pop = stable

Step 3: State the Goal

The gov rep concludes that the Minnesota wolves are more likely to survive and thrive because the growth rate was a lot higher, but the environmentalist responds that the Montana population was already a lot larger, so growth might not have been necessary to keep the population thriving. The Montana population might already have been stable in the first place.

I need to find something that explains this response in a more abstract way: A new piece of evidence changes the way someone would think about the issue addressed in the conclusion (surviving and thriving).

Ⓜ 381

Step 4: Work from Wrong to Right

(A) Introducing additional evidence that undermines an assumption made by the representative	*This sounds pretty good. The environmentalist's statement is a new piece of evidence, and it does undermine the government rep's assumption that growth is a good indicator of likelihood to survive and thrive.*	A ~
(B) Challenging the representative's definition of a critical breeding number	*The environmentalist challenges the rep's assumption about what it takes to survive and thrive, but the environmentalist can't challenge the rep on* critical breeding number, *because the rep never mentions this concept.*	~~B~~
(C) Demonstrating that the critical breeding number of the two wolf populations differs significantly	*The environmentalist mentions the concept of* critical breeding number, *but establishes only that the number of wolves in each population differs significantly, not that the number of wolves needed to achieve the critical breeding number is different.*	~~C~~
(D) Implying that the two populations of wolves could be combined in order to preserve the species	*This might be an interesting strategy, but the environmentalist never mentions it.*	~~D~~
(E) Suggesting that the Montana wolf population grew at a faster rate than stated in the representative's argument	*This is tricky. The environmentalist introduces a new figure, but that figure has to do with the size of the two populations, not the rate of growth. The environmentalist does not dispute the rep's figures for rate of growth.*	~~E~~

Wrong Answer Analysis

In This Chapter...

In this chapter, you will learn about certain common types of traps that the GMAT likes to set for you. You'll also learn how to spot and avoid them!

CHAPTER 16 Wrong Answer Analysis

In previous chapters, you learned about all of the question types along with their common traps or wrong answer types. This chapter is a summary of the "wrong answer" information scattered throughout the question-types chapters, and it also contains additional examples to illustrate the characteristics of these common traps.

The multiple different wrong-answer types are grouped into four big categories:

1. No Tie to the Argument
2. Reverse Logic
3. The Diversion
4. Close but No Cigar

No Tie to the Argument/Conclusion

This wrong-answer type is most commonly found in the five Assumption Family question types: Find the Assumption, Strengthen the Argument, Weaken the Argument, Evaluate the Argument, and Find the Flaw.

Assumption Family question types all contain premises and a conclusion, known collectively as the author's argument. For each of the question types, the correct answer has to affect the overall argument in a specific way. If the choice does not actually affect that argument, then it must be wrong.

Consider this example:

> In order to improve retention of the most productive employees, Q Corp plans to allocate the bonus pool in such a way that the longest-serving employees will earn the highest bonuses.
>
> Which of the following, if true, would strengthen the claim that Q Corp's plan will succeed?
>
> (F) Q Corp also plans to improve healthcare benefits.
> (G) The most productive employees have been with Q Corp an average of 13 years, which is longer than the average employee tenure at the company.

The argument is not just that Q Corp wants to improve employee retention in general. The argument is the *entire plan*: Q Corp will allocate bonuses in a certain way in order to improve employee retention.

The bonus plan will clearly reward the people who have been there the longest. Are they also the most productive employees? Choice (B) bridges this gap by indicating that the most productive employees have indeed worked for the company for a long time.

Note that this choice does not make Q Corp's plan perfect. It's possible that some very productive employees have not been at the company that long, but overall, the plan is more *likely* to be valid. This standard (more likely to be valid) is all that is required for a Strengthen question.

Choice (A) is tempting because it is reasonable to think that improving other benefits will help the overall goal of improving retention of the most productive employees. This might very well be true—but the question doesn't ask you to come up with ways to reach the overall goal. Rather, it asks you to strengthen the *given argument*: that this plan will work in the way described. Choice (A) doesn't say anything about the given plan. It has No Tie to the Argument. Don't dismiss an answer just because it has new language. Instead focus on the logical connection between the answer and the argument.

Some choices are part of a subset of this wrong answer type; they have No Tie to the Conclusion (as opposed to the overall argument or plan). In these cases, a choice might address a premise of the argument but it may have no impact on the conclusion, specifically.

Take a look at this example:

Question	"No Tie to the Conclusion" Wrong Answer
Which of the following, if true, best supports the claim that women who are under 5 feet 10 inches tall cannot have successful careers as basketball players?	Some women who are over 5 feet 10 inches tall are likely to excel at basketball.

In many ways, the wrong answer seems relevant: it's talking about women and basketball; it mentions the "5 feet 10 inch" height threshold. It does not, however, provide any information about women who are under 5 feet 10 inches tall. The conclusion claimed something about this *specific* group of women. If the answer on a Strengthen question does not actually address the given conclusion, then it has No Tie to the Conclusion.

Reverse Logic

One of the most tempting traps is the Reverse Logic trap, when you accidentally pick the opposite of what you really want, such as an answer that strengthens on a Weaken question. Reverse Logic traps occur most frequently on Assumption Family and Evidence Family questions.

One of the most common ways in which you fall into this trap is to misidentify the conclusion, particularly when the argument contains two "sides," or points of view. Consider this example:

> Some companies tie bonuses to company performance as well as personal performance, on the theory that individual performance is only valuable as far as it benefits the company as a whole. This is counterproductive, however, because the highest-performing employees are essentially penalized by receiving a bonus commensurate only with the average performance of the overall company, thereby leading to a lack of motivation to continue to outperform their peers.

What are the claims here? Some companies think that "individual performance is only valuable if it benefits the company as a whole" and set up their bonus plans accordingly. Some unknown person, on the other hand, thinks that this viewpoint is "counterproductive" and will "[lead] to a lack of motivation" on the part of the best employees. Which is the main conclusion?

The author's point of view is always the main conclusion. In this case, the "unknown person" is the author. If a claim is attributed to a particular person or group, that claim is likely *not* the author's claim. A claim that is simply asserted, with no commentary as to who is doing the asserting, must be the author's claim.

16

It would be easy to mix up the claims, though, and that in turn would make it easy to pick a Reverse Logic answer, since the two claims are on opposing sides of the fence.

Consider this problem, using the same argument:

> Some companies tie bonuses to company performance as well as personal performance, on the theory that individual performance is only valuable as far as it benefits the company as a whole in some way. This is counterproductive, however, because the highest-performing employees are essentially penalized by receiving a bonus commensurate only with the average performance of the overall company, thereby leading to a lack of motivation to continue to outperform their peers.
>
> Which of the following, if true, would most seriously undermine the argument above?
>
> (A) The performance of employees who feel they aren't appropriately compensated for their efforts often drops.
>
> (B) High-performing employees typically state that their primary motivation is the satisfaction of a job well done.

In this example, choice (A) strengthens the conclusion instead of weakening it (and it is even easier to fall into this trap if you misidentify the conclusion!). The correct answer, on the other hand, does weaken the author's conclusion by offering a reason why employees might continue to work hard regardless of compensation levels.

The Diversion

Some answers try to mix you up by emphasizing a distracting point or switching terms around to muddle the message. Three wrong answer types fall into this category.

1. Irrelevant Distinction

Consider this argument:

> Students who earn A and B grades are more likely to participate in sports than are students who earn C grades. Therefore, participation in sports helps students achieve higher grades.

You're asked to find an assumption. An incorrect answer might say something like:

> Students who earn A grades participate in sports more frequently than those who earn B grades.

The answer separates, or makes a distinction between, the A and B students. But the argument grouped together the grade-A and grade-B students; it treated them in the same way! The distinction was between those two sets of students and the C students. The answer is an example of an irrelevant distinction; the differences between A and B students don't matter to the argument as given.

These wrong answers tend to show up the most in Assumption Family questions.

2. Real-World Distraction

Tricky wrong answers on Inference questions will try to distract you with reasonable-sounding information that might seem true in the real world. However, the correct Inference answer must be proven using the information in the argument. You cannot prove any wrong answer, as tempting as it may seem.

For example:

> Teachers who switch careers are most likely to leave the teaching profession in their third year of teaching. A majority of teachers who remain in the profession for at least seven years stick with teaching for the remainder of their careers.
>
> Which of the following conclusions can most properly be drawn from the information above?
>
> (A) Most teachers who leave the profession do so because the work is very stressful and the pay poor.
>
> (B) A majority of teachers who leave the profession do so within three years of beginning to teach.
>
> (C) A teacher in his sixth year of teaching is more likely to remain in the profession than one who is in his third year of teaching.

Choices (A) and (B) are both Real-World Distractions. You've probably known at least one teacher who complained about the stress level and pay for the job. You might even have read statistics showing that a high percentage of teachers do leave the profession in the first three years on the job (though the real number is below half). However, neither of those things can be proven from the given argument.

At first, answer choice (C) might seem wrong because it mentions a year that isn't mentioned in the argument. This choice can actually be proven true, though. The third year is the year in which a teacher is *most* likely to leave the profession. Therefore, a teacher in the sixth year (or second year, or twentieth year of his career) must be less likely to leave than the one in his third year.

3. Switching Terms

Some tempting wrong answers will switch terms on you. The answer choice will use actual wording or terminology from the argument but will switch the terms around or pair things that weren't actually paired in the argument. For instance, consider the following statement; what can you infer?

> Studies have shown that holding a blood drive tends to stimulate the participation of members of an organization and increase the number of donations.
>
> (A) Holding a blood drive helps an organization to increase the number of members.

Match the terms. The argument says that the blood drive will increase the number of *donations*, not the number of *members*. Trap answer (A) switched terms! It might be true that the blood drive also increases the number of members, but the argument doesn't indicate anything of the sort! The argument indicates only that the member *participation* is stimulated.

An argument might also use something that seems like a synonym but isn't. For example, an argument might talk about art. One of the answer choices might talk about a museum. Museums do contain art, so that might be okay, but it might not—you need to check whether museums are actually relevant or whether the answer is just trying to get you to think so because museums do have something to do with art. Synonyms are okay if they do actually match the overall argument, but they can also be used as traps.

Close but No Cigar

The final major category consists of those answers that are oh-so-close, but not quite right. These tend to show up most on Structure Family or Explain a Discrepancy questions.

16

One Word Off

The One Word Off variety is simple, in the sense that only one or two words are off. These are also quite difficult and tempting, though, because only a single word could make the difference!

For example, what's the difference between the two answer choices below?

> The first is a prediction that supports a position that the argument concludes.

> The first is a prediction that supports a position that the argument opposes.

Only one word is different—the very last word—and yet that one word changes everything. The first sample answer is describing a premise: something that supports the author's conclusion. The second, on the other hand, is describing a counterpoint: something that *goes against* the author's conclusion. If you're reading too quickly or skim over a word, that can be the difference between picking the right answer and falling for a tempting trap.

Half Right

Answers to Describe the Role questions might be Half Right. For instance, an answer could accurately describe the first boldface statement but not the second. Explain the Discrepancy questions can have a similar problem: the correct answer might address one half of the apparent discrepancy but not the other half. It's impossible to explain a discrepancy without addressing both halves, so don't pick an answer that addresses only one half!

In short, Half Right is just as wrong as all wrong, so make sure to read each answer choice thoroughly.

On the next page, you'll find a summary of all of the wrong answer traps you learned about in this chapter.

16

Wrong Answer Traps

Keep a running list for yourself of the definitions of the wrong answer traps. You'll remember these better if you create a version using your own words.

CR Family	Question Types
Assumption Family	Find the Assumption, Strengthen the Argument, Weaken the Argument, Evaluate the Argument, Find the Flaw
Evidence Family	Inference, Explain a Discrepancy
Structure Family	Describe the Role, Describe the Argument

Type of Trap	Specific Trap	Description
No Tie (most common: Assumption Family)	No Tie to Argument	The answer choice does not affect the overall argument.
	No Tie to Conclusion	The answer choice does not affect the conclusion.
Reverse Logic (most common: Assumption and Evidence Families)	Reverse Logic	Does the opposite of what you want! For example, it strengthens rather than weakens.
The Diversion	Irrelevant Distinction (most common: Assumption Family)	Makes a distinction or comparison between two things that are not necessary to distinguish or compare.
	Real–World Distraction (most common: Inference)	Sounds good in the real world, but the argument doesn't say so.
	Switching Terms	Mixes up actual terms from the argument in a way that changes the meaning. Alternatively, may use synonyms that are too "loose"—check that any synonyms do fit the argument.
Close but No Cigar (most common: Structure Family; Explain a Discrepancy)	One Word Off	Almost right but one or two words mess it up. Read every word!
	Half Right	Does only half of what it should do. For example, it describes one boldface statement correctly but not the other.

16

Problem Set

The problem set consists of problems that you have already seen in earlier chapters of this book. Note: if you have not yet done these problems, then do them normally under the two-minute time constraint for the first time before doing the exercise described below.

For each of the following problems, identify the right answer, and try to articulate *why* each wrong answer is wrong. If you spot a particular category of wrong answer, write that down as well, but remember that the real test won't ask you to classify. Rather, your goal is to train yourself to be able to identify wrong answers accurately and efficiently; the wrong answer categories are just a tool to help you practice this. Also note that some wrong answers may not fit into any of the common categories listed in this chapter.

1. *Gray Wolf Population*

    From the Structure Family

    Government representative: Between 1996 and 2005, the gray wolf population in Minnesota grew nearly 50%; the gray wolf population in Montana increased by only 13% during the same period. Clearly, the Minnesota gray wolf population is more likely to survive and thrive long term.

    Environmentalist: But the gray wolf population in Montana is nearly 8 times the population in Minnesota; above a certain critical breeding number, the population is stable and does not require growth in order to survive.

    The environmentalist challenges the government representative's argument by doing which of the following?

    (A) Introducing additional evidence that undermines an assumption made by the representative
    (B) Challenging the representative's definition of a critical breeding number
    (C) Demonstrating that the critical breeding number of the two wolf populations differs significantly
    (D) Implying that the two populations of wolves could be combined in order to preserve the species
    (E) Suggesting that the Montana wolf population grew at a faster rate than stated in the representative's argument

16

2. *Malaria*

From the Structure Family

In an attempt to explain the cause of malaria, a deadly infectious disease, early European settlers in Hong Kong attributed the malady to poisonous gases supposedly emanating from low-lying swampland. In the 1880s, however, doctors determined that Anopheles mosquitoes were responsible for transmitting the disease to humans after observing that **the female of the species can carry a parasitic protozoan that is passed on to unsuspecting humans when a mosquito feasts on a person's blood.**

What function does the statement in boldface fulfill with respect to the argument presented above?

(A) It provides support for the explanation of a particular phenomenon.

(B) It presents evidence that contradicts an established fact.

(C) It offers confirmation of a contested assumption.

(D) It identifies the cause of an erroneous conclusion.

(E) It proposes a new conclusion in place of an earlier conjecture.

3. *Oil and Ethanol*

From Find the Assumption

Country N's oil production is not currently sufficient to meet its domestic demand. In order to sharply reduce its dependence on foreign sources of oil, Country N recently began requiring all automobiles produced in the country to use a blend of gasoline and ethanol, rather than gasoline alone. Country N produces enough ethanol from agricultural by-products to make up for the gap between its domestic oil production and its current demand for energy.

Which of the following must be assumed in order to conclude that Country N will succeed in its plan to reduce its dependence on foreign oil?

(A) Electric power is not a superior alternative to ethanol in supplementing automobile gasoline consumption.

(B) In Country N, domestic production of ethanol is increasing more quickly than domestic oil production.

(C) Ethanol is suitable for the heating of homes and other applications aside from automobiles.

(D) In Country N, gasoline consumption is not increasing at a substantially higher rate than domestic oil and ethanol production.

(E) Ethanol is as efficient as gasoline in terms of mileage per gallon when used as fuel for automobiles.

16

4.   *MTC and Asthma*

From Find the Assumption

Methyltetrachloride (MTC) is a chemical found in some pesticides, glues, and sealants. Exposure to MTC can cause people to develop asthma. In order to halve the nation's asthma rate, the government plans to ban all products containing MTC.

The government's plan to halve the nation's asthma rate relies on which of the following assumptions?

(A)   Exposure to MTC is responsible for no less than half of the nation's asthma cases.

(B)   Products containing MTC are not necessary to the prosperity of the American economy.

(C)   Asthma has reached epidemic proportions.

(D)   After MTC is used in an area, residual amounts of the chemical can be detected months or years later.

(E)   Dust mites and pet dander can also cause asthma.

5.   *Food Allergies*

From Evaluate the Argument and Find the Flaw

Food allergies account for more than 30,000 emergency room visits each year. Often, victims of these episodes are completely unaware of their allergies until they experience a major reaction. Studies show that 90% of food allergy reactions are caused by only eight distinct foods. For this reason, parents should feed a minuscule portion of each of these foods to their children to determine whether the children have these particular food allergies.

Which of the following must be studied in order to evaluate the recommendation made in the argument?

(A)   The percentage of allergy victims who were not aware of the allergy before a major episode

(B)   The percentage of the population that is at risk for allergic reactions

(C)   Whether some of the eight foods are common ingredients used in cooking

(D)   Whether an allergy to one type of food makes someone more likely to be allergic to other types of food

(E)   Whether ingesting a very small amount of an allergen is sufficient to provoke an allergic reaction in a susceptible individual

16

6.   *Smithtown Theater*

From Strengthen and Weaken

The Smithtown Theater, which stages old plays, has announced an expansion that will double its capacity along with its operating costs. The theater is only slightly profitable at present. In addition, all of the current customers live in Smithtown, and the population of the town is not expected to increase in the next several years. Thus, the expansion of the Smithtown Theater will prove unprofitable.

Which of the following, if true, would most seriously weaken the argument?

(A)   A large movie chain plans to open a new multiplex location in Smithtown later this year.

(B)   Concession sales in the Smithtown Theater comprise a substantial proportion of the theater's revenues.

(C)   Many recent arrivals to Smithtown are students who are less likely to attend the Smithtown Theater than are older residents.

(D)   The expansion would allow the Smithtown Theater to stage larger, more popular shows that will attract customers from neighboring towns.

(E)   The Board of the Smithtown Theater often solicits input from residents of the town when choosing which shows to stage.

7.   *Machu Picchu*

From Strengthen and Weaken

In 2001 the Peruvian government began requiring tourists to buy permits to hike the Inca Trail to the ancient city of Machu Picchu. Only 500 people per day are given permission to hike the Inca Trail, whereas before 2001 daily visitors numbered in the thousands. The Peruvian government claims that this permit program has successfully prevented deterioration of archaeological treasures along the Inca Trail.

Which of the following, if true, most strengthens the argument above?

(A)   Since 2001, Incan ruins similar to Machu Picchu but without a visitor limit have disintegrated at a significantly greater rate than those on the Inca Trail.

(B)   Villages near Machu Picchu have experienced declines in income, as fewer tourists buy fewer craft goods and refreshments.

(C)   Many of the funds from the sale of Inca Trail permits are used to hire guards for archaeological sites without permit programs.

(D)   Since 2001, tourist guides along the Inca Trail have received 50% to 100% increases in take-home pay.

(E)   Due to limited enforcement, the majority of tourists hiking the Inca Trail currently do so without a permit.

8.   *World Bank*

From the Evidence Family

In 2010, China comprised about 10% of the world's gross domestic product (GDP), and its voting share in the World Bank was increased from less than 3% to 4.4%. During the same time frame, France comprised about 4% of the world's GDP and saw its voting share in the World Bank drop from 4.3% to 3.8%.

Which of the following can be logically concluded from the passage above?

(A)   Prior to 2010, China comprised less than 10 percent of the world's gross domestic product.

(B)   Voting share in the World Bank is not directly proportional to each country's share of the world's GDP.

(C)   China's share in the world's gross domestic product is increasing more rapidly than France's share.

(D)   The Chinese government is likely to be dissatisfied with the degree of the increase in its voting share.

(E)   World Bank voting shares are allocated based upon each country's share of the world's GDP during previous years, not during the present year.

9.   *Barcodes*

From the Evidence Family

Two-dimensional barcodes are omni-directional; that is, unlike one-dimensional barcodes, they can be scanned from any direction. Additionally, two-dimensional barcodes are smaller and can store more data than their one-dimensional counterparts. Despite such advantages, two-dimensional barcodes account for a much smaller portion of total barcode usage than one-dimensional barcodes.

Which of the following, if true, most helps to resolve the apparent paradox?

(A)   Many smaller stores do not use barcodes at all because of the expense.

(B)   For some products, the amount of data necessary to be coded is small enough to fit fully on a one-dimensional barcode.

(C)   Two-dimensional barcodes are, on average, less expensive than one-dimensional barcodes.

(D)   Two-dimensional barcodes can also be scanned by consumer devices, such as cell phones.

(E)   One-dimensional barcodes last longer and are less prone to error than two-dimensional barcodes.

Solutions

1. *Gray Wolf Population*

   (A) Introducing additional evidence that undermines an assumption made by the representative

   This is the correct answer.

   (B) Challenging the representative's definition of a critical breeding number

   This answer Switches Terms. The environmentalist discusses critical breeding number, not the representative.

   (C) Demonstrating that the critical breeding number of the two wolf populations differs significantly

   This doesn't fit neatly into one of the standard trap categories. The environmentalist does mention the term "critical breeding number," but does not say that this number differs significantly. Rather, the environmentalist says that the population size differs.

   (D) Implying that the two populations of wolves could be combined in order to preserve the species

   This is a Real-World Distraction answer. It might be an interesting strategy in the real world, but the argument doesn't mention it.

   (E) Suggesting that the Montana wolf population grew at a faster rate than stated in the representative's argument

   This is a Switching Terms answer. The environmentalist does mention a number, but that number does not represent a rate of growth.

2. *Malaria*

   (A) It provides support for the explanation of a particular phenomenon.

   This is the correct answer.

   (B) It presents evidence that contradicts an established fact.

   This doesn't fit neatly into one of the standard trap categories. The boldface text does contradict what people once thought about malaria, but what they once thought was not an established fact.

   (C) It offers confirmation of a contested assumption.

   This is a One Word Off trap—nothing was contested in the argument.

   (D) It identifies the cause of an erroneous conclusion.

   This could be a Reverse Logic trap; you're looking for something that supports the conclusion.

   (E) It proposes a new conclusion in place of an earlier conjecture.

   This is a general Diversion answer; the argument does do this in general, but not the statement in boldface.

16

3.   *Oil and Ethanol*

(A)   Electric power is not a superior alternative to ethanol in supplementing automobile gasoline consumption.

This answer is an Irrelevant Distinction. The argument is about oil and ethanol, not electric power.

(B)   In Country N, domestic production of ethanol is increasing more quickly than domestic oil production.

This doesn't fit neatly into one of the standard trap categories. It looks good at first glance, but isn't actually necessary (which is a requirement for a correct answer on an Assumption question).

(C)   Ethanol is suitable for the heating of homes and other applications aside from automobiles.

This has No Tie to the Argument. What does the heating of homes have to do with the argument?

(D)   In Country N, gasoline consumption is not increasing at a substantially higher rate than domestic oil and ethanol production.

This is the correct answer.

(E)   Ethanol is as efficient as gasoline in terms of mileage per gallon when used as fuel for automobiles.

This answer makes an Irrelevant Distinction. Knowing how efficient the two are generally might help, but they don't necessarily have to be equally efficient. You could also classify this answer as No Tie to the Argument; the relative efficiency of two fuels doesn't inform you about overall dependency of foreign oil.

4.   *MTC and Asthma*

(A)   Exposure to MTC is responsible for no less than half of the nation's asthma cases.

This is the correct answer.

(B)   Products containing MTC are not necessary to the prosperity of the American economy.

This answer has No Tie to the Argument. In the real world, it might be important to evaluate the economic impact of banning MTC, but the argument is solely focused on cutting the asthma rate in half, not the broader economic effect.

(C)   Asthma has reached epidemic proportions.

This is a No Tie to the Argument answer. This answer might explain why there are efforts to reduce the asthma rate, but it doesn't relate to the plan presented in the argument.

(D)   After MTC is used in an area, residual amounts of the chemical can be detected months or years later.

This is a Reverse Logic answer; it weakens the argument. If MTC residue remains for a long time, a ban may not be as effective because some of the MTC from before the ban is still around and could continue to cause asthma.

(E)   Dust mites and pet dander can also cause asthma.

This is an Irrelevant Distinction. The fact that there are other causes of asthma does not affect whether the MTC ban can have the desired effect.

16

5. *Food Allergies*

(A) The percentage of allergy victims who were not aware of the allergy before a major episode

This answer makes an Irrelevant Distinction. Knowing the exact percentage doesn't actually tell you anything.

(B) The percentage of the population that is at risk for allergic reactions

This answer has No Tie to the Argument because it talks about all allergies in general, not just food allergies.

(C) Whether some of the eight foods are common ingredients used in cooking

This doesn't fit neatly into one of the standard trap categories. The argument does not hinge on how commonly used the foods must be in order to warrant testing. Further, the argument does not limit itself to foods that must be cooked.

(D) Whether an allergy to one type of food makes someone more likely to be allergic to other types of food

This answer makes an Irrelevant Distinction; the argument doesn't address whether someone is allergic to multiple types of food.

(E) Whether ingesting a very small amount of an allergen is sufficient to provoke an allergic reaction in a susceptible individual

This is the correct answer.

6. *Smithtown Theater*

(A) A large movie chain plans to open a new multiplex location in Smithtown later this year.

This one can be considered either No Tie to the Argument (a different movie chain doesn't matter to this conclusion) or Reverse Logic (if anything, the new movie theater might take some business from Smithtown Theater, strengthening the author's claim).

(B) Concession sales in the Smithtown Theater comprise a substantial proportion of the theater's revenues.

This one has No Tie to the Conclusion. Knowing this information about concession sales tells you nothing new about the theater's plans to expand.

(C) Many recent arrivals to Smithtown are students who are less likely to attend the Smithtown Theater than are older residents.

This is a Reverse Logic trap because it strengthens the author's claim (and this is a Weaken question).

(D) The expansion would allow the Smithtown Theater to stage larger, more popular shows that will attract customers from neighboring towns.

This is the correct answer.

(E) The Board of the Smithtown Theater often solicits input from residents of the town when choosing which shows to stage.

This sounds good in the real world, but it really has No Tie to the Argument. Two traps for the price of one!

7. *Machu Picchu*

    (A) Since 2001, Incan ruins similar to Machu Picchu but without a visitor limit have disintegrated at a significantly greater rate than those on the Inca Trail.

    This is the correct answer.

    (B) Villages near Machu Picchu have experienced declines in income, as fewer tourists buy fewer craft goods and refreshments.

    This answer has No Tie to the Conclusion. While the declines in income represent a potential downside of the plan, they do not influence the specific claim in the conclusion about preventing deterioration of archaeoligical features.

    (C) Many of the funds from the sale of Inca Trail permits are used to hire guards for archaeological sites without permit programs.

    This is a No Tie to the Argument answer. The argument is about protecting sites along the Inca Trail. The protection of other sites with guards does not influence the argument.

    (D) Since 2001, tourist guides along the Inca Trail have received 50% to 100% increases in take-home pay.

    This answer has No Tie to the Argument. The pay of tourist guides is not related to the protection of the Inca Trail.

    (E) Due to limited enforcement, the majority of tourists hiking the Inca Trail currently do so without a permit.

    This is a Reverse Logic answer that would weaken the argument. This answer states that the permit system may not effectively limit the number of hikers.

8. *World Bank*

    (A) Prior to 2010, China comprised less than 10 percent of the world's gross domestic product.

    No information is given about the growth rate of China's GDP. China's voting shares increased in the World Bank, but the argument doesn't say if that increase resulted from GDP growth.

    (B) Voting share in the World Bank is not directly proportional to each country's share of the world's GDP.

    This is the correct answer.

    (C) China's share in the world's gross domestic product is increasing more rapidly than France's share.

    China has a higher share of GDP than does France, but no information is given about the growth rate of China's GDP. When making numeric comparisons, be careful to distinguish between levels and growth rates.

    (D) The Chinese government is likely to be dissatisfied with the degree of the increase in its voting share.

    This might be reasonable to believe in the real world, but the argument mentions nothing about how the Chinese government feels about anything.

    (E) World Bank voting shares are allocated based upon each country's share of the world's GDP during previous years, not during the present year.

    This is a Switching Terms answer because it includes many words and terms from the argument, however, this answer imposes a cause-and-effect relationship that wasn't given in the argument. The argument never states how GDP, from current or prior years, influences voting shares.

16

9.   *Barcodes*

(A)   Many smaller stores do not use barcodes at all because of the expense.

This choice makes an Irrelevant Distinction. The argument talks about stores that do use barcodes, not stores that don't.

(B)   For some products, the amount of data necessary to be coded is small enough to fit fully on a one-dimensional barcode.

This one is very tempting, but it's also a One Word Off trap. The choice addresses only "some" products— not enough to affect the conclusion.

(C)   Two-dimensional barcodes are, on average, less expensive than one-dimensional barcodes.

This is a Reverse Logic trap. If this choice were true, it would make the discrepancy even more strange, because it offers another reason why people would want to use 2D barcodes.

(D)   Two-dimensional barcodes can also be scanned by consumer devices, such as cell phones.

This can be considered a Reverse Logic trap (because it makes 2D barcodes more attractive) or a No Tie to the Argument trap (because scanning with consumer devices isn't part of the scope of the argument).

(E)   One-dimensional barcodes last longer and are less prone to error than two-dimensional barcodes.

This is the correct answer.

16

UNIT THREE

Reading Comprehension

In this unit, you will learn a process for reading passages effectively without getting too bogged down in the details and for keeping the information organized and accessible as you answer questions. You will also learn how to recognize the different Reading Comprehension (RC) question types, what steps to take to identify the correct answer, and how to avoid trap answers.

In This Unit...

The RC Foundation

In This Chapter...

- How Reading Comprehension Works

- Find the Simple Story

- 4 Steps to the Simple Story

- Answer the Question

In this chapter, you will learn how to read passages efficiently in order to extract the main points you need without getting stuck in unnecessary detail.

CHAPTER 17 The RC Foundation

Picture this:

> You've just received an email from your boss, asking you to review the Summary of Acme Company's annual report before the two of you go into a conference call with Acme's CEO. The Summary is six pages long and the phone call starts in five minutes.
>
> The pressure is on! What do you do?
>
> (A) Speed-read your way through the entire thing. You won't actually remember or understand what you're reading, but hey, you did technically "read" it.
> (B) Start reading carefully, even though you won't be able to finish before the conference call starts.
> (C) Hand in your resignation.
> (D) Read the first paragraph carefully to get oriented, then start picking up the pace. Slow down for the big ideas, but speed up on the details.

The correct answer is (D), of course! You can't possibly read everything carefully in the allotted time, so you prioritize, looking for main ideas while minimizing the details for now. If the conversation does turn to a detail about one of those main ideas, then you'll have a rough idea where to look and can glance quickly through the summary to find the information. In fact, this whole exercise probably sounds a lot like decisions you make every day at work.

Reading Comprehension (RC) on the GMAT is a test of your real-world executive reasoning skills, even though it often feels like a school test. You typically won't have enough time to read everything thoroughly and carefully—the test literally doesn't give you enough time to do that—so you're going to need to prioritize. This unit will teach you how.

How Reading Comprehension Works

On the GMAT, you will probably see a total of three or four Reading Comprehension passages, accompanied by three or four questions each.

The passage will always be on the left side of the screen and one question at a time will appear on the right, as depicted here:

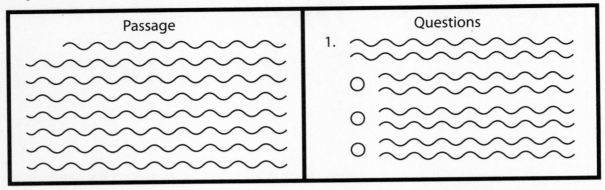

When you answer the first question, a new one will appear in its place. The passage will remain on the left-hand side of the screen. The GMAT will not tell you how many questions you're going to get; you'll know that you're done with the passage when the passage goes away and an entirely new question appears on the screen.

Plan to spend about 1.5 to 2 minutes reading the passage (more on this later) and then an average of about 1.5 minutes per question. (You'll learn more about RC time management in Atlas, your online learning platform.)

The passages range from about 200 words up to about 350 words and from one to four paragraphs. Most people will see two or three shorter passages and one longer one, though this mix can change. The topics are fairly academic, covering areas in hard science, social science, history, and business.

You may see some topics that you enjoy, but you're also likely to see at least one that you don't like much. Try to resist the temptation to dismiss any of the passages as "boring" or "not my topic." If you can convince yourself that the passage is interesting, you'll fare much better on the questions. (Don't worry: This guide will help you to develop this active reading stance!) In the meantime, keep in mind that you're not expected to bring any outside knowledge to the task—whether the passage is about municipal bonds or polypeptide chains, you'll be provided with all of the information you need to answer the questions.

When you start to work through RC problems from *The Official Guide for GMAT Review*, you will see that the passages show line numbers on the left side of the paragraphs, and some questions will make direct reference to a line number. The actual GMAT exam does *not* number the lines in each passage. Instead, when the exam wants to draw your attention to a particular term or phrase in the passage, you will suddenly see that text highlighted in yellow when the relevant question pops up on the screen.

Find the Simple Story

Think back to the annual report challenge. You can't read everything carefully before the meeting. On the other hand, you don't want to just skim over the whole thing or you won't learn anything useful for the meeting.

The goal in situations like this is to find the **Simple Story**: the main points that you would use to summarize that annual report in just a few sentences for your boss. In order to do this, you really do need to read the text, but try to do so selectively, paying attention to the main ideas while setting aside the details for now. Later, if you do need a detail, you can look it up; the report will be right in front of you for the whole meeting.

Try to find the simple story in the passage below. This is a shorter passage, so give yourself approximately 1.5 minutes to read through the passage. At the end, you'll need to answer a question about the main idea of the passage, so keep that in mind as you read; you want the big picture, not the details.

Take any notes that you like (or none at all—it's up to you), but resist the temptation to write on this page. Since the GMAT is administered on a computer, get used to taking notes on a separate piece of scratch paper and looking back and forth between the two.

<u>Bacteria</u>

> Recent research into antibiotic-resistant bacterial strains suggests the need for a reexamination of the frequency with which doctors prescribe antibacterial therapy. One study demonstrated, for example, that most minor bacterial infections will resolve without treatment within 5 to 14 days of onset of symptoms; a course of antibiotics might reduce that time frame by only 1 to 2 days. A second study indicated that the incidence of "superbugs," which have resistance to a wide variety of antibacterial agents, is increasing significantly and that these bugs are more likely to spread among those who have been treated with antibiotics within the past 5 years. In particular, researchers have become alarmed by NDM-1 (New Delhi metallo-beta-lactamase), which is not a single bacterial species, but a multiple-antibiotic-resistant enzyme capable of infecting other strains of bacteria.
>
> It is true that the proliferation of superbugs likely owes a great deal to the mistaken prescription of antibacterial treatment for viral infections, against which such treatment is ineffective, and to the routine addition of antibiotics to livestock feed in order to increase meat yields. Additionally, it is possible that ongoing research into the means by which resistance spreads among bacterial communities may lead to a new generation of antibiotics to which bacteria are unable to develop resistance. Yet these factors do not change the need for individual physicians to be more circumspect about drug therapy when treating cases of true bacterial infection.

Did you stick to the 1.5-minute time frame given? You have a little leeway (30 seconds or so extra), but resist the urge to spend much more time; the real test punishes those who don't manage their time well, and you'll build bad habits if you don't learn to work in the way that the GMAT requires.

If you feel a little panicky about the thought of having to read that fast, take a deep breath and remind yourself that you don't need to understand the annoying details—at least, not right now. You just need to get the big picture straight before the "meeting with your boss" starts.

Can you summarize, in one sentence, the overall idea of this passage? Go ahead and do so.

If you're struggling to do that, you may have gotten distracted by the details. If you took notes, glance at them. Do you have NDM-1 written down?

If so, then you probably got too pulled into the detail; that's very common at this stage. Now you know that you're going to need to retrain yourself to read at a higher level and actually let a lot of detail go (on your first read through).

Now, give yourself about a minute to try the following question:

> The passage is primarily concerned with
>
> (A) discussing research into the common symptoms associated with a particular medical condition
> (B) explaining the frequency with which a certain medical condition is diagnosed
> (C) contrasting the views of doctors and medical researchers with respect to the diagnosis of a particular medical condition
> (D) questioning the current standard of treatment for a particular medical condition
> (E) contending that physicians need to be more careful about distinguishing between two different, but related, medical conditions

Before reviewing the problem, let's talk about how to read the passage and find the simple story in the first place.

The first one to three sentences of a passage lay the groundwork for the entire passage, so at first, read carefully. Pay the most attention to the easier words that really tell you what's going on—not the technical ones that are just there to distract you.

Here's how a very strong test-taker might read the first paragraph. (The bold font represents text the reader pays close attention to.)

Passage Text	Reader's Thoughts
Recent research into antibiotic-resistant bacterial strains **suggests the need for a reexamination of the frequency with which doctors prescribe** antibacterial therapy.	*Hmm. I don't know much about* antibacterial therapy, *but I know that* suggests the need for a reexamination of the frequency *means something's not quite right about how often doctors are using it. Presumably the passage is about to tell me why.*
One study demonstrated, **for example**, that **most minor** bacterial infections will **resolve without treatment** within 5 to 14 days of onset of symptoms;	*Wait, so at least some of the time, you'd get better without even taking drugs?*
a course of antibiotics might reduce that time frame by only 1 to 2 days.	*If you do take drugs, they might not really have a huge impact. Interesting. Okay, so this whole example supports the idea that doctors use antibiotics too much.*
A **second study indicated** that the incidence of "superbugs," which have **resistance** to a wide variety of antibacterial agents, **is increasing significantly**	*I've read stuff before about antibiotic resistance; I'm pretty sure it's not a good thing. And superbug definitely doesn't sound good.*
and that **these bugs are more likely to spread among those who have been treated with antibiotics within the past 5 years**.	*Yay, no weird words here. So these superbug things are definitely bad for people who've been taking antibiotics.*
In particular, researchers have become alarmed by NDM-1 (New Delhi metallo-beta-lactamase), which is not a single bacterial species but a multiple-antibiotic-resistant enzyme capable of infecting other strains of bacteria.	*Uhh. Most of this makes no sense to me, but I get that NDM-1 is bad. It's also a detail, so I really don't care right now. Moving on!*

Right now, you may be thinking: Wait a second—what if I get a question about that detail?

The GMAT test writers might create as many as eight or nine questions for a passage, but you will be given only three or four of those questions. The passage will contain some details that you aren't asked about—and that might be the case for the NDM-1 detail. Do you want to learn about it just because you're very diligent and think it's the right thing to do, even if you never get asked about it?

Of course not! Don't waste time learning details that you might never need, especially when time is so tight. Rather, set the details aside for now. If you do get a question about NDM-1 later, you can return to this text and spend a little time working to understand it.

On to the second paragraph:

Passage Text	Reader's Thoughts
It is true that the proliferation of superbugs likely owes a great deal to the mistaken prescription of antibacterial treatment for viral infections, **against which such treatment is ineffective,**	*It is true that—you use that kind of language when you want to acknowledge some detail that doesn't fit with your overall point.* *The previous paragraph was about* bacterial *infections. Now, it's saying that there are also* mistaken prescriptions *for viral infections. And it's saying that this stuff doesn't even work against viruses anyway.*
and to the routine **addition of antibiotics to livestock feed** in order to increase meat yields.	*And a second reason there are superbugs … this is just another detail, so I can speed up a bit. I've got the big idea: It is true that there are other reasons for the proliferation of superbugs besides those given in the first paragraph.*
Additionally, it is possible that **ongoing research** into the means by which resistance spreads among bacterial communities **may lead to a new generation of antibiotics to which bacteria are unable to develop resistance.**	*An additional example … so this is more of the same? Research might solve the problem longer term.*
Yet these factors **do not change the need for individual physicians to be more circumspect about drug therapy** when treating cases of true bacterial infection.	*Yet! This is going against the ideas just presented. I'm not sure what* circumspect *means, but it looks like the author is coming back to the earlier point—doctors have to be more careful or thoughtful about prescribing these drugs so much.*

Here's the reader's simple story:

> *Something's not quite right about how often doctors are prescribing antibiotics for infections. Two studies support this idea: First, in some cases, the drugs don't help much, and second, something about superbugs.*

> *There are some other potential causes of these superbugs—prescribing antibiotics for infections isn't the only problem—but it's still the case that doctors have to be more careful about using these drugs even for legitimate reasons.*

Notice how much that simple story leaves out. There isn't even a mention of NDM-1, let alone what it is or how it works. That's perfectly fine—if you get a question about it, you can go back to find the relevant text and read in more detail. (Or you could decide that you disliked that detail enough that you would rather guess and move on.)

4 Steps to the Simple Story

Here's the basic process to find your simple story:

Step 1: Get oriented. Read the first sentence or two pretty carefully:

- Understand the topic under discussion and keep an eye out for any main ideas.
- Know the main idea of a paragraph by the time you're done reading that paragraph. You may want to jot down a note. (You'll learn more about taking notes in a later chapter.)
- Read the first paragraph of the passage more carefully than any of the others (when there is more than one paragraph in the passage).

Step 2: Find the main idea of each paragraph. When you start a new paragraph, pay close attention to (at least) the first sentence. Find the main idea of that paragraph—why was it included in the passage?

Step 3: Set aside the details. When you get to examples or other very specific details, focus on *why* the information is present. How does this example fit the overall story? Pay less attention to all of the nitpicky little details.

Step 4: Articulate the simple story. When you're done, pause for a moment to articulate the simple story to yourself. If you had to give someone a 10-second summary of the passage, what would you say?

In subsequent chapters, you'll learn techniques to help you develop the simple story and set yourself up to answer both general and specific detail questions. For now, take a look at how this approach can make the process of answering certain questions easier.

Answer the Question

Now that you have a better idea of how to find the simple story, feel free to try the problem again before you continue reading. Here it is:

The passage is primarily concerned with

(A) discussing research into the common symptoms associated with a particular medical condition

(B) explaining the frequency with which a certain medical condition is diagnosed

(C) contrasting the views of doctors and medical researchers with respect to the diagnosis of a particular medical condition

(D) questioning the current standard of treatment for a particular medical condition

(E) contending that physicians need to be more careful about distinguishing between two different, but related, medical conditions

This is a primary purpose question; you'll learn about this question type in more detail in the General Questions chapter. The correct answer will convey the overall point or main idea of the simple story. Before reading the answers, remind yourself of that story. Then, eliminate answers that go too far beyond the story, that focus too much on certain details without conveying the main idea, or that actually contradict the passage in some way.

The passage is primarily concerned with

(A)   discussing research into the common symptoms associated with a particular medical condition

Incorrect. The passage mentions only that symptoms can resolve without treatment; the symptoms themselves are not discussed.

(B)   explaining the frequency with which a certain medical condition is diagnosed

Incorrect. The first sentence does suggest that the frequency with which antibiotics are prescribed may need to change, but this is not the same as the frequency with which the medical condition is diagnosed in the first place.

(C)   contrasting the views of doctors and medical researchers with respect to the diagnosis of a particular medical condition

Incorrect. The first paragraph does present information that might seem to imply a difference of opinion between doctors and researchers as to whether or how frequently antibiotics should be prescribed—but this is a difference in opinion about treatment. The passage doesn't indicate that the doctors and researchers might disagree about how to diagnose the condition.

(D)   questioning the current standard of treatment for a particular medical condition

CORRECT. The first and last sentences of the passage together indicate that the author believes that doctors may be overprescribing antibiotics—in other words, that the current standard of treatment might not be appropriate. This fits the simple story: The first paragraph presents research to support this opinion, and the second acknowledges other causes of the "superbug" problem before reiterating that the frequency with which antibiotics are used for bacterial infections is still an issue.

(E)   contending that physicians need to be more careful about distinguishing between two different, but related, medical conditions

Incorrect. This is tempting. The passage does mention two types of infections: viral and bacterial. However, the passage doesn't say that doctors are mistakenly diagnosing a bacterial infection when a patient actually has a viral infection. The passage says only that patients with viral infections are sometimes mistakenly treated with antibiotics; it could be that such patients are diagnosed correctly but given an inappropriate treatment.

The only answer that fits with the simple story is answer (D). Take a moment to review and summarize each answer:

(A) Symptoms? Not discussed.

(B) Passage is about frequency of the *treatment*, not frequency of the condition itself.

(C) The *treatment* is the issue, not the diagnosis.

(D) Correct!

(E) The *treatment* is the issue, not the diagnosis.

Note that answers (C) and (E) are incorrect for the same underlying reason, and answer (B) is incorrect for a very similar reason. If you can learn to "abstract" out the trap answers to this level on both Reading Comprehension and Critical Reasoning, you can get quite good at these two question types.

Breaking Down the Passage

In This Chapter...

- Engage with the Passage
- Passage Components
- Language Clues
- Optional Strategy: Breaking Down Complex Sentences
- Problem Set
- Solutions

Ⓜ **413**

In this chapter, you will learn how to break down the different parts of a passage in order to distill the simple story. You will also learn how to separate the big picture from the details and how to handle especially complex sentences.

CHAPTER 18 Breaking Down the Passage

Sometimes, you hit a passage that just speaks to you. You like the topic, the language doesn't seem as challenging, and you might even be somewhat familiar with the technical examples given. When this happens, go with it! Read the passage as though you're reading for pleasure and don't worry as much about building an explicit simple story. (Just be careful not to bring in outside knowledge.)

More often, though, you're not going to get that lucky. Remember the last time you started to read a passage and you wanted to groan aloud because you found the topic boring? Yet you still had to get through the passage and answer questions about it. What to do?

Engage with the Passage

The first step may seem minor, but it will be a real help. Think of someone you know who actually does like the topic. Pretend that you're going to tell her about it later: "Oh, Robyn would like this. I want to remember enough to tell her about the main gist of it." Who knows—you might actually discover that the topic isn't as boring as you thought.

What do you want to remember to tell Robyn? Certainly not some very specific detail four sentences into the second paragraph. Rather, you want to tell her the simple story. Having Robyn in mind will keep you focused on that task. Lean forward a bit in your seat, smile, and do your best to convince yourself that you are reading this passage by choice and not just because you have to.

Passage Components

Do you remember what a thesis statement is? When you were writing academic papers in school, you had to include a thesis statement and provide support for that thesis. You were expected to have an introduction and a conclusion. In many cases, you were even expected to raise questions or acknowledge contrasting points of view, while ultimately showing that your thesis still held.

GMAT passages are, for the most part, excerpts of academic papers. They are much shorter, of course, so they don't contain all of the expected components of an academic work, but certain components will be present.

You do not need to memorize the different components, nor do you need to explicitly label every sentence that you read. If you know what to look for, though, then you'll be better equipped to find the simple story.

The Point

The Point is the thesis statement: It is the single most important message of the passage and the heart of your simple story. The author has written the passage in order to convey the point, even if nothing else gets through to the reader.

Take a look back at the *Bacteria* passage from the last chapter. Where does the author express the point?

> Recent research into antibiotic-resistant bacterial strains suggests the need for a reexamination of the frequency with which doctors prescribe antibacterial therapy. One study demonstrated, for example, that most minor bacterial infections will resolve without treatment within 5 to 14 days of onset of symptoms; a course of antibiotics might reduce that time frame by only 1 to 2 days. A second study indicated that the incidence of "superbugs," which have resistance to a wide variety of antibacterial agents, is increasing significantly and that these bugs are more likely to spread among those who have been treated with antibiotics within the past 5 years. In particular, researchers have become alarmed by NDM-1 (New Delhi metallo-beta-lactamase), which is not a single bacterial species, but a multiple-antibiotic-resistant enzyme capable of infecting other strains of bacteria.
>
> It is true that the proliferation of superbugs likely owes a great deal to the mistaken prescription of antibacterial treatment for viral infections, against which such treatment is ineffective, and to the routine addition of antibiotics to livestock feed in order to increase meat yields. Additionally, it is possible that ongoing research into the means by which resistance spreads among bacterial communities may lead to a new generation of antibiotics to which bacteria are unable to develop resistance. Yet these factors do not change the need for individual physicians to be more circumspect about drug therapy when treating cases of true bacterial infection.

The point is encapsulated in the first and last sentences:

> Recent research into antibiotic-resistant bacterial strains suggests the need for a reexamination of the frequency with which doctors prescribe antibacterial therapy.

> Yet these factors do not change the need for individual physicians to be more circumspect about drug therapy when treating cases of true bacterial infection.

The basic idea is this: *The frequency with which doctors prescribe antibiotics is problematic and doctors have to be more careful.*

This is the single most important idea that the author was trying to convey in writing the passage. If you can't articulate the point, or if you think something else is the point, you are probably going to miss at least some of the questions associated with the passage.

Your simple story will always contain the point. The point can be anywhere in the passage, but it is most often found in the first paragraph or the beginning of the second paragraph. Most of the time, the point will be contained in a single sentence, but occasionally you'll have to combine two or three sentences to get it.

What about the rest of the information in the simple story? Read on.

Support and Background

Some amount of the information in any passage will serve to **Support** the author's point. This support is part of the story.

You may also think of some information as **Background**: It doesn't strongly support the point, but it sets the context for information presented in the passage. Although this information does not strictly support the point, you don't need to distinguish background information from support—you can group it all together. Certainly, you wouldn't want to brush past a whole paragraph without understanding it simply because it looks like background. You need to understand enough of the supporting and background information to build your simple story, but you do not have to thoroughly comprehend or memorize how these details work.

Looking back at the passage, where do you see information that supports the author's point?

The supporting information is contained in the second part of the first paragraph: Two studies support the point. In the simple story, these studies were compressed down to one sentence:

> *Two studies support this idea: First, in some cases, the drugs don't help much, and second, something about superbugs.*

The sentences in the passage contain a whole lot more detail than that, but it is enough to know that these examples support the point. If you are asked a question about any particular supporting detail, you'll know to go back to the latter part of the first paragraph.

Counterpoints, Acknowledgments, and Implications

Some passages will contain **Counterpoints**, information that goes against the author's point (or at least appears to). Passages might also **Acknowledge** a certain point or piece of evidence that does not support the point but that doesn't go against it either.

As with support and background, your goal is to know how the high-level information fits into the simple story, while leaving specific details for later.

Take a look at the passage one more time. Does it contain any counterpoints or acknowledgments?

The second paragraph of the passage begins by acknowledging that there are other possible factors (aside from the treatment of bacterial infections) that are contributing to the superbug problem.

Nevertheless, the author eventually concludes that the original point holds: Doctors have to be more careful about prescribing antibiotics even for legitimate purposes.

Whether you thought of these other factors as counterpoints or as acknowledgments is not all that important. It is important just to recognize that they did not ultimately support the author's point.

Occasionally, passages will contain **Implications** for the future, answering the question, "So what might happen from here or what should we do about the situation?" The *Bacteria* passage does not contain implications, but you could imagine that the author might have discussed a need to fund additional research to establish that the overprescription of antibiotics for bacterial infections is contributing to resistant bacteria. Alternatively, the author might have proposed a government panel to study how to influence doctors to reduce the number of antibiotic prescriptions. Both of those would be implications.

Use all of these components to help you find your simple story. Here is a quick review of the steps.

Step 1: Get oriented. Read the first sentence or two pretty carefully.

- Understand the topic under discussion and keep an eye out for any main ideas.
- Know the main idea of a paragraph by the time you're done reading that paragraph.
- Read the first paragraph of the passage more carefully than any of the others (when there is more than one paragraph in the passage).

Step 2: Find the main idea of each paragraph. When you start a new paragraph, pay close attention to (at least) the first sentence. Find the main idea of that paragraph—why was it included in the passage?

18

Step 3: Set aside the details. When you get to examples or other very specific details, focus on *why* the information is present. How does this example fit the overall story? Pay less attention to all of the nitpicky little details.

Step 4: Articulate the simple story. When you're done, pause for a moment to articulate the simple story to yourself. If you had to give someone a 10-second summary of the passage, what would you say?

Language Clues

Sometimes, specific language in the passage will signal important categories of information that will help you to build your simple story. Keep an eye out for clues about four big categories:

1. Big Picture

2. Foreshadowing

3. Changes of Direction

4. Detail

Big Picture

Big-Picture language introduces or summarizes some kind of main idea. When you see words like these in a sentence, they should almost jump off the page. Don't get distracted by New Delhi metallo-beta-whatever. Pay attention to the big picture!

In the table below are some common language clues that signal a main idea:

Signal	Implication
In general; To a great extent; Broadly speaking; In conclusion; In sum; In brief; Therefore; Thus; So; Hence; As a result; Overall	A generalization or conclusion follows.
First, Second, etc.; To begin with; Next; Finally; Again	Two or more important points or examples are outlined. Pay attention to the overall purpose; *why* is the author mentioning these points or examples?
X argues that; *X* contends that; theory; hypothesis	A named person or group holds a specific theory or opinion.

Foreshadowing

When you watch a movie or television show, you don't just passively gaze at the screen. You are actively engaging with the story, anticipating what might be coming: *Uh oh, the lawyer got distracted by the guy with the gun just as she was piecing together key arguments for the legal case—I bet she's going to make a mistake and mess up in court!* Showing this distraction is a way for the director to foreshadow upcoming events.

Foreshadowing works the same way in writing: The author can drop a clue about something that he plans to say later in the passage. When you spot foreshadowing, you can use it to anticipate the point or other important ideas in the passage.

Given the following as the first sentence of an RC passage, where might you anticipate the passage could go next?

> Given recent company stumbles, it is important to ask: Is the potential return on investment worth the risk?

When an author asks a question in the beginning of a passage, she is almost certainly going to address that question in her passage. She may discuss how a company should weigh the risks and rewards of a potential investment; alternatively, she may provide examples of things that a company should *not* consider. She will probably provide at least one example of how a specific company messed this up or got this right.

How about this opener?

> For some time, government officials disagreed as to where to store high-level radioactive waste.

There are many possibilities for what immediately follows: Perhaps the author will describe the opinions held by different government officials, or perhaps he will explain what caused the disagreement in the first place. However, it seems certain that by the end of the passage the officials will have come to an agreement. The language *for some time*, coupled with the past tense verb *disagreed*, indicates that the problem existed in the past but no longer exists today. At some point, the passage will likely tell you that the officials came to an agreement and determined where to store that nuclear waste.

Here are some examples of common foreshadowing signals:

Signal	Implication
Traditionally; For some time; It was once believed; It had been assumed	Contrast coming up soon; now, things are different
Some (people) claim (believe, define, attribute, etc.); It is true that	Acknowledge a valid opposing point
Statement of a problem or question	Possible fix for problem or answer to question (or statement that it can't be fixed or answered, or more research needs to be done)
Current theory; conventional wisdom	New or different theory or idea coming up soon

The list above is meant to help you to start thinking about foreshadowing, but there are many possible language clues; don't just stick to that list. As you read the first paragraph, look for foreshadowing language to help you anticipate where the passage might be going. The sooner you start to have an idea of the big picture and the point, the better.

Changes of Direction

Change-of-Direction language can signal some kind of twist—a contrast or a qualification that could make for a good test question. In addition, twists can signal a counterpoint or a return to the main point.

In the *Bacteria* passage, the final sentence contains a change-of-direction signal:

> Yet these factors do not change the need for individual physicians to be more circumspect about drug therapy when treating cases of true bacterial infection.

The beginning of that same paragraph acknowledged some information that doesn't actually support the overall point. The appearance of the word *yet* signals that the author is about to change direction and jump back to that point.

18

Here are some common change-of-direction signals:

Signal	Implication
However; Yet; On one hand/On the other hand; While; Rather; Instead; In contrast; Alternatively	Indicate contrasting ideas
Granted; It is true that; Certainly; Admittedly; Despite; Although	Concede a point (author acknowledges or reluctantly agrees)
Actually; In fact; Indeed; Surprisingly	Indicate an unexpected result or phenomenon
Nevertheless; Nonetheless; That said; Even so	Assert a position after conceding a point
Supposedly; It was once thought; Seemingly; For some time	Something appeared to be a certain way, but it really wasn't that way at all

Detail

Certain clues will signal that you should pay less attention on your first read through. When you see these words, still run your eyes over the information, but change your goal: Understand why the information is there, but don't try to understand or remember every last detail given.

Signal	Implication
For example; As an example; In particular; For instance	Provide an example
Furthermore; Moreover; In addition; As well as; Also; Likewise; Too	Add to something that was already said
Likewise; In the same way	Provide a new example or detail that goes along with a previous one
In other words; That is; Namely; So to speak; a semicolon (;)	Restate something that was already said (in this case, you can use whichever set of words is easier for you to interpret!)

Optional Strategy: Breaking Down Complex Sentences

It is not unusual for a GMAT test-taker to read a sentence, pause for a moment, and think, "Huh? I have no idea what that means." The test writers are masters of the complex sentence, so it might be worth your while to take a few pages to practice in-depth reading on a sentence-by-sentence level.

You may or may not need this section. If you are a strong reader who often reads complex material for pleasure or for work, then you have likely already developed your own techniques for breaking down complex sentences into simpler thoughts so that you can digest the full meaning. If that is the case, don't feel that you have to change what already works for you.

If, on the other hand, you can think of at least one "Huh?" moment while reading RC passages, then read on.

What does this sentence mean?

> In a diachronic investigation of possible behavioral changes resulting from accidental exposure in early childhood to environmental lead dust, two sample groups were tracked over decades.

At this point, you may be distracted by the word *diachronic*. If you don't happen to know the meaning of that word, you have plenty of company! Believe it or not, you can ignore those kinds of words. When the test writers toss jargon words at you—scientific terms and the like—one of two things will happen. If you need to know what the word means, then the passage will give you a definition or a contrasting word that lets you figure out the weird word from context. If not, then the passage will just move on, and you should, too. Don't let one unfamiliar word prevent you from processing the rest of the material.

One way to move past such words is to turn them into single letters for ease of reading:

In a D investigation of possible behavioral changes . . .

Here's how a reader might go about stripping that first sentence down to more manageable parts:

Passage Text	Reader's Thoughts
In a diachronic investigation of possible behavioral changes	*Someone was investigating behavior changes.*
resulting from accidental exposure in early childhood to environmental lead dust,	*I don't know what environmental lead dust is, specifically, but I've heard that lead is supposed to be bad for kids. Okay, this makes sense: Some kids were accidentally exposed to lead and someone then investigated some consequences.*
two sample groups were tracked over decades.	*Specifically, they investigated two groups of kids for a long time.*
	Put it all together: Kids were accidentally exposed to lead, and somebody investigated two groups of these kids to see whether their behavior changed over time. *Hmm, I wonder whether the lead did affect the kids? Presumably, the passage will get into that.*

Here are the steps that the reader took:

Steps	Example
1. **Break the sentence down into smaller ideas; ignore technical jargon.**	The reader above read just one idea, then she stopped to understand that one part before continuing to read and add new information. She also ignored the word *diachronic*.
2. **Make connections to things you already know; simplify complex language.**	The reader didn't get flustered by *environmental lead dust*. Instead, she made a connection to something she already knew: Lead is bad for kids. This knowledge went along with what the sentence was saying, helping her to wrap her head around the second part of the sentence.
3. **Link to previous information.**	As the reader understood each new idea, she linked it back to what she'd already read. At the end, she made sure that she had a handle on the entire sentence.
4. **Anticipate.**	Finally, the reader speculated about where the passage might be going. Such anticipation can help keep you actively engaged with the passage—even when the topic isn't your favorite!

As you might guess, breaking down sentences takes time. You won't be able to do this for every sentence in the passage.

Fortunately, you won't need to. First of all, you will actually understand many of the sentences just by reading them once. Second of all, think back to your overall goal: Find the simple story. You don't need to understand every sentence. You only need to understand the sentences that present the big ideas—the ideas that will help you to find the story. When you get to complex sentences about examples or other details, you can just read right over them and keep going.

Try another:

> While *Don Giovanni* is today widely considered Wolfgang Amadeus Mozart's greatest achievement, eighteenth-century audiences in Vienna—Mozart's own city—and the rest of Europe differed greatly in their opinion of a new work unexpectedly mixing traditions of moralism with those of comedy.

Passage Text	Reader's Thoughts
While *Don Giovanni* is today widely considered Wolfgang Amadeus Mozart's greatest achievement,	While *is a huge clue: contrast! I'm guessing that* today *is another important word: The contrast seems to be that DG is considered M's best work* today, *but maybe it wasn't in the past. . . ?*
eighteenth-century audiences in Vienna—Mozart's own city—and the rest of Europe	*There are some details about location, but the important thing is that this part talks about 18th-century audiences. As I suspected, it's talking about the past now, specifically about people who were there when DG was written.*
differed greatly in their opinion of a new work	*They didn't agree—did they all think it was bad? No, it says they* differed greatly *among each other: Some liked it and some didn't. Wait, so what's the contrast?* *Oh, I see. Today, it's widely considered his greatest achievement. Back then, some people liked it and some didn't.*
unexpectedly mixing traditions of moralism with those of comedy.	*This feels like detail. If I get questions about why some people liked it and some didn't, I'll come back here.*
	The basic message: Today, people think DG is M's greatest achievement. In the 18th century, though, the opinion was mixed.

18

Problem Set

For each of the four passages below, take 1.5 to 2 minutes to read the passage and tell yourself the simple story. Then, compare to the version in the solution. There are certainly many ways to convey the same content; just make sure that your version covers all of the big ideas of the passage.

Passage A: Animal Treatment

Over the course of the eighteenth and early nineteenth centuries, educated Britons came to embrace the notion that animals must be treated humanely. By 1822, Parliament
5 had outlawed certain forms of cruelty to domestic animals, and by 1824 reformers had founded the Society for the Prevention of Cruelty to Animals.

This growth in humane feelings was part of
10 a broader embrace of compassionate ideals. One of the great movements of the age was abolitionism, but there were many other such causes. In 1785, a Society for the Relief of Persons Imprisoned for Small Sums persuaded
15 Parliament to limit that archaic punishment. The Society for Bettering the Condition of the Poor was founded in 1796 and a Philanthropic Society founded in 1788 provided for abandoned children. Charity schools, schools
20 of midwifery, and hospitals for the poor were being endowed. This growth in concern for human suffering encouraged reformers to reject animal suffering as well.

Industrialization and the growth of towns
25 also contributed to the increase in concern for animals. The people who protested against cruelty to animals tended to be city folk who thought of animals as pets rather than as live-stock. It was not just animals, but all of
30 nature that came to be seen differently as Britain industrialized. Nature was no longer a menacing force that had to be subdued, for society's "victory" over wilderness was conspicuous everywhere. A new sensibility,
35 which viewed animals and wild nature as things to be respected and preserved, replaced the old adversarial relationship. Indeed, animals were to some extent romanticized as emblems of a bucolic,
40 pre-industrial age.

Passage B: Higher Education

Critics of our higher education system point out the often striking difference between the skills students develop in university courses and the skills desired by employers. Students
5 generally enter university with the expectation that a degree will improve their job prospects, the argument goes, so why not give employers more direct control over the education process? Some commentators have even
10 gone so far as to suggest that traditional postsecondary courses be replaced with short, standardized skills-training workshops.

However, the provision of vocational training is not the goal of most university programs.
15 Rather, universities seek to provide students with experience in a particular field of inquiry, as well as exposure to a wide range of disciplines and worldviews. University students learn to situate themselves not only within the
20 adult world of work and responsibility, but also within the broader streams of historical, social, and physical development that shape and are shaped by their actions and experiences.

It is certainly reasonable to ask whether this
25 vision of education serves the interests of the roughly 2/3 of United States high school graduates who enroll immediately in 2- or 4-year programs after high school. Might some of these students' needs be better met by more narrowly
30 focused vocational programs? Current research suggests that, rather than serving as a reliable engine of social mobility, the United States system of postsecondary education can actually reinforce existing inequalities. However, it is not
35 at all clear that a more employer-oriented system, in which immediate economic need might deter many students from entering academically oriented degree programs, would be any more effective at producing opportunity
40 for traditionally disadvantaged student populations. Further, it is worth considering that the kind of education traditionally provided by universities may confer benefits to society that are not as easily measured as an immediate
45 boost in individual earnings. Before we make any sweeping changes on utilitarian grounds, we ought to consider the utility of the existing order.

18

Ⓜ 423

Passage C: Rock Flour

Although organic agriculture may seem to be the wave of the future, some experts believe that the next stage in agricultural development requires the widespread adoption of
5 something very inorganic: fertilizer made from powdered rocks, also known as "rock flour." The biochemical processes of life depend not only on elements commonly associated with living organisms, such as oxygen, hydrogen,
10 and carbon, but also on many other elements in the periodic table. Specifically, plants need the so-called "big six" nutrients: nitrogen, phosphorus, potassium, calcium, sulfur, and magnesium. In modern industrial agriculture,
15 these nutrients are commonly supplied by traditional chemical fertilizers.

However, these fertilizers omit trace elements, such as iron, that are components of essential plant enzymes and
20 pigments. For instance, the green pigment chlorophyll, which turns sunlight into energy that plants can use, requires iron. As crops are harvested, the necessary trace elements are not replaced and become depleted in the
25 soil. Eventually, crop yields diminish, despite the application or even over-application of traditional fertilizers. Rock flour, produced in abundance by quarry and mining operations, may be able to replenish trace elements
30 cheaply and increase crop yields dramatically.

Not all rock flour would be suitable for use as fertilizer. Certain chemical elements, such as lead and cadmium, are poisonous to humans; thus, applying rock flour containing
35 significant amounts of such elements to farmland would be inappropriate, even if the crops themselves do not accumulate the poisons, because human contact could result directly or indirectly (e.g., via soil
40 runoff into water supplies). However, most rock flour produced by quarries seems safe for use. After all, glaciers have been creating natural rock flour for thousands of years as they advance and retreat, grinding
45 up the ground underneath. Glacial runoff carries this rock flour into rivers and, downstream, the resulting alluvial deposits are extremely fertile. If the use of man-made rock flour is incorporated into
50 agricultural practices, it may be possible to make open plains as rich as alluvial soils.

Passage D: Pro-Drop Languages

In many so-called "pro-drop" or "pronoun-drop" languages, verbs inflect for number and person. In other words, by adding a prefix or suffix or by changing in some other way,
5 the verb itself indicates whether the subject is singular or plural, as well as whether the subject is first person (*I* or *we*), second person (*you*), or third person (*he, she, it,* or *they*). For example, in Portuguese, which is at least
10 partially a pro-drop language, the verb *falo* means "I speak": the –o at the end of the word indicates first person, singular subject (as well as present tense). As a result, the subject pronoun *eu*, which means "I" in Portuguese,
15 does not need to be used with *falo* except to emphasize who is doing the speaking.

It should be noted that not every language that drops its pronouns inflects its verbs. Neither Chinese nor Japanese verbs,
20 for instance, change form at all to indicate number or person; however, personal pronouns are regularly omitted in both speech and writing, leaving the proper meaning to be inferred from contextual clues. Moreover, not every language
25 that inflects its verbs drops subject pronouns in all non-emphatic contexts. Linguists argue about the pro-drop status of the Russian language, but there is no doubt that, although the Russian present-tense verb *govoryu* ("I speak")
30 unambiguously indicates a first person, singular subject, it is common for Russian speakers to express "I speak" as *ya govoryu*, in which *ya* means "I," without indicating either emphasis or contrast.
35 Nevertheless, Russian speakers do frequently drop subject and object pronouns; one study of adult and child speech indicated a pro-drop rate of 40–80 percent. Moreover, personal pronouns must in fact be dropped in
40 some Russian sentences in order to convey particular meanings. It seems safe to conjecture that languages whose verbs inflect unambiguously for person and number permit pronoun dropping, if only
45 under certain circumstances, in order to accelerate communication without loss of meaning. After all, in these languages, both the subject pronoun and the verb inflection convey the same information, so there is no
50 real need both to include the subject pronoun and to inflect the verb.

18

This page intentionally left blank

18

Solutions

Passage A: Animal Treatment

In the 18th and 19th centuries, people in Britain grew concerned about the humane treatment of animals. This was part of a general movement toward more compassionate treatment of others. Industrialization also shifted people's views: In the new industrialized world, nature no longer seemed like a threat.

Passage B: Higher Education

University education doesn't always fit with what employers want, so some people think schools should focus on more job-oriented skills. In the U.S., universities want to teach more than that, but what would be best for students? Maybe the current system doesn't help everyone, but the author thinks the new idea is not necessarily better and wants to be cautious about making changes.

Passage C: Rock Flour

Rock flour, a type of fertilizer made from powdered rocks, could provide a cheap source of nutrients for plants, significantly improving crop yields. While some rock flour might be dangerous, most of it should be safe to use.

Passage D: Pro-Drop Languages

In "pro-drop" languages, the speaker often drops pronouns (*I*, *you*, etc.) because the verb form makes the subject clear. However, these two things don't always go together: Some languages drop pronouns even though the verb doesn't indicate the subject, and some languages keep the pronoun even though the verb also makes the subject clear. The author thinks that some languages allow the speaker to drop the subject pronoun to accelerate communication.

Mapping the Passage

In This Chapter...

In this chapter, you will learn how to make a passage map, a particular way of taking notes that makes you articulate the main points of the passage and prepares you to quickly find the information needed to answer the questions.

CHAPTER 19 Mapping the Passage

You have one more skill to develop before diving into the questions. These passages are complex; even the simple story is several sentences long. You wouldn't want to take the time to write the story out, but it is very useful to jot down certain things. So, you're going to create a **Passage Map**.

A caveat: Your goal is absolutely *not* to take notes the way that you took notes in school. You aren't going to be studying this same passage again weeks from now; once you're done with the passage, you can forget about it forever.

Instead, your goal is to jot down just a few words that will help you to develop and remember your simple story (including the point) and to remember where in the passage to look when you need support to answer a question.

Why Use a Passage Map?

You're going to have to answer two types of questions: general and specific. The passage map will help you to accomplish two important goals:

1. Predict the answers to general questions

2. Know where in the passage to find the details you'll need to answer specific questions

The two goals above will indicate whether you're creating an effective map. If you can't answer general questions based on the information in your map, then you didn't learn enough about the big picture on the first read through. You'll need to practice picking up on the main ideas and major changes in direction.

On specific questions, though, you actually do *not* want to be able to find the answers on your map. If you can, then you likely spent too much time diving into the detail on your read through. The GMAT will always include more detail in the passage than you will need to answer the questions; if you pay careful attention to all of that detail, you may run out of time on the test. You'll actually need to practice minimizing the attention you pay to details, possibly to the point of skimming some information.

Avoid relying too heavily on your memory when answering the detail questions. Remember, this is an "open book" test, and it is full of traps for those who are pretty confident that they remember the details. Check the passage! If you form good habits and apply a consistent and efficient process even on the easier-for-you questions, you'll have a better chance to answer the difficult questions correctly.

Making the Passage Map

Your passage map reflects the simple story, but it will be heavily abbreviated. Your map should include the following information (and not much more):

- The point
- The purpose of each paragraph
- Any other information you would include in the simple story, organized by paragraph

Every reader's map will be different. You have the flexibility to organize in a way that makes sense for you. Of course, this makes creating an answer key to passage mapping a little difficult, but this unit will model the process in a way that provides guidance while leaving your own passage map style up to you.

Try creating a map of the *Bacteria* passage that you saw earlier in this unit. Use any format you like as long as it reflects your simple story.

> Recent research into antibiotic-resistant bacterial strains suggests the need for a reexamination of the frequency with which doctors prescribe antibacterial therapy. One study demonstrated, for example, that most minor bacterial infections will resolve without treatment within 5 to 14 days of onset of symptoms; a course of antibiotics might reduce that time frame by only 1 to 2 days. A second study indicated that the incidence of "superbugs," which have resistance to a wide variety of antibacterial agents, is increasing significantly and that these bugs are more likely to spread among those who have been treated with antibiotics within the past 5 years. In particular, researchers have become alarmed by NDM-1 (New Delhi metallo-beta-lactamase), which is not a single bacterial species, but a multiple-antibiotic-resistant enzyme capable of infecting other strains of bacteria.
>
> It is true that the proliferation of superbugs likely owes a great deal to the mistaken prescription of antibacterial treatment for viral infections, against which such treatment is ineffective, and to the routine addition of antibiotics to livestock feed in order to increase meat yields. Additionally, it is possible that ongoing research into the means by which resistance spreads among bacterial communities may lead to a new generation of antibiotics to which bacteria are unable to develop resistance. Yet these factors do not change the need for individual physicians to be more circumspect about drug therapy when treating cases of true bacterial infection.

Here is the simple story:

> *Something's not quite right about how often doctors are prescribing antibiotics for infections. Two studies support this idea: First, in some cases, the drugs don't help much, and second, something about superbugs.*
>
> *There are some other potential causes of these superbugs—prescribing antibiotics for infections isn't the only problem—but it's still the case that doctors have to be more careful about using these drugs even for legitimate reasons.*

Here's one potential passage map for this story:

① Problem: Drs prescribe antiB a lot—too much?

> 1. Sometimes antiB don't help!
>
> 2. Superbugs ↑ = bad

② Other things cause superbugs, too

> BUT Drs still have to be careful about using antiB Ⓟ

The map reflects the major elements of the story. It clearly delineates the point Ⓟ. It shows what information is in paragraph 1 versus paragraph 2. It mentions the support and the acknowledgment.

This map wouldn't take long to produce, but you can certainly abbreviate more heavily, depending on how strong your short-term memory is.

Here's a more abbreviated version:

① Prob: Drs use antiB a lot—too?

> 1. May not help!
>
> 2. Superbug ☹

19

② Other → superbugs

    STILL Drs must be careful re: antiB Ⓟ

Someone with a great short-term memory and strong RC skills in general might abbreviate to the point that the map resembles hieroglyphics; only she would be able to read it. Here's an example:

① Prob: Drs AB too much

    1. ≠ help

    2. SB

② Other → SB

    Drs must take care w/AB Ⓟ

Now, give yourself about 1.5 minutes to try this problem.

> The research cited in the first paragraph suggests which of the following about antibacterial therapy?
>
> (A) It frequently leads to infection with NDM-1.
>
> (B) It is not generally used to treat minor bacterial infections.
>
> (C) It may help to reduce the incidence of superbugs that are especially hard to treat.
>
> (D) Reducing the rate at which such therapy is used would cause fewer bacteria to develop resistance to antibiotics.
>
> (E) Its short-term benefits, if they exist, may not outweigh the potential harm to the broader population.

This question asks about the studies in the first paragraph. Some of the answers are very detailed, but it's certainly okay to make a quick pass to look for an answer that matches the simple story. If nothing turns up, then go back and analyze the details.

> The studies cited in the first paragraph suggest which of the following about antibacterial therapy?
>
> (A) It frequently leads to infection with NDM-1.
>
> *I don't know! I skimmed the info about NDM-1. Come back later.*
>
> (B) It is not generally used to treat minor bacterial infections.
>
> *They said it is used to treat minor infections—it only reduces treatment time by a couple of days. This one's wrong.*
>
> (C) It may help to reduce the incidence of superbugs that are especially hard to treat.
>
> *I don't know. Come back later.*
>
> (D) Reducing the rate at which such therapy is used would cause fewer bacteria to develop resistance to antibiotics.
>
> *I don't know. Come back later.*
>
> (E) Its short-term benefits, if they exist, may not outweigh the potential harm to the broader population.
>
> CORRECT. *The paragraph does mention that such therapy might reduce the illness by one to two days. This could be a short-term benefit, but the author minimizes this benefit and goes on to discuss a much worse drawback (the superbug). That all fits with the simple story and the first paragraph.*

It's sometimes possible to find the right answer even if you don't yet know why some of the wrong ones are wrong. On the real test, pick (E) and move on. When you're studying, go back afterwards to learn why answers (A), (C), and (D) are wrong.

> (A) It frequently leads to infection with NDM-1.
>
> Incorrect. The passage does say that patients who have used antibiotics within the past five years are more likely to pick up superbugs, but it doesn't indicate how often this happens, especially in the case of NDM-1 in particular. Perhaps this bug is still very rare.
>
> (C) It may help to reduce the incidence of superbugs that are especially hard to treat.
>
> Incorrect. This paragraph mentions nothing about what causes the incidence of superbugs to decrease. In fact, the story hinges on the idea that these superbugs are *increasing*, so this answer contradicts the story.
>
> (D) Reducing the rate at which such therapy is used would cause fewer bacteria to develop resistance to antibiotics.
>
> Incorrect. This is tempting! The question points you specifically to the first paragraph, though, and the first paragraph does not discuss what causes bacteria to become antibiotic-resistant. (The second paragraph does touch on this a bit, but it does not discuss how *antibacterial therapy* might contribute to this phenomenon—read the question carefully!)

In this case, the wrong answers weren't necessarily easy to eliminate, but the right answer was definitely connected to the simple story.

If the correct answer didn't match your take on the passage, you may not have read carefully enough. This typically happens for one of two reasons:

1. You read so quickly that you aren't really taking in what you're reading. Have you ever read something and then realized that you have no idea what you just read and you have to read it again? You'll need to learn to read actively on RC; purposefully looking for the simple story will help.

2. You get distracted by the technical words, the examples, and the minutiae; you're paying so much attention to those details that you forget to tell yourself the simple story. In this case, you're going to have to learn how to strip out the details and concentrate on the big picture.

As this unit progresses, you'll learn techniques to help you overcome these (and other) problems by actively reading for the big picture and using that understanding to simplify the process of answering the questions.

19

Common Notations

You don't have much time to read the passage and make your passage map. The good news is that you'll only need your map for the few minutes it takes you to answer the questions. In fact, you may find that once your map has done its job and helped you to understand the passage, you don't end up looking back at it at all. With this in mind, don't try to create the kind of clear document you might study from in school; you're not really going to be using this map for very long.

Given that, you can abbreviate heavily in your map. Consider the following notations:

Tactic	Passage Language	Abbreviation
Abbreviate technical words or hard-to-pronounce names with a single letter, an acronym, or a much shorter version of the word.	serotonin Mihaly Csikszentmihalyi	S or sero C or MC
Use an arrow to show cause-effect or change over time.	Instability in interest rates can cause investors to avoid bonds.	IR unstable → ppl avoid bonds
Use a colon (:) to attribute an opinion or point of view to a specific person or group.	Many historians believe that economic interests can prolong a war.	H: $$ issues → longer war
Mark examples with parentheses or *e.g.*	A classic example is the behavior of the female sphex wasp.	e.g., ♀ S wasp
Use up and down arrows to indicate increases or decreases.	An increasing number of businesses are expected to reduce benefits for part-time employees.	↑ biz: ↓ ben part-time
Use math and science symbols that you already know.	greater than (or much greater than)	> (>>)
	less than (or much less than)	< (<<)
	change	Δ
	therefore	∴

Problem Set

For each of the four passages below, take 1.5 to 2 minutes to read and map the passage and articulate the simple story.

The solutions present one version of a passage map, but your version will vary; this is fine! The solutions also include simple stories, but you don't need to write these down when you are working through a passage—the passage map should be enough to allow you to put together the simple story.

Passage E: Redlining

In the 1960s, Northwestern University sociologist John McKnight coined the term redlining, the practice of denying or severely limiting service to customers in
5 particular geographic areas, areas often determined by the racial composition of the neighborhood. The term came from the practice of banks outlining certain areas in red on a map; within the red outline, banks
10 refused to invest. With no access to mortgages, residents within the red line suffered low property values and landlord abandonment; buildings abandoned by landlords were then more likely to become
15 centers of drug dealing and other crime, thus further lowering property values.

Redlining in mortgage lending was made illegal by the Fair Housing Act of 1968, which prohibited such discrimination based
20 on race, religion, gender, familial status, disability, or ethnic origin, and by community reinvestment legislation in the 1970s. However, redlining has sometimes continued in less explicit ways and can also
25 take place in the context of constrained access to health care, jobs, insurance, and more. Even today, some credit card companies send different offers to homes in different neighborhoods, and some auto
30 insurance companies offer different rates based on zip code.

Redlining can lead to reverse redlining, which occurs when predatory businesses specifically target minority or low-income
35 consumers for the purpose of charging them more than would typically be charged for a particular service. When mainstream retailers refuse to serve a certain area, people in that area can fall prey to opportunistic smaller
40 retailers who sell inferior goods at higher prices.

Passage F: Tokugawa

The Tokugawa period in Japan (1603–1867) serves as a laboratory for organizational behavior historians for the same reason that Iceland is an ideal location for geneticists—
5 isolation removes extraneous variables. The Tokugawa shoguns brought peace to a land of warring feudal lords. To preserve that tranquility, the Tokugawa shogunate forbade contact with the outside world, allowing only
10 a few Dutch trading ships to dock at one restricted port. Domestically, in pursuit of the same goal, the social order was fixed; there were four classes—warriors [samurai], artisans, merchants, and farmers or
15 peasants—and social mobility was prohibited. The ensuing stability and peace brought a commercial prosperity that lasted nearly two hundred years.

However, as psychologists and social
20 historians have observed, in varying ways, humans often fail to anticipate unintended consequences. In the Tokugawa period, the fixed social hierarchy placed the samurai on top; they and the government were essentially
25 supported by levies on the peasantry, as the other two classes were demographically and economically inconsequential. However, prosperity brought riches to the commercial classes and their numbers burgeoned.
30 Eventually, their economic power dwarfed that of their supposed superiors, the samurai, but the social structure was so ingrained that it was unthinkable to change. By the early nineteenth century, this imbalance between
35 social structure and economic reality eroded the stability of the society. This condition was one of the primary factors that led to the eventual collapse of the shogunate in 1867. In short, the success of the self-imposed order
40 led to its undoing through consequences that were beyond the ken of the founders.

Passage G: Prescription Errors

In Europe, medical prescriptions were historically written in Latin. A prescription for eye drops written in Amsterdam could be filled in Paris, because the abbreviation *OS*
5 meant "left eye" in both places. With the disappearance of Latin as a lingua franca, however, abbreviations such as *OS* can easily be confused with *AS* (left ear) or *per os* (by mouth), even by trained professionals.
10 Misinterpretations of medical instructions can be fatal. In the early 1990s, two infants died in separate but identical tragedies: They were each administered 5 milligrams of morphine, rather than 0.5 milligrams, as the dosage was
15 written without an initial zero. The naked decimal (.5) was subsequently misread.

The personal and economic costs of misinterpreted medical prescriptions and instructions are hard to quantify. However,
20 anecdotal evidence suggests that misinterpretations are prevalent. While mistakes will always happen in any human endeavor, medical professionals, hospital administrators, and policymakers should
25 continually work to drive the prescription error rate to zero, taking simple corrective steps and also pushing for additional investments.

Certain measures are widely agreed upon
30 but may be difficult to enforce, given the decentralization of the healthcare system in the United States. For instance, professional organizations have publicly advocated against the use of Latin abbreviations and other relics
35 of historical pharmacology. As a result, incidents in which *qd* (every day) and *qid* (four times a day) have been mixed up seem to be on the decline. Other measures have been taken by regulators. For instance, the Federal
40 Drug Administration asked a manufacturer to change the name of Losec, an antacid, to Prilosec, so that confusion with Lasix, a diuretic, would be reduced. Unfortunately, there have been at least a dozen reports of
45 accidental switches between Prilosec and Prozac, an antidepressant. As more drugs reach the market, drug-name "traffic control" will only become more complicated.

Other measures are controversial or
50 require significant investment. For instance, putting the patient's condition on the prescription would allow double-checking but also compromise patient privacy. Computerized prescriber order entry (CPOE)
55 systems seem to fix the infamous problem of illegible handwriting, but many CPOE systems permit naked decimals and other dangerous practices. Moreover, since fallible humans must still enter and retrieve the data, any
60 technological fixes must be accompanied by substantial training. Ultimately, a multi-pronged approach is needed to address the issue.

Passage H: Ether's Existence

In 1887, an ingenious experiment performed by Albert Michelson and Edward Morley severely undermined classical physics by failing to confirm the existence of "ether," a
5 ghostly massless medium that was thought to permeate the universe. This finding had profound results, ultimately paving the way for acceptance of Einstein's special theory of relativity.

10 Prior to the Michelson–Morley experiment, nineteenth-century physics conceived of light as a wave propagated at constant speed through the ether. The existence of ether was hypothesized in part to explain the
15 transmission of light, which was believed to be impossible through "empty" space. Physical objects, such as planets, were also thought to glide frictionlessly through the unmoving ether.

20 The Michelson–Morley experiment relied on the fact that the Earth, which orbits the Sun, would have to be in motion relative to a fixed ether. Just as a person on a motorcycle experiences a "wind" caused by her own
25 motion relative to the air, the Earth would experience an "ethereal wind" caused by its motion through the ether. Such a wind would affect our measurements of the speed of light. If the speed of light is fixed with respect
30 to the ether, but the Earth is moving through the ether, then to an observer on Earth light must appear to move faster in a "downwind" direction than in an "upwind" direction.

In 1887, there were no clocks sufficiently
35 precise to detect the speed differences that would result from an ethereal wind. Michelson and Morley surmounted this problem by using the wavelike properties of light itself to test for such speed differences. In their apparatus,
40 known as an "interferometer," a single beam of light is split in half. Mirrors guide each half of the beam along a separate trajectory before ultimately reuniting the two half-beams into a single beam. If one half-beam
45 has moved more slowly than the other, the reunited beams will be out of phase with each other. In other words, peaks of the first half-beam will not coincide exactly with peaks of the second half-beam, resulting in an
50 interference pattern in the reunited beam. Michelson and Morley detected only a tiny degree of interference in the reunited light beam—far less than what was expected based on the motion of the Earth.

This page intentionally left blank

Solutions

Passage E: Redlining

Passage map:

   ① Redlining: deny/limit svc to minorities

   ② Now illegal, but still happens

   ③ Leads to reverse redL: charging more than typical

Simple story:

   Redlining is denying or limiting services to minority customers. It's been illegal since the late '60s, but some businesses still do it. It can also lead to reverse redlining, where businesses do offer service to minority communities, but at a higher price than they would typically charge.

Passage F: Tokugawa

Passage map:

   ① T isolated; fixed social order; peace/stable.

   ② BUT merchants → wealthy, messed up social order, system collapsed. Fixed soc. order was once good, later bad.

Simple story:

   The T period in Japan is good to study because it was isolated. The social order was fixed and it was a really stable era. Later, a "lower" group became wealthy, but the rigid social system stayed. So what helped make things stable at first eventually caused the system to collapse.

Passage G: Prescription Errors

Passage map:

   ① Eur. Rx in Latin, but now errors, dangerous

   ② DK how much error, but maybe lots. Try to ↓

   ③ Pop. measures: no Latin, no similar names

   ④ Other measures controv.: listing condition, computers

Simple story:

   There are many ways to misinterpret medical prescriptions, and this can be dangerous. Some measures—such as eliminating the use of Latin and making names unambiguous—are agreed upon, but others are more controversial.

Passage H: Ether's Existence

Passage map:

   ① 1887, M&M—no ether; made way for Einstein

   ② Old: ether explained how light moved

   ③ Basis for exp: Earth "wind"

   ④ DTL: How M&M showed lack of ether

DTL is an abbreviation for the word *detail*.

Simple story:

   Prior to 1887, scientists thought that space was not "empty," but filled with a substance called ether. In 1887, Michelson and Morley conducted an experiment that involved splitting a beam of light. There was less interference than there should have been if ether existed, so the experiment showed that ether might not actually exist.

General Questions

In This Chapter...

In this chapter, you will learn how to handle general questions. These big-picture questions ask about the primary purpose or main point of the entire passage or of one paragraph in the passage.

CHAPTER 20 General Questions

Reading Comprehension questions can be grouped into two major categories:

1. **General** questions, such as Primary Purpose, Paragraph

2. **Specific** questions, such as Detail, Inference, Specific Purpose

This chapter will cover general questions, which may ask you about the overall purpose of the passage or about the purpose of a specific paragraph. The next chapter will cover specific question types.

You typically won't see more than one general question per passage; in fact, on some passages you won't see any. On average, expect to spend about a minute on each general question.

4 Steps to the Answer

In this chapter, you'll learn how to answer **Primary Purpose** and **Paragraph** questions using a standard 4-step process that you'll use for all RC questions.

Step 1: Identify the question. This chapter will tell you how to recognize that you have a Primary Purpose or a Paragraph question.

Step 2: Find the support. Your initial read of the passage and any map you make will give you a strong idea of the overall point and the purpose of each paragraph. At this stage, you may take a look at your passage map to remind yourself of the big picture, or you may feel comfortable not even doing that. (Note: On specific questions, you *will* have to go back to reread some part of the passage—more on this in the next chapter.)

Step 3: Predict an answer. Take a look at the question again and, using your map or memory, try to formulate a rough answer in your own words. You're not trying to match the correct answer exactly; rather, you're just trying to articulate the *kind* of information you would expect to find in the correct answer.

Step 4: Eliminate and find a match. Evaluate each answer, while keeping in mind your predicted answer. Eliminate any that definitely don't match. When you find a potential match, leave it in and continue to evaluate the remaining answers:

- If you eliminate four answers, great! Pick the remaining one and move on.
- If you still have two or three answers left, compare the answers to the relevant information in your map. If the answers are very similar, you may also compare them to each other.
- If you still have four or five answers left, make sure you are answering the right question! After that, it's probably best to cut your losses: Guess and move on.

Finally, one last word of advice. This might seem obvious, but *every single word* in the answer choice must be supported in order for that choice to be correct. Make sure that you are reading methodically. Don't rush just because you're stressed; saving 10 seconds is not worth the risk of missing a question due to a careless mistake.

Practice Passage: Insect Behavior

Give yourself approximately 4.5 minutes to read the passage below and answer the questions that follow.

At times, insect behavior appears to be explicable in terms of unconscious stimulus-response mechanisms; when scrutinized, it often reveals a stereotyped, inflexible quality.

5 A classic series of experiments were performed on the female sphex wasp. The mother leaves her egg sealed in a burrow alongside a paralyzed grasshopper or other insect, which her larva can eat when it hatches.

10 Typically, before she deposits the grasshopper in the burrow, she leaves it at the entrance and goes inside to inspect the burrow. If the inspection reveals no problems, she drags the grasshopper inside by its antennae. Once the

15 larvae hatch, they feed on the paralyzed insects until ready to spin a cocoon and undergo metamorphosis.

Entomologist Jean-Henri Fabre discovered that if the grasshopper's antennae are

20 removed while the wasp is inside inspecting the nest, the wasp will not drag it into the burrow, even though the legs or ovipositor could serve the same function as the antennae. Later Fabre found more evidence

25 of the wasp's dependence on predetermined routine. While a wasp was performing her inspection of a burrow, he moved the grasshopper a few centimeters away from the burrow's mouth. The wasp brought the

30 grasshopper back to the edge of the burrow, then began a whole new inspection. When Fabre took this opportunity to move the food again, the wasp repeated her routine. Fabre performed his disruptive maneuver

35 forty times, and the wasp's response never changed.

1. The primary purpose of the passage is to

(A) demonstrate, based on examples, that insects lack awareness of their surroundings

(B) argue that insects are unique in their dependence on rigid routines

(C) analyze the maternal behavior of wasps

(D) contrast typical wasp behavior with unconscious behavior

(E) contend that insect behavior can rely on rigid routines that appear to be unconscious

2. Which of the following best describes the purpose of the second paragraph of the passage?

(A) To provide experimental evidence for the thesis articulated in the first paragraph

(B) To introduce a hypothesis about insect behavior

(C) To illustrate the ways in which grasshoppers are unsuitable for the wasp's purposes

(D) To explore the significance of the wasp's varied reactions to certain stimuli

(E) To acknowledge experimental evidence that does not support the author's thesis

Here's one example of a simple story, with the point noted:

The
point

→

Insect behavior is sometimes inflexible or unconscious. Normally, a wasp inspects the burrow and then brings the grasshopper inside. Later, the larvae feed on the grasshopper.

Fabre discovered that the wasp will only *drag a grasshopper by the antennae. He also found that, if the grasshopper is moved during the inspection phase, then the wasp will put the grasshopper back and inspect the burrow again, over and over.*

Hmm. That sounds pretty inflexible—it's as though it can't think or adapt.

That last line is not stated in the passage, but a reader might summarize the simple story in this way.

Here's one example of a passage map:

① Insects: behavior inflex, unconsc
Typ: wasp inspect burrow, bring GH, larvae eat

② F: ONLY drag by antennae
If GH moves, wasp re-inspects, every time

Here's a much more abbreviated version:

① Insect: inflex
Normal behav

② F: weird behav

The second map is so abbreviated that it serves only as a quick reminder of things that the reader already remembers: The normal behavior is described in the first paragraph and the second paragraph has the weird behavior. If your short-term memory is strong, then feel free to use a hyper-abbreviated map like this one. (You might not even write anything at all, but only follow that path if you can maintain a strong mental sense of the passage throughout the process of reading and answering the questions. Don't avoid writing anything simply because you think it will save you time.)

Primary Purpose Questions

Step 1 on any question is to **identify the question type**:

1. The primary purpose of the passage is to

This is a **Primary Purpose** question—the test writers are asking for the point of the whole passage. These are also known as **Main Idea** questions.

Most of the time, these questions will ask you to identify the *primary purpose* of the passage or what the author is *primarily concerned with*. The correct answer should fit with the point that you have articulated to yourself.

Steps 2 and 3 merge for Primary Purpose questions: **Find the support** and **predict an answer**. For Primary Purpose questions, you don't need to go back to the passage. You will already have identified the point—if not, briefly review your map. In the *Insect Behavior* passage, the point is that some insect behaviors seem to be inflexible; the insects can't adapt to changing situations.

Once you have that set in your head, it's time for step 4: **Eliminate and find a match**. For Primary Purpose questions, eliminate any choice that doesn't match the point. For example:

(A) demonstrate, based on examples, that insects lack awareness of their surroundings	*The insect is aware—she sees that the grasshopper has moved and she goes and gets it. The point is about insects' unconscious behavior, not their general awareness. Eliminate.*
(B) argue that insects are unique in their dependence on rigid routines	*The author does argue that insects are dependent on rigid routines but never claims that they are unique in this way. No other types of animals are mentioned. Eliminate.*
(C) analyze the maternal behavior of wasps	*The author uses a couple of examples of wasp behavior to make a more general point about insect behavior; the main point is not that these wasps are making a nest for their offspring. Eliminate.*
(D) contrast typical wasp behavior with unconscious behavior	*The author does not present typical behavior and unconscious behavior as different things. Rather, the typical behavior never changes, even when a disruption of the routine would seem to warrant changing a behavior. Eliminate.*
(E) contend that insect behavior can rely on rigid routines that appear to be unconscious	*CORRECT. The author claims that, at times, insect behavior is inflexible, or rigid, and the insect may not always be capable of responding to an unexpected or changed situation.*

Several types of trap answers appeared in this question.

One word off:	These trap answers mostly look good, but one word isn't supported by the passage, taking the answer choice out of contention. Answer (B) was one word off (*unique*). (Note: This can stretch to a couple of words off!)
Extreme:	These trap answers contain an extreme word, such as *all* or *never*, that is not supported by the passage. It is certainly possible for extreme words to appear in a correct answer, but only if the passage provides direct support for such extreme language. Answer (B) contained an extreme word (*unique*) that was not supported by the passage (sometimes, a wrong answer can fit multiple trap categories!).
Out of scope:	These trap answers will typically touch on aspects of the passage, but will go further than what the passage actually discusses. Sometimes, these answers are just a bit too broad; other times, they are way off. Answer (A) talks about *awareness of their surroundings*, which isn't discussed in the passage.
True but not right:	These answers will typically reflect things that are true according to the passage, but they do not answer the specific question asked. Answer (C) falls into this category. The examples used in the passage *are* about maternal wasp behavior, but the overall point is about a broader topic: the inflexible nature of insect behavior in general.
Direct contradiction:	Answer (D) is an example of a direct contradiction: The passage says the opposite of what this answer choice conveys.

20

Paragraph Questions

In order to answer **Paragraph** questions correctly, you will need to have a strong grasp of the point of the passage as well as the purpose of each paragraph.

Most of the time, Paragraph questions will ask you for one of two things: 1) the purpose of a particular paragraph in the context of the whole passage or 2) the purpose of a particular paragraph in relation to another particular paragraph.

First, identify the question:

  2. Which of the following best describes the purpose of the second paragraph of the passage?

In this case, the question asks for the purpose of the second paragraph in the context of the entire passage.

Second, find the support. Locate paragraph 2 in your map:

> ① Insects: behavior inflex, unconsc
> Typ: wasp inspect burrow, bring GH, larvae eat
>
> ② F: ONLY drag by antennae
> If GH moves, wasp re-inspects, every time

Third, predict an answer. The second paragraph provides examples that support the overall point that insect behavior is inflexible.

Once you have that set in your head, eliminate and find a match. For Paragraph questions, try to disprove each answer. If the answer contains something that wasn't part of the passage, or was restricted to a different paragraph, cross it off.

Before you look at the explanations below, try to label some of the wrong answers using the trap categories you learned on the last problem.

(A) To provide experimental evidence for the thesis articulated in the first paragraph	*CORRECT. The second paragraph does talk about experiments, and those experiments do support what the author claimed in the first paragraph.*
(B) To introduce a hypothesis about insect behavior	*The passage does introduce such a hypothesis, but it does so in the* first *paragraph, not the second one. This is the overall point of the passage, but the question asks about only the second paragraph. (True but not right)*
(C) To illustrate the ways in which grasshoppers are unsuitable for the wasp's purposes	*The passage doesn't say that the grasshoppers are unsuitable. This trap might be set for someone who is reading very quickly or superficially and draws an erroneous conclusion about the experiments with grasshoppers. (Out of scope)*
(D) To explore the significance of the wasp's varied reactions to certain stimuli	*The point of the passage is that the wasp does* not *change her behavior even when the circumstances of her situation change; her reactions do not vary. (Direct contradiction)*
(E) To acknowledge experimental evidence that does not support the author's thesis	*The evidence in the second paragraph does* support *the author's thesis. (Direct contradiction)*

All of the traps here were discussed earlier in the chapter; flip back if you want a refresher on any of the categories.

If a question asks about the entire passage, then you have a Primary Purpose question. Remind yourself of the overall point, using your map as needed.

If the question asks specifically about one paragraph in the context of the whole, then use your map to remind yourself what that one paragraph is about and how it fits into the overall story of the passage.

Try to come up with your own answer to the question before you look at the answers. Then, dive into those answers and start eliminating anything that is too far from what you articulated. Do check all five answers, even after you think you've found the right one. Finally, verify that your final answer matches both the question asked and the answer you articulated to yourself up front.

Don't forget to keep an eye out for the common traps (summarized in your Cheat Sheet on the next page).

20

Primary Purpose Cheat Sheet

Primary Purpose Cheat Sheet

Identify the Question

Primary Purpose:
The primary purpose (or function) of the passage is to . . .

The author of the passage is primarily concerned with . . .

Which of the following most accurately states the purpose of the passage?

Which of the following titles best summarizes the passage?

With which of the following would the author be most likely to agree?

Paragraph:
What is the purpose of the second paragraph?

Which of the following best describes the relationship of the third paragraph to the passage as a whole?

Find the Support

Use your map or overall understanding of the passage.

Predict an Answer

Articulate the point or the purpose of the paragraph *before* looking at the answer choices.

Eliminate

Check all of the answers! Common traps:

Trap	Characteristics
Direct contradiction	The passage says the opposite
Extreme	Extreme word *without support* in the passage
One word off	Looks very tempting but one or two words are wrong
Out of scope	Goes beyond what the passage says
True but not right	The passage does say this, but it does not answer the question asked

Take a photo of this page and keep it with the review sheets you're creating as you study. Better yet, use this page as a guide to create your own review sheet—you'll remember the material better if you write it down yourself. Where appropriate, put it in your own words and you'll remember it even better.

Problem Set

The three passages in this problem set appear in both the General and Specific chapters, but different questions are presented in each chapter.

Give yourself 1.5 to 2 minutes to read each passage and up to 60 seconds to answer each question. After you're done, review your point and passage map before you check the solutions, thinking about ways to improve your process next time. If you come up with ways to improve your map, actually rewrite it to reinforce what you want to do differently next time. Then, check your work against the solution key.

Passage I: Japanese Swords

Historians have long recognized the Japanese sword, or *nihonto*, as one of the finest cutting weapons ever produced. But to regard the sword that is synonymous with the
5 samurai as merely a weapon is to ignore what makes it so special. The Japanese sword has always been considered a splendid weapon and even a spiritual entity. The traditional Japanese adage "the sword is the soul of the
10 samurai" reflects not only the sword's importance to its wielder but also its permanent connection to its creator, the master smith.

Master smiths may not have been
15 considered artists in the classical sense, but each smith exerted great care in the process of creating swords, no two of which were ever forged in exactly the same way. Over hundreds of hours, two types of steel were
20 repeatedly heated, hammered, and folded together into thousands of very thin layers, producing a sword with an extremely sharp and durable cutting edge and a flexible, shock-absorbing blade. It was common, though
25 optional, for a master smith to place a physical signature on a blade; moreover, each smith's secret forging techniques left an idiosyncratic structural signature on his blades. Each master smith brought a high level
30 of devotion, skill, and attention to detail to the sword-making process, and the sword itself was a reflection of his personal honor and ability. This effort made each blade as distinctive as the samurai who wielded it such
35 that today the Japanese sword is recognized as much for its artistic merit as for its historical significance.

1. The primary purpose of the passage is to

    (A) challenge the observation that the Japanese sword is highly admired by historians

    (B) introduce new information about the forging of Japanese swords

    (C) discuss an obsolete weapon of great historical significance

    (D) argue that Japanese sword makers were motivated by honor

    (E) explain the value attributed to the Japanese sword

2. Which of the following is the primary function of the second paragraph?

    (A) To present an explanation for a change in perception

    (B) To determine the historical significance of Japanese swords

    (C) To discuss the artistic aspects associated with creating Japanese swords

    (D) To compare Japanese master smiths to classical artists

    (E) To review the complete process of making a Japanese sword

Passage J: Augustus

Caesar Augustus, founder of the Roman Empire, wrote an account of his life called *Deeds of the Divine Augustus*. It consists of thirty-five numbered sections, each
5   of which records his achievements in a particular field. The first two sections, for instance, describe his role in the civil war that followed Julius Caesar's death, while section twenty-eight enumerates the
10 colonies he founded for his soldiers. Augustus left instructions that the *Deeds* be inscribed on two bronze pillars in Rome, as well as on monuments and temples throughout the empire. Clearly, Augustus
15 intended the *Deeds* to mold his image for posterity.

A number of details in the *Deeds* suggest that Augustus wanted to be remembered as a patriot in the tradition of
20 Cincinnatus. Augustus would have us believe that his political career was driven not by personal ambition, but by a selfless desire to serve Rome and to uphold its ancient liberties and customs. He tells us
25 that his seizure of power was a "liberation from the tyranny of a faction." After he came to power "by universal consent," he returned control of the state to the hands of the Roman senate and people. Emphasizing his
30 humility, he lists numerous occasions on which he declined titles, ovations, and triumphs offered him by the senate.

Few historians accept Augustus's account of his political motivation. Mark Antony's
35 faction was not particularly tyrannical, and Augustus's seizure of power appears to have been motivated mainly by opportunism. In Gibbon's persuasive analysis, Augustus's subsequent restoration of the outward
40 forms of republican government was designed to lend political legitimacy to what was essentially a dictatorship. Augustus's refusal of numerous honors appears to have been part of this same political stagecraft.
45 According to Suetonius, the senate felt obliged to offer Augustus a steady stream of honors. Augustus accepted a great many of these, including the titles of "First Citizen" and "Father of the Country," but refused
50 enough to maintain the appearance of humility.

1. The passage is primarily concerned with

(A) analyzing the literary merits of a text published by a well-known historical figure

(B) explaining a historical inconsistency that has long puzzled scholars

(C) examining the motivations of various leaders during a specific military conflict

(D) challenging the factual evidence detailed in an autobiographical work

(E) evaluating the accuracy of particular claims made in a historical treatise

2. The main purpose of the third paragraph of the passage is to

(A) explain that most of what Augustus wrote in the *Deeds* was untrue

(B) undermine a key aspect of Augustus's attempt to mold his image in the *Deeds*

(C) argue that calling oneself "Father of the Country" is contrary to a ruler's duty of humility

(D) highlight Gibbon's contribution to the scholarly analysis of Roman civic life

(E) contrast Augustus's political motivations with those of Suetonius and Mark Antony

Passage K: Sweet Spot

Most tennis players strive to strike the ball on the racket's vibration node, more commonly known as the "sweet spot." However, many players are unaware of the existence of a second, lesser-known location on the racket face—the center of percussion—that will also greatly diminish the strain on a player's arm when the ball is struck.

In order to understand the physics of this second sweet spot, it is helpful to consider what would happen to a tennis racket if the player's hand were to vanish at the moment of impact with the ball. The impact of the ball would cause the racket to bounce backwards, resulting in a translational motion away from the ball. The tendency of this motion would be to jerk all parts of the racket, including the end of its handle, backward, or away from the ball. Unless the ball happened to hit precisely at the racket's center of mass, the racket would additionally experience a rotational motion around its center of mass—much as a penny that has been struck near its edge will start to spin. Whenever the ball hits the racket face, the effect of this rotational motion is to jerk the end of the handle forward, towards the ball. Depending on where the ball strikes the racket face, one or the other of these motions will predominate.

However, there is one point of impact, known as the center of percussion, which causes neither motion to predominate; if a ball strikes this point, the impact does not impart any motion to the end of the handle. The reason for this lack of motion is that the force on the upper part of the hand would be equal and opposite to the force on the lower part of the hand, resulting in no net force on the tennis player's hand or forearm. The center of percussion constitutes a second sweet spot because a tennis player's wrist is typically placed next to the end of the racket's handle. When the player strikes the ball at the center of percussion, her wrist is jerked neither forward nor backward, and she experiences greatly reduced vibration in the arm.

The manner in which a tennis player can detect the center of percussion on a given tennis racket follows from the nature of this second sweet spot. The center of percussion can be located via simple trial and error by holding the end of a tennis racket between the finger and thumb and throwing a ball onto the strings. If the handle jumps out of the player's hand, then the ball has missed the center of percussion.

1. What is the primary message the author is trying to convey?

   (A) A proposal for an improvement to the design of tennis rackets

   (B) An examination of the differences between the two types of sweet spot

   (C) A definition of the translational and rotational forces acting on a tennis racket

   (D) A description of the ideal area in which to strike every ball

   (E) An explanation of a lesser-known area on a tennis racket that reduces unwanted vibration

2. What is the primary function served by the second paragraph in the context of the entire passage?

   (A) To establish the main idea of the passage

   (B) To provide an explanation of the mechanics of the phenomenon discussed in the passage

   (C) To introduce a counterargument that elucidates the main idea of the passage

   (D) To explain the physics of tennis

   (E) To explain why the main idea of the passage would be useful for tennis players

Solutions

Passage I: Japanese Swords

Historians have long recognized the Japanese sword, or *nihonto*, as one of the finest cutting weapons ever produced. But to regard the sword that is synonymous with the
5 samurai as merely a weapon is to ignore what makes it so special. The Japanese sword has always been considered a splendid weapon and even a spiritual entity. The traditional Japanese adage "the sword is the soul of the
10 samurai" reflects not only the sword's importance to its wielder but also its permanent connection to its creator, the master smith.

Master smiths may not have been
15 considered artists in the classical sense, but each smith exerted great care in the process of creating swords, no two of which were ever forged in exactly the same way. Over hundreds of hours, two types of steel were
20 repeatedly heated, hammered, and folded together into thousands of very thin layers, producing a sword with an extremely sharp and durable cutting edge and a flexible, shock-absorbing blade. It was common, though
25 optional, for a master smith to place a physical signature on a blade; moreover, each smith's secret forging techniques left an idiosyncratic structural signature on his blades. Each master smith brought a high level
30 of devotion, skill, and attention to detail to the sword-making process, and the sword itself was a reflection of his personal honor and ability. This effort made each blade as distinctive as the samurai who wielded it such
35 that today the Japanese sword is recognized as much for its artistic merit as for its historical significance.

Sample passage map (yours will likely differ):

① J sword: not just weapon, spirit

② Master smith: skilled
   how to make
   artistic merit + history

The point (articulate to yourself; don't write): Japanese sword is a weapon *and* a work of art, important to both samurai and smith. The smiths were basically artists.

1. First, identify the question type:

The primary purpose of the passage is to

The wording here indicates that this is a Primary Purpose, or Main Idea, question. Glance at your map (find the support) and remind yourself of the point (predict the answer). Finally, go to the answers to find a match.

(A) *challenge the observation that the Japanese sword is highly admired by historians*

The passage does not challenge the idea that historians admired the swords; the entire passage reflects great admiration for the swords and their makers. (Direct contradiction)

(B) *introduce new information about the forging of Japanese swords*

The second paragraph does talk about how swords are forged, but does not present this information as *new*. Moreover, information about the forging process is only one part of the passage; it is not the overall point of the passage. (One word off)

(C) *discuss an obsolete weapon of great historical significance*

An *obsolete* weapon would no longer be in use today; the passage does not indicate that Japanese swords are no longer used or no longer produced. (One word off)

(D) *argue that Japanese sword makers were motivated by honor*

The passage does indicate that the swords were a reflection of the master smith's personal honor, but this is a narrow detail; it is not the point of the entire passage. (True but not right)

(E) *explain the value attributed to the Japanese sword*

CORRECT. The passage does explain the value of the sword to the samurai (in the first paragraph—"the sword is the soul of the samurai") and to the master smith (in the second paragraph).

2. First, identify the question type:

    Which of the following is the primary function of the second paragraph?

This is a Paragraph question. Next, find the support (second paragraph of your map) and predict an answer. The master smith was an artist; the swords were effectively the smith's artwork. Sometimes, they even signed the swords!

Finally, check the answers to find a match.

(A) *To present an explanation for a change in perception*

The passage does not indicate that a general *change* in perception has occurred. Rather, the author is putting forth his own idea that smiths might be considered artists. (Out of scope)

(B) *To determine the historical significance of Japanese swords*

The last sentence of the paragraph does mention the historical significance, but the rest of the paragraph focuses on the forging process and the *artistic merit*. The paragraph does not discuss the historical significance. (Out of scope)

(C) *To discuss the artistic aspects associated with creating Japanese swords*

CORRECT. The second paragraph begins by indicating that the smiths *may not have been considered artists in the classical sense*, but goes on to underscore the uniqueness of the finished products (no two were forged the same way, the swords were often signed, the finished product was a reflection of the smith's personal honor and ability). The last sentence indicates that the swords are highly regarded for their *artistic merit*.

(D) *To compare Japanese master smiths to classical artists*

While the passage does imply that the smiths might be considered artists, there is no mention of actual classical artists, nor is any comparison made. (Out of scope)

(E) *To review the complete process of making a Japanese sword*

The passage does provide some details of the sword-making process, but it does not review the *complete* process. (Extreme)

20

Passage J: Augustus

Caesar Augustus, founder of the Roman Empire, wrote an account of his life called *Deeds of the Divine Augustus*. It consists of thirty-five numbered sections, each
5 of which records his achievements in a particular field. The first two sections, for instance, describe his role in the civil war that followed Julius Caesar's death, while section twenty-eight enumerates the
10 colonies he founded for his soldiers. Augustus left instructions that the *Deeds* be inscribed on two bronze pillars in Rome, as well as on monuments and temples throughout the empire. Clearly, Augustus
15 intended the *Deeds* to mold his image for posterity.

A number of details in the *Deeds* suggest that Augustus wanted to be remembered as a patriot in the tradition of
20 Cincinnatus. Augustus would have us believe that his political career was driven not by personal ambition, but by a selfless desire to serve Rome and to uphold its ancient liberties and customs. He tells us
25 that his seizure of power was a "liberation from the tyranny of a faction." After he came to power "by universal consent," he returned control of the state to the hands of the Roman senate and people. Emphasizing his
30 humility, he lists numerous occasions on which he declined titles, ovations, and triumphs offered him by the senate.

Few historians accept Augustus's account of his political motivation. Mark Antony's
35 faction was not particularly tyrannical, and Augustus's seizure of power appears to have been motivated mainly by opportunism. In Gibbon's persuasive analysis, Augustus's subsequent restoration of the outward
40 forms of republican government was designed to lend political legitimacy to what was essentially a dictatorship. Augustus's refusal of numerous honors appears to have been part of this same political stagecraft.
45 According to Suetonius, the senate felt obliged to offer Augustus a steady stream of honors. Augustus accepted a great many of these, including the titles of "First Citizen" and "Father of the Country," but refused
50 enough to maintain the appearance of humility.

Sample passage map (yours will likely differ):

① Aug: Deeds
    achvmnt; publicize good image

② Patriot, selfless, humble...
    But was it true?

③ Not really
    manipulate opinion

The point (articulate to yourself; don't write): Augustus wrote *Deeds* to present himself as altruistic, but most historians think he was merely justifying his own moves to gain power. It's like he was presenting one (much more positive) view of himself on social media while actually being very different in real life.

1. First, identify the question type:

    The passage is primarily concerned with

This is a Primary Purpose, or Main Idea, question. Check your passage map (or your memory!) to predict the kind of information the answer should include.

Finally, look for a match in the answers.

(A) *analyzing the literary merits of a text published by a well-known historical figure*

The text was published by a well-known person, but the point of the passage is not to analyze the *literary* value. Rather, the author is analyzing the disconnect between how Augustus presented his own motivations (in a very positive light) and what historians think about Augustus's motivations (not so positive).

(B) *explaining a historical inconsistency that has long puzzled scholars*

The passage does discuss something that might be called an *inconsistency*, but there is no indication that scholars have been puzzled. Rather, it seems that most historians are in agreement that the way Augustus presented his motivations is not particularly truthful. And it's probably a stretch to call this an *inconsistency*; rather, Augustus presumably knew that he was being disin-genuous when he claimed to be acting from selfless motives.

(C) *examining the motivations of various leaders during a specific military conflict*

While the passage does mention a couple of other leaders besides Augustus, it is not focused on assessing the motivations of all of them during a particular conflict. The passage focuses on what historians thought of *Augustus's* motivations.

(D) *challenging the factual evidence detailed in an autobiographical work*

The passage definitely challenges part of what Augustus wrote in *Deeds*, but it does not challenge the *factual* evidence. He did, apparently, found colonies for his soldiers and so on (or at least the passage doesn't dispute this). Rather, the passage challenges what Augustus claimed about his own *motivations* in taking the actions he did.

(E) *evaluating the accuracy of particular claims made in a historical treatise*

CORRECT. Augustus makes particular claims in *Deeds*—that he was selfless, that he was humble, that he apparently was motivated by a desire to serve others. The passage then indicates that historians doubt this self-view and believe his actions were likely *designed to lend political legitimacy to what was essentially a dictatorship.*

2. First, identify the question type:

The main purpose of the third paragraph of the passage is to

This is a Paragraph question. When you are asked to find the main purpose of a paragraph, look for a topic sentence. This paragraph begins with the topic sentence "Few historians accept Augustus's account of his political motivation," which suggests that Augustus's own account of his political motivation might not have been very accurate.

(A) *explain that most of what Augustus wrote in* the Deeds *was untrue*

This answer choice is too extreme. While the paragraph does dispute *part* of the *Deeds*, it does not claim that *most* of it is untrue. Paragraphs 1 and 2 indicate that the *Deeds* cover many aspects of Augustus's career, and that the portion being disputed consists only of *a number of details*.

(B) *undermine a key aspect of Augustus's attempt to mold his image in the* Deeds

CORRECT. The paragraph tries to under-mine one key aspect of the *Deeds*: Augustus's account of his political motivation.

(C) *argue that calling oneself "Father of the Country" is contrary to a ruler's duty of humility*

The paragraph mentions the title *Father of the Country*, but does so as part of an anecdote regarding how Augustus turned down certain honors in order to pretend to show humility. The paragraph does not conclude that accepting this one title is contrary to the concept of humility.

(D) *highlight Gibbon's contribution to the scholarly analysis of Roman civic life*

Gibbon's contribution to the topic is intro-duced in order to support the main point: that Augustus's motivations were less about altruism and more about his own drive for power. In addition, *Roman civic life* is a broad topic, spanning many people and many centuries, whereas the paragraph only cites Gibbon's views on one man's actions.

(E) *contrast Augustus's political motivations with those of Suetonius and Mark Antony*

The paragraph says nothing about Suetonius's motivation. Similarly, the passage says little about Mark Antony's motives. It is there-fore not correct to say that this paragraph contrasts Augustus's motivation with those of Suetonius and Mark Antony.

Passage K: Sweet Spot

Most tennis players strive to strike the ball on the racket's vibration node, more commonly known as the "sweet spot." However, many players are unaware of the
5   existence of a second, lesser-known location on the racket face—the center of percussion—that will also greatly diminish the strain on a player's arm when the ball is struck.

In order to understand the physics of this
10 second sweet spot, it is helpful to consider what would happen to a tennis racket if the player's hand were to vanish at the moment of impact with the ball. The impact of the ball would cause the racket to bounce backwards,
15 resulting in a translational motion away from the ball. The tendency of this motion would be to jerk all parts of the racket, including the end of its handle, backward, or away from the ball. Unless the ball happened to hit precisely
20 at the racket's center of mass, the racket would additionally experience a rotational motion around its center of mass—much as a penny that has been struck near its edge will start to spin. Whenever the ball hits the racket
25 face, the effect of this rotational motion is to jerk the end of the handle forward, towards the ball. Depending on where the ball strikes the racket face, one or the other of these motions will predominate.

30 However, there is one point of impact, known as the center of percussion, which causes neither motion to predominate; if a ball strikes this point, the impact does not impart any motion to the end of the handle.
35 The reason for this lack of motion is that the force on the upper part of the hand would be equal and opposite to the force on the lower part of the hand, resulting in no net force on the tennis player's hand or forearm.
40 The center of percussion constitutes a second sweet spot because a tennis player's wrist is typically placed next to the end of the racket's handle. When the player strikes the ball at the center of percussion, her wrist is
45 jerked neither forward nor backward, and she experiences greatly reduced vibration in the arm.

The manner in which a tennis player can detect the center of percussion on a given
50 tennis racket follows from the nature of this second sweet spot. The center of percussion can be located via simple trial and error by holding the end of a tennis racket between the finger and thumb and throwing a ball onto the
55 strings. If the handle jumps out of the player's hand, then the ball has missed the center of percussion.

Sample passage map (yours will likely differ):

① 2 SS (↓ strain), one less known

② if hand disappear?

③ center perc = no motion, ↓↓ vibration

④ find center perc

The point (articulate to yourself; don't write): People usually know about one sweet spot but not the other. Both reduce vibration in the arm. (Plus lots of technical details—ignore for now!)

1.   First, identify the question type:

What is the primary message the author is trying to convey?

This is a Primary Purpose, or Main Idea, question. Glance at your map to remind yourself of the point before you go to the answers.

(A)   *A proposal for an improvement to the design of tennis rackets*

The passage doesn't talk about this at all. (Out of scope)

(B)   *An examination of the differences between the two types of sweet spot*

It does talk about two different types of sweet spot. Leave this in for now.

(C) *A definition of the translational and rotational forces acting on a tennis racket*

One paragraph did mention these forces, but that was only one paragraph. This is not the point of the whole thing. (True but not right)

(D) *A description of the ideal area in which to strike every ball*

The passage does say that striking the ball at a sweet spot can reduce vibration, but it never says that spot is the ideal area in which to strike *every* ball. (Extreme)

(E) *An explanation of a lesser-known area on a tennis racket that reduces unwanted vibration*

It does talk about this. Leave this in.

Compare answers (B) and (E) to the support in the passage. The first paragraph mentions both sweet spots. After that, though, the passage focuses just on the lesser-known one; it doesn't go back and forth contrasting the two. Answer (E) is more appropriate than answer (B).

The correct answer is (E).

2. First, identify the question type:

What is the primary function served by the second paragraph in the context of the entire passage?

This is a Paragraph question. Glance at your map and articulate the purpose of the second paragraph to yourself before you check the answers.

The second paragraph begins with the text *In order to understand the physics of this second sweet spot.* It then goes into lots of detail about what would happen if the player's hand vanished and various forces and … wait! Don't get sucked into the detail. The first sentence is probably enough: This is how the second sweet spot works. Check the answers.

(A) *To establish the main idea of the passage*

The first paragraph establishes the main idea. The second paragraph provides detail about how the second sweet spot works. (Out of scope)

(B) *To provide an explanation of the mechanics of the phenomenon discussed in the passage*

CORRECT. The second paragraph does explain the physics, or the *mechanics*, of the phenomenon (the second sweet spot) mentioned in the first paragraph.

(C) *To introduce a counterargument that eluci-dates the main idea of the passage*

The second paragraph does elucidate (or explain) the main idea, but it is not a counterargument to anything. (One word off)

(D) *To explain the physics of tennis*

The paragraph does discuss the physical forces relevant to the sweet spot, but it does not explain all of the physics behind the game of tennis. That would be a very long paragraph! (Out of scope)

(E) *To explain why the main idea of the passage would be useful for tennis players*

The first and third paragraphs explain why the main idea is useful: to reduce vibration in the arm. The second paragraph does not do this. (True but not right)

Specific Questions

In This Chapter...

In this chapter, you will learn how to handle the most commonly asked specific questions on the GMAT. You'll learn how to use your passage map to efficiently find relevant details, what analysis each type of question requires, and how to identify the correct answer and avoid trap answers.

CHAPTER 21 Specific Questions

Most of the questions you will see on the GMAT will ask you about specific details in the passage. On average, expect to spend about 1.5 minutes on each specific question.

Here are the three most common types of specific questions:

1. **Detail questions.** These questions ask you to find a specific detail explicitly stated in the passage.

2. **Inference questions.** On these, the correct answer will *not* be stated explicitly in the passage, but it can be proven true using information stated in the passage.

3. **Specific Purpose questions.** These questions ask you *why* the author mentions a specific piece of information or employs a particular example.

You may occasionally see another type, such as a Strengthen or Weaken question. These are more commonly given on Critical Reasoning questions; if you do see one on Reading Comprehension, you can use the same strategies that you use for CR.

4 Steps to the Answer

You'll use the same process you learned for general questions in order to answer specific questions:

Step 1: Identify the question. This chapter will tell you the common language to expect for the different question types.

Step 2: Find the support. Expect to go back into the passage for all specific questions. Use your map to quickly figure out where to go, then read the relevant one to three sentences. Do not skip this step! Many specific questions have trap answers designed specifically to catch people who don't look back at the passage.

Step 3: Predict an answer. Take a look at the question again and, using the relevant passage text, try to formulate a rough answer in your own words. But there's a caveat: This won't work 100 percent of the time. This chapter will explain what to do when you can't predict the answer.

Step 4: Eliminate and find a match. Do a first pass through the answers, crossing off anything that is definitely wrong. Leave in any potential matches for your predicted answer as well as any for which you're not sure (whether you think they might be right or wrong). Don't spend time debating an answer choice (yet). When you're done with your first pass, see what you have left:

- If you have eliminated four answers, great! Pick the remaining one and move on.

- If you still have two or three answers left, compare the answers to the relevant information in the passage. If the answers are very similar, you may also compare them to each other. Use this to narrow down to the best answer of the remaining options.

- If you still have four or five answers left, make sure you didn't misread the question! After that, it may be best to cut your losses: Guess and move on.

Practice Passage: Electroconvulsive Therapy

21

Give yourself approximately 8 minutes to read the passage below and answer the four questions that follow. Mimic real test conditions. Answer the questions in the order given; pick an answer before you move to the next one, and don't return to a question you've already answered.

Electroconvulsive therapy (ECT) is a controversial psychiatric treatment involving the induction of a seizure in a patient by passing electricity through the brain. While
5   beneficial effects of electrically induced seizures are evident and predictable in most patients, a unified mechanism of action has not yet been established and remains the subject of numerous investigations. ECT is extremely
10 effective against severe depression, some acute psychotic states, and mania, though, like many medical procedures, it has its risks.

Since the inception of ECT in 1938, the public has held a strongly negative conception
15 of the procedure. Initially, doctors employed unmodified ECT. Patients were rendered instantly unconscious by the electrical current, but the strength of the muscle contractions from uncontrolled motor seizures often led to
20 compression fractures of the spine or damage to the teeth. In addition to the effect this physical trauma had on public sentiment, graphic examples of abuse documented in books and movies, such as Ken Kesey's *One
25 Flew Over the Cuckoo's Nest*, portrayed ECT as punitive, cruel, overused, and violative of patients' legal rights.

Modern ECT is virtually unrecognizable from its earlier days. The treatment is
30 modified by the muscle relaxant succinylcholine, which renders muscle contractions practically nonexistent. Additionally, patients are given a general anesthetic. Thus, the patient is asleep and
35 fully unaware during the procedure, and the only outward sign of a seizure may be the rhythmic movement of the patient's hand or foot. ECT is generally used in severely depressed patients for whom psychotherapy
40 and medication prove ineffective. It may also

be considered when there is an imminent risk of suicide, since antidepressants often take several weeks to work effectively. Exactly how ECT exerts its effects is not known, but
45 repeated applications affect several neurotransmitters in the brain, including serotonin, norepinephrine, and dopamine.

ECT has proven effective, but it is not without controversy. Though decades-old
50 studies showing brain cell death have been refuted in recent research, many patients do report loss of memory for events that occurred in the days, weeks, or months surrounding the ECT. Some patients have also
55 reported that their short-term memories continue to be affected for months after ECT, though some doctors argue that this memory malfunction may reflect the type of amnesia that sometimes results from severe
60 depression.

1. According to the passage, why has ECT been viewed negatively by the public?

    (A) Though ECT is effective in many cases, the medical community is not certain exactly how it works.

    (B) Early incarnations of ECT often resulted in physical trauma to the patient.

    (C) Effective use of ECT requires exposure to concerning medications, such as muscle relaxants and anesthesia.

    (D) ECT does not benefit individuals with anxiety disorders.

    (E) ECT cannot be performed without subsequent loss of memory in the patient.

2. Which of the following can be inferred about the way in which the modern form of ECT works?

    (A) Greater amounts of the neurotransmitters serotonin, norepinephrine, and dopamine seem to reduce symptoms of depression.

    (B) ECT cannot be used prior to attempting psychotherapy or medication.

    (C) Succinylcholine completely immobilizes the patient's body.

    (D) ECT often works faster than antidepressants.

    (E) One ECT treatment is often sufficient to reduce symptoms of depression significantly.

3. The author mentions amnesia as a possible side effect of severe depression in order to

    (A) acknowledge one of the possible negative side effects associated with ECT

    (B) emphasize the seriousness of severe depression as a debilitating disease

    (C) introduce a possible alternative cause for short-term memory loss reported by some patients

    (D) draw a connection between brain cell death and short-term memory loss

    (E) refute claims that ECT is responsible for any form of amnesia in patients

4. Each of the following is cited in the passage as a current or historical criticism of electroconvulsive therapy EXCEPT

    (A) ECT may cause the death of brain cells and memory loss

    (B) in certain cases, ECT was portrayed as a means to punish individuals

    (C) ECT had the potential to be used in inappropriate situations

    (D) early forms of ECT did not adequately protect patients from secondary harm brought on by the treatment

    (E) repeated applications of ECT affect several neurotransmitters in the brain

The questions above represent four distinct question types. The following sections will each cover one type and provide an explanation of the relevant question. First, here's what a reader might be thinking while reading the passage and jotting down a map:

ECT (electricity → seizure) has positives and negatives. Don't know how it works, but it is effective against depression and some other things.

Public doesn't like ECT. Early forms caused serious bodily trauma. Books and movies depicted it as cruel and abusive.

Modern ECT is much better. No trauma. Still don't know how it works but it helps really depressed people who can't get help in other ways.

It still has drawbacks, though, primarily around memory loss.

ECT + / −	
+	−
① treats depression	how work?
②	public percep trauma
③ Modern = no trauma helps v. depr. ppl	cruel, etc.
	how work?
④	memory loss

Here's a simple story for the passage:

ECT was pretty bad at first but it's much better now. They don't really know how it works, but it does work for severe depression. Even though ECT is better now, it still has some drawbacks.

Detail Questions

Detail questions typically include the language *according to the passage* (or something very similar). If you see this language, then you are being asked to find a particular piece of information, explicitly stated somewhere in the passage, that answers that particular question. The first question is a Detail question:

1. According to the passage, why has ECT been viewed negatively by the public?

Most of the time, the question stem will provide enough information to tell you where in the passage to look for the answer. Where does this particular question stem signal that you should look?

The question stem specifically references the public's negative view of ECT. This concept is the topic sentence of the second paragraph, so your passage map would likely contain some reference to this idea.

Your map, then, tells you where to go for step 2 of the process (find the support). Return to paragraph 2 and read as far as you need to in order to get an idea of why people disliked ECT:

Since the inception of ECT in 1938, the public has held a strongly negative conception of the procedure. Initially, doctors employed unmodified ECT. Patients were rendered instantly unconscious by the electrical current, but the strength of the muscle contractions from uncontrolled motor seizures often led to compression fractures of the spine or damage to the teeth. In addition to the effect this physical trauma had on public sentiment, graphic examples of abuse documented in books and movies, such as Ken Kesey's *One Flew Over the Cuckoo's Nest*, portrayed ECT as punitive, cruel, overused, and violative of patients' legal rights.

Use this information to try to predict the answer (step 3 of the process). First, people experienced some serious types of physical trauma (spinal fractures, damage to the teeth). Second, books and movies portrayed ECT as abusive and cruel. The correct answer should address one or both of those two topics.

Time for step 4: Eliminate and find a match! Try to identify any trap answer types that you have already learned.

(A) Though ECT is effective in many cases, the medical community is not certain exactly how it works.

The passage does say this, but it does not say that this is why people dislike ECT. (True but not right)

(B) Early incarnations of ECT often resulted in physical trauma to the patient.

CORRECT. This matches the first of the two reasons given in paragraph 2: Initially, people often experienced serious physical injuries when undergoing ECT treatment.

(C) Effective use of ECT requires exposure to concerning medications, such as muscle relaxants and anesthesia.

The passage does state that ECT now uses muscle relaxants and anesthesia, but the passage does not call these medications concerning. If anything, the passage seems to consider these advances positive because they allow the patient to be asleep and fully unaware. (Could be considered either One word off or True but not right)

(D) ECT does not benefit individuals with anxiety disorders.

The passage does not mention individuals with anxiety disorders. (Out of scope)

(E) ECT cannot be performed without subsequent loss of memory in the patient.

The last paragraph does mention that ECT can result in memory loss, but does not say that this side effect is always present. (Nor does the passage mention public perception with respect to memory loss.) (Extreme)

As you work through the answers, your thought process might be something along these lines:

(A) *Not one of the two reasons I stated before.*

(B) *Yes, this was one of the reasons I stated. Leave in.*

(C) *Not one of the two reasons I stated before.*

(D) *Not one of the two reasons I stated before.*

(E) *Not one of the two reasons I stated before. I do remember the passage saying something about this though, and memory loss is obviously not good. Leave in for now.*

   Hmm, (B) vs. (E). Answer (B) is an exact match for what I said, so I'm going to go for it. If I didn't have such a good match, I'd go and check the part that talked about memory loss.

If you do want to check the passage for the memory loss information, use the same process. Check your map; where was that info?

Paragraph 4. Reread the relevant text: *Many patients do report loss of memory for events that occurred in the days, weeks, or months surrounding the ECT. Some patients have also reported that their short-term memories continue to be affected for months after ECT.*

Check that against the choice. First, this text says *many*, not *all*, patients experience memory loss, so this is an *extreme* trap. Second, this paragraph is not where the passage discussed why the public has such a negative view of ECT.

The wrong answers represent several common traps, all of which were first presented in the General Questions chapter. For a quick review, reference your Cheat Sheet at the end of that chapter.

If you see a question that begins *According to the passage*, you almost certainly have a Detail question. Use your map to figure out what paragraph you'll need; in this case, the concept of negative public perception was a good clue to look in the second paragraph.

Whenever possible, try to formulate an answer to the question before you look at the answer choices. Note that there may be more than one possibility. In this case, the correct answer could have talked about the bodily trauma or about the depictions in books and movies.

At times, you may struggle to understand certain parts of a passage, in which case you may not be able to predict an answer. In this case, do one of two things. If you think you understand the main points in the relevant text, use that to try to eliminate some answers before you guess. (Sometimes, you might be able to eliminate all four wrong answers!)

If you don't understand the text well enough to pick up the main points, then guess and move on. (Don't be stubborn and waste valuable time that you could use elsewhere; when you don't get it, admit that to yourself and move on right away.)

Inference Questions

Inference questions ask you to find an answer that must be true based on information presented in the passage—but the information in the correct answer will *not* be explicitly given to you in the passage.

For example, if your boss tells you that Acme Company is your company's most important client, what can you infer?

You might imagine that Acme is responsible for a larger chunk of the company's revenue than is any other client. This is a reasonable inference in the real world, but it will lead you to a wrong answer on the GMAT. Why? Because it doesn't *have* to be true. Perhaps Acme is the company's most prestigious client. Perhaps your boss is good friends with Acme's CEO.

In fact, you have no idea *why* Acme is the most important client. The boss just stated a fact and didn't give you any insight into the reason for that fact.

The GMAT is never asking you to come up with reasonable real-world inferences. Rather, it is asking you to deduce what *must be true* given the available evidence.

So if Acme is the company's most important client, what else has to be true?

For starters, your company has to have at least one other client. If Acme were the only client, then your boss couldn't call it the *most important* client.

If one of the company's other clients is Widgets Incorporated, you could also correctly infer that Widgets is not the company's most important client—that spot is already taken by Acme!

Which problem in the *Electroconvulsive Therapy* set was the Inference problem? The wording of the question stem will tell you:

2.   Which of the following can be inferred about the way in which the modern form of ECT works?

In this case, the word *inferred* is in the question stem. When you see any form of the words *infer*, *imply*, or *suggest*, you have an Inference question.

Now, find the support (step 2). *Modern ECT* is first mentioned in the third paragraph, so look there to find and reread the relevant text. Step 3 (predict an answer), however, is pretty tough: The paragraph is all about how ECT works. In this case, it would be tough for anyone to try to predict an answer in advance.

Instead, return to the third paragraph to remind yourself of the type of information it contains, then start to check the answers, crossing off anything you cannot prove to be true based on information from that paragraph. Here's the third paragraph:

> Modern ECT is virtually unrecognizable from its earlier days. The treatment is modified by the muscle relaxant succinylcholine, which renders muscle contractions practically nonexistent. Additionally, patients are given a general anesthetic. Thus, the patient is asleep and fully unaware during the procedure, and the only outward sign of a seizure may be the rhythmic movement of the patient's hand or foot. ECT is generally used in severely depressed patients for whom psychotherapy and medication prove ineffective. It may also be considered when there is an imminent risk of suicide, since antidepressants often take several weeks to work effectively. Exactly how ECT exerts its effects is not known, but repeated applications affect several neurotransmitters in the brain, including serotonin, norepinephrine, and dopamine.

Think big picture; don't get too caught up in the details. The modern form of ECT is much safer for patients—they're asleep and won't have the same issues that caused injuries before. Modern ECT can be very effective for depression and risk of suicide. Move to the answers and check them against the paragraph:

(A) Greater amounts of the neurotransmitters serotonin, norepinephrine, and dopamine seem to reduce symptoms of depression.	*The third paragraph does mention these neurotransmitters and that ECT is effective for depression. The technical detail is annoying, so leave this in for now; if you still have more than one choice left at the end, then you can examine this more closely.*
(B) ECT cannot be used prior to attempting psychotherapy or medication.	*Whenever you see an extreme word, check whether the passage justifies the usage. In this case, the third paragraph does not justify the use of the word* cannot; *it says only that those other therapies are tried first at least some of the time. (Extreme)*
(C) Succinylcholine completely immobilizes the patient's body.	*Another extreme word! Check it. The second sentence states that* succinylcholine *renders muscle contractions practically nonexistent. The qualifier* practically *means the muscle contractions are almost* gone, *but not* entirely. *The word* completely, *then, is too extreme. (Extreme)*
(D) ECT often works faster than antidepressants.	*The third paragraph does mention antidepressants; leave this in for now.*
(E) One ECT treatment is often sufficient to reduce symptoms of depression significantly.	*The passage does not discuss the number of treatments necessary to reduce symptoms significantly. At one point, it does mention* repeated applications, *so, if anything, it appears that more than one treatment might be typical. (Out of scope)*

Compare (A) and (D).

(A) *Scan for these words; they appear in the last sentence. What's the message? Nobody really knows how ECT works, just that it affects these neurotransmitters—but it doesn't say that ECT results in* greater *amounts of these things, just that they are* affected. *The word* greater *in the answer choice isn't supported. (One word off)*

(B) *CORRECT. The third paragraph states that ECT* may also be considered when there is an imminent risk of suicide, since antidepressants often take several weeks to work effectively. *If ECT is used as an emergency intervention for suicide, because antidepressants take a while to work, then it must be true that ECT often works more quickly than antidepressants.*

If you see a question that contains some form of the words *infer, imply,* or *suggest,* then you know you have an Inference question. In most cases, the question stem will also contain some specific info that will help you to determine which paragraph you'll need. In this problem, a key term in the question stem (*modern ECT*) is mentioned for the first time at the beginning of the third paragraph.

If you can, try to formulate an answer to the question before you look at the answer choices. Note that, sometimes, the question stem will be too vague to predict a solid answer in advance (this can happen on any type of specific question). When this happens, remind yourself of the main points in any relevant paragraph(s) or sentences and then start to test the answers. (If you know that you don't understand the question well enough to formulate an answer for that reason, consider guessing and moving on.)

If you find yourself struggling with RC Inference questions, you may want to consider using Critical Reasoning to help bolster your inference skills. CR Inference questions work the same way, so you may find that you learn this more easily for CR and can then come back and apply your skills to RC.

On either question type, it can be helpful to analyze your work by comparing each answer choice carefully to the supporting text (after you have finished solving the problem). This will help you learn to distinguish a valid inference from an answer choice that goes too far.

Specific Purpose Questions

Specific Purpose questions are not as common as either Detail or Inference questions, but you can expect to see at least one on the Verbal section of the GMAT. These questions ask you for what purpose, or why, the author mentions a specific piece of information—so they are often called **Why** questions for short.

As with Inference questions, you can't just repeat back what the passage explicitly states. Instead, you have to do a little bit of processing. For example, consider this information:

> Silicon chip manufacturers struggle to maintain profit margins due to the exorbitantly high overhead costs associated with building semiconductor factories. Such factories typically cost a minimum of two billion dollars to build and may be obsolete within three to five years. As such, the manufacturers seek out customers who need very high volumes of products, allowing the overhead costs to be spread out over a large number of units.

Here's the question:

> The author states that semiconductor factories may become obsolete within three to five years of being built in order to

Why does the author talk about this particular detail? In the prior sentence, the author asserts that *chip manufacturers struggle to maintain profit margins* because these factories have *exorbitantly high overhead costs,* so she is providing information to support her contention that these costs really are so high as to impact profit significantly. The correct answer might say something like:

> emphasize the unusually high costs associated with manufacturing silicon chips

Here's the Specific Purpose question from the ECT passage:

> 3. The author mentions amnesia as a possible side effect of severe depression in order to

What similarities can you spot between the semiconductor question stem and the one above? Both talk about the *author.* Both finish with *in order to.* Specific Purpose questions are typically structured to say *the author* (mentions some specific detail) *in order to,* and then you have to fill in the blank with the answer that explains *why* the author mentioned that particular detail.

So, where did the author of the ECT passage talk about amnesia and severe depression?

You may not have noted this very specific detail about amnesia in your map, so you may have to go on a hunt. The passage mentions *severe depression* in three out of the four paragraphs, so don't scan for those key words. Instead, scan for the word *amnesia*. One more clue: Amnesia is a type of memory loss. You might have noted or you may remember that the last paragraph talks about memory loss. Here's the relevant text from the fourth paragraph:

> Some patients have also reported that their short-term memories continue to be affected for months after ECT, though some doctors argue that this memory malfunction may reflect the type of amnesia that sometimes results from severe depression.

On to step 3: Formulate your own answer to the question. *Why* does the author bring up amnesia in the context of severe depression?

Some people appear to attribute short-term memory problems to ECT; this is consistent with much of the rest of the passage, which discusses negative side effects and risks associated with ECT. The second half of the quoted text, however, indicates that some doctors think that these symptoms might actually be caused by the depression itself. In other words, it's possible that this particular side effect is not actually a result of ECT.

The author, then, is pointing out that not every possible negative effect is definitely due to ECT. What answer choice goes along with this idea? (Also, try to identify any wrong answer traps that you have already learned.)

(A) acknowledge one of the possible negative side effects associated with ECT	*The passage does talk about many negative side effects associated with ECT, but the reference to amnesia is intended to introduce the idea that certain side effects actually might not be due to ECT. (Direct contradiction)*
(B) emphasize the seriousness of severe depression as a debilitating disease	*This choice sounds very tempting; in the real world, amnesia is a very serious issue and severe depression is a debilitating disease. However, depression is mentioned only as a possible alternative cause; the passage does not state that the amnesia is definitely a result of the depression. (True but not right)*
(C) introduce a possible alternative cause for short-term memory loss reported by some patients	*CORRECT. The first half of the sentence brings up patient reports of memory loss due to ECT. The second half indicates a different potential cause: Some doctors think this memory loss might actually be due to depression.*
(D) draw a connection between brain cell death and short-term memory loss	*The fourth paragraph mentions both brain cell death and short-term memory loss. The passage does not connect the two ideas, however. In fact, it says that reports of brain cell death have been refuted, though memory loss is still in evidence. (Mix-up)*
(E) refute claims that ECT is responsible for any form of amnesia in patients	*The sentence does offer a possible alternative cause, but ECT is not definitively ruled out as one possible cause. (Extreme)*

The wrong answers represent several common traps, one of which hasn't shown up in earlier problems. A **Mix-Up** is a tricky trap in which the test writers use wording straight from the passage to convey a different meaning than what is presented in the passage. They are expecting you to think it sounds familiar and jump on the choice without giving it too much thought, and in fact that's exactly what many test-takers do.

In answer (D) above, the keywords used are all straight from the passage. The meaning of the answer, however, does not fit with the author's reason for mentioning amnesia. In fact, the answer does not even convey what the passage really said.

In order to is the most common clue that you are facing a Specific Purpose question; if the question says the author brought up some detail *in order to* do something, then you're trying to figure out why the author brought up that detail.

As for all specific questions, use your map to figure out what paragraph you'll need; in this case, the words *amnesia* and *severe depression* indicated the fourth paragraph.

Whenever possible, try to formulate an answer to the question before you look at the answer choices. If you can't, remind yourself of the main points in any relevant sentences or paragraphs and then start to test the answers.

EXCEPT Questions

Any question type can also be written as an **EXCEPT question**; most of the time, when you see an EXCEPT question, you'll be dealing with a Detail question or an Inference question.

Here is the fourth question from the ECT passage. What question type is it?

4. Each of the following is cited in the passage as a current or historical criticism of electroconvulsive therapy EXCEPT

The language *each of the following is cited* indicates that this is a Detail question. The information in four of the answers is explicitly stated in the passage. The fifth answer, the one *not* cited in the passage, will be the correct answer.

Follow the same process you would normally use for a Detail question, with one twist.

It would be inefficient to try to find all of the criticisms of ECT in the passage first and only then go check the answers to find the matches. Instead, go straight to the answers and work backwards: Use the keywords to try to find the information in the passage. If you've spent more than about 20 seconds on an answer and still haven't found it in the passage, leave it and move to the next answer.

As you work, label the answers either True or False on your scrap paper. On this problem, true (or T) means that the answer is indeed cited in the passage as a criticism of ECT. False (or F) means that it is not. Cross off the four T answers and pick the odd one out, the lone F answer.

Also, note one important thing about the question: It asks for *current or historical criticism*, so something that was once criticized but is no longer considered problematic today would still count as a criticism of ECT.

(A) ECT may cause the death of brain cells and memory loss.

T. The fourth paragraph mentions that very old research showed brain cell death (even though that research has been refuted today) and that memory loss is an ongoing concern.

(B) In certain cases, ECT was portrayed as a means to punish individuals.

T. Line 26 indicates that ECT was portrayed as punitive.

(C) ECT had the potential to be used in inappropriate situations.

T. Tricky! Line 26 indicates that ECT was portrayed as over-used. *If a treatment is overused, then at least some of those uses shouldn't be happening, or are inappropriate.*

(D) Early forms of ECT did not adequately protect patients from secondary harm brought on by the treatment.

T. Lines 19–21 indicate that early forms of ECT often led to compression fractures of the spine or damage to the teeth.

(E) Repeated applications of ECT affect several neurotransmitters in the brain.

CORRECT. F. Lines 45–47 do mention that ECT affects neurotransmitters, but this information is not presented as a criticism *of ECT. Rather, it is presented as a partial means of understanding how ECT works.*

The standard wrong answer trap categories don't necessarily apply to EXCEPT questions. The four wrong answers are "right" in the sense that they were truly in the passage. The one correct answer on an EXCEPT question (the false one) can fall into one of the standard trap categories. Which trap does answer (E), above, represent?

According to the passage, it is true that ECT affects neurotransmitters, but it is false that this was *cited in the passage as a current or historical criticism* of ECT. So answer (E) is a variation of a True but not right trap answer.

EXCEPT questions are not a separate type of question; any of the main question types could be presented as an EXCEPT question. Use your usual clues to identify the question type. Then, work backwards: Go straight to the answers and try to find them in the passage. You're going to cross off the four true answers (for which you will find support in the passage) and select the one false answer.

Specific Question Cheat Sheet

21

Specific Question Cheat Sheet

Identify
the Question

Detail:	Most common: *Accoring to the passage...*
	indicates explicitly ...
	mentions (or proposes) which of the following ...
Inference:	Most common: *infer, imply, suggest, provides support for...*
	author would be most likely to describe (or *predict*) X
Specific Purpose:	Most common clue: *in order to*
	The author's reference (to X) *serves primarily to...*
EXCEPT:	Any can also be EXCEPT questions. Use keywords from the answers to find the support in the passage.

Find the
Support

Use your map to find the specific paragraph needed. If you can't, go to the answers to try to work backwards. If this doesn't work, guess and move on.

Predict
an Answer

Try to formulate an answer in your own words. If you can't, go to the answers to try to work backwards. If this doesn't work, guess and move on.

Eliminate

Check all of the answers! Common traps include the following:

Trap	Characteristics
Direct contradiction	The passage says the opposite.
Extreme	Extreme word *without support* in the passage.
One word off	Looks very tempting but one or two words are wrong.
Out of scope	Goes beyond what the passage says.
Mix-up	Uses words directly from the passage, but the meaning is not what the passage says.
True but not right	The passage says this (or it's true in the real word), but it does not answer the question asked.

Take a photo of this page and keep it with the review sheets you're creating as you study. Better yet, use this page as a guide to create your own review sheet—you'll remember the material better if you write it down yourself. Where appropriate, put it in your own words and you'll remember it even better.

Problem Set

The three passages in this problem set appear in both the General and Specific chapters, but different questions are presented in each chapter.

After you're done, review your point and passage map before you check the solutions, thinking about ways to improve your process next time. If you come up with ways to improve your map, actually rewrite it to reinforce what you want to do differently next time. Then, check your work against the solution key.

Passage I: Japanese Swords (6 minutes)

Historians have long recognized the Japanese sword, or *nihonto*, as one of the finest cutting weapons ever produced. But to regard the sword that is synonymous with the
5 samurai as merely a weapon is to ignore what makes it so special. The Japanese sword has always been considered a splendid weapon and even a spiritual entity. The traditional Japanese adage "the sword is the soul of the
10 samurai" reflects not only the sword's importance to its wielder but also its permanent connection to its creator, the master smith.

Master smiths may not have been
15 considered artists in the classical sense, but each smith exerted great care in the process of creating swords, no two of which were ever forged in exactly the same way. Over hundreds of hours, two types of steel were
20 repeatedly heated, hammered, and folded together into thousands of very thin layers, producing a sword with an extremely sharp and durable cutting edge and a flexible, shock-absorbing blade. It was common, though
25 optional, for a master smith to place a physical signature on a blade; moreover, each smith's secret forging techniques left an idiosyncratic structural signature on his blades. Each master smith brought a high level
30 of devotion, skill, and attention to detail to the sword-making process, and the sword itself was a reflection of his personal honor and ability. This effort made each blade as distinctive as the samurai who wielded it such
35 that today the Japanese sword is recognized as much for its artistic merit as for its historical significance.

1. Which of the following can be inferred about the structural signature of a Japanese sword?

   (A) It is an inscription that the smith places on the blade during the forging process.

   (B) It refers to the particular characteristics of a blade created by a smith's unique forging process.

   (C) It suggests that each blade can be traced back to a known master smith.

   (D) It reflects the soul of the samurai who wielded the sword.

   (E) It refers to the actual curved shape of the blade.

2. Each of the following is mentioned in the passage EXCEPT

   (A) Every Japanese sword has a unique structure that can be traced back to a special forging process.

   (B) Master smiths kept their forging techniques secret.

   (C) The Japanese sword was considered by some to have a spiritual quality.

   (D) Master smiths are now considered artists by most major historians.

   (E) The Japanese sword is considered both a work of art and a historical artifact.

3. The author explains the way in which swords were made in order to

    (A) establish that the Japanese sword is the most important handheld weapon in history

    (B) claim that the skill of the samurai is what made each Japanese sword unique

    (C) support the contention that the master smiths might be considered artists as well as craftsmen

    (D) illustrate that master smiths were more concerned with the artistic merit of their blades than with the blades' practical qualities

    (E) demonstrate that the Japanese sword has more historical importance than artistic importance

Passage J: Augustus (6.5 minutes)

Caesar Augustus, founder of the Roman Empire, wrote an account of his life called *Deeds of the Divine Augustus*. It consists of thirty-five numbered sections, each
5 of which records his achievements in a particular field. The first two sections, for instance, describe his role in the civil war that followed Julius Caesar's death, while section twenty-eight enumerates the
10 colonies he founded for his soldiers. Augustus left instructions that the *Deeds* be inscribed on two bronze pillars in Rome, as well as on monuments and temples throughout the empire. Clearly, Augustus
15 intended the *Deeds* to mold his image for posterity.

A number of details in the *Deeds* suggest that Augustus wanted to be remembered as a patriot in the tradition of
20 Cincinnatus. Augustus would have us believe that his political career was driven not by personal ambition, but by a selfless desire to serve Rome and to uphold its ancient liberties and customs. He tells us
25 that his seizure of power was a "liberation from the tyranny of a faction." After he came to power "by universal consent," he returned control of the state to the hands of the Roman senate and people. Emphasizing his
30 humility, he lists numerous occasions on which he declined titles, ovations, and triumphs offered him by the senate.

Few historians accept Augustus's account of his political motivation. Mark Antony's
35 faction was not particularly tyrannical, and Augustus's seizure of power appears to have been motivated mainly by opportunism. In Gibbon's persuasive analysis, Augustus's subsequent restoration of the outward
40 forms of republican government was designed to lend political legitimacy to what was essentially a dictatorship. Augustus's refusal of numerous honors appears to have been part of this same political stagecraft.
45 According to Suetonius, the senate felt obliged to offer Augustus a steady stream of honors. Augustus accepted a great many of these, including the titles of "First Citizen" and "Father of the Country," but refused
50 enough to maintain the appearance of humility.

1. The passage mentions "monuments and temples" (line 13) primarily in order to make the point that Augustus

   (A) built imposing edifices throughout the empire as a demonstration of his benevolence

   (B) recognized that religion was important to the senate and people of Rome

   (C) sought to shape future perceptions by disseminating his manuscript across multiple important sites

   (D) was more a dictator consolidating his power than a patriot helping his people

   (E) wanted to serve Rome and uphold its ancient liberties and customs

2. It can be inferred from the passage that, in Augustus's day, Cincinnatus was remembered as

   (A) someone unlikely to put his own interests before those of the state

   (B) a notably patriotic emperor

   (C) an intensely ambitious man

   (D) the founder of the libertarian faction in Roman politics

   (E) the bravest defender of Rome's ancient liberties and customs

3. According to the passage, which of the following is an assertion made in the *Deeds*?

    (A) Augustus was victorious in the civil war that followed Julius Caesar's death.

    (B) The example of Cincinnatus was an inspiration to Augustus in times of conflict.

    (C) Augustus's restoration of republican forms gave political legitimacy to his regime.

    (D) Augustus brought freedom to Rome.

    (E) Augustus accepted the title of "First Citizen" in a spirit of humility.

Passage K: Sweet Spot (6.5 minutes)

Most tennis players strive to strike the ball on the racket's vibration node, more commonly known as the "sweet spot." However, many players are unaware of the
5 existence of a second, lesser-known location on the racket face—the center of percussion— that will also greatly diminish the strain on a player's arm when the ball is struck.

In order to understand the physics of this
10 second sweet spot, it is helpful to consider what would happen to a tennis racket if the player's hand were to vanish at the moment of impact with the ball. The impact of the ball would cause the racket to bounce backwards,
15 resulting in a translational motion away from the ball. The tendency of this motion would be to jerk all parts of the racket, including the end of its handle, backward, or away from the ball. Unless the ball happened to hit precisely
20 at the racket's center of mass, the racket would additionally experience a rotational motion around its center of mass—much as a penny that has been struck near its edge will start to spin. Whenever the ball hits the racket
25 face, the effect of this rotational motion is to jerk the end of the handle forward, towards the ball. Depending on where the ball strikes the racket face, one or the other of these motions will predominate.
30 However, there is one point of impact, known as the center of percussion, which causes neither motion to predominate; if a ball strikes this point, the impact does not impart any motion to the end of the handle. The
35 reason for this lack of motion is that the force on the upper part of the hand would be equal and opposite to the force on the lower part of the hand, resulting in no net force on the tennis player's hand or forearm. The center of
40 percussion constitutes a second sweet spot because a tennis player's wrist is typically placed next to the end of the racket's handle. When the player strikes the ball at the center of percussion, her wrist is jerked neither
45 forward nor backward, and she experiences greatly reduced vibration in the arm.

The manner in which a tennis player can detect the center of percussion on a given tennis racket follows from the nature of this
50 second sweet spot. The center of percussion can be located via simple trial and error by holding the end of a tennis racket between the finger and thumb and throwing a ball onto the strings. If the handle jumps out of the
55 player's hand, then the ball has missed the center of percussion.

1. The author mentions a penny that has been struck near its edge in order to

   (A) illustrate what happens at the lesser-known center of percussion

   (B) argue that a penny spins in the exact way that a tennis racket spins

   (C) illustrate the difference between two types of motion

   (D) draw an analogy to help explain a type of motion

   (E) demonstrate that pennies and tennis rackets do not spin in the same way

2. According to the passage, which of the following occurs when a ball strikes the racket strings on a sweet spot?

   (A) The jolt that accompanies most strokes will be more pronounced.

   (B) The racket experiences rotational motion but not translational motion.

   (C) The racket experiences translational motion but not rotational motion.

   (D) The player experiences less vibration in the arm holding the racket.

   (E) The center of mass and the center of percussion coincide.

3. Which of the following can be inferred about the forces acting on the racket handle?

(A) A player whose grip is anywhere other than at the end of the racket's handle will experience a jolting sensation when striking the ball.

(B) Striking a ball at the well-known sweet spot will result in fewer vibrations than striking it at the lesser-known sweet spot.

(C) Striking a ball on the vibration node will impart some amount of motion to the handle of the racket.

(D) Depending on where the ball strikes, the handle will experience either translational or rotational motion.

(E) If the player's hand could disappear at the moment of impact, the racket would drop straight to the ground.

Solutions

The solutions show a sample passage map and the point, as well as explanations for each answer choice. No simple story is provided, but do try to develop that level of understanding of the passage when creating your map. Where appropriate, wrong answers have been labeled by wrong answer category.

Passage I: Japanese Swords

Historians have long recognized the Japanese sword, or *nihonto*, as one of the finest cutting weapons ever produced. But to regard the sword that is synonymous with the
5 samurai as merely a weapon is to ignore what makes it so special. The Japanese sword has always been considered a splendid weapon and even a spiritual entity. The traditional Japanese adage "the sword is the soul of the
10 samurai" reflects not only the sword's importance to its wielder but also its permanent connection to its creator, the master smith.

Master smiths may not have been
15 considered artists in the classical sense, but each smith exerted great care in the process of creating swords, no two of which were ever forged in exactly the same way. Over hundreds of hours, two types of steel were
20 repeatedly heated, hammered, and folded together into thousands of very thin layers, producing a sword with an extremely sharp and durable cutting edge and a flexible, shock-absorbing blade. It was common, though
25 optional, for a master smith to place a physical signature on a blade; moreover, each smith's secret forging techniques left an idiosyncratic structural signature on his blades. Each master smith brought a high level
30 of devotion, skill, and attention to detail to the sword-making process, and the sword itself was a reflection of his personal honor and ability. This effort made each blade as distinctive as the samurai who wielded it such
35 that today the Japanese sword is recognized as much for its artistic merit as for its historical significance.

Sample passage map (yours will likely differ):

① J sword: not just weapon, spirit

② Master smith: skilled
how to make
artistic merit + history

The point (articulate to yourself; don't write): Japanese sword is a weapon *and* a work of art, important to both samurai and smith. The smiths were basically artists.

1. First, identify the question type:

Which of the following can be inferred about the structural signature of a Japanese sword?

The wording *can be inferred* indicates that this is an Inference question. Next, the question asks about the *structural signature* of a sword. Look at your map; in which paragraph would that information likely be found? The second paragraph talked about how the smiths forged the swords, so go to that paragraph and scan for the phrase *structural signature*.

The relevant sentence says:

It was common, though optional, for a master smith to place a physical signature on a blade; moreover, each smith's secret forging techniques left an idiosyncratic structural signature on his blades. (lines 24–29)

The sentence references both a *physical signature* and a *structural signature*, so the structural signature must not be a literal signature. Further, the sentence indicates that each smith's structural signature is distinctive to the individual (*idiosyncratic*), a result of that smith's *secret forging techniques*.

(A) *It is an inscription that the smith places on the blade during the forging process.*

This refers to the physical signature, not the structural signature. (True but not right)

(B) *It refers to the particular characteristics of a blade created by a smith's unique forging process.*

CORRECT. This matches the information articulated in step 3 (predict an answer). Each smith's process resulted in a structural signature unique to that smith.

(C) *It suggests that each blade can be traced back to a known master smith.*

Tricky! The passage does say that a structural signature is unique to one smith, but it does not say that records survive indicating specifically who that smith was. A historian might be able to tell that three blades came from the same smith, but she may not be able to tell who that smith was. (Out of scope)

(D) *It reflects the soul of the samurai who wielded the sword.*

The first paragraph does include a quote about the soul of the samurai, but this information is not presented in relation to the information about the structural signature. (Mix-up)

(E) *It refers to the actual curved shape of the blade.*

Careful: If you have ever seen a samurai sword, then you may remember that it is curved—but the passage doesn't say so! In any case, since the signature is individual to the smith, something that all swords had in common wouldn't be helpful here. (Out of scope)

2. First, identify the question type:

Each of the following is mentioned in the passage EXCEPT

The question indicates that four of the answers *are* mentioned in the passage, so this is a Detail EXCEPT question. The question is too vague to formulate an answer in advance, so work backwards: Go straight to the first answer choice and try to find it in the passage.

(A) *Every Japanese sword has a unique structure that can be traced back to a special forging process.*

True. This is mentioned in the second paragraph (lines 26–29): *each smith's secret forging techniques left an idiosyncratic structural signature on his blades.*

(B) *Master smiths kept their forging techniques secret.*

True. This is mentioned in the second paragraph (lines 26–27): *each smith's secret forging techniques.*

(C) *The Japanese sword was considered by some to have a spiritual quality.*

True. This is mentioned in the first paragraph (lines 6–8): the *sword has always been considered a splendid weapon and even a spiritual entity.*

(D) *Master smiths are now considered artists by most major historians.*

CORRECT. False. The passage does not say this. Some people may recognize the smiths as artists (see answer E below), but there is no indication that this view is held by *most major historians.* (Extreme)

(E) *The Japanese sword is considered both a work of art and a historical artifact.*

True. This is mentioned in the last sentence of the second paragraph (lines 35–37): the *sword is recognized as much for its artistic merit as for its historical significance.*

3. First, identify the question type:

The author explains the way in which swords were made in order to

The *in order to* language indicates that this is a Specific Purpose (Why) question. Paragraph 2 explains how the swords were made; why did the author include this information?

The beginning and end of the paragraph provide clues. First, the author says that smiths may not have been considered artists *in the classical sense*, foreshadowing the idea that perhaps they could still be considered artists. The end of the passage indicates that the forging process resulted in such a distinctive blade that the sword is now recognized for its artistic merit as well as its historical significance.

(A) *establish that the Japanese sword is the most important handheld weapon in history*

The passage does call the Japanese sword *one of the finest cutting weapons ever produced* (lines 2–3), but this is not quite as strong as calling it the most important handheld weapon in history. In any case, this is not the author's purpose in describing how the sword was made. (Extreme)

(B) *claim that the skill of the samurai is what made each Japanese sword unique*

The passage claims that the smith's secret forging techniques, not the skill of the samurai, made a blade unique. (Direct contradiction)

(C) *support the contention that the master smiths might be considered artists as well as craftsmen*

CORRECT. The default definition for the smiths is craftsmen, but the detailed information about the forging process, as well as the opening and closing sentences, indicate that the smiths might be considered artists as well.

(D) *illustrate that master smiths were more concerned with the artistic merit of their blades than with the blades' practical qualities*

The passage discusses both the artistic merits and the practical qualities of the swords, but the passage does not indicate whether the smiths thought one was more important than the other. (Out of scope)

(E) *demonstrate that the Japanese sword has more historical importance than artistic importance*

The last sentence does talk about both of these concepts, but it does not indicate that one is more important than the other. (Out of scope)

Passage J: Augustus

Caesar Augustus, founder of the Roman Empire, wrote an account of his life called *Deeds of the Divine Augustus*. It consists of thirty-five numbered sections, each
5 of which records his achievements in a particular field. The first two sections, for instance, describe his role in the civil war that followed Julius Caesar's death, while section twenty-eight enumerates the
10 colonies he founded for his soldiers. Augustus left instructions that the *Deeds* be inscribed on two bronze pillars in Rome, as well as on monuments and temples throughout the empire. Clearly, Augustus
15 intended the *Deeds* to mold his image for posterity.

A number of details in the *Deeds* suggest that Augustus wanted to be remembered as a patriot in the tradition of
20 Cincinnatus. Augustus would have us believe that his political career was driven not by personal ambition, but by a selfless desire to serve Rome and to uphold its ancient liberties and customs. He tells us
25 that his seizure of power was a "liberation from the tyranny of a faction." After he came to power "by universal consent," he returned control of the state to the hands of the Roman senate and people. Emphasizing his
30 humility, he lists numerous occasions on which he declined titles, ovations, and triumphs offered him by the senate.

Few historians accept Augustus's account of his political motivation. Mark Antony's
35 faction was not particularly tyrannical, and Augustus's seizure of power appears to have been motivated mainly by opportunism. In Gibbon's persuasive analysis, Augustus's subsequent restoration of the outward
40 forms of republican government was designed to lend political legitimacy to what was essentially a dictatorship. Augustus's refusal of numerous honors appears to have been part of this same political stagecraft.
45 According to Suetonius, the senate felt obliged to offer Augustus a steady stream of honors. Augustus accepted a great many of these, including the titles of "First Citizen" and "Father of the Country," but refused
50 enough to maintain the appearance of humility.

Sample passage map (yours will likely differ):

① Aug: Deeds
   achvmnt; publicize good image

② Patriot, selfless, humble...
   But was it true?

③ Not really
   manipulate opinion

The point (articulate to yourself; don't write): Augustus wrote *Deeds* to present himself as altruistic, but most historians think he was merely justifying his own moves to gain power. It's like he was presenting one (much more positive) view of himself on social media while actually being very different in real life.

1. First, identify the question type:

The passage mentions "monuments and temples" (line 13) primarily in order to make the point that Augustus

The question asks *why* the passage mentions *monuments and temples,* so this is a Specific Purpose (Why) question. In order to answer this question, reread the sentence in which *monuments and temples* are mentioned, as well as any nearby sentences that also address this topic: "Augustus left instructions that the *Deeds* be inscribed on two bronze pillars in Rome, as well as on monuments and temples throughout the empire. Clearly, Augustus intended the *Deeds* to mold his image for posterity."

The word *clearly* is a signal that the second sentence provides the author's interpretation of the information contained in the first sentence. The information about *monuments and temples* is provided as evidence for the author's view that Augustus was using the *Deeds* to make himself look good to future people/history, essentially.

(A) *built imposing edifices throughout the empire as a demonstration of his benevolence*

It is not clear whether Augustus built the monuments and temples discussed in the passage. The passage indicates only that he left instructions to inscribe his text on these edifices.

(B) *recognized that religion was important to the senate and people of Rome*

The passage does not provide any information on Augustus's attitude towards religion.

(C) *sought to shape future perceptions by disseminating his manuscript across multiple important sites*

CORRECT. The purpose of mentioning the *monuments and temples* is to make the point that Augustus wanted to *mold his image for posterity*. The phrase *shape future perceptions* in this answer choice conveys that same meaning.

(D) *was more a dictator consolidating his power than a patriot helping his people*

In general, the author does make the case that historians believe Augustus was a dictator. But that case is made later in the passage. The section discussing the *monuments and temples* is still explaining what Augustus's motivations were, not what later historians thought of him.

(E) *wanted to serve Rome and uphold its ancient liberties and customs*

The author of the passage is *not* claiming that Augustus truly *wanted to serve Rome and uphold its ancient liberties and customs*; rather, the author says that this is a claim that *Augustus would have us believe*. Rather, the author uses the section on *monuments and temples* to start to establish that Augustus wanted people to *believe* that he was a certain way, not that he really was that way.

2. First, identify the question type:

It can be inferred from the passage that, in Augustus's day, Cincinnatus was remembered as

This is an Inference question. What must be able to be inferred (i.e., what must be true) about Cincinnatus, given the evidence in the passage?

The name of Cincinnatus occurs only once, early in paragraph 2: "A number of details in the *Deeds* suggest that Augustus wanted to be remembered as a patriot in the tradition of Cincinnatus." The text indicates explicitly that (1) Cincinnatus was a patriot, (2) Cincinnatus was part of a tradition, and (3) Augustus wanted to be remembered as someone like Cincinnatus. More information can be inferred from the next sentence, which says "Augustus would have us believe that his political career was driven not by personal ambition, but by a selfless desire to serve Rome and to uphold its ancient liberties and customs." Since the first sentence says that Augustus wanted to be remembered as being like Cincinnatus, and the second sentence spells out in more detail how Augustus wished to be remembered, you can infer that Cincinnatus was seen as conforming broadly to this description: someone whose "political career was driven not by personal ambition, but by a selfless desire to serve."

(A) *someone unlikely to put his own interests before those of the state*

CORRECT. As noted above, Cincinnatus was remembered as a patriot whose "political career was driven not by personal ambition, but by a selfless desire to serve." In other words, he was remembered as a man who would be unlikely to put his own interests ahead of anyone else's interest, including that of the state.

(B) *a notably patriotic emperor*

The passage does indicate that Cincinnatus was a patriot, but not that he was an emperor. It is possible to serve one's country without being an emperor.

(C) *an intensely ambitious man*

Cincinnatus was *not* motivated by personal ambition; this answer choice says the opposite.

(D) *the founder of the libertarian faction in Roman politics*

The passage provides information about Cincinnatus's selfless and patriotic motivation, but says hardly anything about what he actually did. There is no basis for inferring that he founded a political faction.

(E) *the bravest defender of Rome's ancient liberties and customs*

It may be reasonable to infer from the passage that Cincinnatus was a *defender* of Roman *liberties and customs*. It is not clear that he was *brave*, however, since the concept of bravery is not mentioned. And there is no basis at all to infer that he was *the bravest* (i.e., braver than anybody else) defender of those liberties and customs.

3. First, identify the question type:

According to the passage, which of the following is an assertion made in the Deeds?

This is a Specific Detail question. Your task is to find the specific detail asked about in the question.

To justify an answer choice, you need to be able to point to one or two sentences in the passage that explicitly indicate that the assertion in question appears specifically in the *Deeds*.

Many of the wrong answer choices are superficially attractive, because they sound like statements that *could* have appeared in the *Deeds*, or because they repeat key words from elsewhere in the passage.

(A) *Augustus was victorious in the civil war that followed Julius Caesar's death.*

The passage says that the *Deeds* describe Augustus's *role in the civil war that followed Julius Caesar's death*, but it does not say whether the *Deeds* claimed that Augustus was *victorious* in that war. It may seem

reasonable to *infer* that Augustus described himself as the victor in that conflict, but the question is not asking for an inference.

(B) *The example of Cincinnatus was an inspiration to Augustus in times of conflict.*

In commenting on Augustus's motivation for writing the *Deeds*, the passage does suggest that Augustus wanted to seem like Cincinnatus. However, the passage does not indicate whether Cincinnatus is ever mentioned in the *Deeds*.

(C) *Augustus's restoration of republican forms gave political legitimacy to his regime.*

In paragraph 3, the passage says that, *according to Gibbon*, Augustus's restoration of *the outward forms of republican government* was designed to give legitimacy to Augustus's regime. The passage does not, however, indicate whether a similar assertion is made in the *Deeds*.

(D) *Augustus brought freedom to Rome.*

CORRECT. The passage says that, according to the *Deeds*, Augustus's *seizure of power was a "liberation from ... tyranny."* The phrase *liberation ... from tyranny* is quoted directly from the *Deeds*, so the *Deeds* did indeed claim that Augustus brought freedom to Rome.

(E) *Augustus accepted the title of "First Citizen" in a spirit of humility.*

In the last paragraph, the passage mentions Augustus's acceptance of the title of *First Citizen*. However, the passage does not say that the *Deeds* mentions this title or the spirit in which Augustus accepted it.

Passage K: Sweet Spot

Most tennis players strive to strike the ball on the racket's vibration node, more commonly known as the "sweet spot." However, many players are unaware of the existence of a second, lesser-known location on the racket face—the center of percussion—that will also greatly diminish the strain on a player's arm when the ball is struck.

In order to understand the physics of this second sweet spot, it is helpful to consider what would happen to a tennis racket if the player's hand were to vanish at the moment of impact with the ball. The impact of the ball would cause the racket to bounce backwards, resulting in a translational motion away from the ball. The tendency of this motion would be to jerk all parts of the racket, including the end of its handle, backward, or away from the ball. Unless the ball happened to hit precisely at the racket's center of mass, the racket would additionally experience a rotational motion around its center of mass—much as a penny that has been struck near its edge will start to spin. Whenever the ball hits the racket face, the effect of this rotational motion is to jerk the end of the handle forward, towards the ball. Depending on where the ball strikes the racket face, one or the other of these motions will predominate.

However, there is one point of impact, known as the center of percussion, which causes neither motion to predominate; if a ball strikes this point, the impact does not impart any motion to the end of the handle. The reason for this lack of motion is that the force on the upper part of the hand would be equal and opposite to the force on the lower part of the hand, resulting in no net force on the tennis player's hand or forearm. The center of percussion constitutes a second sweet spot because a tennis player's wrist is typically placed next to the end of the racket's handle. When the player strikes the ball at the center of percussion, her wrist is jerked neither forward nor backward, and she experiences greatly reduced vibration in the arm.

The manner in which a tennis player can detect the center of percussion on a given tennis racket follows from the nature of this second sweet spot. The center of percussion can be located via simple trial and error by holding the end of a tennis racket between the finger and thumb and throwing a ball onto the strings. If the handle jumps out of the player's hand, then the ball has missed the center of percussion.

Sample passage map (yours will likely differ):

① 2 SS (↓ strain), one less known

② if hand disappear?

③ center perc = no motion, ↓↓ vibration

④ find center perc

The point (articulate to yourself; don't write): People usually know about one sweet spot but not the other. Both reduce vibration in the arm. (Plus lots of technical details—ignore for now!)

1. First, identify the question type:

    The author mentions a penny that has been struck near its edge in order to

The *in order to* language indicates that this is a Specific Purpose (Why) question. Paragraph 2 mentions the penny; why did the author include this information?

Here's the relevant text (lines 19–24):

> Unless the ball happened to hit precisely at the racket's center of mass, the racket would additionally experience a rotational motion around its center of mass—much as a penny that has been struck near its edge will start to spin.

The first part of the sentence talks about a certain motion that the tennis racket experiences—don't worry too much about exactly what it means. After the dash, the *much as a penny* language indicates that this example is an analogy: The racket is spinning in the same way that the penny would spin. The author uses this analogy to help the reader understand what is happening to the racket.

(A) *illustrate what happens at the lesser-known center of percussion*

This choice is tricky. The beginning of the third paragraph indicates that the motion described at the end of the second paragraph is *not* what happens at the center of percussion; if you spot that, you can eliminate this choice, but that's a pretty specific detail. Even if you miss that, though, it's enough to find another answer choice that does match your pre-stated idea—so keep looking. (Direct contradiction)

(B) *argue that a penny spins in the exact way that a tennis racket spins*

The author is trying to draw a parallel between the two but does not say that they spin in the *exact* same way. (Extreme)

(C) *illustrate the difference between two types of motion*

The paragraph does talk about two types of motion, but the penny example applies just to one of them. (True but not right)

(D) *draw an analogy to help explain a type of motion*

CORRECT. The penny analogy explains how the tennis racket spins.

(E) *demonstrate that pennies and tennis rackets do not spin in the same way*

The analogy indicates that they spin in a similar way. (Direct contradiction)

2. First, identify the question type:

According to the passage, which of the following occurs when a ball strikes the racket strings on a sweet spot?

The language *according to the passage* indicates that this is a Detail question. A large portion of the passage talks about what happens when a ball strikes a racket on a sweet spot. Where should you look?

When the question is this broad, find the first mention of the topic. This first mention will give you the main idea and you can eliminate some answers. If you cannot eliminate all four, then you can go to the next mention of the topic and use that to eliminate until you get down to one answer (or you can decide that you'd rather guess and move on).

The first paragraph indicates that there are two sweet spots and that striking a ball there will *greatly diminish the strain on a player's arm.*

(A) *The jolt that accompanies most strokes will be more pronounced.*

This goes against the basic idea that the strain will *diminish*. (Direct contradiction)

(B) *The racket experiences rotational motion but not translational motion.*

(C) *The racket experiences translational motion but not rotational motion.*

Answers (B) and (C) talk about the same two forces, so deal with them together. The second paragraph does talk about these forces, but the details are pretty technical. Check the remaining answers first to see whether one matches your predicted answer; if so, you never have to check the technical detail.

(D) *The player experiences less vibration in the arm holding the racket.*

CORRECT. This is the basic benefit of the sweet spot: When a player hits a ball there, the strain, or vibration, felt in the arm is lessened.

(E) *The center of mass and the center of percussion coincide.*

Because answer (D) already works, dismiss this answer.

In the case of answers (B), (C), and (E), the test writer is trying to slow you down. You aren't required to assess each answer choice in order; when you hit something that requires a deeper dive, check the other answer choices first.

Striking the ball at a sweet spot can result in both translational and rotational motion, so answers (B) and (C) are both wrong. The passage never indicates a time when the center of mass and center of percussion would be in the same location, so answer (E) is also wrong.

3. First, identify the question type:

Which of the following can be inferred about the forces acting on the racket handle?

The word *inferred* indicates that this is an Inference question. The forces acting on the racket handle are first discussed in paragraph 2.

Warning: This passage is a hard one and this question is seriously challenging. If you like the topic, feel free to delve into the technical details. If you don't, summarize only the high-level points, or just guess right now and move on. (And on the real test, be a little pleased—yes, pleased!—that you earned such a hard question.)

The question asks specifically about the *racket handle.* Scan the second paragraph for mentions of the handle. Translational motion moves the racket handle backward. Rotational motion jerks the handle forward.

The third paragraph adds that if a ball strikes the center of percussion, there will be *no* motion at the end of the handle.

(A) *A player whose grip is anywhere other than at the end of the racket's handle will experience a jolting sensation when striking the ball.*

The passage does not address what would happen if the player gripped the racket somewhere other than the end of the handle. The "sweet spot" describes where the ball strikes the strings, not where the player holds the racket. (Out of scope)

(B) *Striking a ball at the well-known sweet spot will result in fewer vibrations than striking it at the lesser-known sweet spot.*

The passage does not address which sweet spot might result in fewer vibrations. (Out of scope)

(C) *Striking a ball on the vibration node will impart some amount of motion to the handle of the racket.*

CORRECT. This is a very tricky answer! The third paragraph indicates that striking the ball at the center of percussion will result in no motion—and the author further specifies that this lack of motion occurs only when the ball is struck at this one location. If the ball strikes any *other* point on the racket, then the handle will experience some motion. The vibration node is the well-known sweet spot (see the first paragraph), so it qualifies as a spot other than the center of percussion.

(D) *Depending on where the ball strikes, the handle will experience either translational or rotational motion.*

If the ball is struck at the center of percussion, it will experience neither type of motion. If the ball is struck elsewhere, it will experience both types of motion. (Direct contradiction)

(E) *If the player's hand could disappear at the moment of impact, the racket would drop straight to the ground.*

The second paragraph states that, if the player's hand somehow disappeared, then the racket would bounce backward, among other motions. (Direct contradiction)

This last problem was incredibly hard. Even if you didn't find the support for (C), congratulate yourself if you were able to eliminate some of the incorrect answers. Also, notice that the second question in the set, while also a Detail question, was easier to answer because it did not require as much technical understanding of the passage. If you are having trouble following a very technical passage, you may get lucky and be offered a specific question that you can answer with only a high-level understanding. However, it's likely that at least one question will require enough technical understanding that the best choice may be to guess quickly and move on.

Extra Problem Set

In This Chapter...

- Problem Set

- Solutions

In this chapter, you will gain additional practice on all aspects of Reading Comprehension problems: reading and mapping the passage and answering questions of all types.

CHAPTER 22 Extra Problem Set

Time to put it all together! This chapter contains four passages with either four or five accompanying questions each. (Note: The real test will give you either three or four questions per passage.)

Each title is followed by a suggested length of time to give yourself to complete the passage and all questions. You can, of course, choose to spend extra time—but on the real test, that time will have to come from other questions. (If you receive extended time on the test, adjust accordingly.)

Problem Set

Passage L: The Invention of TV (8 minutes)

   In the early years of television, Vladimir Zworykin was considered the device's inventor, at least publicly. His loudest champion was his boss, David Sarnoff, then president of RCA and
5 a man regarded even today as "the father of television." Current historians agree, however, that Philo Farnsworth, a self-educated prodigy who was the first to transmit live images, was television's technical inventor.
10   In his own time, Farnsworth's contributions went largely unnoticed, in large part because he was excluded from the process of introducing the invention to a national audience. Sarnoff put televisions into living
15 rooms, and Sarnoff was responsible for a dominant paradigm of the television industry that continues to be relevant today: advertisers pay for the programming so that they can have a receptive audience for their
20 products. Sarnoff had already utilized this construct to develop the radio industry, and it had, within ten years, become ubiquitous. Farnsworth thought the television should be used as an educational tool, but he had little
25 understanding of the business world, and was never able to implement his ideas.
   Some argue that Sarnoff simply adapted the business model for radio and television from the newspaper industry, replacing the
30 revenue from subscriptions and newsstand purchases with that of television set sales, but Sarnoff promoted himself as nothing less than a visionary. Some television critics argue that the construct Sarnoff implemented has played
35 a negative role in determining the content of the programs themselves, while others contend that it merely created a democratic platform from which the audience can determine the types of programming it
40 desires.

1. The primary purpose of the passage is to

   (A) correct public misconceptions about Farnsworth's role in developing early television programs

   (B) debate the influence of television on popular culture

   (C) challenge the current public perception of Vladimir Zworykin

   (D) chronicle the events that led from the development of radio to the invention of the television

   (E) describe both Sarnoff's influence on the public perception of television's inception and the debate around the impact of Sarnoff's paradigm

2. Which of the following best illustrates the relationship between the second and third paragraphs?

   (A) The second paragraph dissects the evolution of a contemporary controversy; the third paragraph presents differing viewpoints on that controversy.

   (B) The second paragraph explores the antithetical intentions of two men involved in the infancy of an industry; the third paragraph details the eventual deterioration of that industry.

   (C) The second paragraph presents differing views of a historical event; the third paragraph represents the author's personal opinion about that event.

   (D) The second paragraph provides details that are necessary to support the author's opinion, which is presented in the third paragraph.

   (E) The second paragraph presents divergent visions about the implementation of a technology; the third paragraph further explores one of those perspectives.

3. According to the passage, the television industry, at its inception, earned revenue from

    (A) advertising only

    (B) advertising and the sale of television sets

    (C) advertising and subscriptions

    (D) subscriptions and the sale of television sets

    (E) advertising, subscriptions, and the sale of television sets

4. The passage suggests that Farnsworth might have earned greater public notoriety for his invention if

    (A) Vladimir Zworykin had been less vocal about his own contributions to the television

    (B) Farnsworth had been able to develop and air his own educational programs

    (C) Farnsworth had involved Sarnoff in his plans to develop, manufacture, or distribute the television

    (D) Sarnoff had involved Farnsworth in his plans to develop, manufacture, or distribute the television

    (E) Farnsworth had conducted research into the type of programming the audience most wanted to watch

Passage M: Life on Mars (7.5 minutes)

Because of the proximity and likeness of Mars to Earth, scientists have long speculated about the possibility of life on Mars. As early as the mid-seventeenth century, astronomers
5 observed polar ice caps on Mars, and by the mid-nineteenth century, scientists discovered other similarities to Earth, including the length of day and axial tilt. But in 1965, photos taken by the Mariner 4 probe revealed a
10 Mars without rivers, oceans, or signs of life. Moreover, in the 1990s, it was discovered that Mars, unlike Earth, no longer possessed a substantial global magnetic field, allowing celestial radiation to reach the planet's surface
15 and solar wind to eliminate much of Mars's atmosphere over the course of several billion years.

More recent probes have investigated whether there was once liquid water on Mars.
20 Some scientists believe that this question is definitively answered in the affirmative by the presence of certain geological landforms. Others posit that alternative explanations, such as wind erosion or carbon dioxide oceans,
25 may be responsible for these formations. Mars rovers *Opportunity* and *Spirit*, which began exploring the surface of Mars in 2004, have both discovered geological evidence of past water activity. In 2013, the rover *Curiosity*
30 found evidence that the soil on the surface of Mars is approximately 2 percent water by weight. These findings substantially bolster claims that there was once life on Mars.

1. The passage is primarily concerned with which of the following?

   (A) Disproving a widely accepted theory

   (B) Initiating a debate about an unproven theory

   (C) Presenting evidence in support of a recently formulated claim

   (D) Describing various discoveries made concerning the possibility of life on Mars

   (E) Detailing the findings of the Mars rovers *Opportunity*, *Spirit*, and *Curiosity*

2. Each of the following discoveries is mentioned in the passage EXCEPT

   (A) Wind erosion and carbon dioxide oceans are responsible for certain geological landforms on Mars.

   (B) Mars does not have a substantial global magnetic field.

   (C) Mars had water activity at some point in the past.

   (D) The length of a day on Mars is similar to that on Earth.

   (E) The axial tilt of Mars is similar to that of Earth.

3. The passage suggests which of the following about polar ice caps?

   (A) Until recently, the ones on Mars were thought to consist largely of carbon dioxide.

   (B) By 1965, the ones on Mars had disappeared.

   (C) They are also found on Earth.

   (D) Their formation is tied to length of day and axial tilt.

   (E) They indicate that conditions on the planet Mars were once very different than they are at present.

4. Which of the following pieces of evidence, if found on Mars, would most support the claim that Mars once held life?

    (A) Carbon dioxide oceans

    (B) Celestial radiation and solar wind

    (C) High daily level of sunlight reaching the planet's surface

    (D) Volcanic eruptions

    (E) A significant global magnetic field

Passage N: Fossils (9 minutes)

In archaeology, as in the physical sciences, new discoveries frequently undermine accepted findings and give rise to new theories. This trend can be seen in the
5 reaction to the recent discovery of a set of 3.3-million-year-old fossils in Ethiopia, the remains of the earliest well-preserved child ever found. The fossilized child was estimated to be about 3 years old at death,
10 female, and a member of the *Australopithecus afarensis* species. The *afarensis* species, a major human ancestor, lived in Africa from earlier than 3.7 million to 3 million years ago. "Her completeness, antiquity, and age at
15 death make this find unprecedented in the history of paleoanthropology," said Zeresenay Alemseged, a noted paleoanthropologist. Other scientists said that the discovery could reconfigure conceptions about the lives and
20 capacities of these early humans.

Prior to this discovery, it had been thought that the *afarensis* species had abandoned the arboreal habitat of its ape cousins. However, while the lower limbs of this fossil supported
25 findings that *afarensis* walked upright, its gorilla-like arms and shoulders suggested that it retained the ability to swing through trees. This has initiated a reexamination of many accepted theories of early human
30 development. Also, the presence of a hyoid bone, a rarely preserved bone in the larynx that supports muscles of the throat, has had a tremendous impact on theories about the origins of speech. The fossil bone is primitive
35 and more similar to that of apes than to that of humans, but it is the first hyoid found in such an early human-related species.

1. The primary purpose of the passage is to

(A) discuss a controversial scientific discovery

(B) contrast varying theories of human development

(C) support a general contention with a specific example

(D) argue for the importance of a particular field of study

(E) refute a widely believed myth

2. The passage quotes Zeresenay Alemseged in order to

(A) qualify the main idea of the first paragraph

(B) provide contrast to the claims of other scientists

(C) support the theory regarding the linguistic abilities of the *afarensis* species

(D) support the stated significance of the discovery

(E) provide a subjective opinion that is refuted in the second paragraph

3. It can be inferred from the passage's description of the discovery of the fossil hyoid bone that

(A) *Australopithecus afarensis* was capable of speech

(B) the discovered hyoid bone is less primitive than the hyoid bone of apes

(C) the hyoid bone is necessary for speech

(D) the discovery of the hyoid bone necessitated the reexamination of prior theories about speech

(E) the hyoid bone was the most important fossil found at the site

4. Each of the following is cited as a reason that the fossils discovered in Ethiopia were important EXCEPT

    (A) the fact that the remains were those of a child

    (B) the age of the fossils

    (C) the location of the discovery

    (D) the presence of a bone not usually discovered

    (E) the intact nature of the fossils

5. The impact of the discovery of the hyoid bone in the field of archaeology is most closely analogous to which of the following situations?

    (A) The discovery and analysis of cosmic rays lend support to a widely accepted theory of the origin of the universe.

    (B) The original manuscript of a deceased nineteenth-century author confirms ideas about the development of an important work of literature.

    (C) The continued prosperity of a state-run economy stirs debate in the discipline of macroeconomics.

    (D) Newly revealed journal entries by a promi-nent Civil War–era politician lead to a questioning of certain accepted historical interpretations about the conflict.

    (E) Research into the mapping of the human genome gives rise to nascent applications of individually tailored medicines.

22

22

Passage O: Chaos Theory (8 minutes)

Around 1960, mathematician Edward Lorenz found unexpected behavior in apparently simple equations representing atmospheric air flows. Whenever he reran his model with
5 the same inputs, different outputs resulted, although the model lacked any random elements. Lorenz realized that tiny rounding errors in the initial data mushroomed over time, leading to erratic results. His findings
10 marked a seminal moment in the development of chaos theory, which, despite its name, has little to do with randomness.

Lorenz's experiment was one of the first to demonstrate conclusively that unpredictability
15 can arise from deterministic equations, which do not involve chance outcomes. In order to understand this phenomenon, first consider the non-chaotic system of two poppy seeds placed in a round bowl. As the seeds roll to
20 the bowl's center, a position known as a point attractor, the distance between the seeds shrinks. If, instead, the bowl is flipped over, two seeds placed on top will roll away from each other. Such a system, while still not
25 technically chaotic, enlarges initial differences in position.

Chaotic systems, such as a machine mixing bread dough, are characterized by both attraction and repulsion. As the dough is
30 stretched, folded, and pressed back together, any poppy seeds sprinkled in are intermixed seemingly at random. But this randomness is illusory. In fact, the poppy seeds are captured by "strange attractors," staggeringly complex
35 pathways whose tangles appear accidental but are in fact determined by the system's fundamental equations.

During the dough-kneading process, two poppy seeds positioned next to each
40 other eventually go their separate ways. Any early divergence or measurement error is repeatedly amplified by the mixing until the position of any seed becomes effectively unpredictable. It is this "sensitive dependence
45 on initial conditions" and not true randomness that generates unpredictability in chaotic systems, of which one example may be the Earth's weather. According to the popular interpretation of the "Butterfly Effect," a
50 butterfly flapping its wings causes hurricanes. A better understanding is that the butterfly

causes uncertainty about the precise state of the air. This microscopic uncertainty grows until it encompasses even hurricanes. Few
55 meteorologists believe that we will ever be able to predict rain or shine for a particular day years in the future.

1. The primary purpose of this passage is to

   (A) explain how non-random systems can produce unpredictable results

   (B) trace the historical development of a scientific theory

   (C) distinguish one theory from its opposite

   (D) describe the spread of a technical model from one field of study to others

   (E) contrast possible causes of weather phenomena

2. According to the passage, what is true about poppy seeds in bread dough, once the dough has been thoroughly mixed?

   (A) They have been individually stretched and folded over, like miniature versions of the entire dough.

   (B) They are scattered in random clumps throughout the dough.

   (C) They are accidentally caught in tangled objects called strange attractors.

   (D) They are bound to regularly dispersed patterns of point attractors.

   (E) They are in positions dictated by the underlying equations that govern the mixing process.

3. According to the passage, the small rounding errors in Lorenz's model

    (A) rendered the results unusable for the purposes of scientific research

    (B) were deliberately included to represent tiny fluctuations in atmospheric air currents

    (C) had a surprisingly large impact over time

    (D) were at least partially expected, given the complexity of the actual atmosphere

    (E) shrank to insignificant levels during each trial of the model

4. The passage mentions each of the following as an example or potential example of a chaotic or non-chaotic system EXCEPT

    (A) a dough-mixing machine

    (B) atmospheric weather patterns

    (C) poppy seeds placed on top of an upside-down bowl

    (D) poppy seeds placed in a right-side-up bowl

    (E) fluctuating butterfly flight patterns

Solutions

The solutions show a sample passage map and the point, as well as explanations for each answer choice. No simple story is provided, but do try to develop that level of understanding of the passage when creating your map. Where appropriate, wrong answers have been labeled by wrong answer category.

Passage L: The Invention of TV

In the early years of television, Vladimir Zworykin was considered the device's inventor, at least publicly. His loudest champion was his boss, David Sarnoff, then president of RCA and
5 a man regarded even today as "the father of television." Current historians agree, however, that Philo Farnsworth, a self-educated prodigy who was the first to transmit live images, was television's technical inventor.
10   In his own time, Farnsworth's contributions went largely unnoticed, in large part because he was excluded from the process of introducing the invention to a national audience. Sarnoff put televisions into living
15 rooms, and Sarnoff was responsible for a dominant paradigm of the television industry that continues to be relevant today: advertisers pay for the programming so that they can have a receptive audience for their
20 products. Sarnoff had already utilized this construct to develop the radio industry, and it had, within ten years, become ubiquitous. Farnsworth thought the television should be used as an educational tool, but he had little
25 understanding of the business world, and was never able to implement his ideas.
   Some argue that Sarnoff simply adapted the business model for radio and television from the newspaper industry, replacing the
30 revenue from subscriptions and newsstand purchases with that of television set sales, but Sarnoff promoted himself as nothing less than a visionary. Some television critics argue that the construct Sarnoff implemented has played
35 a negative role in determining the content of the programs themselves, while others contend that it merely created a democratic platform from which the audience can determine the types of programming it
40 desires.

Sample passage map (yours will likely differ):

① VZ = inventor
   S = father of TV
   really F

② F not part of process, focus edu
   S made comm (same as radio)

③ S just adapt? or visionary?
   Some see S neg, some pos

The point (articulate to yourself; don't write): Farnsworth really invented TV, but he didn't know how to turn it into a business. Sarnoff used the radio model to make television big business. People have differing feelings about his role.

1. First, identify the question type:

    The primary purpose of the passage is to

The wording indicates that this is a Primary Purpose question. Glance at your map and remind yourself of the point before you go to the answers.

(A) *correct public misconceptions about Farnsworth's role in developing early television programs*

   The passage does correct the misconceptions about Farnsworth's role. This is only a detail of the passage, however; most of the passage talks about Sarnoff's development of the business model for television. (True but not right)

(B) *debate the influence of television on popular culture*

   The passage does not delve into popular culture. (Out of scope)

(C) *challenge the current public perception of Vladimir Zworykin*

Zworykin is not the focus of the passage, nor does the passage say anything about *current* public perception of Zworykin; it only indicates that he was once considered the inventor of the technology. (Out of scope)

(D) *chronicle the events that led from the development of radio to the invention of the television*

The passage is not about the events that led to the invention of television, nor is it about radio. Radio is only mentioned because Sarnoff used a similar business model to launch the business of television. (Out of scope)

(E) *describe both Sarnoff's influence on the public perception of television's inception and the debate around the impact of Sarnoff's paradigm*

CORRECT. The passage does describe how Sarnoff made television popular; some critics think that his role was positive while others think that it was negative. Notice that this is the only answer choice that mentions Sarnoff. He is featured prominently in every paragraph, so any answer choice representing the point of the passage should not mention other people while ignoring him.

2.   First, identify the question type:

Which of the following best illustrates the relationship between the second and third paragraphs?

This is a Paragraph question. Glance at your map and articulate to yourself the relationship between the second and third paragraphs before you check the answers.

The second paragraph explains how Sarnoff made television a commercial success and why Farnsworth was not able to do so. The third paragraph expands on Sarnoff's work, indicating both positive and negative views.

(A) *The second paragraph dissects the evolution of a contemporary controversy; the third paragraph presents differing viewpoints on that controversy.*

Perhaps the fact that the wrong man was initially credited with television's invention could be considered a controversy, but that controversy is not contemporary, nor is it the purpose of the second or third paragraphs. (Out of scope)

(B) *The second paragraph explores the antithetical intentions of two men involved in the infancy of an industry; the third paragraph details the eventual deterioration of that industry.*

The second paragraph might be described in this way, but the third paragraph does not talk about the deterioration of television. Rather, the industry was (and is!) a success. Perhaps it didn't live up to Farnsworth's hopes, but the passage doesn't describe any decline—in fact, Farnsworth's vision didn't get off the ground. (Direct contradiction)

(C) *The second paragraph presents differing views of a historical event; the third paragraph represents the author's personal opinion about that event.*

The second paragraph provides historical details of the launch of television, not different views of the launch. The third paragraph does not present the author's personal opinion. (Out of scope)

(D) *The second paragraph provides details that are necessary to support the author's opinion, which is presented in the third paragraph.*

The author does not provide his own opinion; rather, he conveys the opinions of others (*some argue; some television critics argue*). (Out of scope)

(E) *The second paragraph presents divergent visions about a new technology; the third paragraph further explores one of those perspectives.*

CORRECT. The second paragraph does present the two different visions held by Farnsworth and Sarnoff. The third paragraph does provide additional information about Sarnoff's particular vision.

3. First, identify the question type:

According to the passage, the television industry, at its inception, earned revenue from

The language *according to the passage* indicates that this is a Detail question. The passage discusses television revenues in the second and third paragraphs. Search for the information.

Paragraph 2 (line 18): *advertisers pay for the programming*

Paragraph 3 (lines 29–31): *replacing the revenue from subscriptions and newsstand purchases with that of television set sales*

(A) *advertising only*

Revenue was also earned from the sale of TV sets. (True but not right)

(B) *advertising and the sale of television sets*

CORRECT. Revenue was earned from advertisers and the sale of TV sets.

(C) *advertising and subscriptions*

(D) *subscriptions and the sale of television sets*

(E) *advertising, subscriptions, and the sale of television sets*

Choices (C), (D), and (E) mention subscriptions. Subscriptions were used in the newspaper industry, not the television industry. (Mix-up)

4. First, identify the question type:

The passage suggests that Farnsworth might have earned greater public notoriety for his invention if

The word *suggests* signals that this is an Inference question, so you will need to go back to the passage. Farnsworth's contributions are discussed in the second paragraph:

[Farnsworth] was excluded from the process of introducing the invention to a national audience ... Farnsworth thought the television should be used as an educational tool, but he had little understanding of the business world, and was never able to implement his ideas. (lines 12–26)

If Farnsworth hadn't been excluded, maybe he would have earned more acclaim. Alternatively, if he had understood business better, then he might have earned more acclaim. Look for an answer with a similar meaning.

(A) *Vladimir Zworykin had been less vocal about his own contributions to the television*

The passage says that Sarnoff, not Zworykin himself, was vocal about Zworykin's contributions. (Mix-up)

(B) *Farnsworth had been able to develop and air his own educational programs*

It's possible that if Farnsworth had been able to follow through on his goal of using television for education, he would have earned public acclaim, but the passage says nothing to indicate this. Because he had little understanding of business, his programs might not have been great successes even if he had been able to produce them. (Out of scope)

(C) *Farnsworth had involved Sarnoff in his plans to develop, manufacture, or distribute the television*

There is no indication that Farnsworth had any such plans. Rather, it would have helped Farnsworth to be involved with Sarnoff's plans. (Mix-up)

(D) *Sarnoff had involved Farnsworth in his plans to develop, manufacture, or distribute the television*

CORRECT. If Farnsworth hadn't been excluded, then he might have garnered acclaim as Sarnoff and Zworykin did.

(E) *Farnsworth had conducted research into the type of programming the audience most wanted to watch*

The passage indicates that Farnsworth had little understanding of the business world; even if he knew what audiences wanted to watch, he wouldn't necessarily have known how to build a successful business model. (Out of scope)

Passage M: Life on Mars

Because of the proximity and likeness of Mars to Earth, scientists have long speculated about the possibility of life on Mars. As early as the mid-seventeenth century, astronomers
5 observed polar ice caps on Mars, and by the mid-nineteenth century, scientists discovered other similarities to Earth, including the length of day and axial tilt. But in 1965, photos taken by the Mariner 4 probe revealed a
10 Mars without rivers, oceans, or signs of life. Moreover, in the 1990s, it was discovered that Mars, unlike Earth, no longer possessed a substantial global magnetic field, allowing celestial radiation to reach the planet's surface
15 and solar wind to eliminate much of Mars's atmosphere over the course of several billion years.

More recent probes have investigated whether there was once liquid water on Mars.
20 Some scientists believe that this question is definitively answered in the affirmative by the presence of certain geological landforms. Others posit that alternative explanations, such as wind erosion or carbon dioxide oceans,
25 may be responsible for these formations. Mars rovers *Opportunity* and *Spirit*, which began exploring the surface of Mars in 2004, have both discovered geological evidence of past water activity. In 2013, the rover *Curiosity*
30 found evidence that the soil on the surface

of Mars is approximately 2 percent water by weight. These findings substantially bolster claims that there was once life on Mars.

Sample passage map (yours will likely differ):

① Life on M?
   + sim to E
   − diff too

② Water? debate
   recent: yes, water

The point (articulate to yourself; don't write): Debate about life on Mars. Positives and negatives, but the big deal was the discovery of water, increasing the chance that there was life on Mars.

1. First, identify the question type:

The passage is primarily concerned with which of the following?

This is a Primary Purpose question. Glance at your map and remind yourself of the point before you go to the answers.

(A) *Disproving a widely accepted theory*

There is no widely accepted theory, just speculation. Plus, that speculation is more positive than negative! (Out of scope)

(B) *Initiating a debate about an unproven theory*

The passage does discuss a potential theory (that there may once have been life on Mars), but the passage itself does not initiate any debate. Rather, it reports on various findings and opinions of others. (Out of scope)

(C) *Presenting evidence in support of a recently formulated claim*

The earliest mentioned interest in Mars was in the mid-seventeenth century; this is not recent. (One word off)

(D) *Describing various discoveries made concerning the possibility of life on Mars*

CORRECT. The passage does describe various discoveries made in the mid-seventeenth and mid-nineteenth centuries, as well as more recent discoveries that concern the possibility of life on Mars.

(E) *Detailing the findings of the Mars rovers* Opportunity, Spirit, *and* Curiosity

The passage does discuss this, but the rovers are details; they are not the overall point of the passage. (True but not right)

2. First, identify the question type:

Each of the following discoveries is mentioned in the passage EXCEPT

The question indicates that four of the answers *are* mentioned in the passage, so this is a Detail EXCEPT question. The entire passage is about discoveries, so go straight to the first answer choice and try to find it in the passage.

(A) *Wind erosion and carbon dioxide oceans are responsible for certain geological landforms on Mars*

CORRECT. False. The passage says only that wind erosion or carbon dioxide *may* be responsible for certain geological landforms, not that they *are*. This is an unusual form of an Extreme answer: Though the word *are* is not an extreme word itself, it is more extreme than *may*. (Extreme)

(B) *Mars does not have a substantial global magnetic field*

True. The first paragraph says that Mars *no longer possessed a substantial global magnetic field* (lines 12–13).

(C) *Mars had water activity at some point in the past*

True. The second paragraph says that *Mars rovers* Opportunity *and* Spirit … *discovered geological evidence of past water activity* (lines 25–29).

(D) *The length of a day on Mars is similar to that on Earth*

True. The first paragraph discusses Mars's *similarities to Earth, including the length of day* (lines 7–8).

(E) *The axial tilt of Mars is similar to that of Earth*

True. The first paragraph discusses Mars's *similarities to Earth, including the … axial tilt* (lines 7–8).

3. First, identify the question type:

The passage suggests which of the following about polar ice caps?

The word *suggests* points to an Inference question. The passage mentions polar ice caps in the first paragraph:

As early as the mid-seventeenth century, astronomers observed polar ice caps on Mars, and by the mid-nineteenth century, scientists discovered other similarities to Earth, including the length of day and axial tilt. (lines 3–8)

The second half of the sentence states that scientists discovered *other* similarities to Earth, implying that polar ice caps are also a similarity between the two planets.

(A) *Until recently, the ones on Mars were thought to consist largely of carbon dioxide.*

The passage does mention carbon dioxide, but not in the context of polar ice caps. (Mix-up)

(B) *By 1965, the ones on Mars had disappeared.*

The passage does mention that photos taken in 1965 showed that Mars was *without rivers, oceans, or signs of life* (line 10), but this sentence makes no reference to the polar ice caps. (Mix-up)

(C) *They are also found on Earth.*

CORRECT. The sentence says that scientists discovered *other* similarities to Earth, implying that the earlier discovery (polar ice caps) is also similar to what is found on Earth.

(D)   *Their formation is tied to length of day and axial tilt.*

The passage mentions length of day and axial tilt as examples of other similarities to Earth, but it does not indicate that those had anything to do with the formation of polar ice caps. (Out of scope)

(E)   *They indicate that conditions on the planet Mars were once very different than they are at present.*

It's possible that conditions were once very different, but the passage does not provide any information to indicate that this is the case. (Out of scope)

4.   First, identify the question type:

Which of the following pieces of evidence, if found on Mars, would most support the claim that Mars once held life?

The words *most support the claim* indicate that this is a Strengthen question. Both paragraphs discuss characteristics that indicate the possibility of life. Because there are so many possible indicators, work backwards from the answers and try to find them in the passage. First, though, remind yourself that the passage also discusses characteristics that are incompatible with life. Read carefully!

(A)   *Carbon dioxide oceans*

The second paragraph mentions that carbon dioxide oceans, rather than water, might be responsible for certain landforms, and the passage makes clear that water is an important indicator of possible life. Carbon dioxide oceans, then, would weaken the evidence for water presence and thus *decrease* the chances of life. (Weaken)

(B)   *Celestial radiation and solar wind*

The first paragraph mentions celestial radiation and solar wind in the context of a scenario in which there is *not* life. (Weaken)

(C)   *High daily level of sunlight reaching the planet's surface*

You might posit that abundant sunlight would improve the odds of life, but the passage does not provide any information about this. (Out of scope)

(D)   *Volcanic eruptions*

The passage does not provide any information about volcanic eruptions. (Out of scope)

(E)   *A significant global magnetic field*

CORRECT. The first paragraph says that scientists posited that life could exist on Mars due to the similarities between Earth and Mars. However, Mars, unlike Earth, does *not* have a substantial global magnetic field, and this difference between Mars and Earth is presented as a negative in the debate about life on Mars. The implication, then, is that a global magnetic field would be positive evidence in favor of life on Mars.

Passage N: Fossils

In archaeology, as in the physical sciences, new discoveries frequently undermine accepted findings and give rise to new theories. This trend can be seen in the
5   reaction to the recent discovery of a set of 3.3-million-year-old fossils in Ethiopia, the remains of the earliest well-preserved child ever found. The fossilized child was estimated to be about 3 years old at death,
10   female, and a member of the *Australopithecus afarensis* species. The *afarensis* species, a major human ancestor, lived in Africa from earlier than 3.7 million to 3 million years ago. "Her completeness, antiquity, and age at
15   death make this find unprecedented in the history of paleoanthropology," said Zeresenay Alemseged, a noted paleoanthropologist. Other scientists said that the discovery could reconfigure conceptions about the lives and
20   capacities of these early humans.

22

Prior to this discovery, it had been thought that the *afarensis* species had abandoned the arboreal habitat of its ape cousins. However, while the lower limbs of this fossil supported
25 findings that *afarensis* walked upright, its gorilla-like arms and shoulders suggested that it retained the ability to swing through trees. This has initiated a reexamination of many accepted theories of early human
30 development. Also, the presence of a hyoid bone, a rarely preserved bone in the larynx that supports muscles of the throat, has had a tremendous impact on theories about the origins of speech. The fossil bone is primitive
35 and more similar to that of apes than to that of humans, but it is the first hyoid found in such an early human-related species.

Sample passage map (yours will likely differ):

① new disc → undermine old
new theories eg child fossil

② 2 things changed w/child
walking / limbs
speech / hyoid

The point (articulate to yourself; don't write): New discoveries change old ideas and give rise to new theories. A detailed archaeological example illustrates this overall point. The discovery of a particular skeleton led researchers to reexamine theories about early human life.

1. First, identify the question type:

    The primary purpose of the passage is to

This is a Primary Purpose question. Glance at your map and remind yourself of the point before you go to the answers.

(A) *discuss a controversial scientific discovery*

The passage does not indicate that the discovery was in any way controversial. (Out of scope)

(B) *contrast varying theories of human development*

The passage does discuss how certain theories about early human development have changed over time, but it does not contrast different theories. (Out of scope)

(C) *support a general contention with a specific example*

CORRECT. The first sentence of the passage makes a general contention (*In archaeology . . . new discoveries frequently undermine accepted findings* [lines 1–3]). The rest of the passage provides a specific example (the Ethiopian fossils) that supports that contention.

(D) *argue for the importance of a particular field of study*

The author does not make a case about the *importance* of archaeology (or any other field) specifically. (Out of scope)

(E) *refute a widely believed myth*

A *myth* is a traditional story or belief that may or may not be strictly factual. A *myth* is not what the passage describes: new evidence that led researchers to revise an existing theory. (Out of scope)

2. First, identify the question type:

    The passage quotes Zeresenay Alemseged in order to

The *in order to* language indicates that this is a Specific Purpose (Why) question. Return to the passage and articulate in your own words why the author quoted Alemseged in paragraph 1.

"Her completeness, antiquity, and age at death make this find unprecedented in the history of paleoanthropology," said Zeresenay Alemseged, a noted paleoanthropologist. Other scientists said that the discovery could reconfigure conceptions about the lives and capacities of these early humans. (lines 14–20)

The author is trying to use this example to support the point that discoveries can give rise to new theories. Alemseged's quote reinforces the idea that the discovery of this set of fossils is extremely significant (*unprecedented*), as does the fact that other scientists agree with Alemseged in this respect.

(A) *qualify the main idea of the first paragraph*

To qualify a piece of information is to limit or diminish it. Alemseged's quote does the opposite: It reinforces the point. (Direct contradiction)

(B) *provide contrast to the claims of other scientists*

Alemseged's quote emphasizes the importance of the discovery. The other scientists mentioned share this perspective. (Direct contradiction)

(C) *support the theory regarding the linguistic abilities of the* afarensis *species*

Linguistic abilities are mentioned at the end of the second paragraph, but Alemseged's quote is about the general significance of the find and it doesn't provide any support for a particular theory. (Mix-up)

(D) *support the stated significance of the discovery*

CORRECT. This choice matches the answer predicted above.

(E) *provide a subjective opinion that is refuted in the second paragraph*

Alemseged's opinion is reinforced, not refuted, by the second paragraph, which delves into the important consequences of the discovery. (Direct contradiction)

3.   First, identify the question type:

It can be inferred from the passage's description of the discovery of the fossil hyoid bone that

This is an Inference question. The hyoid bone was mentioned in the second paragraph:

This has initiated a reexamination of many accepted theories of early human development. Also, the presence of a hyoid bone, a rarely preserved bone in the larynx that supports muscles of the throat, has had a tremendous impact on theories about the origins of speech. The fossil bone is primitive and more similar to that of apes than to that of humans, but it is the first hyoid found in such an early human-related species. (lines 28–37)

The first sentence sets up the idea that the hyoid discovery was an example of the need to reexamine some earlier theory. Specifically, it had a *tremendous impact on theories about the origins of speech* (lines 33–34). Since it was the earliest hyoid bone found in a human-related species, perhaps it indicates that speech may have arisen earlier than previously thought.

(A) Australopithecus afarensis *was capable of speech*

This is tempting but goes too far. The passage relates the hyoid to speech but does not provide information as to whether *afarensis* could actually speak. (Out of scope)

(B) *the discovered hyoid bone is less primitive than the hyoid bone of apes*

Check the last sentence of the paragraph. Tricky! The sentence calls the bone primitive and similar to that of apes, but does not say that it is less primitive than the ones found in apes. (Out of scope)

(C) *the hyoid bone is necessary for speech*

The passage does connect the hyoid bone to speech, but does not provide information that would imply that the bone is *necessary*. (Extreme)

(D) *the discovery of the hyoid bone necessitated the reexamination of prior theories about speech*

CORRECT. Leading into the hyoid example, the passage talks about discoveries leading to a reexamination of many accepted theories. The passage then says that the hyoid discovery has had a *tremendous impact* (line 33) on prior theories. The implication is that the hyoid discovery has also resulted in a reexamination of those prior theories.

(E) *the hyoid bone was the most important fossil found at the site*

The discovery of the hyoid was certainly important, but the passage provides no information about which discovery was the most important. (Extreme)

4. First, identify the question type:

    Each of the following is cited as a reason that the fossils discovered in Ethiopia were important EXCEPT

The question indicates that four of the answers *are* mentioned in the passage, so this is a Detail EXCEPT question. Most of the passage discusses fossil discoveries, so go straight to the first answer choice and try to find it in the passage.

(A) *the fact that the remains were those of a child*

    True. Alemseged's quote indicates that the *age at death* was important (lines 14–16).

(B) *the age of the fossils*

    True. Alemseged's quote indicates that the *antiquity* of the bones was important (line 14).

(C) *the location of the discovery*

    CORRECT. False. While the geographic location of the discovery is given in the passage, the location was not cited as a reason that the fossils were important.

(D) *the presence of a bone not usually discovered*

    True. The hyoid example indicates that the bone is *rarely preserved* (line 31) and that it was the *first hyoid found in such an early human-related species* (lines 36–37). The passage says that the discovery of the hyoid bone had a *tremendous impact* (line 33).

(E) *the intact nature of the fossils*

    True. Alemseged's quote indicates that the *completeness* of the bones was important (line 14).

5. First, identify the question type:

    The impact of the discovery of the hyoid bone in the field of archaeology is most closely analogous to which of the following situations?

This is an unusual question that does not fall into one of the common categories; it's more like a Critical Reasoning question. It is asking you to make an analogy to the situation presented in the passage. You may or may not see an RC question like this on the test.

The hyoid is mentioned in the second paragraph, so read the appropriate text and ask yourself what the *impact of the discovery* was. Then, examine the answers to find a match.

The bone was the first hyoid found for this species, and it had a *tremendous impact on theories about the origins of speech* (lines 33–34). Find a similar situation in the answers.

(A) *The discovery and analysis of cosmic rays lend support to a widely accepted theory of the origin of the universe.*

    The hyoid discovery led to a reexamination of an existing theory. In this answer, the new evidence supported the existing theory.

(B) *The original manuscript of a deceased nineteenth-century author confirms ideas about the development of an important work of literature.*

    The hyoid discovery led to a reexamination of an existing theory. In this answer, the new evidence confirmed the existing theory.

(C) *The continued prosperity of a state-run economy stirs debate in the discipline of macroeconomics.*

    The hyoid discovery inserted an important new piece of information into the conversation; this choice does not mention anything about new information or evidence.

(D) *Newly revealed journal entries by a prominent Civil War-era politician lead to a questioning of certain accepted historical interpretations about the conflict.*

    CORRECT. The hyoid discovery, like the newly revealed journal entries in this choice, led to a questioning of certain interpretations or theories.

(E) *Research into the mapping of the human genome gives rise to nascent applications of individually tailored medicines.*

The hyoid discovery had an impact on previously formulated theories. This choice does not address previous applications or theories.

Passage O: Chaos Theory

Around 1960, mathematician Edward Lorenz found unexpected behavior in apparently simple equations representing atmospheric air flows. Whenever he reran his model with
5 the same inputs, different outputs resulted, although the model lacked any random elements. Lorenz realized that tiny rounding errors in the initial data mushroomed over time, leading to erratic results. His findings
10 marked a seminal moment in the development of chaos theory, which, despite its name, has little to do with randomness.

Lorenz's experiment was one of the first to demonstrate conclusively that unpredictability
15 can arise from deterministic equations, which do not involve chance outcomes. In order to understand this phenomenon, first consider the non-chaotic system of two poppy seeds placed in a round bowl. As the seeds roll to
20 the bowl's center, a position known as a point attractor, the distance between the seeds shrinks. If, instead, the bowl is flipped over, two seeds placed on top will roll away from each other. Such a system, while still not
25 technically chaotic, enlarges initial differences in position.

Chaotic systems, such as a machine mixing bread dough, are characterized by both attraction and repulsion. As the dough is
30 stretched, folded, and pressed back together, any poppy seeds sprinkled in are intermixed seemingly at random. But this randomness is illusory. In fact, the poppy seeds are captured by "strange attractors," staggeringly complex
35 pathways whose tangles appear accidental but are in fact determined by the system's fundamental equations.

During the dough-kneading process, two poppy seeds positioned next to each
40 other eventually go their separate ways. Any early divergence or measurement error is repeatedly amplified by the mixing until the

position of any seed becomes effectively unpredictable. It is this "sensitive dependence
45 on initial conditions" and not true randomness that generates unpredictability in chaotic systems, of which one example may be the Earth's weather. According to the popular interpretation of the "Butterfly Effect," a
50 butterfly flapping its wings causes hurricanes. A better understanding is that the butterfly causes uncertainty about the precise state of the air. This microscopic uncertainty grows until it encompasses even hurricanes. Few
55 meteorologists believe that we will ever be able to predict rain or shine for a particular day years in the future.

Sample passage map (yours will likely differ):

① L: diff results from rounding errors
  chaos theory (not random)

② not chaos: bowl + poppy seeds

③ chaos: bowl + dough
  attract, repulse

④ not random, depends on start cond
  butterfly

The point (articulate to yourself; don't write): Lorenz discovered something about chaos theory (which is not really about randomness). Non-chaotic systems are predictable. Chaotic systems increase initial differences, so even though they are not actually random, they are hard to predict.

1. First, identify the question type:

The primary purpose of this passage is to

This is a Primary Purpose question. Glance at your map and remind yourself of the point before you go to the answers.

(A) *explain how non-random systems can produce unpredictable results*

CORRECT. The passage does explain how chaotic (*non-random*) systems aren't actually predictable. The passage gives the example of poppy seeds kneaded into bread dough until their position *becomes effectively unpredictable* (lines 43–44).

(B) *trace the historical development of a scientific theory*

The passage does discuss some of Lorenz's contributions to chaos theory, but the passage does not trace the entire historical development of the theory. (Out of scope)

(C) *distinguish one theory from its opposite*

Only one theory (chaos theory) is mentioned in the passage. The passage does contrast two systems (non-chaotic and chaotic), but these are not both theories, nor is the overall point to contrast these two systems. (Out of scope)

(D) *describe the spread of a technical model from one field of study to others*

The passage does not discuss multiple fields of study. (Out of scope)

(E) *contrast possible causes of weather phenomena*

The end of the passage does mention the weather, but there is no mention of different possible causes of weather phenomena. Even if there were, this would be detail, not the point. (Out of scope)

2. First, identify the question type:

According to the passage, what is true about poppy seeds in bread dough, once the dough has been thoroughly mixed?

The language *according to the passage* indicates that this is a Detail question. The bread dough concept is introduced in the third paragraph and continued in the fourth paragraph. Start with the third paragraph:

> As the dough is stretched, folded, and pressed back together, any poppy seeds sprinkled in are intermixed seemingly at random. But this randomness is illusory. In fact, the poppy seeds are captured by "strange attractors," staggeringly complex pathways whose tangles appear accidental but are in fact determined by the system's fundamental equations. (lines 29–37)

After the dough is mixed, then, the seeds have separated based on some equations, but it's not possible to predict how. See whether there's a match in the answers; if not, try the fourth paragraph.

(A) *They have been individually stretched and folded over, like miniature versions of the entire dough.*

The paragraph indicates that the dough is stretched and folded over, not the seeds. (Mix-up)

(B) *They are scattered in random clumps throughout the dough.*

The paragraph specifically indicates that the movement is *not* random. (Direct contradiction)

(C) *They are accidentally caught in tangled objects called strange attractors.*

"Strange attractor" is a technical name for a complex, tangled pathway. There are no tangled objects. Moreover, there is nothing accidental about the movement. (Mix-up)

(D) *They are bound to regularly dispersed patterns of point attractors.*

The seeds are not in regularly dispersed patterns; the patterns are so complex that the outcome is *seemingly at random* (line 32). Later, in the fourth paragraph, the passage makes clear that the final positions are not predictable (and therefore not regularly dispersed) even though they are actually governed by equations. (Out of scope)

(E) *They are in positions dictated by the underlying equations that govern the mixing process.*

CORRECT. The final sentence of the third paragraph indicates that the system's fundamental equations determine the final position of the poppy seeds.

3. First, identify the question type:

According to the passage, the rounding errors in Lorenz's model

The language *according to the passage* indicates that this is a Detail question. The first paragraph introduces Lorenz's model and the rounding errors:

> Edward Lorenz found unexpected behavior in apparently simple equations representing atmospheric air flows. Whenever he reran his model with the same inputs, different outputs

resulted—although the model lacked any random elements. Lorenz realized that tiny rounding errors in his analog computer mushroomed over time, leading to erratic results. (lines 1–9)

The rounding errors were tiny at first but mushroomed (got much larger) over time, such that the final results of seemingly similar starting points could be quite different.

Since the question stem contains the first half of a sentence that the answer choices finish, remind yourself of the text before reading the answers: *The rounding errors in Lorenz's model . . .*

(A) *rendered the results unusable for the purposes of scientific research*

The passage does not indicate whether Lorenz was still able to use the results for his purposes. If anything, the errors led to a positive, not negative, result: The erratic results led to *a seminal moment in the development of chaos theory* (lines 10–11). (Out of scope)

(B) *were deliberately included to represent tiny fluctuations in atmospheric air currents*

Lorenz did not deliberately include the rounding errors. At first, he did not realize that they were present and couldn't understand why he kept getting different results. (Direct contradiction)

(C) *had a surprisingly large impact over time*

CORRECT. The rounding errors were so tiny that Lorenz did not notice them immediately, but they *mushroomed over time* until they produced different results even with seemingly the same inputs. The passage describes this behavior as *unexpected*.

(D) *were at least partially expected, given the complexity of the actual atmosphere*

The rounding errors were simply computer errors; the passage does not indicate that they resulted from the complexity of the atmosphere. (Mix-up)

(E) *shrank to insignificant levels during each trial of the model*

On the contrary, the rounding errors grew a great deal, or *mushroomed*, over time. (Direct contradiction)

4. First, identify the question type:

The passage mentions each of the following as an example or potential example of a chaotic or non-chaotic system EXCEPT

The question indicates that four of the answers *are* mentioned in the passage, so this is a Detail EXCEPT question. The entire passage talks about both chaotic and non-chaotic systems, so it's not possible to formulate an answer in advance. Go straight to the first answer choice and try to find it in the passage.

(A) *a dough-mixing machine*

True. The first sentence of the third paragraph indicates that a *machine mixing bread dough* (lines 27–28) is an example of a chaotic system.

(B) *atmospheric weather patterns*

True. The fourth paragraph mentions one possible example of a chaotic system as *Earth's weather* (lines 48–50).

(C) *poppy seeds placed on top of an upside-down bowl*

(D) *poppy seeds placed in a right-side-up bowl*

Answers (C) and (D) discuss the poppy seed examples. True. The second paragraph describes both examples as non-chaotic systems (lines 18–19).

(E) *fluctuating butterfly flight patterns*

CORRECT. False. While it is true that the passage discusses a *butterfly flapping its wings* (line 50), the passage does not mention anything about butterfly flight patterns.

Applying to
Business School?

chedule a free, 30-minute consultation at **www.mbamission.com/consult**, nd start getting answers to all your MBA admissions questions!

Vhy mbaMission?

 More than 20 years of MBA admissions consulting experience, with thousands of acceptances and $20M+ in scholarships earned annually

 Ranked number one MBA admissions consulting firm by GMAT Club and *Poets&Quants*

 Dedicated, full-time team of carefully selected and meticulously trained MBA admissions experts

 Exclusively recommended by Manhattan Prep, Powered by Kaplan since 2009

 Extensive, unparalleled library of free business school content

 Services available for all stages of the application process

Go beyond books. Try us for free.

Starter Kit

Ready for more? Sign up to get loads of free reading, practice, and resources/tools to keep you going with your GMAT studies.

Trial Class

Want to get a taste of what our live classes are like? Attend the first session for free, no strings attached.

Free Events

Join a free workshop to learn valuable informatio taught by one of our expert instructors.

Try our classes and products for FREE at
kaptest.com/gmat.

Not sure which is right for you?

Try all three!

Or give us a call and we'll help you figure out the best fit for you.

Prep made personal.

Whether you're looking to enroll in a comprehensive course or get personalized 1-on-1 instruction, we've got you covered.

Our Manhattan Prep instructors aren't just 99th-percentile scoring **GMAT experts**—they're experienced teachers who will go the extra mile to help you hit your top score.

Check out what our students have to say about Manhattan Prep:

★ Trustpilot
★★★★★

"Deciding to take this class was the best decision I made in my GMAT journey.... I would strongly recommend anyone take a class at Manhattan Prep..."
Allison, Manhattan Prep GMAT Student 10/17/23

★ Trustpilot
★★★★★

"I've recommended Manhattan Prep to many friends and coworkers looking to study for the GMAT and truly think it is the best decision to get through this phase!"
Aman, Manhattan Prep GMAT Student 6/27/23

★ Trustpilot
★★★★★

"Hands down best materials / course on the market."
Sam, Manhattan Prep GMAT Student 5/25/23

★ Trustpilot
★★★★★

"Highly recommend taking GMAT Manhattan Prep. They do an amazing job breaking down the test and giving you the tools to be successful."
Glodie, Manhattan Prep GMAT Student 1/10/22

★ Trustpilot
★★★★★

"There are SO many useful strategies that are covered on the Manhattan Prep online portal and during class. ... These are game changers, since it really helps you structure your studies."
Neil, Manhattan Prep GMAT Student 3/29/23

MANHATTAN PREP
POWERED BY KAPLAN

Contacts us at 800-576-4628 or gmat@manhattanprep.com for more information about your GMAT study options.